Attitudes to
other religions

*Comparative religion
in seventeenth-
and eighteenth-century
Britain*

For
Gwyneth, Katharine
and Robert
with thanks

those fictional works which pretend to an eastern source in order to comment on life in Europe or to gain interest in their exhortations. In Britain Lyttleton's *Letters from a Persian*, Goldsmith's *Citizen of the World* and the Earl of Chesterfield's *Oeconomy of Human Life* are examples of this fictional form. They suggest that there was at least a latent hope that the East might have some secrets and insights for the West to learn. There was, though, no corresponding expectation concerning the 'new world' of the American continents, the 'dark continent' of Africa and, at the end of our period, the newest discoveries in Australasia. The only minor exception to this judgement is that a few proponents of natural religion apparently believed that their idea of a 'noble savage' would be found to be actualised if groups of people could be discovered in territories which had not suffered the corruptions of civilisation.

Most of the discussions of other religions, however, were not given in answer to a question asking simply for information nor to one about the enlightenment to be found in some other faith. They were the product of questions about the truth of Christianity, either of Christianity as a whole or of some particular aspect of it. By far the greater part of the treatments of other religions in our period is thus only properly appreciated as part of debates about Christianity and as attempts to justify positions and answer questions raised in those debates. Whatever interest there may have been in acquiring information about other religions, the discussions about them generally arose from and sometimes only make sense in terms of contemporary debates about the content and credibility of the Christian faith.

The majority of the authors whom we will be discussing were not primarily interested in other religions as viable faiths. Neither were they concerned to engage in serious dialogue with the adherents of these religions as opposed, in some cases of missionary concern, to attempting to persuade them of the error of their ways. They were interested in other religions because and to the extent that they saw in them ways of justifying their own understanding of authentic belief, of overcoming objections to it and of defeating opposing beliefs. Hugo Grotius, for example, as part of his attempt to verify Christian belief in his widely read *The Truth of the Christian Religion*, offers a 'Confutation' of the 'particular Errors, and . . . special Arguments' which adherents of other faiths 'use to oppose' Christianity.[3] Similarly Charles Leslie's *The Truth of Christianity Demonstrated* considers the cases of what he lists as the four religions to be found in the world '*viz.* Christianity, Judaism, Heathenism, and Mahometism' in coming to his conclusion that the rivals of

Christianity are to be regarded as corruptions of the one true religion which is Christianity.[4] This concern with other religions as a way of establishing a theological judgement is also illustrated by the way that Toulmin, a Unitarian, compares Christ with Socrates, Confucius and Mahomet in order to affirm the superiority of Christ's character against those who deny his unique status as 'the Author and Finisher of our Faith'.[5] Even Reland's sympathetic study of Islam is not free from an avowal of such an apologetic interest. If we can take him at his word, his intention is to provide an accurate account of that faith and to refute the lies that have been told about it so that 'we may be able to attack it with sure Blows' and 'valid Reasonings' by knowing the truth about it.[6] As for Lessing's plea for mutual toleration in the parable of the rings in *Nathan the Wise*, this expresses his critical view of all positive religions and of the arguments used to claim superiority for any of them. It does not reflect an interest in other religions for their own sake. Lessing is suggesting that the Jew, the Christian and the Muslim should 'each endeavour to vie with both his brothers in displaying the virtue' of his faith with 'gentleness, benevolence, forbearance' and 'inward resignation to the godhead' without pretending to be able to show that his faith is the authentic one.[7]

In most cases, then, references to other religions in the theological writings of the seventeenth and eighteenth centuries are to be interpreted primarily with reference to contemporary discussions about the nature and verification of Christian belief. The treatment of Judaism and Islam was generally concerned to show that these religions were not supported by the kinds of convincing argument that could be advanced in the case of Christianity, while the treatment of the remaining religions was intended to show that they offered no serious challenges to Christianity.

What has been widely overlooked, though, in previous studies of religious thought in this period is the degree of interest that was shown in other religions, even if it was only to refute them. When Henry Smith wrote *Gods Arrow against Atheists*, he attacked 'Atheisme and Irreligion' and defended 'the Church of England' as 'the true Church of God' against Papists, Brownists and Barrowists. Such arguments might be expected from a popular preacher in later Elizabethan England. What is surprising, though, is that he also felt it necessary to confute 'the Gentiles, and all Infidels of the World' and even to devote a chapter to showing 'the religion of Mahomet to be a false and wicked Religion'.[8] Two centuries later, when Beilby Porteus produced his *Summary of the Principal Evidences of the Christian Revelation* which was 'designed chiefly for the use of young persons' in his diocese of London, the Bishop included a chapter comparing 'Christ and Mahomet, and their respective religions'. His conclusion that the religion of the former is 'derived from God' while that of the latter 'is confessedly the invention of man' is not at all unexpected in view of the status of the author and the intention of the book.[9] What is interesting is that the Bishop considered it important to include the comparison at all. In this respect, though, as we shall see, his work is not at all unusual.

Before, then, we consider how other religions were treated in seventeenth- and eighteenth-century works and why they were so treated, we need to appreciate why they were discussed at all. To untangle this story it is important to see the discussions against the background of the religious thought of the period.

II

Background

Religious debates in the seventeenth and eighteenth centuries were deeply concerned about the question of truth. Believers were not content to regard the contents of their faith merely as a matter of private choice, even less as a culturally conditioned conviction or a socially imposed set of behaviour patterns. Throughout this period the corrosive effects of the modern appreciation of the human and cultural relativities of understanding had not yet eaten so far into general consciousness as to produce widespread despair about the possibility of justifying the truth of religious beliefs. Although Descartes and Locke classically mark the opening of the modern era in thought as they concentrate attention on the question of the proper bounds and structure of knowledge rather than on questions about what is actually known, their works do not express doubts about the possibility of establishing the truth of the beliefs at the heart of Christian theism. On the contrary, they include important attempts to show the truth of those beliefs.

While some challenged their arguments and others presented different ones, there was widespread consensus on two principles in the period from the publication of their works until the end of the eighteenth century. It was only then that the classical age of reason and enlightenment declined under the combined effects of Kant's critical philosophy and the Romantic movement. The first of these principles is that religious faith is fundamentally a matter of assent to certain truths. The second is that these truths can be determined to be such by the proper use of human reason. What believers have to do, therefore, is to show that it is their beliefs rather than any others that express the final and complete truth about God and humanity and their proper relationship.

While these principles were generally accepted, it was also increasingly apparent that there was no such consensus about the actual content of that final and complete truth. The divisions following the Reformation destroyed for the inhabitants of western Christendom the illusion that all reasonable people will agree about their religious convictions. Not all disagreement could be convincingly condemned as the obvious result of sin, pride, obstinancy or ignorance. Although attempts were made to dismiss disagreements in this way, especially by preachers advertising their wares, by the beginning of the seventeenth century it was becoming clear to many who investigated the problems that it was not as easy to decide where the truth lay as convinced partisans wished to maintain.

Furthermore, disputes about religious beliefs did not only concern disagreements within Christendom. As well as feeling a need to justify their convictions against other Christians, the religious literature of the period indicates how some Christians also considered that the truth of their faith was not finally secure unless they could meet, at least to their own satisfaction, the challenges implicit in the beliefs of other religions. Even though the treatment of these rivals might seem today to be rather cursory, at least an attempt was made to offer some arguments to verify the superiority of Christianity. When, for example, Richard Baxter in *The Reasons of the Christian Religion* moved on from discussing 'Natural Religion or Godliness' to the matter of 'Christianity and Supernatural Revelation', he 'found it' his 'duty to enquire what *other men* thought in the world, and what were the reasons of their several beliefs' so that he might share whatever knowledge they had attained. After a brief but not wholly unsympathetic survey, though, he decided that while the religions of 'the meer Naturalists, called commonly Heathens and Idolaters', the Jews and the Muslims shared some of the truths to be found in Christianity, they contained no truth that was not found in Christianity and much that was defective.[1] What is noteworthy, though, is not the conclusion of his survey but the fact that he and many others felt obliged to conduct such surveys at all.

As has already been suggested, the debates about the truth of belief in this period were linked to a growing recognition of reason as the final authority for deciding what is true in matters of religious belief as in all else. Appeals to other authorities – ecclesiastical bodies, sacred texts, private illumination or personal conviction – were increasingly found to provide no bases for agreement. In the disputes during and after the Reformation, it seemed that no faction found any difficulty in finding some plausible authority to justify its own position and to condemn those of its opponents. The resulting impasses led to bigotry, persecution and even war. Frustrated over attempts to secure agreement, some considered that violence was justified in order to establish conformity to what they were convinced to be the truth. Gradually, though, it was accepted that the use of force was no satisfying way to settle disputes about religious truth. It might compel outward conformity but it could not produce conviction. Revulsion at the consequences of persecution thus combined with the absence in practice of any other agreed authorities to lead people to view reason as the only proper basis for establishing religious beliefs and for resolving religious disputes.

An early example of the appeal to reason can be found in Herbert of Cherbury's *De Veritate*, one of the first purely metaphysical treatises by an English author. It seems that Herbert's observations of religious persecution in France encouraged him, while ambassador there, to complete this study of the nature and conditions of true understanding. In his doctrine of the common notions he considered that he had established a universally acceptable criterion for the rational solution of conflicts. William Chillingworth, a junior contemporary of Herbert, in his *Religion of Protestants, A Safe Way to Salvation* (1638), likewise urged the appeal to reason as the way to resolve the conflicts over authority and over the interpretations of authority which lay at the core of the disagreements between Roman Catholics and Protestants. As the century progressed, the authority of reason as the final basis of decision was further affirmed by the Cambridge Platonists. In the works of Whichcote, Culverwel, Smith, Cudworth and More, reason is treated as the final arbiter of both natural and revealed religion. It is 'the candle of the Lord' bestowed on every person for this purpose. Henry More was so convinced of the power of reason to determine where the truth lies in such matters that he suggested that there should be international discussions between the adherents of different religions, as well as liberty for individuals to profess what they decided to be 'the best Way to serve God'.[2]

It was John Locke, however, who established the canon of reason in such a way that it dominated theological discussions for over a century following the publication of his *Essay Concerning Human Understanding* in 1690. He classically described the authority of reason in religious matters when he wrote that 'he governs his Assent right, and places it as he should, who in any Case or Matter whatsoever, believes or disbelieves, according as Reason directs him'. Only so, in his view, will a person use 'the Light and Faculties G O D has given' for discovering 'Truth'.[3]

A few theologians questioned the validity or, more often, the all-embracing character of this canon of reason so far as it applied to matters of religious belief. Among them were John Edwards and John Hutchinson whose rejection of the canon of reason was based on a commitment to the Bible, Edmund Gibson and William Law whose doubts were based on doctrinal considerations, and Peter Browne and John Ellis whose reservations were derived primarily from their analyses of the limits of human reason. Furthermore, among those who accepted the canon of reason there was often fundamental disagreement about what should count as a reasonable argument. Anthony Collins and John Wesley, for example, might both 'appeal' to 'men of reason' but what the advocate of 'Free-thinking' understood to be right reason and what it showed to be true is very different from the arguments and conclusions presented by the energetic organiser of the Methodist revival. Nevertheless, in spite of a few doubts about the principle of the canon of reason and the much greater disagreements about its application, theological debates for over a century from the time of Locke are generally characterised by the fact that the participants felt obliged to show that their understanding of correct belief is the valid conclusion of rational arguments. Not only a major radical like Matthew Tindal claims that the canon of reason alone can prevent religious beliefs being 'irrational and unlawful, debasing the Dignity of Mankind, and effacing the Image of God implanted in them'.[4] Such a scourge of the 'deists' as Charles Leslie similarly holds that 'reason is reason to all the World: And nothing can be true, for which there is not a reason sufficient to convince Gain-sayers'.[5]

The quotations from Tindal and Leslie come from passages in which the author is concerned to verify his view of correct belief in the face of the challenges of other religions. By far the greatest effect of the adoption of the canon of reason in theology, however, was to stimulate debate within Christianity about the nature and content of correct belief. Several parties were engaged in this struggle. The lines of battle crossed each other in what are sometimes confused and confusing ways. Each party had to be careful lest, in repelling one attack, it used arguments which exposed it to attack from a different direction. For instance, those who held that assent to the Christian revelation rests on a foundation of natural theology[6] had to take care, on the one hand that their care for natural theology as a basis for belief did not make them vulnerable to the charge that they showed thereby that revelation is unnecessary since the natural theology is sufficient for religion, and on the other hand that their case for the revealed parts of belief could not be used to show the untenability of any natural theology.

Among the roughly distinguishable groups involved in these intellectual battles were those who held that natural religion, whose truths are discernible by reason, is available to and sufficient for all people (the various positions often described as 'deistic' generally belonged to this group), those who claimed that the Christian revelation is a necessary restatement of an originally pure natural religion which has become hopelessly corrupted, those who claimed that Christian belief rests upon but goes beyond natural religion and natural theology, and those who maintained that all authentic belief has initially to be revealed but then can and should be confirmed by rational arguments. There were also sceptics who identified the proper limits of reason in order to cast doubt on the rational tenability of any religious belief, and fideists who used the identification of those limits to deny that reason has any legitimate role in determining religious belief. Finally there were those who used reason to confirm some parts and reject other parts of traditional Christian doctrine. Examples of this last group can be found in the disputes about the nature of Jesus Christ which were increasingly affected during the eighteenth century by rational appraisals of the Biblical evidence. Each theologian thus found that he not only had to defend his views against a variety of opponents outside his doctrinal camp. He often also had to be on his guard against unreliable 'supporters' who supposedly shared his position. The result was a period of lively, sometimes virulent, often passionate, frequently erudite, and generally clear theological argument.

It is this situation which provides the background to discussions of other religions at this time and which frequently provides the clue to a proper appreciation of the ways in which they were treated. Although there are some attempts simply to describe what was held and practised in other religions, most of the references to them arise as part of arguments concerning the reasonableness of some understanding of Christian belief. John Rogers' references to Islam in his *Necessity of Divine Revelation* is a typical case. Against those who use internal arguments to defend the Bible's revelatory status, maintaining that 'the excellent Effects, the Comforts and Illuminations' which are to be found in the Bible are proof of its being 'a Divine Revelation', Rogers points out that 'a *Mahometan*' who 'feels the same Effects from the *Alcoran*' could 'offer the same Proof for his Superstition'.[7] Later he refutes 'the Romanists Way of proving the Authority of Scripture from the Infallibility of their Church', by pointing out that a similarly unsatisfactory circular 'proof' could be offered by a Muslim for his scriptures: 'I believe the *Alchoran* to be true, because the *Mufti*, who is infallible, affirms it to be so; and I believe the *Mufti* to be infallible, because the *Alchoran* says he is so.'[8] Indeed Rogers even allows that the Muslim's case might be more plausible than the Roman Catholic's because the former's scriptures might positively affirm the infallibility of the Mufti. His remarks illustrate how some theologians used their knowledge of other religions to support their arguments in the religious controversies of the time.

There are five ways in which references to other religions were used in theological debates in this period. Some theologians claim to find in other religions evidence which backs their own theological understanding. There are, for example, those who seek to justify their claims about the possibility of a natural knowledge of God by arguing from evidence taken from other religions that such a knowledge was available before and is still available outside the area of the Christian revelation. A contrary argument is brought forward by others who refer to different evidence taken from other religions to support their view that no such authentic knowledge is naturally available.

A second way of using other religions is as theological 'mud' to sling at opponents. Some theologians consider that they can discredit the beliefs and practices of an opponent by showing how they resemble those of a 'heathen' religion. It is for this reason that Roman Catholic practices are sometimes compared to those of ancient paganism and Socinian beliefs to Islamic ones.

Thirdly, the cases of certain other religions are examined in order to show that the kinds of argument adduced in favour of some set of Christian beliefs cannot be used to confirm, perhaps even more strongly, the beliefs of those other religions. The need for such examination arose particularly when Christian claims about divine revelation faced the challenge of Islam. It was not possible, for example, to verify claims about the finality of the Christian revelation by straightforward references to its 'miraculous' propagation in view of the evidence of the rapid and extensive spread of Islam. If the argument from propagation were to be convincing, it was important to show that the spread of Islam could be explained in a non-miraculous manner, whereas that of Christianity could not.

Fourthly, other religions are described in order to show that there are no credible rivals to Christianity as a reasonable faith. It was widely considered in this respect that the truth of one set of beliefs can be significantly confirmed by showing the rational unsatisfactoriness of other religions. Charles Blount thus professes to want 'to declare the absurd and monstrous Doctrines of the Heathenish Superstition' and their 'blind Conjectures' in accordance with the principle that

As the lustre of an Oriental Diamond is more clearly perceived, when compared with counterfeit Stones; so Christianity appears in its greatest Glory and Splendor, when compared with the obscurity of Paganism: the Deformity of the one, serving but as a foyl to the Beauty of the other. Nor doth the Divinity of our Scriptures ever better appear, than when compared with the Follies of the *Talmud*, and *Alcharon*, or the Constitutions of the Heathen Law-givers . . .[9]

However ironic may be Blount's affirmation of this principle, others regard it as an important way of establishing the truth of their under-standing of Christianity. They attempt to destroy the supposed attrac-tiveness of other faiths by describing what are claimed to be their actual beliefs and practices. Benjamin Whichcote thus briefly dismisses Islam for measuring truth by the '*Longest Sword*' and Judaism by 'the *Most Voices*'.[10]

Generally this way of arguing tendentiously compares the best forms of the faith being confirmed with the worst aspects of the others. Equally searching attention is not given to possible objections to the former. David Hume points to the unsatisfactoriness of this way of using other religions when he remarks that 'if nothing were requisite to establish any popular system, but the exposing the absurdities of other systems, every votary of every superstition could give a sufficient reason for his blind and bigotted attachment to the principles, in which he has been edu-cated'.[11]

Finally, as the counterpart of the previous argument, references to other religions are employed to enhance the readers' appreciation of the merits of Christianity and to promote their devotion to it. It is this intention that Alexander Ross claims for his *Pansebeia*. According to his preface, the 'different opinions' of 'all religions in the world' are not merely exposed so that 'we may see their deformity and avoid them'. By contrasting it with errors we perceive the excellence of the truth; by learning of the worldwide acknowledgement of 'a Divinity' we are taught 'the impudency' of atheism and of the view that counts 'all Religions but inventions of humane policy'; by observing the dedication of other worshippers we are shown our lack of zeal; by becoming aware of 'the confused multitude of Religions in the World' we will perceive our fate 'if once we forsake the right way'; by reading about 'old dreams of ancient Hereticks' we will recognise the need to weed out the present 'rabble of vain, phantastical, or prophane opinions' that distract the country; lastly, by discovering 'the wretched condition of a great part of the World, buried as it were, in the darkness of ignorance, and the tyranny of superstition', we should be induced to be thankful for our status, pity the wretches who do not share it, and take care to preserve it.[12]

A similar point is made by Joseph Pitts in his account of Islam. His description of his experiences in Muslim lands shows that he had been impressed by their devotion to their faith. It is not surprising, then, that he remarks in his preface that

> It is a Shame, indeed, to *Christians*, to take a View of the Zeal of those poor blind *Mahometans*; which in the following Account will be found to be in many Things very strict. If they are so zealous in their false Worship, it must needs be a Reprimand to Christians, who are so remiss in the *True*.[13]

In this way, then, the study of other religions was used and defended as a way to promote the cause of Christianity and deepen the commitment of its adherents. It was supposed to enhance their appreciation of its reasonableness and to stir their zeal in its observance.

Since the treatments of other religions often 'use' those religions to defend and attack positions in contemporary theological debates about Christianity, it is not surprising that the supposed evidence about those religions is sometimes twisted to suit apologetic needs. The use of other religions is in practice sometimes an abuse. However, what materials about them were available to British theological writers in the seventeenth and eighteenth centuries? Except for Islam, ancient Judaism and, to a lesser extent, contemporary Judaism, there was for much of the period and concerning most of the world little reliable evidence for them to work on.

A great deal of the material that was used came from the authors of ancient Greece and Rome. When Toland, for example, writes in the third of his *Letters to Serena* about 'The Origin of Idolatry, and Reasons of Heathenism', fifty-five pages discuss ancient times and only three and a bit 'the present Heathens' – and then mainly to point out that they 'agree very much with the Antients' in the content and variety of 'their Opinions'.[14] Hume's discussion of the origin of religion likewise largely refers to materials from ancient Greece and Rome.[15] This dependence on classical literature in discussions about origins would have seemed appropriate to many readers because current opinion about the age of mankind would have placed these materials significantly nearer the time of those origins than contemporary reports about world religions.

It is not, however, only in attempts to identify the origins of religion that we find that references are mostly to classical literature. There was for much of the period a widespread, though declining, prejudice in favour of its authors. In spite of the excitement occasioned by new discoveries, Sir William Temple was not alone in preferring ancient to modern learning. He held that there were giants in those days in comparison with whom contemporary thinkers have little to offer:

> Let it come about how it will, if we are Dwarfs, we are still so, though we stand upon a Giant's Shoulders; and even so placed, yet we see less than he, if we are naturally shorter sighted, or if we do not look as much about us, or if we are dazzled with the Height, which often happens from Weakness either of Heart or Brain.[16]

In any case, whatever counter-arguments might be offered to Temple's judgement, the educational practices of the time meant that educated people were well versed in classical authors and that it was their information which most readily came to mind when non-Christian beliefs and practices were being discussed.

When, for instance, Herbert of Cherbury wishes to demonstrate that all people fundamentally acknowledge the five common notions of religion, and when Halyburton seeks to refute his argument, by far the greater part of the evidence that is presented is taken from classical authors.[17] Towards the end of our period the situation had changed in that more information about other religions was easily available. When, therefore, East Apthorp proposes to determine whether mankind, using human reason, is able to discover 'a religion worthy of God and man', he suggests that the evidence to be considered should include

> the Vedam, the Zend-avesta, the Sadder, the Koran; the Mysteries, Oracles, and religions of gentilism . . . the intricacies of Philosophy . . . and . . . the recitals of living manners in ancient or modern travellers . . . and the discoveries of the moderns respecting the state of savage life, especially on the continent and islands of the new world.[18]

The comprehensiveness of his proposals, however, is not carried through in practice. The notes at the end of his study do include references to works on 'the eastern religions and books of authority', to reports on religious customs in New Zealand, Mexico and Peru, and to Confucius and Chinese religion.[19] These references, though, take up just over six pages of a discussion in which over one hundred and fifty pages refer to reports from classical authors.[20]

While Apthorp does not do much more than briefly mention travellers' reports, other authors use them to a greater extent to provide information about other religions. Such sources, though constituting a sizeable and popular body of literature by the end of the eighteenth century, often give distorted and superficial accounts of the religions they describe. This is how Holwell judged many travellers' reports:

> His telling us such and such a people . . . worship this stock, or that stone, or monstrous idol; only serves to reduce in our esteem, our fellow creatures, to the most abject and despicable point of light. Whereas, was he skilled in the language of the people he describes, sufficiently to trace the etymology of their words and phrases, and capable of diving into the mysteries of their theology; he would probably be able to evince us, that such seemingly preposterous worship, had the most sublime rational source and foundation.[21]

Not only did many travellers from the West lack these linguistic skills, they also generally failed to appreciate fully the need to understand such things within their total cultural context.[22] Furthermore they often lacked a theological awareness and empathy which would have helped them to perceive the religious significance of what they were told and observed. The result is that many of the descriptions of other religions derived from their reports, often at second or third hand, are misleading. As Dow put it in 1768, 'modern travellers have accordingly indulged their talent for fable, upon the mysterious religion' of the people visited.[23] Their prejudices perverted their understanding. Even when they are correct in individual details, they frequently convey a general impression which fails to do justice to the religion being treated. The extracts from Stackhouse's *Compleat Body of Divinity* illustrate the kind of presentation that can result from relying on such sources.[24]

The third source of information was, of course, the original materials of other religions. For most of the period, and for most religions, they were not readily accessible. Even where they were available, as was especially the case with Judaism and Islam, they were often not used. As late as 1785, Toulmin, while giving two references to chapters in the Koran, shows no qualms about reporting that the 'Authorities' for his treatment of Mahomet are Prideaux, Addison, Rollin and *The New and General Biographical Dictionary*.[25] Prideaux's own work, however, shows that Arabic sources were far from unknown. The 'Account of the

Authors Quoted' appended to his *True Nature of Imposture Fully Displayed in the Life of Mahomet* (first published in 1697) lists over thirty 'Arabic Authors'.[26] Even if Prideaux's selection and use of them is not as unprejudiced as he would like to be thought, he clearly was aware of the need to find trustworthy authorities for his work.[27]

Throughout the period, though, Christian apologists show themselves to be ready to reject the original materials of other religions as the biased products of the gullible minds of their adherents. They do not consider that their own theological intentions may equally well have produced prejudiced misunderstanding. Reland describes a common attitude when he complains that anyone who wishes to study Islam is sent to secondary, sometimes polemical, works and to poor translations of the Koran:

> He is not advis'd to learn the *Arabick*, to hear *Mahomet* speak in his own Tongue, to get the *Eastern* Writings, and to see with his own Eyes, not with other Peoples: Because 'tis not worth while (say many) to undergo so much Trouble and Fatigue, only to consult the Dreams and Ravings of a Fanatick.[28]

Partly because of this attitude, works like Pococke's *Specimen Historiae Arabum*, Hyde's *Tractatus Alberti Bobovii de Turcarum Liturgia*,[29] Reland's *Short System of the Mahometan Theology* and Sale's important translation of the Koran (as well as the earlier, much poorer one by Ross from du Ryer's French translation) are not as common as the interest in other religions might lead one to expect.

Pococke's work initially led to a burst of enthusiasm for Arabic studies but his correspondence shows that it soon declined in spite of his efforts and those of his successor, Hyde. One of those who did seek to follow their example was Simon Ockley. His difficulties in preparing *The History of the Saracens*, the first volume of which appeared in 1708 and the second in 1718, illustrate the problems facing those who attempted, in scholarly fashion, to refer to original materials. Although vicar of Swavesey in Cambridgeshire and, from 1711, Professor of Arabic at Cambridge, he had to travel to Oxford to work in the Bodleian Library which, he reported, is 'without question, the best furnished with Oriental Manuscripts of any in *Europe*'.[30] Having gained access to its resources, however, his problems were not over, as he indicated in a letter to his daughter. In the case of one of the most useful manuscripts, Al Wakidi's history, he had great problems in deciphering the text:

> I am forced sometimes to take three or four lines together, and then pull them

all to pieces to find where the words begin and end; for oftentimes it is so written, that a word is divided as if the former part of it was the end of the foregoing word, and the latter part the beginning of another; besides innumerable other difficulties known only to those that understand the language.[31]

A further problem was that the Bodleian, for all its riches from the collections of Laud, Pococke, Hyde and Selden,[32] lacked important texts. It contained, for example, only two of the twelve volumes of history written by Al Wakidi and Ockley wished that funds could be found to remedy the gaps by judicious purchases in the East.[33] The situation was not unusual. Even where there was a desire to consult original materials, it was not easy to find them.

As for texts from Persia, India and further east, the situation was generally even more difficult. Some knowledge of Chinese religious thought had come out of the Roman Catholic missionary activity there – and the controversies they aroused in Rome. A letter by Sir William Jones reveals that in 1769 he took up Chinese with the aid of the collection which Philippe Couplet and others produced, *Confucius, Sinarum Philosophus sive Scientia Sinensis Latine Exposita* (Paris, 1687).[34] Apthorp knew of a version of Confucius' books in Latin printed at Prague in 1711 and Toulmin refers to *The Morals of Confucius* 'printed in London, 1691' (a translation of a French work compiled by La Brune or Cousin and published in Amsterdam in 1688).[35] For much of the period, though, there was not much material easily accessible. Only in the later part of the eighteenth century do we find the beginnings of sustained attempts to make texts from India and surrounding areas available in European languages. In 1762 Anquetil-Duperron returned to France with 180 manuscripts from his travels in India and in 1771 published his pioneering *Zend-Avesta, ouvrage de Zoroastre*. Among the first important translations of Indian texts into English are Halhed's *A Code of Gentoo Laws* (1776), Wilkin's *The Bhagvat-Geeta, or Dialogues of Kreeshna and Arjoon* (1785) and Sir William Jones' *Institutes of Hindu Law: or, The Ordinances of Menu* (published in Calcutta in 1794). The knowledge of the literature, artefacts and institutions of this part of the world was greatly advanced from this time by Sir William Jones' efforts through the foundation of the Asiatic Society of Bengal in 1784 and the publication of its journal, *Asiatick Researches*, which first appeared in 1788. Many of the articles in this journal indicate a move into a study of these materials in their own right which contrasts with the polemical motivation of most previous work. This, though, marks the end of our period. For most of it the original sources available for the study of other religions tend to be limited or unreliable or somewhat inaccessible. The general practice of most writers on the subject was to repeat the views – and errors – of earlier secondary works.

Where original materials and direct reports about other religions were available, problems arose about how to interpret them. In most cases the selection and treatment is basically dictated by ulterior motives. Authors pick out the elements which suit their intentions, some hostile and others sympathetic to the religions being reviewed, and ignore the rest. At times this produces oddly mixed results. Pitts' account of Islam emphasises the way he was bludgeoned into that faith (presumably in order to excuse his conversion)[36] while indicating overall that he was favourably impressed by its adherents' faithfulness. Burder attempts to arouse support for missionary work both by pointing to the wicked and pitiful state of 'poor benighted Pagans' and by shaming Christians through references to the way infidels keep their religious laws.[37]

Herbert of Cherbury is conscious, though, of the impossibility of attempting 'to study with an impartiall minde . . . all the seuerall Religions'. It would involve learning every language, reading all the relevant books and conferring with those 'learned men' throughout the world who might be able to edify him. No one, in his opinion, could enjoy the financial means, strength for travel, memory and judgement required by such a task. He therefore proposes to meet the methodological problem of determining the 'meanes to attaine euerlasting Salvation' by fixing 'upon some fundamentall Articles agreed vpon by all' the religions which he could discover and then considering 'how farre they might Conduce to my Salvation'.[38] What this involves in practice is seen in his *De Religione Gentilium*. Here he adduces evidence to show that the philosophers and priests among the ancients held, among other basic doctrines, that repentance alone provided the means of atonement with God. Apparently contrary evidence is explained away on one or more of three grounds. First, it is held that not all uses of a word such as 'God' are univocal. Consequently some statements about God which seem to contradict his thesis are held on examination not to be about God at all.[39] Secondly, other conflicting statements are judged to be the result of genuine mistakes or priestly perversions of true understanding.[40] Thirdly, it is argued that many of what seem to be claims to the contrary are in fact to be seen as using symbolical or mystical modes of expression to convey the doctrine which Herbert upholds.[41]

This somewhat 'heads I win, tails you lose' method of treating the

ATTITUDES TO
OTHER RELIGIONS

Comparative religion
in seventeenth-
and eighteenth-century
Britain

DAVID A. PAILIN

Manchester University Press

© David A. Pailin 1984

Published by Manchester University Press
Oxford Road, Manchester M13 9PL
and 51 Washington Street, Dover,
New Hampshire 03820, USA

British Library cataloguing in publication data
Pailin, David A.
    Attitudes to other religions.
    1. Religions – Great Britain – History
    I. Title
    291′0942   BL80.2
    ISBN 0-7190-1065-9

Library of Congress cataloging in publication data
Attitudes to other religions.
    Includes index.
    1. Religions – Early works to 1800 – Addresses, essays, lectures. 2.
Religious thought – Great Britain – History – 17th century. 3. Religious
thought – Great Britain – History – 18th century. I. Pailin, David A.
(David Arthur), 1936–
BL87.A87 1984   291′.09′032   83-20652
ISBN 0-7190-1065-9

Photoset by Elliott Brothers & Yeoman Ltd.,
Woodend Avenue, Liverpool 24
Printed in Great Britain
by Butler & Tanner Ltd, Frome and London

Contents

READINGS

Contents

Preface

Since the aim of this study is to introduce readers to seventeenth- and eighteenth-century views on 'other religions', I have deliberately allowed the authors studied to speak as far as possible in their own words and with their own forms of spelling, punctuation and italicisation. In this way I hope that something of the flavour as well as of the content of their writings may be conveyed, even though the selection of their materials inevitably means that they are presented as I see them. No author, least of all one who seeks to include a collection of readings, can avoid responsibility for what is included and what omitted. My choice of readings, though, has been guided by two principles. The first is to seek to illustrate the range of views that are to be found in the two centuries covered by this study; the second is not to provide extracts from such texts as Hume's *Natural History of Religion* which are easily accessible in modern editions. The result, I hope, is to present a selection of texts which are not accessible outside major libraries and which give a sample of the materials which antedate the modern investigation of religions. In the introductory chapters I provide a guide to their appreciation. In this way I wish to contribute to our understanding both of a neglected aspect of seventeenth- and eighteenth-century British thought and of the early story of the study of 'comparative religion' as it is called in Manchester.

One result of the attempt to keep close to the original texts is that some styles and designations which are now rejected frequently appear. Not only, for instance, do I write 'Mahomet' and 'Koran' because that is how they generally appear in the literature of this period, but, in the quotations, Muslims are often spoken of as 'Mahometans'. I recognise that such usages may today be properly criticised but I trust that readers will accept that I have no desire in any such practice to cause offence, only to be true to the originals which are cited. Similarly I have no desire to defend what is sometimes said about 'other religions' and their faithful, only to indicate that such remarks were made. One of the fruits of such a study as this is to show how 'pride and prejudice' so often affect understanding. We may not be free from such influences today but by considering what happened in the past our consciousness of their dangers may be heightened.

An earlier form of some of this material, now probably hardly recognisable, appeared in *Religion* I, autumn 1971, and I am grateful to the Board of that journal for permission to use it in this work. My thanks are also due to John Banks and Catherine Annabel of the Manchester University Press for their patience and encouragement over a long period and, above all, to Gwyneth, Katharine and Robert for providing a happy environment for my work.

Hazel Grove   *David A. Pailin*
4 July 1983

The author and publishers are deeply indebted to

THE SPALDING TRUSTS

for a generous grant in aid of publication

I

Introduction

The first commandment, 'You shall have no other god to set against me', reminds us that at no time has humanity shared a common religion. Even the self-confident adherents of the most intolerant faiths have had to admit that in practice theirs is not (yet) a universal faith, however ill-founded they might regard its rivals. Although persecution might exclude rivals from the territory of a sect or nation, travel beyond its frontiers has shown that other systems of belief are possible. The result has been an interest in 'other religions' which is probably as old as religion itself. 'Comparative religion', at least as the attempt to show the superiority of one's own beliefs, is by no means a post-Enlightenment discipline.

The story of the trial of power between Elijah and the prophets of Baal in I Kings 18 is a record of what was supposed to be such a demonstration on behalf of the 'true' religion of Israel. From the formative days of Christianity there have been frequent attempts to demonstrate the error of Judaism in continuing that faith. Paul's prayer that the Jew might come to the salvation revealed in Christ (cf. Romans 10, 1 ff) and Justin Martyr's *Dialogue with Trypho* (c. 135 A D) mark early stages in a story of literary controversy as well as of less rational forms of confrontation. The attacks, though, have not all come from one side. Abelard's *Dialogue of a Philosopher with a Jew and a Christian*, for example, has a contemporary Jewish parallel in *The Kuzari* of Judah Halevi, a Spanish Jew who wrote in 1140 how a king of the Khazars was persuaded of the truth of the Jewish religion after hearing cases put by a philosopher, a Christian and a rabbi.

The other continuing objects for Christian apologetics in the ancient and medieval world were sceptical philosophy and Islam. Although the ancient cults largely died out with the ancient world – or, perhaps, are to be seen as having been absorbed and transmuted into Christian cults, there was a persistent worry about a threat from 'reason'. Apologists considered it important to try to show that 'the philosopher' who properly appreciated the dictates of reason must approve the truth of Christianity. This task was often linked with Christian apologetics against Islam, especially since a large part of the medieval knowledge of ancient philosophy was transmitted by way of Muslim commentators. Aquinas' *Summa Contra Gentiles*, finished in 1264, is a classic attempt to use the commonly agreed authority of reason, guided by the newly fashionable Aristotelean understanding, to demonstrate the truth of Christian belief and, by comparison, the error of any other. It was ostensibly intended as a manual for Christian missionaries in Spain but it may also be seen as a defence of Christianity against sceptics within Christendom.

The aim of this study, however, is not to provide a general history of 'comparative religion' but to draw attention to one hitherto neglected chapter in that story, namely, the treatment of 'other religions' in British literature (i.e., literature published in Britain though not necessarily by British authors) from the end of the sixteenth to the start of the nineteenth century. What, though, is meant by 'other religions' and why these temporal boundaries?

The phrase 'other religions' here basically refers to 'non-Christian religions' but internal debates within Christianity, both between denominations and about the role and significance of natural theology, make it impracticable to define the notion too closely. As with the label 'deist', so what each theologian regards as 'other religions' is determined by his own view of what is to be included within his own religion and what excluded. Some Protestant theologians, for example, treat Socinianism and even Roman Catholicism as 'other religions' while certain advocates of 'natural religion' in effect regard all positive religions, including Christianity, as 'other religions'. As for the compendia of religions published during this period, they often fail to discriminate between religions enjoying widespread support and minor sects. The descriptions in Alexander Ross' *Pansebeia* (first published in 1653), for example, not only cover Judaism, Islam, Calvinism and Lutheranism but also include the religions of the ancient Phoenicians and of Sumatra and such sects as the naked Adamites and the Antidicomarianites. At the end of our period William Hurd's *New Universal History . . . of All the Religions* (first published in 1788) similarly not only describes major world faiths but also such minor groups as the Southcottians, Muggletonians and Cowherdians. The range of materials mentioned in discussions of 'other religions' in this period is vast. It is also often entertaining.

The period to be covered in this study starts about the time when discussions of religion were beginning to be influenced by investigations into the proper limits of human understanding and by the recognition of the canon of reason as the way to solve religious disagreements. In particular it begins in the early years of the author of the first British treatise on comparative religion. Herbert of Cherbury was probably born in 1583. His *De Religione Gentilium* ('*The Religion of the World*') was completed in 1645. It was not published, however, until 1663 when Isaac Vossius saw it through the press in Amsterdam. Much of Herbert's data is taken from Gerard Vossius' *De Theologia Gentili*, published in 1641. Whereas, however, Vossius claimed to be seeking to reveal the errors of heathen religion, Herbert interpreted the evidence in terms of his understanding of human reason and, in particular, as confirming the general perceptibility of the common notions which he had laid down in his *De Veritate* ('*On Truth*'), first published in Paris in 1624. In this way he sought to show that, despite the distortions introduced into religion by priestcraft, there is a universal divine providence recognisable by and offering salvation to all people.

The close of this study is marked by the first moves towards what may be described as the scientific investigation of religions. By the end of the eighteenth century the sceptical influences of the Enlightenment had combined with growing knowledge of the world beyond Christendom to produce a situation in which 'other religions' could become objects of study rather than errors to be controverted. Although, as we shall see, there were a few attempts at unprejudiced study of other religions in earlier decades, it was not until rational doubts about the credibility of traditional Christian doctrines had coincided with an appreciation of the actuality of other belief-systems that such studies began to flourish. Even so, many of the studies of comparative religion that have appeared since the start of the nineteenth century have been tainted by an often unacknowledged prejudice in favour of Christianity. If these treatments of other religions have not been directed by a desire to show the superior status of Christian belief, they have arisen from a concern to discover its background and context. Other studies that have not suffered from this 'Christian' prejudice have often reflected another – that of a secularism which desires to show the crudity and incredibility of all religions. Nonetheless, at the start of the nineteenth century the study of other religions can be held to have entered a new phase.[1] Knowledge of them and the ways of appreciating them developed dramatically. This study ends as that phase begins for it has a different story to tell.

In his *Autobiography*, R. G. Collingwood observes that

> You cannot find out what a man means by simply studying his spoken or
> written statements . . . In order to find out his meaning you must also know
> what the question was (a question in his own mind, and presumed by him to
> be in yours) to which the thing he has said or written was meant as an
> answer.[2]

Whatever the validity of this remark as a general hermeneutical principle, it provides an illuminating approach to understanding when we
consider what was written about other religions in the seventeenth and
eighteenth centuries.

Some of the materials were simply written to meet a growing demand
for information, often about hitherto unknown parts of the world.
Travellers' tales have always fascinated many people. As the knowledge
of the world increased, reports of voyages and geographical dictionaries
appeared which helped both to satisfy and to stimulate interest in what
happened and what was thought elsewhere. At this level the materials
furnish the answer to the simple question, 'What do other people actually
believe and do?' Behind this question lies no theological motive but basic
human inquisitiveness, both antiquarian and current. The readers, for
example, of Thomas Bankes' *System of Universal Geography* could be
expected to be as much interested in the Mexicans' 'passion for strong
liquors' as in their methods of performing human sacrifice. Accordingly,
the more bizarre, exotic and odd the reports, the more they answered
this somewhat superficial demand for information. Indeed, some of the
works of this sort seem to have found in the descriptions of religious acts
a way of titillating their readers under the unexceptionable guise of
education!

Few of the works from the period under review anticipate that religious 'turn to the East' movement which has enjoyed a certain vogue in
recent decades. Those who were disillusioned with Christianity did not
on the whole investigate the ancient religions of the East in the hope that
they might find there what they vaguely craved but had not found in
Christendom. The information available, even when adapted and mag-
nified by a sympathetic imagination, was not generally sufficient nor of
such a quality to provide an attractive faith for self-consciously 'enlightened' people. Where the fascination of the East is obvious, though, is in

evidence is fairly typical throughout the period. Most of the theologians involved in commenting on other religions were advocates for a point of view and that point of view controlled what they selected as evidence and what they did with it. It is common, for example, to find Christian apologists interpreting evidence from other religions as pointing to Christian claims. Horsley and Porteus both repeat the old Christian argument that at the time of Jesus' birth there 'prevailed . . . over the whole East, an ancient and fixed opinion, that there should arise out of Judaea a person who should obtain dominion over the world'.[42] Porteus refers to Suetonius and Tacitus in support; Horsley to 'the Oracles of the Cumaean Sibyl' preserved in Rome and 'the work of Hystaspes, a Persian Magus of high antiquity'.[43] Horsley also holds that 'the sages of the Pythagorean and Platonic schools had some obscure and distorted apprehensions' of the doctrines of immortality, hell and 'even of the trinity of persons'. While now mixed with corrupting additions by priests, these notions had been preserved from the original 'pure religion' of mankind.[44] In this way certain remarks, taken in isolation, are interpreted as evidence for ideas which are historically quite alien to them.

Methodological disagreements over the way to interpret texts are seen in the treatment of Indian materials in the latter half of the eighteenth century. Alexander Dow, for example, denies that 'human reason was ever so depraved' that men would worship 'the work of hands' as 'the creator of the universe'. Maintaining that 'common sense, upon the affairs of religion, is pretty equally divided among all nations', he interprets the supposed polytheism of the Brahmins as 'no more than a symbolical worship of the divine attributes'.[45] By this means they attempt to represent indirectly what they recognise to be impossible for people to imagine directly. Holwell similarly holds that the words 'Birmah', 'Bistnoo' and 'Sieb' (Brahma, Vishnu and Shiva) are used in personal and figurative senses to 'represent what the Bramins call the three first and great attributes of God'.[46]

Others, however, suspect that such interpretations are a more sophisticated way of falling into the error which Holwell and Dow allege against many travellers' reports, namely, of reading the material in terms of one's own prejudices. Halhed, on the one hand, criticises the attempts 'by the learned and ingenious of Europe' to construe 'the extravagant fables' of 'the mythology of the Gentoos' as 'sublime and mystical symbols of the most refined morality'. He rejects such procedures as unfair since they fail to respect the way in which those scriptures are 'literally esteemed as the immediate revelations of the Almighty'. It is illegitimate to use allegorical and mystical modes of interpretation to foist 'upon the plain and literal' meaning of pagan mythology senses which pander to our vanity by making them conform with our own beliefs.[47] Warren Hastings, on the other hand, suggests that sometimes the problem is not one of failing to recognise the integrity of the texts but one of failing to be able to grasp their content. If the insights into the deity expressed in certain texts have come as a result of prolonged spiritual discipline, they may only be apprehensible by those who have shared such discipline and thereby acquired new faculties for understanding. As a result:

> When the text is rendered obscure from such causes, candor requires that credit be given to it for some accurate meaning, though we may not be able to discover it; and that we ascribe their obscurity to the incompetency of our own perceptions, on so novel an application of them, rather than to the less probable want of perspicuity in the original composition.[48]

Hastings and Halhed agree, though, as has already been noted, that the ideas and values expressed in the texts of other religions are only properly appreciated when they are understood in terms of their cultural, social and economic context.[49] Many of those who discussed other religions would probably have assented to this as a principle.[50] In practice, as we shall now see, few came near to observing it. Usually it was on the basis of poor evidence and in a prejudiced frame of mind (as advocates for a position) that theologians in the age of reason approached other religions. We now turn to consider how their views of other religions were influenced by the theological debates which provoked them.

III

The question
of natural religion

Discussions about natural religion in the seventeenth and eighteenth centuries are confused by a lack of agreement about the meaning of the phrase. For some, 'natural religion' refers to the religious truths which all people can in theory determine by the use of their reason, either by considering the character of reality or by investigating the contents of their understanding. For others it is the religion which God had revealed to Adam and which, in principle or in practice, has been transmitted from Adam to all humanity. For some, 'natural religion' denotes the beliefs and practices of those who are 'natural' human beings – unaffected, that is, by civilisation; for others it means the religion of those who are untouched by divine revelation – usually those outside the influence of Judaism, Christianity and, since Mahomet is often held to have adapted many of his ideas from Jewish and Christian teaching, Islam. For some, talk about natural religion has a primarily empirical reference while for others it is normatively used in a theoretical way. For some, natural religion is a human product which shows that valid religious faith can only be derived from a divine revelation. Confusions thus arise because those involved in the theological debates of the time are often not at all clear about the different senses in which the phrase 'natural religion' is being used. As a result they sometimes fail to recognise that the denial of 'natural religion' in one sense is quite compatible with the affirmation of it in another sense and that evidence which tells against one view does not therefore tell against another.

It is in terms of this complicated and confused situation that references to natural religion must be understood. Evidence about the beliefs and practices found in other religions is seen to be important in many of the debates about the status and significance of natural religion but what is regarded as significant evidence and what it is held to indicate depends on which view of natural religion is being considered and against what kind of criticism.

One important strand in religious understanding of the period maintains the validity, goodness and sometimes even the complete sufficiency of what it regards as natural religion. Herbert of Cherbury's affirmation of the five common notions of religion is a classical example of this position. In his *De Veritate* ('*On Truth*'), first published in 1624, he argues that there are certain 'common notions' concerning religion which all normal human beings will recognise to be true once they have apprehended them. These 'common notions' cover the existence and nature of God, the duty of worshipping him, the connection of piety with virtue, atonement through repentance and the reality of punishment or reward after this life. Although Herbert says that he cannot judge 'whether these means are sufficient to prepare us for eternal salvation', it is quite clear that he considers that they must be.[1] His conviction that God is a universal providence leads him to hold that the way of salvation must be available to all people. Consequently, he argues that only if 'penitence and faith in God' are enough for salvation will 'the wretched mass of men' be able to find 'grace and inward peace'.[2] In general, while he may not be prepared in principle to deny that the five common notions may need augmentation, he is prepared to declare that they constitute 'the only Catholic and uniform Church' through which alone 'salvation is possible'. The principles which they express, furthermore, have been 'universally accepted by every religion, age and country'.[3]

In *De Veritate* Herbert declares himself to be 'content' to have managed to show how 'the human mind informed by the Common Notions has been able in every age and place to apprehend' the fundamental principles of religion.[4] His demonstration of this universal ability largely rests in *De Veritate* upon the validity of his metaphysical understanding of truth. Later, in *De Religione Gentilium* ('*The Religion of the World*'), he attempts to show how the evidence about the religious beliefs and practices found in the world, in spite of corruptions by self-seeking priests, actually agrees with what he has established in theory.[5]

Herbert's philosophical doctrine of the common notions was widely, though perhaps erroneously, held to have been discredited by Locke's attack on innate principles.[6] The view that there is a universal natural religion, whether or not influenced by Herbert's own works, nevertheless has considerable support in the period. It is frequently claimed that some basic religious beliefs are common to all humanity even if they are not held to be built into the basic structure of our understanding (Herbert describes the common notions as 'divinely inscribed in the understanding itself')[7] nor are identical with Herbert's five principles.[8]

In fiction, this view had been put forward by Ibn Tufayl's medieval story of Hayy Ibn Yokzan which the Quaker George Keith published in an English translation in 1674. It tells how a child alone on a desert island arrives by his own intelligence at the basic truths of religion. The story may have influenced Defoe's ideas for *Robinson Crusoe*. Whether or not this is so, Defoe describes a form of natural religion in his treatment of the religious insights of Friday and of Will Atkins' native wife. Friday believes in 'one old Benamuckee' who is 'older' than and lives 'beyond' all things, whom all things worship ('All things do say O to him') and who is the resort of the dead. His religion is also, to Crusoe's distaste, infected by priestcraft. When Crusoe tries to teach him about the devil, Friday discomforts him by his 'meerly natural and innocent' questions about why God does not either destroy the devil now or, if he repents, pardon him. Defoe in this way portrays the native, a 'natural' man, as not only showing how 'the meer notions of nature . . . guide reasonable creatures to the knowledge of a God, and of a worship or homage due' to him, but also as enjoying a basic theological awareness which allows him to see inherent difficulties in certain beliefs which are supposedly derived from revelation. Friday's natural religion, however, while generally good as far as it goes, is held by Robinson Crusoe to be much in need of augmentation and correction by the truths of the Christian revelation.[9]

How, then, were references to other actual religions used to support, modify or criticise claims about natural religion?

Some theologians in the period regard what is said about natural religion as empirical claims about universally accepted religious beliefs and, therefore, as open to empirical tests which would show whether or not they are justified. There is, however, uncertainty about how these tests are to be carried out. Not only are there disagreements over the interpretation of evidence about the actual character of religious beliefs and practices found in the world, but there is also a lack of clarity about what constitutes universality. Those who hold that the universality refers to all places and ages, including the present, seem obliged to show that contemporary reports support their position. To maintain, for example, that monotheism is a tenet of natural religion in this strong empirical sense would involve showing that all parts of humanity, perhaps in spite of appearances, are basically committed to belief in one God.

The difficulty of showing that there is any such basic uniformity of belief in contemporary humanity led in some cases to modifications of the empirical element in claims about natural religion. Some treatments of natural religion, for instance, regard the empirical universality of its beliefs as referring not to a contemporary state of affairs but to some supposedly universal acceptance in an original and pure (i.e. 'natural') state of humanity. This latter state is then more or less strongly contrasted to the present corrupt state of humanity.[10] Deviations in religious beliefs and practices found in the world from those theoretically ascribed to natural religion are thus explained in a way that harmonises with and is clearly influenced by doctrines of the 'fallen' state of humanity. They are manifestations of how humanity over the centuries has perverted the natural, God-given state of things. At the same time, it is frequently held that the original beliefs of natural religion, since they do belong to what is natural and fundamental to humanity, can still be traced, albeit faintly, in distorted forms in contemporary religions.

It is this range of understanding of the empirical implications of talk about natural religion that lies behind various attempts to show that a particular belief can be regarded in some way or other as universal – and of counter-arguments that it is not universal and so is either not part of natural religion or evidence that there is no such thing as natural religion. The fundamental belief in this respect is that in the reality of one God. The first of Herbert of Cherbury's common notions of religion is that 'there is some supreme divinity' ('Esse Supremum aliquod Numen'). Whatever opinions may have been held about his metaphysical defence of this belief, there was no doubt that the case for natural religion would be significantly challenged if it could be shown that it is not universally accepted. Conversely there was also a widespread opinion that numbers are significant in deciding what is true. Some express this by explicitly endorsing the principle of the *consensus gentium* as a valid truth-test.[11] Others are more circumspect. Holding, as Culverwel puts it, that reason is 'this great and Royal gift of our Creatour' and 'the Candle of the Lord' within every person, they consider that what people using their reason generally agree to be true is most likely to be such.[12] Consequently it was felt that the greater the number and spread of people that could be shown to believe in the reality of God, the more the atheistic position is shown to be false.

Attempts are thus made to show empirically that some monotheistic belief is universal, or at least was so in humanity's original state, both in order to support claims for natural theology and in order to confute atheism. Alexander Ross, for example, speaks of 'the impudency' of atheists in view of that fact that 'no Nation hath been so wretched as to deny a Deity, and to reject all Religion' for religion is as much a distinguishing feature of humanity as rationality.[13] Ralph Cudworth similarly rebuts atheism by showing the universality of monotheistic belief. In *The True Intellectual System of the Universe* he claims to show that 'the *Generality* of Mankind in all Ages' have at least had an 'Anticipation in their Minds, concerning the *Real* and *Actual Existence*' of God. In a way that has similarities to Herbert of Cherbury's method of dealing with the same problem, he investigates the apparent counter-evidence of polytheism and argues that it does not undermine his case. Those 'Pagans' who assert '*Many Gods* (which were *Understanding Beings Superiour to men*)' are claimed also to acknowledge '*One Chief* and *Sovereign* Numen, the *Maker* of them all'. Thus, after reviewing an enormous range of materials, almost wholly from ancient authors, he concludes that 'those few *Atheists*' who are to be found 'are no other than the *Monsters* and *Anomalies* of Humane Kind'.[14]

Locke too admits that there is some evidence that not all people are monotheists and he is at pains to deny that the idea of God is innate.[15] Nevertheless he does not see this as casting doubt on the proper universality of belief in God, but maintains that God 'hath spread before all the World, such legible Characters of his Works and Providence, and given all Mankind so sufficient a light of Reason' that 'the Precepts of Natural Religion are plain, and very intelligible to all Mankind'.[16] Those who deny the reality of God go against 'Reason, and the natural Propensity of their own Thoughts'.[17] Locke thus defends the universality of natural religion by reference to what all people ought to recognise if they only reasoned correctly, and thus overcomes any problems created by empirical evidence that some people do not in fact accept its doctrines.

Others, as has been indicated already, avoid problems created by evidence about actual beliefs by asserting that the universal entertainment of a pure monotheism existed in the original state of humanity. This true belief has been greatly corrupted in different parts of the world since that time, but traces of it can still be found. This argument is not only applied to belief in God. Charles Blount's *The Oracles of Reason* includes a passage from Thomas Burnet's *Archaeologiae Philosophicae* in which it is claimed that 'the *Siamese Brachmins*' maintain doctrines about the earth which they could only know by tradition 'from the very times of *Noah* . . . and the Antediluvian Sages'. In this way Burnet finds support for his own *Theory of the Earth* in the opinions of 'the Modern

Pagans' although he has also to admit that their preservation of the tenets of the ancients is 'quite overwhelmed with *Trash* and *Filthiness*, being for the most part clogg'd with fabulous Additions'.[18] The distinction in these arguments between preservation and corruption was made in practice, of course, on the basis of what did and what did not back the beliefs being advanced.

For some writers the corruption of the original natural religion dates from the Fall. The loss to mankind which has resulted is a frequent theme in the period. Joseph Glanvill went so far as to maintain that pre-lapsarian Adam was so well equipped that he had no need of 'a *Galilæo*'s tube' (a telescope) to observe 'the Coelestial magnificence'. His 'natural Opticks' were powerful enough. Furthermore, 'whereas we patch up a piece of Philosophy from a few industriously gather'd, and yet scarce well observ'd or digested experiments', Adam's scientific understanding was 'compleatly built, upon the certain, extemporary notice of his comprehensive, unerring faculties'.[19] Robert South in a sermon contrasts the present sorry state of humanity with that originally enjoyed by Adam. To him the truths of religion were plain and pure: today religious understanding is widely distorted.[20]

East Apthorp similarly writes of human nature as now 'a palace in ruins, whose broken columns and disranged marbles, shew its original magnificence'. Adam's fall has led to 'the traductive disorder and corruption of humanity'. The distortion of religion, though, is seen by Apthorp as dating from the Flood. Before the Flood, religion was 'untainted with idolatry' – the errors of 'the first race of men' were 'practical and moral' rather than religious. It was only after the Flood that 'a portentous idolatry gradually overspread the earth'.[21] Another writer who accepts the view that the corruption of the natural religion of humanity only occurred after the time of the Flood is Chevalier Ramsay. He uses it as part of his claim that the different religions all descend from one 'great Man or Legislator', identified by some as Enoch and by others as Noah. He holds that this is the person whom the Chinese call 'Fohi; the Indians Zoroaster; the Chaldeans, Douvanai; the Egyptians, Thoyt; the Phenicians, Taaut; the Latins, Mercury; the Greeks, Hermes; the Arabians, Adris or Edris; the Gauls, Teutatis'. This person's instruction was preserved at first in the form of 'hieroglyphics' which continued for some time 'much the same in all nations' but whose true meaning was eventually forgotten. In this way 'the Pagans fell by degrees into gross idolatry and wild superstition'.[22] Nevertheless, in spite of the 'degradations, adulterations, and misinterpretations' of the original teaching, Ramsay attempts to show at length how there 'still remains some hints, rays, and vestiges' of it in 'the mythologies, and religions of all nations'.[23]

Ramsay has an extensive view of 'the great principles' of this religion whose traces he finds throughout the world.[24] Others are less ambitious in their claims about the vestiges of the original pure religion which remain. Nevertheless, whether they date the beginning of its corruption to the Fall or to the Deluge, there are a number who support claims about the reality of natural religion by reference to supposed evidence of beliefs which have been transmitted from some original state of humanity.

When this kind of argument is applied to theistic beliefs, we find that Humphrey Prideaux, for example, suggests that polytheistic views were introduced into the world by 'the *Babylonians* or *Chaldeans*, who were the first form'd State after the Flood'. Their polytheism, however, is held to presuppose an ultimate monotheism since the gods who are worshipped are said to be seen as mediators between humanity and the '*One Supreme God*'.[25] Leland, who considers that the universal natural religion is derived from an original revelation to Adam, criticises some Christian commentators for misunderstanding the polytheism of ancient philosophers and erroneously regarding them as monotheists. Nevertheless he does find that many of 'the nations which are usually looked upon as illiterate and barbarous' have managed to preserve 'the antient tradition' of 'one Supreme Divinity'. To justify this claim he refers to 'the latest and best accounts' of 'the most intelligent Hottentots', 'the Negroes of Guiney', 'several tribes and nations' of India, and the inhabitants of Ceylon, America, Peru and Florida. At the same time, though, he recognises that most of them consider this supreme God to be too remote to be interested in human affairs, and consequently worship the inferior deities who are held to control the affairs of this world.[26]

Others, however, recognise that the evidence for the universality of any set of beliefs is weak. Bernard Mandeville follows a typical sceptical line on this point (though a line followed by Locke in attacking innate principles)[27] when he argues that neither in morals nor in religion is there any universal agreement about what is to be accepted. What seems obvious to one person is not to another: what the former sees as demanded by nature is seen by the latter as but the teaching of 'the Force of Custom'. Thus, to seek universally agreed beliefs is to embark on 'a Wild-Goose-Chase'.[28] Thomas Halyburton, from the side of belief in revelation, looks at each of Herbert of Cherbury's five common notions of religion and similarly adduces evidence that they were not universally accepted. Some of his evidence is taken from Herbert's *De Religione*

Gentilium since he doubts the justifiability of the interpretations employed to reconcile that material to the doctrine of the common notions. Much of his other evidence comes from Hornbeck's *De Conversione Gentilium* and classical authors. For instance, he cites reports showing that 'the Egyptians and Grecians of old' as well as 'the Sabeans, several Americans and inhabitants of Africa' recognise as God only the sun, moon and stars while 'the Phenicians, Britons of old, and their famed Druids, and perhaps most nations' ascribed the names of God to the sun.[29]

Those who accept the force of this kind of evidence but nevertheless want to affirm some kind of natural theology accordingly try to make their claims about it without implying some form of universality which could be empirically refuted. They have to present an understanding of natural theology which does not maintain that its doctrines are universally recognised nor ever were so according to historical records, even if they may argue that reasonable people everywhere ought to recognise them. Thomas Stackhouse's views illustrate the uncertain – even ambivalent or contradictory – attitudes that sometimes resulted. On the one hand he accepts that Herbert of Cherbury's five principles express 'the sound part' of ancient pagan religion. He maintains that no people, however 'rude and barbarous', have ever failed to acknowledge 'one Supreme Deity' and claims that some of the five principles are to be found, among many errors, in the contemporary religions of China, Japan, Peru and Canada.[30] On the other hand he admits that the errors of polytheism and idolatry have existed from ancient times and are still widespread, producing absurd and conflicting religious beliefs.[31] In such ways, then, the evidence of other religions is seen as casting at least some doubt on the validity of regarding claims about natural religion as descriptions of beliefs which are actually held by all people.

Critics of the notion of a natural religion also advance the contents of beliefs that are actually entertained in other religions as evidence that there is no significant insight into religious truth shared by or even, perhaps, naturally available to all people. These critics thus attack the notion of a natural religion by listing what seems to them and their readers to be clear absurdities in the doctrines of other religions. If, they suggest, people actually believe these bizarre and sometimes mutually contradictory notions, especially those in the supposedly more 'natural' states of humanity (i.e., those least 'corrupted' by civilisation), then it cannot reasonably be held that there is a significant natural religion which provides sound understanding of the fundamental truths of religion.[32] The existence of such understanding as a natural possession, it is assumed in this argument, would prevent the adoption of such bizarre beliefs.

It is this argument which lies behind many of the lists of strange and odd and (to contemporary readers) self-evidently erroneous beliefs in other religions – and also behind attempts by defenders of natural religion like Herbert of Cherbury to rebut the argument by showing that these are accidental mistakes and corruptions which do not destroy the basic substance of the universal natural religion. Alexander Ross, for example, attacks natural religion by suggesting that the religions which are 'most consonant to natural Reason' are 'the barbarous and butcherly Religions of the *Gentiles*, in sacrificing men, in worshipping stocks and stones, &c'.[33] This is a form of argument especially favoured by those who challenge all forms of religious belief. Thomas Hobbes holds that 'there is almost nothing that has a name, that has not been esteemed amongst the Gentiles, in one place or another, a God, or Divell'.[34] David Hume, on the basis of the ancient classics and a few travellers' tales, refers in his *Natural History of Religion* to various beliefs throughout the world. Although he allows 'almost universal' agreement about the existence of some 'invisible, intelligent power in the world', he denies that it has any real significance since it is attached to so many conflicting or, to him, unacceptable beliefs. He reminds his readers, for example, of reports that 'the C H I N E S E when their prayers are not answered, beat their idols . . . The E G Y P T I A N mythologists . . . said, that the gods, pursued by the violence of earth-born men, who were their enemies, had formerly been obliged to disguise themselves under the semblance of beasts' and that 'in very barbarous and ignorant nations, such as the A F R I-C A N S and I N D I A N S, nay even the J A P O N E S E . . . worship may be paid to a being, whom they confess to be wicked and detestable'.[35]

Herbert of Cherbury's third common notion of religion maintains that there is universal recognition that 'the connection of virtue and piety' is the most important part of religion. This connection is worked out in lives directed by conscience and marked by hope, faith, love, joy, blessedness, purity and holiness. The fifth principle, furthermore, backs these moral aspects of religion with assertions of *post mortem* rewards and punishments. At this point at least, Herbert's views agree with a widespread understanding of religion in the seventeenth and eighteenth centuries. Religious faith was primarily judged not by its theological sophistication but by its practical expressions. Believers and nonbelievers agree at this point. Wesley calls his followers to the pursuit of scriptural holiness while Voltaire responds to the variety of dogmas by having the Eternal decree that 'we will never judge any . . . on their chimerical ideas, but solely on their actions'.[36]

It is at this point that the empirical understanding of natural religion runs into its most serious difficulties. If it was hard to find empirical evidence for the universal acceptance of the doctrines of natural religion, it was practically impossible to justify empirically the claim that the moral aspects of natural religion prevail throughout the world. Not even the most subtle exegesis of the evidence could hide the fact that in some religions what seem to others to be abhorrent practices are not only tolerated but even inculcated. Defoe in a work of fiction can present 'poor honest Friday' as a loyal, morally good natural man – allowing, that is, for some cultural relativity in ethical codes[37] – but the morality of other religions in practice seems to many theologians to provide decisive evidence against regarding natural religion as a universal and commendable phenomenon.

Since religion was generally regarded as essentially linked to morality, there was no escape from this conclusion by distinguishing between religious doctrines and moral practices. Instead, the theological battles of the period resulted in people being more confident of their moral commitments than of their religious understanding and consequently judging religious doctrines by their moral concomitants. To display, therefore, the moral evils ordained or permitted by other religions is seen as a powerful way both of condemning those religions and of falsifying the claim that there is a universal natural religion to which all people basically assent. There is, though, some confusion at this point because not all theologians are as prepared as Defoe to recognise the cultural relativity of the recognition of some moral values. Some are confident enough about their own version of ethics to consider that it is the only possible one and that all offences against it are *ipso facto* morally indefensible. Others are less parochial but nevertheless consider that certain actions are so manifestly evil that no genuine religion can tolerate them.

It is, then, as attacks on the notion of natural religion, taken as having some empirical reference, that we should understand many of the references in the theology of this period to the supposed moral evils sanctioned by other religions. Charles Leslie, for example, attacks those whom he regards as deist advocates of natural religion by referring to

the indulgence of fornication and uncleanness among the Heathen, and their human sacrifices (most abhorrent to the God of holiness and mercy) and the filthy obscenity of their very *sacra*; besides the great defect of their morals, which knew no such things as humility, forgiveness of injuries, loving their enemies, and returning good for evil . . . and by the word *humilitas*, they meant only a lowness and dejection of mind, which is a vice. . . . You may see pride and self-conceit run through all their philosophy, besides their principle of increasing their empire, by conquering other countries who did them no harm, whom they called barbarians.[38]

In this passage Leslie is primarily referring to the world of ancient Greece and Rome which provides for him the earliest evidence of natural religion. As for its contemporary manifestation, he suggests in another work that 'the Hottentotes of the *Cape of Good Hope*' who are 'hardly distinguishable from beasts' show what 'nature left to it self would do'.[39] John Wesley similarly refers to contemporary heathens as being in many cases

inferior to the beasts of the field. Whether they eat men or no, (which indeed I cannot find any sufficient ground to believe,) they certainly kill all that fall into their hands. They are, therefore, more savage than lions, who kill no more creatures than are necessary to satisfy their present hunger. See the real dignity of human nature! Here it appears in its genuine purity . . .[40]

While Wesley is prepared to allow that some heathens are 'quite of another spirit, being taught of God, by his inward voice, all the essentials of true religion',[41] he sees 'The Religion of Nature truly delineated' (the title of a book by Wollaston) in the practices of the Chicasaws who torture their captives to death and who do 'nothing but eat and drink and smoke, from morning till night'.[42] Thomas Secker similarly comments on the 'Barbarities' of the Indian tribes bordering English settlements in North America.[43] On the other side of the globe, Lord Anson found a contrast between the reports of some missionaries about the 'exemplary' nature of 'the morality and justice' of the Chinese and the 'timidity, dissimulation, and dishonesty' which he experienced in his dealings with them.[44]

Among the many attacks of this kind on the notion of natural religion is that by Edmund Gibson in his *Second Pastoral Letter* as Bishop of London in 1730. Much of the letter is taken up with evidence from ancient philosophers to support the claim that the corruptions and insufficiency of a natural religion determined by human reason proves the 'great Need, and Expedience of a Divine Re[ve]lation'.[45] There is,

however, a section in the letter where Gibson considers the evidence of
'Books of Travels and other authentick Accounts' about 'the State of
Religion' in countries 'where Natural Reason is their only Guide'. Bas-
ing his account on Millar's survey in his *Propagation of Christianity*,
Gibson reports that

> *Idolatry* has been found in almost every Country that has been discover'd,
> and, in many of them Rites of Worship very wicked and abominable. In
> [Formosa, and the Philippine Islands] some, they were perform'd by *Women*,
> who in performing them laid aside all natural Shame and Modesty . . . In
> [Bisnagar and Nasinga] some Places, the People cut off Pieces of their own
> Flesh and threw them to their Idol, and in [Ceylon, Mexico, Peru, Ter-
> rafirma, Virginia] many others they were found to offer *human* Sacrifices . . .
> The Objects of their Worship were the [Tartary Philippine Islands, Guinea:
> Ausico and Jagos and Monomotapa, (all in Africa) Zocotara, an Island near
> Africa, Chili, Peru, Terrafirma, Canada, Florida, Hispaniola, Virgina] Sun,
> Moon and Stars, the four [Ceylon] Elements . . . [Goa] Apes, [Ceylon]
> Elephants, [Congo and Angola, in Africa] Serpents, Vipers, Dragons,
> Tygers, Herbs . . . and in many Places [Ceylon, Java, Philippine Islands,
> Aethiopia, Virginia] Evil Spirits . . . Among their D O C T R I N E S, and
> Heads of Belief, were found these that follow. [Tartary] Two Gods, one of
> Heaven, the other of Earth . . . [Siam] One God above the Rest, becoming
> so, by first passing thro' a Multitude of Bodies; [Malabar] Gods subject to
> various Changes, and limited to certain Times of Government; [Malabar,
> Ceylon, Japan, Florida] Providence concerning itself only about the great
> Affairs of the World; [Indians, Tartars, Florida] The Transmigration of
> human Souls into the Bodies of Beasts; [The Bramins] Pagods eating and
> drinking like Men . . . Many P R A C T I C E S have been found among
> them, that are abominable; [East-Indies, Guinea] Women burning them-
> selves with their Husbands, when dead . . . [Jagos (in Africa) Brazil, His-
> paniola] Eating Men's Flesh, and Shambles for selling it . . . [Almost every
> where in Pagan Countries] Having a Number of Wives and Concubines, and
> putting away Wives at Pleasure; [Ceylon] Exposing and killing their Chil-
> dren, if born under an unhappy Planet, or [Formosa] born before the Mother
> was of such an Age, or [China] if the Parents found themselves over-charged.

According to Gibson, these 'Instances of Corruption in Worship, Doctrine, and Practice' which prevail in 'the Heathens World' show that
natural religion, so far as it depends on our rational powers, is an
inadequate guide to belief and action.[46]

Some of the attacks on natural religion by reference to beliefs and
practices in other religions have a 'heads I win, tails you lose' way of

dealing with the evidence. On the one hand, the critics point to the absence of universal and sound doctrines and practices among the other religions. On the other hand, where true doctrines and commendable practices are found among other religions, it is argued that this is due either to the gracious activity of God among the adherents of the other religions or to borrowings from the Judaeo-Christian revelation. Reference has already been made to Wesley's recognition of the activity of the 'inward voice' of God among some of the heathen. Isaac Barrow similarly has a broad view of God's concern. In his second sermon on 'The Doctrine of Universal Redemption' Barrow urges that God's grace 'is not like the Sea, which if it overflow upon one Shore, must therefore retire from another'. Consequently God 'is no less able, no less ready than he ever was to afford help to his poor Creatures, where-ever it is needful or opportune'. In spite, then, of 'the Torrent of natural Pravity' which prevails among men, 'we may at least discern and shew very conspicuous Footsteps of divine Grace . . . even among *Pagans*' where they reveal a knowledge of God's will and manifest 'Qualities and Actions' which 'we can hardly deny to have been the Gifts of God'. It is their adherence to these which will ensure for them at least 'some Part . . . or an imperfect kind of Salvation'.[47] Barrow's recognition of the universal scope of God's providence does not lead him as far as it leads Herbert of Cherbury but it does allow him to accept the good parts of other religions. A similarly qualified but generous spirit is found in Richard Baxter's *Reasons of the Christian Religion*. It does not worry him if 'Pythagoras, Socrates, Plato, the Japonian Bonzii, the Indian Bramenes' or any others are found to teach the truth, for all truth is 'God's truth' and we should not be surprised if 'a God of so much goodness' blesses it, 'who ever be the messenger of it'.[48]

The alternative way of showing that the evidence of correct beliefs in other religions does not support claims about a natural religion was by arguing that these beliefs were derived from the Jewish and Christian tradition of revelation – including in some cases pre-Mosaic revelations contained in that tradition. Theophilus Gale goes to great lengths to argue that 'The wisest of the Heathens stole their choicest Notions and Contemplations, both Philologic, and Philosophic, as wel Natural and Moral, as Divine, from the sacred Oracles' of the Jewish tradition. In defending this thesis he claims the concurrence of such 'learned Papists' as Stenchus Eugubinus and Ludovicus Vives and of such Protestant divines as the Scaligers, Serranus, Vossius, Sandford, Heinsius, Bochart, Jackson, Hammond, Usher, Preston, Owen and Stillingfleet.[49] The same case is put forward by John Edwards. While claiming that the ancient pagan writers confirm what is recorded in the Bible, he maintains that there is an 'unanswerable' argument that 'the Old Testament is the First and Antientest Book that ever was extant, and therefore, when the *Pagan* Writers mention things in this Book, they took them thence, or from those Persons who had them out of these Writings'.[50] It is clear to him that

> *Moses*'s Laws and the Customs of the Patriarchs were not borrowed from the Pagans (as some have imagin'd,) but that the *Chaldeans, Phoenicians*, and *Egyptians*, yea, that the *Arabians* and *Persians* . . . and that the *Greeks* and Latins have derived their Mysteries from the *Hebrews*, and that all the Gentile Theologers borrowed their Great Truths from the Books of the Old Testament.[51]

As Gale's list of supporters suggests, there were many who were prepared to follow this line of argument to reconcile their convictions about the primacy and superiority of a Biblical faith with the presence of parallel ideas in other traditions. Edward Stillingfleet traces agreements between 'Heathen Mythology' and the 'Scripture-history' of 'the first Ages of the World' to humanity's common origin as 'the Posterity of Noah'.[52] Humphrey Prideaux and John Leland see all authentic religious understanding as being derived from divine revelations which started with Adam immediately after his creation. Thus Prideaux suggests that the universality of a '*Notion* of a *Mediator* between *God* and *Man*' is best explained by a revelation to a 'common Parent' of all people[53] while Plato's approximation to 'the truth in divine Matters' came from having 'conversed with the *Jews*' and read their 'sacred Books' when travelling in 'the East'. Aristotle in turn received similar instruction.[54] Leland puts it that 'there is great reason to believe' that 'an original Revelation' was given to 'the first parents and ancestors of the human race' which is the source of the 'knowledge of Religion and Letters' throughout the world.[55] Another to use the argument from derivation is Patrick Delaney. He claims that '*Brama* was *Abram*' (and so the Bramins are descended from Abraham – as is 'well known'). He also holds 'Hystapes and Zoroaster' followed Abraham in introducing 'the worship of God at altars only, without temples' and that knowledge of 'the holy revealed will of God', of writing and of the sciences of 'astronomy and geometry' was 'propagated throughout the world' from the teaching which Abraham gave to his household.[56]

The complexity of the arguments about natural religion and of the use of the evidence of other religions is further illustrated by Hugo Grotius' evaluation of apparent agreements between pagan beliefs and those of the Jewish and Christian religions. He regards them neither as evidence for natural religion nor as material to be explained away as cases of borrowing but as offering support for Biblical claims.[57] Thus he finds it significant that 'the most antient Tradition among all Nations', particularly among those 'who were Strangers to the *Jewish* Religion' is 'exactly agreeable to the Relation of *Moses*'. For example, Moses' 'Description of the Original of the World, is almost the very same as in the antient *Phoenician* Histories . . . and a good Part of it is among the *Indians* and *Egyptians*' from whom the Greeks and Romans learnt about it. The 'Memory of the Seven Days Work' is found 'not only among the *Greeks* and *Italians* . . . but also amongst the *Celtae* and *Indians*'. The story of Adam and Eve is said to be found still 'amongst the *Heathen* dwelling in *Peru*, and the *Philippine* Islands' while the story of the Flood is found in 'Cuba, Mechoacana, Nicaraga' today as well as in ancient writers.[58] In order to use the parallel beliefs of other religions as evidence supporting Christian beliefs, Grotius has to presuppose their independence of the Mosaic tradition. His apologetic treatment of this evidence, that is, is based on an understanding of its origin which is contradicted by theologians like Gale, Edwards, Prideaux and Leland because of the different form of their apologetic arguments for the Biblical materials.

So far as the notion of natural religion is concerned, there are three major responses to empirical evidence that no belief (or at least no significant system of beliefs) is universal, that many absurd things are believed in other religions and that many abominable practices are tolerated or even ordained by other religions. The responses are scepticism about all religion, an intellectual re-understanding of what is meant by natural religion, and an emphasis on the role of revelation in any satisfactory religious understanding. We will consider each of these responses briefly, for they reflect different ways in which people evaluate the significance of other religions during this period.

The sceptical response is found in writers such as Hobbes, Hume, Bolingbroke and Voltaire. They consider that the evils and absurdities of other religions cast doubt on the validity of all forms of religious belief. Hobbes sees the natural state of human life as 'solitary, poore, nasty, brutish, and short' and religion as reflecting this. While reason may lead to an intellectual monotheism, the 'Naturall seed of *Religion*' as practised is the fear of the unknown and the desire to control the future. According to Hobbes the vast variety of religious beliefs and practices is the result of 'the different Fancies, Judgements, and Passions of severall men' which produce 'as many Gods, as there be men that feigne them'.[59] By interpreting the contradictions and absurdities of other religions as evidence of their human origin, Hobbes in effect casts doubt on the validity of any religious belief, in spite of his apparently approving comments about the cosmological argument and supernatural revelation.

In *The Natural History of Religion* Hume powerfully develops this sceptical appraisal. He claims that, whatever reason may conclude,[60] empirical investigations of 'the religious principles which have, in fact, prevailed in the world' show them to be more like 'sick men's dreams' or 'the playsome whimsies of monkeys in human shape, than the serious, positive, dogmatical asserations of a being, who dignifies himself with the name of rational'.[61] Polytheism is held to be the original form of religion, in spite of being the less rational. This is what is indicated by 'the most ancient records' and by 'our present experience concerning the principles and opinions of barbarous nations'.[62] Additionally, it is improbable that people would descend from an initial monotheism to the less rational form of religion found in polytheism.[63] This initial polytheism was the result of primitive people imaginatively projecting the unknown forces which control their life as personal beings, and of their attempts to influence those forces for their well-being.[64] This view of the primitive forms of religion is also used by William Robertson in his study of India. He suggests that 'man in the more early stage of his progress' regards a separate deity as responsible for 'every event which attracts his attention, or excites his terror'. Both the ancient Greeks and the Indians 'believed, that over every movement in the natural world' and in human society, no matter how trivial, 'a particular deity presided'.[65] These gods are the products of human imagination.

Hume, though, not only uses the evidence of other religions to discredit religious belief in terms of its origins: he also claims, again on the basis of both the empirical evidence and the intrinsic rationality of the matter, that polytheism is in some respects much superior in its moral consequences to monotheism, even though the latter is the more rational belief.[66] Referring to 'Machiavel' (and anticipating Nietzsche), he suggests, with faint reservations,[67] that 'the doctrines of the CHRIST-IAN religion' fit people 'for slavery and subjection' whereas polytheism promotes 'activity, spirit, courage, magnanimity, love of liberty, and all the virtues which aggrandize a people'.[68] The evidence of the beliefs and practices of religions, including Christianity, leads Hume to conclude that 'the whole is a riddle, an ænigma, an inexplicable mystery'. The proper response is to suspend judgement concerning religion and to escape from the 'fury and contention' of quarrelling superstitions 'into the calm, tho' obscure, regions of philosophy'.[69]

Robertson, a friend of Hume, was a Presbyterian minister and leader in the Church. It is not surprising, then, that he mostly confines his remarks about the immoral consequences of religion to its superstitious forms in ancient Greece and Rome and particularly in India. He does not draw any general conclusions about religion, and explicitly distinguishes between more primitive superstitions and the 'true religion' that is 'the offspring of reason cherished by science'.[70] What he does point out, though, is that as the deities are 'distinguished, either by ferocity of character or licentiousness of conduct' so the behaviour expected of their adherents follows the same patterns. Some believers practise all kinds of rigorous mortifications. Others link 'the gratification of sensual desire and the rites of public religion', resulting 'in scenes of indulgence too indecent to be described'. In worship 'in the Pagodas' women sing and dance and 'it is difficult to say, whether they trespass most against decency by the gestures they exhibit, or by the verses which they recite'.[71] Whatever, that is, may be the case with rational 'true religion',[72] what is found in practice does not enhance the standing of other actual religions.

An interesting variant of the use of evidence about religion to promote scepticism about actual religions is provided by Bolingbroke. In one of his 'Fragments or Minutes of Essays' he argues that in China 'natural religion seems to have been preserved more pure and unmixed' longer than in any other state. This natural religion, though, was almost wholly a matter of observing 'the order of nature' and deducing morality from it. It was held to be unlawful to attempt to discover anything about the attributes and activity of God. According to Bolingbroke the resulting understanding much better suited 'the purposes of true religion' than the 'artificial theology and superstition' which 'philosophers, legislators, and priests have devised'.[73] In this way, therefore, he used the contrast between the supposedly non-theistic character of pure natural religion (defending it as the result of a proper respect for the ineffability of the divine) and the theistic claims of actual religions to cast doubt on the truth and usefulness of the latter.

Probably the most sceptical response to the evidence of other religions, though, is not by a British author but by a Frenchman, Voltaire. He has no qualms about using reports of Christianity as well as the evidence of other religions to support his scepticism about all actual religions. Christianity for him is, in effect, one of the 'other religions' – even if the most important one – which stand over against his agnostic theism.[74] Time and time again in the *Philosophical Dictionary* he ridicules the doctrines, behaviour and quarrels of believers, often in a delightfully amusing way. His conclusion – which is a warning to students of religion – can be seen in his article on the 'Theologian':

> I knew a real theologian once . . . He knew the Brahmins, the Chaldeans, the Ignicoles, the Sabeans, the Syrians, the Egyptians, as well as he knew the Jews; he was familiar with the various readings of the Bible . . . The more he grew truly learned, the more he distrusted everything he knew. As long as he lived, he was forbearing; and at his death, he confessed he had squandered his life uselessly.[75]

Such is Voltaire's sceptical response to empirical evidence about religion – and his view of the value of studying it!

The second response to the evidence of other religions is to maintain that talk about natural religion should not be confused with empirical assertions about actual religions but treated as descriptions of theological understanding which, in theory at least, all people of good sense can and should discern. This renders claims about natural religion invulnerable to attacks based on the evidence of the actual states of other religions. What such evidence is allowed to show is not the unsatisfactoriness of natural religion but the degree to which it has been corrupted.

This in effect is Herbert of Cherbury's position, for his common notions of religion are identified by metaphysical reflection as being true *a priori*. Although he also indicates that his religious understanding can be empirically verified, his way of doing this is to sift the evidence according to the common notions and thereby to declare apparently contrary materials to be the product of error or priestcraft. Tillotson likewise regards 'the Idolatries of *the Heathen*' as 'a Corruption of *Natural Religion*' which 'grew out of . . . the vicious Temper and Disposition of Mankind'.[76] Following Paul in Romans I, 20 ff, he holds that the heathen 'did not live up to that Knowledge which they had of God' potentially but 'offended against the Natural Light of their own Minds'. Their philosophers 'lost the truth by too much subtilty about it, and . . . disputed themselves into doubt and uncertainty about those things which were naturally known'.[77] Prideaux also sees the origin of 'so many false *Religions* among Mankind' in 'Corruptions insensibly growing on' the 'Natural Religion' which 'God gave unto Man . . . when he first created him'.[78]

Matthew Tindal's Christianity as Old as the Creation is often judged to be the classic statement of the 'deist' position – the position, that is, of those who are critical of some of the traditional claims of Christianity and in particular of its emphasis on revealed truths. In this work the divorce between natural religion and what actually is believed by the numerous 'traditional Religions' is clearly stated:

> By Natural Religion, I understand the Belief of the Existence of a God, and the Sense and Practice of those Duties, which result from the Knowledge, we, by our Reason, have of him, and his Perfections . . . and of the Relation we stand in to him, and to our Fellow-Creatures; so that the Religion of Nature takes in every Thing that is founded on Reason and Nature of Things.[79]

In this way Tindal, accepting the canon of reason without reservation, establishes a position from which he can criticise all actual beliefs and practices, including those of Christianity. A further illustration of this view of natural religion is provided by Lessing. While he accepts that positive religions may be unavoidable because of the way people differ over the contents of 'the religion of nature', nevertheless he asserts that 'the best revealed or positive religion is that which contains the fewest conventional additions to natural religion, and least hinders the good effects of natural religion'.[80]

In such ways, then, theologians attempt to deflect the threat to the idea of natural religion posed by what is found in other religions by distinguishing their natural religion, derived from reason and nature, from the actual doctrines and practices found in the world. They are, however, still vulnerable to attacks which use other religions as examples of the errors and evils into which people of apparently sound reason can still fall. Gibson, for example, argues that defenders of natural religion cannot claim that the 'monstrous Opinions and Practices' of the heathen are due to their 'Measure of Reason' being 'low and imperfect' since in other worldly affairs they seem 'to be skilful and dextrous enough'.[81] Culverwel, though, is among those who are not impressed by assaults on the reliability of human reason. He describes attempts to replace the authority of reason by that of revelation as an 'Oriental Invention'. He has no sympathy for stratagems whereby reason as the 'Candle of the Lord within' everyone is rejected in favour of 'the word of two, or three Hebrew Doctours, that tell you of a voice' which they spread 'like unfaithful

Ecchoes, with *false*, and *imperfect* rebound'.[82]

The kind of position which Culverwel is rejecting constitutes the third response to the evidence of other religions in relation to natural religion, the view that the state of other religions proves the need for revelation if a true, pure and complete religion is to be established in the world. This lies behind many of the references to other religions made by theologians who seek to show the reasonableness of specifically Christian doctrine.

Some theologians maintain that no authentic knowledge of God at all is possible apart from divine acts of revelation. Archibald Campbell concludes from examining mainly classical authors that 'mankind . . . in the exercise of their natural powers and faculties' alone cannot come to a knowledge of even the basic elements of natural religion. For this they stand 'in *absolute* need . . . of supernatural revelation'.[83] John Ellis[84] and John Leland likewise consider that all people have always had, at least potentially, some knowledge of God, but only because the first revelation of the divine was given to Adam and has been transmitted from him to all his descendants. Further revelations by God have been necessary, though, because in the tradition, as is shown by the state of other religions, the reports of the original revelation have become corrupted. It is thus argued at length that examination of pagan philosophy shows that it is unable to arrive at any clear, unerroneous and stable notions of God, morality and immortality. Leland sums up his case in the thesis that 'mankind stand in great need of Divine Revelation to guide and instruct them aright even in the main articles of what is usually called Natural Religion' and that such revelation has been given by God, reaching its climax in 'the Christian Revelation as contained in the Holy Scriptures'.[85] This view of human reason is entertained by Francis Bacon early in our period. He claims that theological understanding, unlike that of the natural sciences, 'ought to be derived from the word and oracles of God, and not from the light of nature, or the dictates of reason'.[86] Towards the end of the period, Apthorp concludes from reflections on various religions that we will be able to serve God acceptably only if first we have been taught by him what to believe and do.[87]

Most of the defenders of the Christian faith in these centuries, however, are not as radical as Campbell, Ellis and Leland in their doubts about the competence of human reason. They do not deny the possibility of any valid natural theology but claim, in contrast to such advocates as Tindal, that the religious understanding which people can reach by their reason alone is inadequate to meet their religious needs, and is liable to be corrupted by errors and human prejudices. Revelation is thus needed to purify and augment what reason may in principle be able to establish. The evidence of other religions is, therefore, not considered by these theologians to imply the impossibility of any non-revelatory knowledge of God. What it does show is the religious insufficiency and intellectual uncertainty of such knowledge.

Samuel Clarke's Boyle Lectures for 1704 and 1705 are a classic statement of the kind of Christian apologetic which rests the revealed truths of religion on a foundation of doctrines established by some kind of natural theology. According to Clarke, reason can demonstrate a number of propositions about the being and attributes of God. Divine revelation, however, is also needed because while there have been 'wise and brave and good Men' among the heathen who have tried to discover, teach and practise 'the Duties of natural Religion', they have never 'been able to reform the World, with any considerably great and universal Success'. This is because they have been 'very *Few* . . . intirely *ignorant* of some Doctrines, and very *doubtful and uncertain* of others, absolutely necessary for the bringing about that great end'.[88]

Other examples of this argument are not hard to find. Many of them, though, are not as optimistic as Clarke about what reason can satisfactorily determine. They thus place even greater stress on the need for revelation, without ruling out in principle any form of valid natural theology. Baxter, for example, sees 'the Light and law of Nature' as having been suitable to people with 'uncorrupted reason' and 'undepraved mind' but as now needing the aid of 'some recovering medicinal Revelation' – as all the religions found in the world testify.[89] Gibson, as has already been noted, likewise regards the state of other religions as proving 'the Insufficiency of *Natural Reason* to be a Guide in Religion'. There is thus 'Need and Expedience of a Divine Revelation'.[90] Halyburton claims that 'a very overly consideration of the religions in the heathen world' will show that in practice what people by their own powers can determine about religion does not have 'the least appearance of satisfying' as a religion since it can provide neither an adequate knowledge of God's nature nor, even more importantly, of his way of salvation as made known in the Christian dispensation.[91] According to Toulmin, only the Christian revelation makes known men's moral duty 'in its full extent', providing 'the full and ample assurances of forgiveness' and 'the most effectual and universal remedy against the fears of death'.[92] By such theses, then, Christian theologians defended the necessity of the Christian revelation, claiming that the evidence of other religions shows that outside that revelation religion is never complete, never certain and often highly corrupt and erroneous.

The relationship between views of natural religion and the evidence of other religions is complicated in the writings of the seventeenth and eighteenth centuries. It is time, however, to consider other aspects of the attitudes to other religions displayed in this period.

IV

Pride and prejudice in
the study of actual religions

Whatever their evaluation of contemporary debates about the reasonableness of Christianity, theologians of this period had no doubts about
the superiority of their own beliefs and practices. Apart from a few
people who were captured by Muslims or who found it expedient to flee
into Turkish territory,[1] those who reject Christianity do not turn to
other actual religions. They leave Christianity for some form of deism or
scepticism which they judge to be superior to and is primarily formed in
reaction against Christian beliefs. The pride and prejudice which lie
behind this sense of superiority hinder their appreciation of other religions. Theologians in particular find it difficult, if not impossible, to treat
other religions seriously and sympathetically. They are so engrossed in
defending their own versions of Christianity against fellow-Christians
and sceptics and, in most cases, so isolated from significant contact with
adherents of other faiths, that they cannot envisage other religions as
viable faiths expressing the ultimate concerns of vast numbers of intelligent people. Instead, even such a distinguished orientalist as Thomas
Hyde tends to treat other religions as matters of curiosity, ridicule and
amazement. In his preface to Bobovius' description of the 'Turkish
Liturgy' he suggests that it is reasonable to regard it as true because it
'discovers their Folly so freely, and gives us Christians Occasion to laugh
at their *Mysterys*'. The 'Nonsense and Folly' of other religions are thus
seen as ways of 'confirming all others more strongly in the *true Religion*'
of Christianity.[2]

When the relative truth of other religions is evaluated, it is either
Christianity or some self-consciously rational development of Christianity that provides the norm for religious truth and the head of the
hierarchy of religions. The usual division of the other religions is a

simple threefold one into 'Paganism, Judaism' and 'Mahometanism'.[3] John Wesley's hierarchy of 'the several sorts of Faith' may initially seem more sophisticated. It ascends from that of a 'Materialist' through those of 'Deists', of 'Heathens, with which I join that of Mahometans', of ancient and modern Jews to that of Roman Catholics before culminating in 'the proper faith of Protestants'.[4] Its refinements, however, express Wesley's judgements on divisions within Christendom rather than a discriminating view of non-Christian faiths. In this it is typical of the period. Even as late as 1792, William Carey's tables of the populations and religions of the countries of the world recognise several forms of Christianity but otherwise distinguish only between Pagans, Jews and Mahometans (noting, though, that in Persia the Mahometans are 'of the Sect of Ali').[5] What is not doubted is that the place of Christianity, in some form, is at the top.

For most of the period, furthermore, there was little awareness of the need to approach other religions in their own terms.[6] Reland urges anyone who wishes to dispute with Muslims 'to learn the *Arabick* . . . to get the *Eastern* Writings, and to see with his own Eyes' but he appreciates that this advice is unusual. The common opinion is that it is not worth-while 'to undergo so much Trouble and Fatigue, only to consult the Dreams and Ravings of a Fanatick'. Most people fail to recognise that Muslims have as much 'Sense and Reason' as other people and that their faith has commended itself in large areas of the world by what is at least an 'Appearance of Truth'. If, therefore, it is to be exposed as 'a very base Religion', it must be as a result of careful efforts to understand it accurately.[7]

Reland's plea, however, generally goes unheard. Even if some commentators see, like Thomas Hyde, that there are *'shining Examples'* of 'Moral and Theological Virtues' as well as ridiculous beliefs and practices in other religions,[8] their modes of understanding and evaluation are largely moulded by their contemporary Christian culture. For instance, descriptions of other religions are basically controlled by the concepts of classical and contemporary European thought. John Holwell may warn his readers that 'ignorance, superstition and partiality to ourselves, are too commonly the cause of presumption and contempt of others' and may result in holding 'in utter detestation and contempt' the religious views of others. Nevertheless, his translation of the 'Gentoo Shastah' is so distorted by the imposition of Christian terms that it seems now to be impossible to identify the original.[9] Christian apologists, furthermore, often employ the traditional argument that where true understanding is found in other religions, it is due to the unperceived activity of the Spirit of God whose nature is correctly acknowledged by Christians. Thus Richard Baxter claims that the 'light and mercy' found in 'Socrates, Plato, Cicero, Seneca, Antonine, Epictetus, Plutarch, &c.' came from the eternal *Logos* redemptively displayed in Christ.[10] By such an argument the finality of the Christian faith is supposedly reconciled with instances of truth elsewhere.

The domination of contemporary Christian modes of understanding is also to be seen in the way that the concepts of other religions are often explicitly identified with those of European thought. Although some such comparisons are unavoidable if people of one culture are to be introduced to the ideas of another, the method was sometimes used so uncritically that it must have hindered rather than helped understanding. Charles Wilkins, for instance, describes 'the most learned *Brahmans* of the present times' as 'Unitarians according to the doctrines of Kreeshna'.[11] A commentary on Hindu literature reports that 'GAUTAMA corresponds with ARISTOTLE; CANA'DA with THALES; JAIMINI with SOCRATES; VYA'SA with PLATO; CAPILA with PYTHAGORAS; and PATANJ-ALI with ZENO'. It does, however, go on to admit that 'an accurate comparison between the *Grecian* and *Indian* Schools would require a considerable volume'.[12] Others are not so cautious about reading the history of other nations in terms of Biblical reports. William Whiston, for example, considers that such stories as those of Cain and Lamech provide clues to explaining the distribution of 'the White, and Black, and Copper-colour'd and Olive-colour'd People of the World'.[13] At the same time, his interpretation of the Biblical account of the extent of the Flood is guided by what he regards as independently known about such parts of the world as China and America.[14] In other studies he revives, as he says, 'Dr. *Giles Fletcher*'s famous Discovery, that the *Tartars* are no other than the ten Tribes of *Israel*: Which have been so long sought for in Vain'.[15] Marshall's comment that Europeans 'created Hinduism in their own image' applies to the interpretation of all non-Christian religions.[16] It is not surprising, therefore, that the other religions are regarded as confused and inferior. They are not only judged by the standard of Christian religious understanding; they are also described in Christian terms.

This assumption of the superiority of Christianity does not mean that everything in other religions is dismissed as utterly worthless.[17] Those who hold certain views about natural religion expect to find some true religious understanding throughout the world, while others who find correct beliefs and sound moral practices in other religions see them as evidence that the grace of God is not confined to professing Christians. Richard Hooker, for example, tempers his understanding of the inescapable obligation to establish the one true religion with the recognition that there was something of value, though mixed with considerable error, in the ancient Britons' belief in the transmigration of souls and the Romans' belief in divination.[18] Stackhouse speaks well of Confucius' moral teaching and of the Peruvians' notion of God. He suggests that the beliefs of the Japanese followers of 'Siaka' are 'in the main Intendment of them true' and that their behaviour puts Christians to shame.[19] John Wesley finds the 'inward voice' of God in 'that Mahometan . . . who . . . wrote the life of Hai Ebn Yokdan' since that story, although suspected by Wesley of being fictitious, 'contains all the principles of pure religion and undefiled'.[20] Comments such as these, however, express only a rather condescending recognition that Christianity is not the sole repository of truth and goodness. They are usually combined with the affirmation that Christianity alone provides the way of salvation. Thus while Thomas Hyde acknowledges that Muslims 'worship the *true God*' and are often exemplary in their alms-giving, justice and other virtues, he also states that what they build 'in the Day of Distinction shall not be able to endure the *fiery Trial*'.[21]

Where other religions are considered theologically, their inferiority is detailed under different heads corresponding to the different arguments used to show the reasonableness of Christian belief. Leaving aside the treatments of Judaism and Islam for separate treatment later, we find that other religions are widely criticised, first, because their beliefs are held to be intrinsically erroneous and seriously defective. Such judgements, of course, are determined by the critics' (Christian) norms for what is reasonable, good, true and complete. Although, towards the end of our period, Nathaniel Halhed maintained that 'we are not justified' in judging 'the Hindoo religion' by 'the known and infallible truth of our own',[22] generally, as has been noted, such reservations were lacking both in principle and in practice.[23] Grotius condemns pagan worship as misdirected and its views of fate as contrary to moral responsibility. Barrow judges pagan claims to revelation to be confused and mutable products of 'human invention or suggestion Diabolical'. Gibson, an orthodox Anglican bishop, and Hume, a probing questioner of belief, agree in condemning pagan worship on the ground that it is usually idolatrous and frequently 'very wicked and abominable'. Tillotson dismisses heathen religion as 'plainly defective, both in the Knowledge of God . . . and the Precepts of a good Life . . . and the assurances of Immortality' – which are for him and for most of his contemporaries the foundation, rule and motive of true religion and morality.[24]

However, while there is general agreement about the overall unacceptability of the beliefs and practices found in other religions, there are disagreements about how far those beliefs and practices are to be interpreted in ways that reduce their *prima facie* erroneousness. A few people are prepared to acknowledge that there may be cases where other religions contain views which are more plausible than Christian ones on some matter – John Holwell, for example, asserts that the doctrine of the Fall can only be expressed without insult to God if we deny with the Bramins that God is prescient of the actions of free agents.[25] On the other hand there are a number of sympathetic reporters who are willing to suggest that the scriptures of other religions are to be understood as using fables and allegories to express basically correct ideas – metaphysical, religious or moral. Herbert of Cherbury, for instance, suggests that the worship of the sun is to be interpreted as intending 'nothing but a *Symbolical* Worship' of 'the *Supreme God*'.[26] Alexander Dow claims Indian support for regarding the different deities of Hinduism as representations of the different attributes of one God. Whatever 'the more ignorant Hindoos' may think, sophisticated 'Brahmins' see the 'long list of inferior' divinities as 'merely allegorical' descriptions of the different attributes of the one God.[27] Others, in contrast, object to such corrective interpretations, maintaining that the scriptures of the other religions are to be understood literally and hence are manifestly false. Isaac Watts and Andrew Fuller thus reject attempts to interpret away polytheistic errors in other religions.[28] In the end, the answer to this hermeneutical question seems to be determined by the judgement that is desired, rather than the judgement by any attempt to answer that question independently.

Other religions are criticised, secondly, because they permit and even inculcate practices that seem immoral to Christian eyes. William Paley speaks of 'the sacred rites of the Western Polytheism' as 'licentious', and the public rites of the East as having 'a more avowed indecency'.[29] Joseph White describes 'the religious creed of the Gentoos' as one of 'the most barbarous idolatry', involving 'mortifications which strike at the root of every lawful and innocent enjoyment'. After mentioning some of the more notorious, he concludes that it is a religion which, unlike 'the pure and rational religion of Jesus', is 'shocking to our reason and to our finer sensibilities'.[30] Even though less tendentious surveys like Bernard

Picart's *Ceremonies and Religious Customs of the Various Nations* acknowledge virtuous elements in the practices of other religions, the overall impression which they leave is that other religions are morally eccentric, if not in certain respects outrightly perverse, in the eyes of British readers. They are also seen as widely corrupted by priestcraft.[31]

The cultural as well as religious conditioning of such judgements can be illustrated by a couple of sentences from a chapter in Picart entitled 'Of the Civility of the *Americans*; their Virtues and Vices':

> They are ignorant of every Thing we call Decorum, and lay the least Restraint imaginable on the Impulses of Nature; they neither have that Reservedness, that Neatness, nor that Discretion, which the Arts of Politeness inspire us with, and have but a very imperfect Knowledge of the Respect which is to be observed among Equals, or between Master and Servant . . . In a Word, if we except the Submission they pay to their respective Chiefs, the Respect they pay their Elders, and that of Children to their Parents, we may affirm, they despise all those Principles on which Politeness is founded.[32]

The adherents of other religions are thus in effect condemned because they would not fit easily into the drawing-rooms of London society and might appear disrespectful to squires and parsons in the shires! It is argued, furthermore, that the rejection of Christianity by adherents of other religions is partly explicable by their 'great corruption of manners' and the way in which 'the purity of the precepts of the Gospel' stands opposed 'to their vitious inclinations'.[33] The assumption of the truth of current 'Christian' morality is thus used both to condemn other religions and to show why their adherents are hard to convert to Christianity.

Other religions are criticised, thirdly, because they are not supported by what are regarded as sound, rational arguments based on convincing 'facts' of history. In the religious controversies of this time, claims to divinely revealed understanding are particularly held to be authenticated by the evidence of accompanying miracles, the fulfilment of prophecies, the intrinsic power of the faith to gain converts and the character of its founder. In the case of other religions, it is argued that their revelations are not backed by any such evidence. Grotius, as well as arguing that pagan religions are not accompanied either by miracles or by fulfilled prophecies, claims that they are shown to be false by their lack of intrinsic power to propagate themselves or even to persist 'Wheresoever humane Force was wanting' to support them.[34] Tillotson denies that there are any authentic miracles to prove the case of other religions: 'the Miracles wrought . . . to confirm false Doctrines, as such as do some way or other confute themselves; or if they be real, are sufficiently detected to be the pranks of the Devil, and not the great and glorious Works of God. Such were the Miracles of the Heathen Deities.'[35] Pagan oracles, furthermore, have never been able to foretell the future with any accuracy and so do not provide an argument from prophecy for the truth of their faiths.[36] Tillotson also argues that pagan religions are only able to continue and spread where they receive the aid of secular forces and because they suit 'the vicious Temper and Disposition of Mankind'.[37] They lack the self-authenticating power of a true religious faith. Francis Atterbury applies historical criticism to the reports of miracles by '*Mango-Copal, Amida, Brama* and *Zaca*'. His conclusion is that 'the Reporters of these Facts are so much later than the Facts themselves, that 'tis impossible to have any Rational Assurance concerning the Reality of them'.[38] Paley similarly argues that both in ancient Greece and Rome and in contemporary India, 'the prevailing mythology' is 'destitute of any proper evidence' because its supposed origin dates from times 'long anterior to the existence of credible history, or of written language'.[39]

By such arguments, defenders of Christianity seek to establish that so far as positive religions are concerned, the choice facing humanity is that, as Baxter puts it, 'Christianity or nothing is the way'.[40] Sometimes problems arise for such defences, however, when critics suggest that similar objections may be raised against the Christian evidences. Conyers Middleton's exposé of 'the *pretended miracles* and *pious frauds* of the *Romish Church*', as continuing the practice of forgery used by pagan priests, appealed to Protestants wanting to strengthen their case against Roman Catholicism.[41] At the same time, it worried some that Middleton's views seemed at least to hint that the basic Christian arguments from miracle might not be invulnerable.[42] Such doubts are largely responsible for the numerous eighteenth-century discussions of the historical accuracy of the reports of Jesus' resurrection, in an attempt to find one conclusive item of evidence that will show that Christian claims to revelation are divinely authorised. Another source of concern arose from the growth of the missionary movement. To those Christian apologists who hold that the truth of Christianity is shown by its miraculous power to gain converts in its first centuries, it is disturbing that contemporary Christian missions have such a lack of success. The heathen do not come flocking in. Paley concludes from this that Christ and his apostles must have 'possessed means of conviction' which are not presently available.[43]

On the whole, though, it is widely felt that whatever problems may face a positive assertion of Christian evidences, the other religions have nothing satisfactory to offer in justification of their claims to revelation.

A fourth argument against paganism takes the form of showing, at least to the Christian advocate's satisfaction, that the founder of Christianity is superior in status, wisdom, power and moral goodness to the founders of other religions. Negatively, John Jortin argues that 'the *Gentiles* ought not to have slighted and rejected the Gospel upon account of the low estate and sufferings of Christ and his Apostles'. Both their reason and their teachers should have taught them that 'temporal happiness', wealth and esteem are not signs of wisdom, virtue and 'the favour of God'.[44] Positively, Christ's character is variously compared to those of Mahomet, Socrates, Confucius, Buddha and Zoroaster, for instance, in order to establish 'a stronger conviction' of Christ's 'superior dignity and worth' than is produced by an examination of his character alone.[45]

Leaving till later comparisons with Mahomet and Moses, we find, for example, that Joshua Toulmin compares Socrates and Christ with reference to their background, education, experience, teaching, character, style of life and behaviour at death. Although Socrates was a great teacher and a good man, indeed possibly 'a kind of Type of Christ to the Heathens',[46] Toulmin asserts that 'the divine Jesus . . . with much greater purity and perfection inculcated the same principles'. Not only is Socrates charged with accepting the religion of his day. He is also accused of a lack of 'purity and decorum' because he wrestled with Alcibiades and taught Theodata how to snare admirers! His irony is said to indicate 'superciliousness' and his behaviour in writing verses the night before his death that his 'behaviour was not uniformly great'.[47]

Similar arguments are used to show the inferiority of Confucius to Christ. Toulmin's comparison of their conduct is along the lines of 'whatever you can do, I can do better'! Confucius' teaching is held to be the product of human thought whereas, according to Toulmin, 'we are naturally led' by the evidence to hold that '*divine* communications' were the source of Christ's teaching.[48] This judgement is somewhat modified by the suggestion that, for all the limitations of his teaching, some of Confucius' remarks may show that he was divinely 'inspired with a foreknowledge of the coming of the Saviour of the World'.[49] This claim, though, in effect reinforces the assertion of Christ's superiority, since it gives to Confucius the role of preparing the Chinese for the reception of Christian preachers.

Although there are numerous references to what must be Buddhist doctrines and practices, Buddhism itself is often not clearly distinguished as a separate religion. It is not identified as such, for example, in Alexander Ross' *View of All Religions in the World* when he mentions, albeit rather briefly, the religions found in the territories of south-east Asia. For most of our period, the relative paucity and confused state of information about religions east of Persia results in those religions being described according to political and geographical divisions, with all that pertains to a particular country or region being bundled together in a somewhat undiscriminating pot-pourri.

There is considerable confusion, in particular, over the identification of Buddha (or 'Sommona Codom' or 'Siaka' or the Chinese 'Fo' as he is variously called). Thomas Stackhouse repeats Siamese and Japanese reports that he was originally a prince in Ceylon.[50] Hugh Farmer speaks of Buddha as 'the most celebrated of the Samanean doctors, who was born near seven hundred years before Christ'. His doctrine has been adopted in India, Japan, China, Siam and Tartary and he is 'honoured as a god'.[51] Sir William Jones makes several attempts to identify Buddha. In his discourse 'On the Hindu's' in 1786 he maintains that 'W O D or O D E N, whose religion . . . was introduced into *Scandinavia* by a foreign race, was the same with B U D D H A whose rites were probably imported into *India* nearly at the same time, though received much later by the *Chinese*, who soften his name in F Ó'.[52] A year later, in his discourse 'On the Arabs', Jones conjectures that Buddha was a person who 'travelled eastward from *Ethiopia*, either as a warrior or as a lawgiver, about a thousand years before C H R I S T and whose rites we now see extended' as far as Japan.[53] In a dissertation, 'On the Chronology of the Hindus', written in 1788, however, Jones mentions the 'strange diversity of opinion' which he finds among 'the different *Pandits*' whom he has consulted about the date of Buddha.[54] His conclusion now is that the 'Hindus' have probably 'confounded' two Buddhas. One of them was the ninth (and so far the last) 'of the *Avátara's*, or *Descents*, of the Deity'; the other perhaps one of 'his followers in a later age' who 'attempted to overset the whole system of the *Bráhmans*'.[55] Jones' final comment is that 'if the learned *Indians* differ so widely in their accounts' about the time of the Buddha's appearance as 'the ninth Avátar', we may justifiably 'suspect the certainty of all the relations concerning even *his* appearance', let alone those concerning earlier figures.[56] Generally, where the Buddha is mentioned, and it is not often, he is presented as a teacher of moral precepts and the transmigration of souls, whom some adherents erroneously worship as a God, not as a significant rival to Christ.

Discussions of Zoroaster and his followers are not uncommon although the treatment of the latter is more often in terms of the Magi of ancient Persia than with reference to contemporary Parsees.[57] The pride and prejudice which colours the appraisal of other religions is frequently displayed; for example, Zoroastrian doctrines are presented either as intrinsically mistaken or, where they contain elements that are true, as derived from Jewish sources. It is sometimes suggested, furthermore, that Zoroaster not only learned his ideas from others but also set himself up as a prophet in order to enjoy the prestige which he envied in the Jewish prophets. In no way are he and his followers seen as rivals to Christ and Christianity.

As with the case of the Buddha, there is some confusion about the date of Zoroaster. Ralph Cudworth speaks of him as being 'of so great Antiquity, that Writers cannot well agree about his Age'. He describes him, rather confusedly, as a polytheist who worshipped many gods while acknowledging 'one Supreme' God as the 'only Fountain and Original of all Good' and asserting that there is 'an Evil Daemon Coeternal with God, and Independent on him'.[58] Cudworth links Zoroastrian teaching with Mithraism and sees it as consequently including beliefs which hint at the doctrine of the Trinity.[59] A major advance in knowledge about Zoroastrianism came with the publication of Thomas Hyde's Historia Religionis Veterum Persarum in 1700, which places Zoroaster in the reign of Darius Hystaspes.[60] Although not everyone was immediately convinced, what is generally important to those who discuss Zoroaster is to make it clear that there are no reasonable grounds for regarding him as a source of revealed insights into the divine. John Leland, for instance, presents a 'heads I win, tails you lose' kind of argument to this effect. If Hyde is correct, Zoroaster is to be seen as having 'derived his notions of God . . . from the Mosaic and Prophetical writings' while if Zoroaster lived in patriarchal times, his doctrines 'may be supposed to have preserved considerable remains of the antient primitive religion'.[61] John Holwell repeats other reports that Zoroaster visited 'Indostan . . . about the time of Romulus' in order to be instructed by the 'Bramins North West of the Ganges . . . in the doctrines and worship instituted by the Chatah and Aughtorrah Bhades'. He is also said to have 'been initiated in all the mysteries, and learning, of the Egyptians'.[62] Generally, though, the major source of his instruction in religious truth is held to be Jewish. He is said not only to have been a Jew but also to have been the servant of one of the prophets. According to Prideaux this prophet is probably to be identified as Daniel although others have been mentioned, ranging from Elias to Ezra.[63]

There were some doubts about the authenticity of the materials ascribed to Zoroaster by Hyde. Hugh Farmer, for example, refers to two learned gentlemen who maintain that the supposed fragments of Zoroaster given by Hyde are 'the rhymes of a modern priest who lived about three centuries ago'. This is part of his attempt to show that the ancient Persians (whom he describes as 'a barbarous people') fit his theory that the ancient heathens worshipped human spirits.[64] On the whole, however, Zoroaster is not attacked by questioning the evidence about him but by appraising its significance. Whatever the respectability of his sources, Zoroaster's use of them is condemned. Holwell allows that his moral instruction may bear 'the stamp of divine' but judges his 'system of theology' to be one of 'madness'. On the basis of 'Bramah's *Shastah*' there was raised 'an aerial superstructure, wild and incomprehensible' which propagated 'an unintelligible jargon of divinity'.[65] Prideaux, who follows the more usual line in seeing Zoroaster as basically influenced by Jewish ideas, introduces him as 'the greatest Impostor, except *Mahomet*'. He shared 'all the craft and enterprising boldness of that *Arab*' but was more learned. While he took his doctrine of God from the Jewish scriptures, 'the crafty Impostor' dressed it up 'in such a style and form' as would suit the 'old Religion of the *Medes* and *Persians*'.[66] As for claims that he foretold the coming of Christ, these are said to have come from 'the *Legendary* writings of the Eastern Christians'.[67] Since, then, his moral and religious teachings are a mixture of borrowings and personal adaptations, Zoroaster is not perceived as any threat to the significance of Christ. If anything, comparisons between the two are held to highlight the unique status of the latter. As for current followers of Zoroastrian beliefs, those surviving in Persia are in oppressed conditions while a colony of them in Bombay are described as 'a poor, harmless sort of people, zealous in their Superstition, rigorous in their Morals, and exact in their Dealings, professing the worship of one God only . . . '.[68] Implicit in such comments is the judgement that while such people may provide trustworthy trading partners, their religion presents no threat to the primacy of the Christian faith.

Where apologists for a divine revelation in Christ argue that his life and teaching offer an intrinsic verification of his significance, they sometimes use tendentious comparisons not only with the central figures of other religions such as Buddha and Zoroaster but also with major

thinkers such as Socrates in order to highlight their claim. Joshua Toulmin, for example, argues that Christ's teaching about immortality is
certain in contrast to the 'surmises and conjectures' of the 'philosophers
of antiquity'.[69] He taught openly whereas 'the lectures of the antient
Philosophers were not open to all men'. He was generous in temper,
frank and able to confirm his teaching by 'visible and notorious works of
power' which they could not emulate.[70] Whereas 'the Founders of all
false religions' invented 'some whimsical mortification', the Christian
religion is thoroughly reasonable.[71] As for Christ's 'instructions in virtue', they are 'pure and perfect'.[72] In these ways, then, the internal
evidences of Christianity are held to show it to be 'of divine origin'. For
Toulmin they confirm Christ's status as a supreme 'Teacher' and
'Prophet';[73] for others who did not share his Unitarian hesitations, they
also showed Christ's personal divinity.

Evidence about the antiquity of some of the other religions, particul-
ary the Egyptian, Chinese and Hindu, presented problems for Christian
apologists. Critics of Christian belief use this evidence in two ways.
Some employ it to challenge the truth of the Biblical materials. Sir
William Jones might confess that since he is 'attached to no system', he
can accept or reject 'the Mosaick history' according to the evidence.[74]
Those who, as believers, see themselves as fundamentally committed to
some understanding of Christianity tend to assume that Christian faith
involves assent to what the Bible records. They regard it as necessary,
therefore, to uphold the Biblical story whatever the apparent evidence
from other religions;[75] otherwise, as Voltaire points out, those who
maintain that 'God dictated' the Bible will have to admit that 'God
evidently is not an expert in chronology'.[76]

Nathaniel Halhed indicates one aspect of this problem of chronology.
He suggests that Hindu scriptures cast doubt on 'the Mosaic chronology
as generally received' by presenting 'plausible accounts' of remoter ages
than that chronology allows for. Furthermore, agreements between the
laws of Moses and those of the Hindus may be explained as due to the
early transplantation of 'the doctrines of Hindostan . . . into Egypt'
where they were learnt by Moses.[77] Similar assertions of the relative
novelty and derivative nature of the Jewish scriptures are made by
Voltaire: only 'ignorance and fanaticism' maintain that the Pentateuch is
older than the books of Sanchuniathon, of Thout, and of the first
Zerdusht, the Shasta, the Vedas and the five Kings of the Chinese.[78]
Whereas Voltaire, however, was unsympathetic to Christian claims,
Halhed affirms a Christian orthodoxy. He states that ultimately he has 'a

most unshaken reliance' upon 'divine revelation' and prefers it to the sceptical suspicions of human reason.[79] Sir William Jones rejects this trump-card of faith when used by Hindus to defend their records.[80] As for Christianity, he defends the Biblical accounts of the first stages of humanity on the grounds that the earliest Hindu records are 'chiefly *mythological*' and that their historical reports cannot be trusted 'farther back than about two thousand years before CHRIST'.[81] He also argues that Moses' piety precludes any idea that he would have borrowed parts of the Egyptian mythology.

A different use of evidence about antiquity to threaten Christian faith rests on the assumption that truth and age go together. In the preface to *The Travels of Cyrus*, for example, Andrew Ramsay states that he judges the Orientals and then the Egyptians to be purer in their theology than the Greeks and the Romans. His aim is 'to shew that the earliest opinions of the most knowing and civilized nations come nearer the truth than those of latter ages'.[82] This preference for the past – often held to be the location of a presumed golden age – is widespread. It leads some to assume that the first state is the best, an assumption which lies behind many of the attempts to locate the original unity and derivation of religions. Some of the results today seem more ingenious than ingenuous. Colonel Pearse, for example, links the Hindu festival of Bhavání with English maypole customs to suggest that there is 'a strong affinity' between Hinduism and 'the old religion of *Britain*' while Reuben Burrow suggests possible links between the ancient monuments of Egypt, Ireland and India – and possibly also the Tower of Babel.[83] John Holwell holds that the Bramins have the 'truly original' religious tenets and that these were later learnt from them by the Egyptians, Persians, Greeks and Romans.[84] Sir William Jones, on the other hand, describes 'the system of *Indian* theology invented by the *Bráhmans*' as 'the first corruption of the purest and oldest religion'.[85] Jones places the origin of humanity in Iran[86] and claims that the initial 'general union' of religion is shown by similarities in the religions of Greece, Rome, Egypt, India, China, Persia, Phrygia, Phoenice, Syria, 'some of the southern kingdoms and even islands of *America*' and among the Goths.[87] He sees this as confirmation of 'the truth and sanctity of the *Mosaick* History' as found in the early chapters of Genesis.[88] Patrick Delaney, as has been mentioned, provides a variant derivation by holding that '*Brama* was *Abram*' and so the Bramins are descended from Abraham.[89]

In such ways, then, various Christian apologists evaluate and interpret the chronological materials of other religions in order to make them cohere with, if not positively to confirm their beliefs. Others prefer an easier way, attacking the evidence as in principle unreliable. Collyer, for instance, rejects the suggestion that 'the Mosaical ordinances' may have been derived from the Egyptians on the grounds that God would not 'ordain such customs as the Devil himself was author of'.[90]

Joseph Butler in his *Analogy of Religion* defends the revealed elements in Christian belief against the objections of critics who hold that natural theology is sufficient by arguing, among other things, that the difficulties which these critics find in the revealed elements are also to be found in the doctrines of their natural theology. This form of argument is also used to defend the truth of Christianity against the other religions. As Hugo Grotius puts it, 'there have not been wanting some amongst the Heathen, who have said those Things singly, which in our Religion are all put together' and are clearly true while 'if there be any thing in the Christian Religion difficult to be believed, the like is to be found amongst the wisest of the Heathen'.[91] Such a mode of reasoning is, of course, significant only for those who accept that Christianity is the true faith. In the hands of others like Hume and Voltaire this kind of argument provides another way of discrediting Christian beliefs. Voltaire, for example, argues that the rational difficulties of Christian beliefs and the absurd practices which Christians sometimes adopt show that Christianity is no more acceptable than any other religion. In spite of the explanations of learned commentators – 'subtle and exquisite minds, excellent metaphysicians, men free from prejudices, and not at all pedantic'[92] – Christians have no right to feel superior to the adherents of other religions. Considering how some Christians behave, how dare they 'make fun of Laplanders, Samoyedes, and Negroes!'[93]

Nevertheless, writers of this period do make fun of other religions. They are so convinced of the correctness of their own positions that they often do not bother to argue against other religions, being content to describe them as obvious absurdities in order to highlight their own superiority. Sometimes they even maintain that the more learned among the followers of the other religions share their scepticism.[94] Consequently there are far more descriptions of other religions than serious attempts to refute them. Whereas, then, Lessing's parable of the three rings in *Nathan the Wise* suggests that between the faiths of Jew, Muslim and Christian the true one is undiscoverable, and others, like Herbert of Cherbury, advocate the study of religions in order to discover 'which among the several religions in the world, is the purest, chastest, and best',[95] the more typical attitude, though, (even if it is rarely expressed so blatantly) is that of George Fox who summons Jews, Turks and Chinese to acknowledge Christ. To 'the Emperor of China, and his Subordinate Kings and Princes', he writes that 'God is come to Rule, and his Son Christ to uphold all things'. None will be accepted by the living God except those 'who are in the Light, which is Christ his Son'.[96] There are no hesitations about the truth of Christianity here.

The variety of descriptions of other religions produced in the seventeenth and eighteenth centuries reflects growth in knowledge of as well as of popular interest in other parts of the world. The range of references is as extensive as the known world. As the period progresses, and especially towards its end, there appears an increasing number of studies intended simply to provide information about other peoples and not to support a particular position in current theological debates. Outside discussions of Christianity, Judaism and Islam, though, religions tend to be treated as nationally or geographically defined entities which are largely indistinguishable from the society, politics and even culture of their adherents.[97]

Throughout the period the fate of non-Christians is often a cause of concern. Herbert of Cherbury's desire to appreciate the universality of God's providence leads him to assert that 'in matters relating to eternal salvation no model of Faith . . . is given, beyond what is common to all mankind'.[98] In the same vein, ' A . W .' in Blount's *Oracles of Reason* asserts that 'no Revealed Religion is necessary to future Happiness' for it cannot 'be made known to all men'.[99] The common view among Christians, however, is that salvation comes through Christ. In the prayer of consecration at Holy Communion Anglicans remind themselves that Jesus Christ made 'a full, perfect, and sufficient sacrifice, oblation, and satisfaction for the sins of the whole world'. As Richard Kidder puts it, 'Our Lord rescued us, and saved us, we contributed nothing toward our deliverance. He is the Saviour of mankind: Our intire deliverance is to be ascribed to him'.[100] The problem is whether those who have never heard of Christ's saving work are covered by it or whether their unculpable ignorance results in their eternal damnation?

Thomas Halyburton is prepared to answer 'Yes' to this question. He judges all people to be guilty before God and so as having 'forfeited any claim' to God's favour. They should not, therefore, complain if God chooses that acceptance of the gospel in faith be 'the only effectual mean of acceptance with and justification before God'.[101] It is not that those who do not hear the gospel are unfairly deprived but that those who do receive it are undeservedly fortunate. Halyburton's position is shared by many. Where they feel that God's justice in this needs defence, they argue that the evil deeds of the heathen offend against natural laws which all people can appreciate and should obey. Others, though, such as Thomas Rymer, see this understanding of the gospel message as producing a 'heavy Prejudice against the Christian Scheme'. It makes a mockery of the 'universality of Christ's Merits' if 'so great a Majority of Mankind' is condemned 'to eternal Misery, for want of such Faith in Christ as they never cou'd attain to'.[102]

Isaac Barrow recognises the unlimitedness of God's grace. He responds to the problem of the salvation of non-Christians by suggesting that Christians should be content with affirming Christ as the 'Saviour of all Men' and not perplex themselves about how his saving grace is imparted to others.[103] Rymer holds that those 'to whom Christ is in no Degree reveal'd' are not in that respect 'criminally defective in their Faith': their 'future Happiness' is secured by living according to the Faith that is made known to them.[104] John Wesley, for all his insistence on the gospel of justification and sanctification by grace, similarly asserts, in a sermon on the text 'Without Faith it is impossible to please him' (Hebrews 11, 6), that 'no more . . . will be expected' of Heathens 'than the living up to the light they had'.[105] Alexander Ross even allows that God sometimes blesses 'the professors of false Religions, and punisheth the contemners thereof' because a false religion 'when conscientiously practised' stands for some acknowledgement of a divinity and of social order.[106] Richard Baxter accepts that the heathen are to be judged according to their understanding, but has doubts about their ability to show the repentance and holiness of life that is properly required of them.[107] He seeks to solve the problem of their salvation by distinguishing between 'Christ's procurement of our pardon and salvation by his sacrifice' and 'Christ as the object of man's faith, or as believed in by man'.[108] The former alone is necessary for salvation, and has been available from the creation of humanity. It is not restricted in its effectiveness to those who recognise it.[109] John Tillotson similarly considers that the good among the heathen were accepted by God and 'not excluded from the Blessing of the *Messias*, tho' they were ignorant of him'.[110]

The problem of reconciling the universality of salvation to Christian claims for Christ is complicated, though, by two other considerations. First, it is recognised by some that if non-Christians are to be judged according to their lights, contemporary 'deists' who reject the Christian revelation might claim the same conditions for their salvation. It is presumably in order to counter such a claim that Isaac Watts is led to indicate a distinctly unpleasant future for non-Christians:

> If the heathen or infidel nations, with all their sincerity, are described in the New Testament as having no hope of eternal life, even where the gospel had not been published, surely much less ground is there for hope, where the gospel is known and refused.[111]

Even if some 'mollifying sense' may be put on what the Bible says about the heathens who have not heard the gospel, no such amelioration will be applicable to those who have rejected it.

Secondly, claims that the heathen have some way of salvation apart from a recognition of Christ threaten one of the main motives behind the development of missionary activities. Thomas Wilson urges 'serious' Christians who find themselves 'among the Heathens' to take up the missionary task. They are to try to convince them that they are liable to be punished 'most severely in the Life which is to come' for worshipping Gods which are really 'evil Spirits'.[112] Somewhat ironically, then, those who are concerned enough about non-Christians to ensure that they hear the Christian message of salvation also tend to maintain that otherwise they will suffer for no fault of their own. The gospel they present seems to work in them a humanity which is apparently lacking in its God!

Thomas Stackhouse represents the perplexity which many share. On the one hand he accepts that there is no other way to redemption than that effected by Christ. On the other he recognises that it would 'seem very hard' if some were excluded from 'the Benefit of this Act of Grace' simply because 'they did not lay hold on what they never heard of'. His solution is to affirm that God will judge them according to their understanding, that God will compensate them hereafter for their 'melancholy' state in this world, and that God can make known to them what is necessary for salvation between this life and the day of judgement. In such ways he will be 'infinitely kind to them'.[113] Later Stackhouse returns to the issue and, perhaps justifiably, decides that it is 'a Mystery past our Comprehension' how the saving work of Christ, the divine nature and the salvation of the heathen world are reconciled to each other.[114]

With such views of other religions, it is not surprising that, like Robinson Crusoe, theologians of this period find 'an infinite satisfaction' in living where they do and 'not where the people, given up by Heaven to strong delusions, worship the devil'.[115] Tillotson describes 'the difference between the Christian Religion and all others . . . profest in the World' as 'almost equal to that betwixt *light* and *darkness*'. Only 'passion, or prejudice, or interest, or some other faulty Principle' prevents a person from assenting to Christianity.[116] In his view, the errors of the heathen are parasitic upon the truth of Christianity and thereby they confirm it.[117] At best, the doctrines of the heathens are 'mythological fables, invented to express some moral virtues or vices, or the history of nature, and power of the elements, &c.'.[118] At worst, they are dismissed out of hand as monstrous in thought and deed. The pride and prejudice which lies behind such attitudes is illustrated by Isaac Watts' thanks to God who, by his 'rich and peculiar grace . . . has appointed our birth in Great Britain, where the name of Christ and his gospel are known, while millions of our fellow-creatures, made of the same flesh and blood, are travelling onward to eternity, with few or none of these advantages'.[119]

There were, however, two religions which could not be so cavalierly dismissed – Judaism and Islam. If Christianity were to be seen to be the true religion, its apologists needed to show by sound reasons why the claims of Judaism and Islam must be judged to be false.

V

The treatment of Judaism

Theological comments about the Jewish religion in the seventeenth and eighteenth centuries are frequently confused because it is not clear, at times apparently even to the authors, whether they refer to Judaism as the religion of the Old Testament, as the religion of a people up to and at the time of Christ, as the religion of a people since that time, or as a contemporary faith. Although most treatments of Judaism are largely concerned with the adequacy and permanence of the religion of the Old Testament (generally regarded as a single, coherent faith), there are some references to later beliefs and practices. Alexander Ross, for example, deals first with Biblical reports and then turns to what is observed to happen now in synagogues in various places on the Continent.[1] He describes the current practices of the Jews as being 'Rabbinical rather than Mosaical' and claims that Jews defend this on the grounds that 'they are not tied to the Rites of *Moses*, because they are not in their own Land'.[2] Picart's work is another exception to the concentration on Biblical forms of Judaism, for the materials which he uses describe a wide range of 'the customs and ceremonies of the present Jews'.[3] Often, though, the lack of any great degree of historical awareness combines with considerable ignorance about contemporary Jewish ways[4] to lead commentators to concentrate on Biblical evidence. If this seems somewhat lacking in intellectual awareness, it should be remembered that most theologians in this period (as well as since the development of historical consciousness) would also have regarded Biblical materials as the proper source for discovering the true nature of contemporary Christian faith.

Whatever Christian commentators in this period mean when they refer to Judaism, however, they cannot treat it in the same way as other non-Christian faiths. They are unable to dismiss it as utterly worthless since, whatever the influences that have moulded post-Biblical Judaism, in the Old Testament Christians accept the Jewish holy scriptures as the first part of their own. Admittedly, Christians can claim that the relationship with God represented in the old covenant has been replaced by the gospel of the New Testament. In practice, though, most Christians seem happy to range over the whole Bible from Genesis to Revelation in selecting authoritative passages for guiding Christian faith and practice. Christian advocates, furthermore, generally consider it necessary to acknowledge that 'the *Jewish* Religion . . . had its birth from the revelation and appointment of God'.[5] On the one hand, therefore, they have to defend the divine revelation contained in the Old Testament, both against the advocates of natural religion who argue that no revelation is needed, and against sceptical critics who use the contents of the Old Testament to attack its authority. Among such critics is Thomas Chubb who concludes that 'the *Jewish* revelation, in the gross (whatever may be the case of some particular branches of it) cannot well be admitted as *divine*, without offering some kind of *violence* to the human mind'. It presents, for instance, unworthy portraits of God and commands ceremonies which are 'a *battery* against *virtue* and *true religion*'.[6] On the Continent, Voltaire delights in pointing out parts of the Old Testament that are far from obviously divine.[7] On the other hand Christian apologists, because they are Christian, have also to show that the truth and finality of the divine revelation in the New Testament is not rendered superfluous or invalid by acceptance of the Old Testament as divinely revealed. Henry More, for example, seeks to do this by asserting that while 'God himself was the Institutor of the Religion of the Jews', and that while that religion is far superior to '*Paganism*', nevertheless it only prefigures in shadowy types the 'rich Discoveries of the Gospel'.[8]

The difficulty facing Christian apologists is that solutions to one problem are liable to aggravate the other. The more the Old Testament is held to contain a revelation from God necessary to people's well-being (in opposition to advocates of some form of natural religion), the harder it becomes to hold that it had to be superseded by that of the New Testament, at least without implying some deficiency in God's initial revelation. Conversely, the more the normative status of the revelation in the New Testament is stressed, the harder it becomes to show that the Old Testament must be regarded as from God. In practice, as Voltaire teasingly points out, Christians show 'a strange prejudice', for they 'abhor the Jews' while insisting that 'everything written by them . . . bears the inprint of Divinity'.[9] The opening of *The Questions of Zapata* points to the dilemma facing the Christian advocate:

1. How ought I to proceed with the object of showing that the Jews, whom we burn by the hundred, were for four thousand years God's chosen people?
2. How could God, whom one cannot without blasphemy regard as unjust, forsake the whole earth for the little Jewish tribe, and then abandon this little group for another? . . .
4. If God is the God of Abraham, why do you burn the children of Abraham? And, when you burn them, why do you recite their prayers? How is it that, since you worship the books of their law, you put them to death for observing that law?[10]

The usual solution offered by Christian apologists to the problem of the status of the Jewish religion, in view of the place of the Old Testament in the Christian canon of holy scripture, is that the Jews have failed to understand the Old Testament correctly. As Baxter puts it, a correct understanding of the Old Testament 'will confute the *Jews* rejection of Jesus Christ'. It is not 'what they have from God' which is to be rejected but what they erroneously deny.[11] More virulent anti-Jewish polemicists like William Romaine go on to point out that while Christians accept that the Old Testament is as much of 'divine authority' as the New, the contents of both being 'true in all their parts, and worthy of that all-wise God, by whose inspiration they were written', it should not be forgotten what is said in the New Testament 'about the Jews, who crucified Christ'.[12] Whatever status might therefore seem to belong to the Jewish religion in view of Old Testament texts has to be corrected in the light of New Testament remarks about the Jews, it being assumed that modern Jews share their condemnation.

A theologically more sophisticated expression of the problem posed by the Old Testament is raised by the claim that what it records was revealed by God. The question arises of how it can be claimed that a divine revelation is defective and so needed to be replaced or augmented by that of the New Testament. To judge a revelation to be defective seems to cast aspersions on God, suggesting either that he is mutable[13] or that the earlier revelation he gave was unsatisfactory. Isaac Barrow tackles this problem, asserting on the one hand that the goodness, wisdom and justice of God make it highly reasonable to expect that God will reveal his nature and humanity's duty and, on the other, that what God did reveal as the Jewish religion was 'in many respects defective'.[14] He nevertheless maintains that this latter judgement does not impute anything unbecoming to God's perfection. God may quite properly make 'so imperfect a Revelation', first, because there can be no reason why God may not choose to delay giving all or part of the revelation needed by people and, secondly, because the revelation found in the Old Testament is suited primarily to the 'stupid . . . fickle . . . and stubborn' spirit of the Jews. It can, therefore, be regarded as a proper revelation by God to the Jews but one which is not suited to 'the rational nature' of the mature humanity which Barrow sees in his contemporaries.[15]

A more sympathetic presentation of this latter point is offered by Thomas Burnett. He sees the nature of God's revelation as guided – and limited – by the pedagogical needs of the Jews. Because they had been 'bred up in hard labour, under the oppressions of Tyranny', they had become 'a very dull, and stupid people'. Consequently, God graciously condescends to their capacities, reducing his moral commands to what they could remember and presenting 'the most important truths to them' in the form of 'Emblems and Figures' which they could grasp.[16] Their ceremonial observances similarly are to instruct them in God's ways. Although Burnett is aware of the dangers of 'Fanciful Invention' at this point, he does suggest that

> When Swines Flesh, for Instance, was made Unclean, to them, it might be for Instruction in Righteousness, as well as other Ends, that they might by this be taught to avoid the brutal Nature of that Creature, that as he wallows in the Mire, when full, so they should not wallow in sin, which is usually represented under the notion of Filth, nor abuse their Plenty to Sensuality, and Licentiousness. When they are forbid to eat Birds of Prey, 'tis to teach them, that they must not live by Rapine; and by Fish without Scales, that delight in Mud, they were taught to avoid all Earthly-mindedness, and all base and mean designs, and practices.[17]

Presumably implicit in such remarks is the view that 'free-born' Britons with their better understanding no longer need such educational aids.

One other widespread view is that in the Jewish faith God provided symbols of what later, in his own time, he would make known directly. The defectiveness of the earlier revelation thus does not indicate imperfection in God but rather his plan for and control over the processes of history. Ross, for example, sees the structure and utensils of Solomon's temple as divinely foreshadowing the Christian dispensation: 'the Altar of Burnt-offerings did signifie our Eucharist, and the Brazen-Sea our Baptism' while the 'Holy Oyl with which the Priest was anointed, shadowed the Graces of the Spirit'.[18]

Having in such ways tried to answer (and in many cases ignored) the tricky problem of how to reconcile the divine origin of the Jewish religion with its defectiveness, Christian theologians criticise Judaism on a number of counts. Their comments not only reflect New Testament strictures on the Jews and current anti-Jewish polemic, but are also shaped to some extent by current arguments for the truth of Christianity.

In the first place, the particularity of Judaism is adduced as evidence against it. Judaism is claimed to be imperfect because it is not the product of a revelation to all people. It is based on a special revelation to a particular group and is conditioned by their allegedly peculiar character and calling. Various of its supposed characteristics are specified as showing that it lacks that 'due condition of generality and amplitude' of the revelation needed by humanity as a whole.[19] Thus it is held that God does not make known all his will therein, that its stress on ritual rather than on moral and spiritual rules is unsatisfactory for the rational nature of people, that it imposes unattainable duties and provides no real hope of forgiveness of sins,[20] that it offers only temporal rewards for good living, and that it has no promise of immortality.[21] The Jewish revelation, therefore, is unable to bring salvation to humanity. Even when account is taken of God's later revelations through the prophets as well as of his fundamental ones through Abraham and Moses, it is still held to be the case that 'the whole *horizon* of heavenly truth was not disclosed' to the Jews. The Old Testament's revelation is thus 'so scant, and pinched' and so 'ill proportioned' to the glory of God and the needs of humanity that Judaism cannot reasonably be regarded as representing God's final instruction for humanity.[22] Indeed, as John Tillotson points out, the 'Jewish Religion' is not only 'very destitute of Arguments to prove, that it was either an universal, or perfect, or final revelation of God's Will to Mankind'. It also contains explicit statements in 'the Law and the Prophets' that a 'Messias' would come as 'the Author of a more perfect Law and Institution' to be revealed to all people.[23] According to Isaac Watts, the only 'dispensations of grace' that were 'designed for all the nations of the earth' before the coming of Christ were those given to Adam and Noah, 'the two common fathers of all mankind'. Those given to Abraham and Moses were confined to a family and its posterity as constituting 'the jewish nation'.[24]

It is interesting to note, though, that when such arguments are pressed by the radical Thomas Chubb against the Old Testament revelation,

John Leland finds it necessary to defend what he regards as the Christian position by asserting that God's special relationship to the Jews 'is no way inconsistent with God's universal care and providence towards mankind'. Furthermore, he maintains, in the face of such criticisms as those of Chubb, that the idea of God and the moral laws in the Mosaic covenant are 'unquestionably holy and excellent'.[25] Leland's remarks illustrate how judgements about Judaism in this period are influenced as much by the nature of the question at issue as by the nature of Judaism itself. When Christian apologists are facing radical critics who deny the need for or reality of divine revelation, they find considerable value as well as authenticity in the Jewish revelation.[26] When, in contrast, they are considering the position of Christianity in relation to Judaism, they do not deny the latter's revelation, but cast doubt on its lasting significance.[27]

Following on the claim that the revelation conveyed by the Old Testament is, at best, only partial, Christian apologists argue, secondly, that Judaism was never intended by God to be the final and permanent expression of his relationship with humanity. One way of assessing the rival claims of Judaism and Christianity which does not cast slurs on the former, is to hold that what was given by Moses and what was given by Christ perfectly corresponds in each case to the state of the world at that time.[28] The more common assessment, though, holds that Judaism offers only 'a Part and the Beginning of Truth' and was always intended to find its completion in Christianity.[29] Isaac Barrow, like others who offer this argument, puts it that Judaism was 'not designed for perpetual obligation and use: . . . it was, according to its design, temporary and mutable'. He emphasises those parts of the Old Testament which foretell a future state in which the Jewish law will be superseded by a Messianic revelation, and the historical evidence of God's abandonment of the Jews and his abrogation of their rites in the destruction of Jerusalem, the end of their sacrifices and their dispersion. He thus concludes that 'we may justly suppose genuine *Judaism* no where to be found; that it cannot be, nor is indeed any where practised'.[30]

The essential impermanence of the Jewish religion is affirmed on various counts. Alexander Ross, after giving six reasons why 'God instituted so many festival days' which show how their rites strengthened the Jewish faith, adds a seventh. This is that they also 'represented' Christ 'the promised Messiah'. Thus 'every sacrifice and oblation' is said to 'shadow forth his death and passion' and it is the latter event alone which is held properly to give 'eternal Redemption'.[31]

William Berriman similarly maintains that the Jewish religion, as enunciated in the Old Testament, contains clear signs of its eventual replacement. Long before the advent of Christ brought its obscurities to an end, Jews recognised that their dispensation points to 'some farther Design' that lies 'deeper than the Surface'. The Law is seen as having provided 'a standing Prophecy of *Christ*' and the Psalmist, by meditating upon it, as having attained through its 'Clouds and Shadows' some 'Glimmering of the *Gospel* Light' that was to come.[32]

As well as pointing to indications of impermanence to be found within the Jewish religion, Christian commentators also stress what they regard as its deficiencies.[33] One of the arguments that sometimes appears in this respect is that the Jews had no knowledge of immortality. The claim, though, is disputed. For example, Leland accepts that 'the belief of a future state obtained among that people' even though it is not mentioned in the law of Moses,[34] while Farmer maintains such a belief was so universally accepted in the ancient world that there was no need for Moses to inculcate it.[35] Others, however, perhaps partly as a result of seeking anti-Jewish arguments, come to a different conclusion from the apparent absence of Old Testament teaching on the matter. Henry More, for instance, is prepared to allow that Moses himself and the prophets 'understood the Mystery of *Immortality*' but he holds that 'the *Generality* of the *Jews* were locked up' in a '*lower* kind of *Dispensation*' which promised only the enjoyment and pains '*of this Natural Life*'. The '*Blessings* and *Cursings* of the *Law* were merely Temporal' and it was only with Christ that assurance of 'Eternal Joy' appeared.[36] Thomas Burnett similarly maintains that 'there does not seem to have been . . . a sufficient Revelation of a future State' given to the Jews.[37] Although William Warburton concludes from such evidence that 'the Divine Legation of Moses' must be divine just because it does not claim the sanction of future rewards and punishments for what it ordained, he recognises that many will find his conclusion paradoxical.[38] The general opinion is that 'the Belief of another Life is always necessary to the practice of Virtue' and that 'without a thorough sense of it' there is always great danger of immorality prevailing.[39] Consequently, where the evidence is judged to show that the Jews had no such 'thorough sense', it is considered that their religion is shown thereby to be seriously flawed. The superiority of the Christian faith, in contrast, is that 'Jesus Christ hath assured us of the certainty, . . . nature and greatness of that future happiness' in a manner that surpasses anything that was available before him.[40]

Another argument used to show the deficiency of the Jewish faith refers to the supposed moral state of the Jews, especially in the time of Christ. Burnett, for example, not only asserts that the Law had been unable to avoid corrupting interpretations, but claims that it had been unable to prevent the Jews becoming 'so profligately Wicked' that they would have been destroyed by God 'if the *Romans* had not come against them'. The ways of the old faith were thus shown to be 'ineffectual' and as needing replacement by 'a New Revelation' if both the behaviour and the erroneous ideas of the Jews were to be reformed.[41]

The impermanence of the Jewish faith is also held to be shown by the current state of the Jews. Their dispersion and the destruction of their temple are not only regarded as divine punishment for their rejection of Jesus as the Messiah – an argument which will be discussed later. They are also God's way of indicating that the religion enshrined in the law of Moses has come to an end.[42] Burnett, for example, sees their condition as manifesting God's will that they should no longer 'keep themselves separate and observe that dispensation' which required them to worship only at Jerusalem'.[43] Picart's treatment of 'The Customs and Cere-monies of the Present Jews', largely derived from the Jewish scholar Leon of Modena (1571–1648), reflects a rather curial view of religion when it sees the crucial factor for Judaism in the destruction of Jerusalem not in the end of the temple rituals but in the end of 'the *Sanhedrim* or grand Consistory, to whose Decisions all the *Jews* were under an indis-pensable Obligation to submit'. While it describes how the Jews have attempted in this situation to preserve their traditions and discipline, its own conclusion is clear: 'it is very evident, that the Religion of the *Jews* was to subsist no longer entire' once they had been banished from Jerusalem.[44] So far as Christian commentators are concerned, the status and responsibility for being the people of God have, since the time of Christ, been inherited by the Christian church.[45] This point of view lies not only behind Picart's presentation of Christ, the pope and the councils as the replacements for Moses, Joshua and the Sanhedrin, but probably also behind the indications of how the patterns of Christian church life have copied those of Judaism.[46]

A third kind of argument used by Christian apologists to demonstrate the superiority of their faith to that of Judaism is by reference to the miracles which are held to have accompanied and verified their respec-tive revelations. In the religious controversies of the seventeenth and eighteenth centuries, it is widely accepted that miracles, as events due to God's agency, are God's primary way of confirming claims to revealed understanding of his nature and will. As Richard Kidder puts it, 'A

Miracle hath always been a good proof of a Doctrine, and ever acknowledged to be very convincing . . . A true miracle is an attestation from
Heaven: We cannot think that God will set his seal to a lye, or to a truth of
little moment and concern'.[47] In cases where conflicting claims to revelation each adduce miracles in confirmation of their claim, the conclusive
witness of God is held to be with the one that is accompanied by the
greatest miracles. Accordingly, as part of his case for the truth of the
Christian religion against the Jews, Kidder seeks to 'compare our
Saviour's Miracles with those true and divine Miracles which *Moses*
wrought' in order to 'shew that the works which *Jesus* did, were greater
works than ever were done by any other person whatsoever'.[48] He does
not deny that Moses produced 'mighty works' which gave 'sufficient
credit' to his mission but argues that Jesus' superiority is divinely proved
by the greater number, power and goodness of his mighty works.

Kidder's argument here is typical of many. Although Christian
apologists, in order to defend the Biblical records of divine revelation
against critics such as Chubb, might speak of 'the Mosaic constitution' as
'attended at its first establishment with the most glorious and amazing
demonstrations of a divine power and majesty',[49] when they turn to the
question of Judaism as a rival religion, they assert that Christianity's
promulgation was accompanied by even greater miracles. Jewish objections to the divine origin of Christ's miracles are rebutted. George
Stanhope, for example, takes up such Jewish charges as that his miracles
were the result of 'Magick and Diabolical Enchantments' and that his
resurrection was not publicly demonstrated.[50] Generally the rebuttals
are along the lines that whatever doubts in this respect can be raised
against the accounts of Christ's miracles can be raised even more
strongly against those of Moses. Positively, it is maintained that the
miracles of Christ are far better attested than any which the Jews can
claim in support of their religion. Consequently, Jewish doubts about
Christianity's authentication by miracles can only succeed at the cost of
using arguments which apply with more force against the divine authentication of the Jewish religion.[51] According to Leslie, then, the Jews face
this dilemma:

> you can never demonstrate the truth of the matters of fact of *Moses* by any
> arguments or evidences which will not as strongly evince the truth of the
> matters of fact of *Christ*: And, on the other hand, you cannot overthrow the
> matters of fact of *Christ*, but you must by the same means destroy those of
> Moses.

The logic of the case, as Leslie sees it, is that the Jews are bound 'either to renounce *Moses* or to embrace *Christ*'. He regards this choice as a 'happy necessity' for them![52]

Christian apologists in this period often suggest that the propagation of Christianity in its early decades can only be understood as miraculous. The nub of the argument is that God enabled Christianity to conquer the world, in spite of its humble origins, because it is the true faith, hence, its supposed successful spread provides further evidence for its truth.[53] Although the argument can now be seen to depend on partial and tendentious views of history and geography, it enjoyed wide acceptance. It is used to develop a fourth case against Judaism in two ways.

One way is through the argument that Christianity's superiority to Judaism is shown by its ability to gain converts to its faith in spite of adverse circumstances. Francis Atterbury, for example, maintains that the Jewish religion, even though backed by some miracles, 'will not admit of any Comparison with the *Christian*' since it was first established among the Jews by a national 'Deliverer, under whose Conduct and Command they then entirely were, and in a Place, where they had no Communication with the rest of the World'.[54] Christianity, in contrast, is presented as having had to face sophisticated and hostile opponents and yet as having overcome them.

The other way in which the argument from propagation is used to attack Judaism is by pointing to Judaism's failure to gain converts. Its apparent unwillingness and inability to spread its faith is held to indicate its inferiority to Christianity. Grotius points out that the Jewish religion 'has received no remarkable Increase since Christ'.[55] Francis Atterbury maintains that this is due to the intrinsic constitution of Judaism: 'by its original Frame and Intention' it was 'limited as to Place, Persons, and Time' whereas Christianity in contrast was intended from the beginning 'to be diffus'd throughout the World'.[56] The Jews may have been dispersed throughout the world but they do not use their situation as an opportunity to convert the world to their faith. Rather, as Jacob Bryant puts it, they exist 'every where distinct': 'Rivers run downwards through many outlets to the sea, and are soon blended and lost in the ocean: But the Jews are like the waters of Styx, which remain unmixed wherever they flow, and retain their bitterness to the last'.[57] Unconverting and unconverted, Judaism persists as both inferior and an affront to the universal character of the Christian religion.

A fifth, and the most common, argument which is used against the Jews is that their faith looks forward to a Messiah who has in fact already come. Here seventeenth- and eighteenth-century theologians use traditional Christian arguments to maintain that Jesus was the promised Messiah. The Jews are fundamentally in error because they fail to see that their own records and their history since the death of Christ combine to show that the Messiah must already have appeared. Christian apologists argue positively that all the expectations concerning the Messiah have been fulfilled by and in Jesus and negatively, that the plight of the Jews is a divine punishment for their rejection of him.

The more popular form of the positive side of the argument is illustrated by such pamphlets as George Fox's *A Declaration to the Jews, for them to Read over; in which they may see that the Messiah is come, according to their own Prophets . . .* and his *A Looking-Glass for the Jews: Wherein they may clearly see that the Messiah is come, by the Prophets in the Old Testament (above Sixteen hundred Years since) and the manifest Testimonies since . . .*[58] Here the argument, so far as it is one, consists of quotations from the Old Testament which are applied to Jesus and to the Jews in order to show his status and the predicted error of their repudiation of him. Charles Leslie, in his *Short and Easy Method with the Jews*, similarly has no doubts that the prophecies about the Messiah have been clearly fulfilled in the life of Jesus. He points to the 'confusion' to which 'the Jews are brought' when they attempt to force 'their way thro' the plain predictions of the *Messiah*' in order to deny that 'our *Jesus* did, and does exactly answer to the several marks given of the *Messiah* by the Prophets'.[59] Sometimes the apologists show more zeal for their cause than scholarly awareness. Jacob Bryant, for example, may be on defensible ground when he holds that the Jews 'confess that no one antecedent to Christ could claim the character of Messiah' but his argument that Jesus must be the Messiah since 'we are certain that nobody since had any pretensions to it' is hard to justify.[60]

The Christian case for the Messiahship of Jesus is argued for at length by Richard Kidder in the three volumes of *A Demonstration of the Messias, in which the truth of the Christian Religion is proved especially against the Jews.* The first volume of this work appeared in 1684 and the third in 1700, part of it having been presented as Boyle Lectures for 1693 and 1694. Kidder bases his argument on the claim that Jews and Christians agree in acknowledging that the Old Testament is divine and that 'there was a *Messias* promised, and described' in it. No one, furthermore, 'hath any just cause to call in question' the factual accounts about Jesus given in the New Testament. On this basis he attempts to show in detail that the events of Jesus' life – its circumstances, what he did and what he suffered – exactly accomplished the genuine predictions which had been made about the Messiah.[61]

> In a word, the things foretold of the *Messias*, and fulfilled in *Jesus* were so
> *many*, and so *strangely fulfilled*, so much without any humane assistance, and
> so *contrary* to all *expectation*, and all the endeavours used to hinder the foretold
> event that he who considers these things with care must believe that *Jesus* is
> the *Christ* and that his Religion is true.[62]

As for the Jews' continuing allegiance to Moses, Kidder argues that on
four counts Jesus is to be preferred to Moses: his miracles were greater
than those of Moses and divinely authenticated his claim to be the
Messiah;[63] his predictions about the future were more detailed and more
impressively fulfilled;[64] the reports in the tradition about Jesus are more
reliable than those about Moses;[65] and there are better reasons to accept
the gospels than 'to receive the five Books of Moses'.[66] Kidder's conclusion is that the Christian has 'sufficient Motives of Credibility' for his
beliefs which are the same in kind but better in quality than those which
the Jews have for their allegiance to the law of Moses.

Kidder's case comprehensively covers the points made by many
others against the Jews.[67] Their arguments, though, are not simply
directed against the Jews. Even though the Jews provide the ostensible
and even the actual main object of these attacks, the arguments used are
also part of current Christian apologetics against those who consider the
truths established by natural theology to be sufficient and doubt the
Christian understanding of the significance of Jesus. As Kidder admits in
his preface, he wants to defend 'our common Christianity' for the benefit
of 'the Christian Reader' as well as to engage in controversy with the
Jews. He thus intends to deal with texts in the Bible which have been
'perverted by some men, and scoffed at by others'.[68] Certainly many of
the problem texts and Biblical inconsistencies which are dealt with under
the head of Jewish objections to the credibility of the gospels are such as
were also being presented by radical critics of Christian orthodoxy.[69]
Here, as elsewhere, the debate about other religions provides a way of
dealing with current questions raised about traditional Christian belief.

The negative side of the argument for the Messiahship of Jesus is the
claim that the sorry state of the Jews since the time of Jesus is a divine
punishment for their rejection of him. Picart's text is one of the rare
places in this debate which recognises that the Jews interpret their
misfortunes as 'Matter of Glory and Triumph' on the grounds that they
are a result of the position of their nation as 'the Heart of the Universe'

which must suffer for the indispositions of the other parts. As Picart's text observes, 'all Christian Divines' see the same misfortunes as 'particular Marks of Reprobation' which come from 'the Hand of God'.[70] It is a theme which Christian apologists sometimes display an uncharitable delight in presenting. Laurence Echard speaks of God making 'a dreadful Example' of the Jews, treating them as 'miserable Objects of divine Wrath, and fully ripen'd for Vengeance' because they opposed the gospel and were guilty of 'our Saviour's and his Saints Blood'.[71]

The depth of anti-Jewish feeling which could be roused by this point is illustrated by William Romaine's attacks in 1753 on the parliamentary bill for permitting the naturalisation of Jews. In two pamphlets on the issue, he not only asserts that the Jews are being punished for rejecting Jesus as the Christ but also claims that any attempt to ease their situation would be to interfere with God's judgement on them.[72] He is fully convinced that contemporary Jews are guilty of 'the highest act of treason' for

> they defend their ancestors' rebellion; they justify the crucifying of the Son of God; and, if they had him in their power, they would crucify him again. Their books are full of the bitterest curses and blasphemies against Jesus Christ, and they say such shocking things of him, as we dare not repeat.[73]

Although Romaine asks his readers to pray for the conversion of the Jews,[74] his pamphlets generally display unbending hostility towards them. The proper concern of the Jews should be 'to become christians' rather than 'to become Englishmen' for as Jews they suffer 'their present blindness and dispersion' as 'the heavy judgments of God . . . for rejecting Jesus'.[75] The Bible declares that they are to suffer dispersion 'over the earth as fugitives and vagrants' until they repent. To grant them naturalisation is to turn their punishment into a reward and thereby to 'act directly against providence' and 'frustrate, so far as man is able, the truth of God's infallible prophecies'.[76] Instead they must be seen to 'deserve every discouragement under which providence has put them' for 'their crime' consists in resisting God.[77] To establish the Jews as citizens in England would be to incorporate those who judge Jesus to have been 'an impostor and a blasphemer' in a state whose laws 'are built upon the certainty' of his being the Messiah.[78] Romaine even alleges that it would place 'our constitution' in danger, for the Jews expect a Messiah in England whose 'character will be like Oliver Cromwell's (I leave the reader to judge what an accomplished villain then he will be)' and who will have 'us all led in chains attending his Messiah's triumphal car'.[79]

In view of such attitudes, it is not surprising that the Naturalisation Bill produced, as Smollett says, 'violent debates' in parliament 'in which there seemed to be more passion than patriotism, more declamation than argument'.[80] Although the Act was initially passed in both Houses in 1753 and received the royal assent, it was repealed in the same year in the following session of parliament because it had aroused such resentment in the country. However Jews might regard their situation, a large number of English people regarded their state as a divine punishment for the rejection of Jesus during and since his lifetime. It was a punishment that they were unwilling to ease.

Anti-Jewish prejudice also has a dominant role in a sixth argument which is used against the Jews, that since they have no sound reasons for their refusal to be converted to Christianity, their opposition to the truth (as Christians see it) must be due to culpable obstinacy.

The antecedent of this argument is justified by arguing that the Jewish objections to Christian belief are ill-founded. Their supposed problems with the New Testament are met in general terms by many writers who defend the reliability of its records. Some, such as Kidder, go on to deal with particular issues presented by alleged inconsistencies, inaccuracies and misquotations in the New Testament which are supposed to create obstacles for the Jews. By various forms of exegesis it is claimed that they constitute no genuine objections to its credibility.[81] Jewish objections to Christian doctrines are held to be equally lacking in force. Grotius, for example, suggests that the Jewish claim that Christians worship many gods is due to a misunderstanding of Trinitarian doctrine while their claim that Christians worship a created being is due to a misunderstanding of Christological doctrine.[82]

The consequent of this argument allows Christian apologists to move into the attack. Apparently confident that the truth of their own position is so evident as to need no defence (and conveniently overlooking the current disputes in religious thought), they condemn the Jewish refusal to assent to Christianity as morally perverse. John Tillotson, for instance, describes the Jews as a great pattern of infidelity. Largely on the basis of the New Testament, he accuses them of

1. Monstrous Partiality, in denying that which had greater Evidence than other matters which they did believe.
2. Unreasonable and groundless Prejudice.
3. A Childish kind of Perverseness.

4. Obstinacy and pertinacious persisting in Error.
5. Want of Patience to consider and examine what can be said for the Truth.
6. Rudeness, and boisterous falling into uncivil terms.
7. Fury and outragious Passion.
8. Infidelity is usually attended with bloody and inhuman Persecution.[83]

John Jortin is in some ways more understanding about why the Jews rejected (and still do reject) Jesus as the Christ but nevertheless holds that 'one great and general cause' of their infidelity is their 'wickedness': 'vice weakens the understanding' and hinders it from discerning the truth.[84] In particular the Jews are said to have been prejudiced against Jesus' gospel because it is spiritual, places morality above rites, demands sacrifice and challenges their traditional authorities.[85]

Other authors do not expound the New Testament's charges against the Jews but make allegations about Jewish character and practices since the Biblical period. Whereas Beilby Porteus stresses that the prophecies fulfilled by Jesus are contained in books kept by the Jews and so must be authentic,[86] Thomas Stackhouse accuses them of corrupting the text of the Old Testament, changing their interpretation of its meaning and preferring the oral 'Tradition of their Fathers' to written reports in order to evade the claims of Christianity. In these ways they 'evacuate the *written* Word of God, and the Evidence, which it produces against them' and so 'preclude themselves from all Possibility of being converted'.[87] From such attacks it is only a short step to mudslinging. According to Isaac Barrow, Jews are 'vain and superstitious . . . proud and arrogant, churlish and soure, ill-natured and false-hearted toward all men'. They are 'deservedly offensive and odious . . . the scorn and obloquy of all Nations'.[88] Alexander Ross describes them as 'a blind, hard hearted, stiff-necked people' who 'are given up to a reprobate sense'.[89] At this point, anti-Jewish slander is liable to be a substitute for argument. Ross, for example, goes on to charge Jews with being 'merciless Extortioners, and cunning in the Art of poysoning' while their religion is made up of 'ridiculous ceremonies' with 'Rabbinical fables, Cabbalistical whimseys' and 'Thalmudical Traditions'.[90] Romaine not only complains of their economic power but descends to personal abuse:

You know a Jew at first sight. And what then are his distinguishing features? . . . It is not his dirty skin, for there are other people as nasty; neither is it the make of his body, for the Dutch are every whit as odd . . . But look at his eyes. Don't you see a malignant blackness underneath them, which gives them such a cast, as bespeaks guilt and murder?[91]

It is amusing to note that Romaine also complains about the Jews' bad manners in defending themselves in a pamphlet![92]

Richard Baxter even summons Mahomet to the Christian side against the Jews: 'Mahomet himself confesseth Christ to be a true Prophet . . . and condemneth the Jews for rejecting him.'[93] Charles Leslie's *Short and Easy Method with the Jews*, though, indicates that references to Mahomet can also be used by Jews against Christianity. One supposed Jewish objection to Christianity is based on a supposed parallelism between Christ and Mahomet. According to this objection, if Christians maintain that God ordained changes in the true religion through Christ, they can have no sure ground for rejecting Islamic claims that further changes were ordained by God through Mahomet. Leslie replies to this first by a *tu quoque* argument, reminding the Jews that this is the objection which the Samaritans urge against Judaism. Secondly, he denies the parallel between Christ and Mahomet on the grounds that Mahomet neither fulfilled prophecies nor confirmed his teaching by genuine miracles. As for Jewish insistence on the authority of the tradition of their fathers, he claims that this is an empty argument since it is one which other religions, including Islam, can use in their own defence.[94]

It would be a mistake, however, to consider that all the treatments of Judaism in this period are wholly hostile. Descriptions such as those contained in Picart's 'Customs and Ceremonies of the Present Jews' are naturally sympathetic to Judaism when they come from Jewish sources, and provide material for a positive appreciation of Jewish beliefs and practices.[95] According to Picart's preface, 'the Jews are not only remarkably devout, but charitable too' and 'we cannot sufficiently admire the modest and serious Behaviour of the Jews, when they are going to their Morning Prayers'.[96] Although 'the excessive Strictness of some superstitious *Jews*' is criticised, the overall treatment draws attention to commendable aspects of their faith and seeks to rebut the calumnies that have been laid against them.[97] Attention is also drawn to the ways in which they have been and are still persecuted and it is suggested the 'abject Condition to which they have been reduced' contributes both to 'making them more wicked' and to their secrecy.[98] Alexander Ross, in spite of the hostile comments already quoted, similarly provides a largely straightforward account of modern as well as of ancient Jewish practices and of the reasons for them.[99]

In general, Christian theologians have an ambivalent attitude towards the Jews. Most of them clearly find it difficult, if not impossible, to regard Judaism as a viable religious option for their day. They share

Leslie's conclusion that rational examination of the situation shows that
Jews today are 'under the necessity, either of rejecting *Moses*, or embracing of Christianity'.[100] At the same time, the more perceptive of them
recognise that there are many factors which make it unlikely that Jews
will in any numbers turn to Christianity.[101] Among the factors cited by
Richard Kidder, for example, are the scandalous lives of many Christians, the careful education of Jewish children, the weak arguments often
used against Judaism by Christians, offensive doctrines and practices
which Jews find especially in the church of Rome, the divisions of
Christianity, the insincerity and wickedness of many converts and the
treatment by Jews of those converts.[102] The way that the Jews are
customarily treated, and Christians' ignorance about them (an ignorance
which Kidder holds to be fostered by the Jews who seek to buy up
whatever collections of Jewish books that have come into Christian
hands), 'render the Hope of their *Conversion* very faint and small'.[103]

What, though, ensures that Christian theologians are never prepared
to write off Judaism completely is its origin in the revelation recorded in
the Old Testament. Against the Jews, Christian apologists may affirm
that the Jewish faith is based on a partial and temporary revelation which
is inadequate for salvation and which finds its completion in Christianity. The adherents of that faith, however, do not present anywhere near
as pressing a problem as those who cast doubt on the need for anything
more than natural religion and, in particular, on traditional Christian
understanding of the Biblical revelation. In replying to such critics
Christian apologists generally consider it essential to insist that the
Jewish religion, so far as it is based on the Old Testament, is derived
from a genuine revelation from God.

In accordance with this need to defend the Biblical revelation against
those who question its necessity, some theologians argue that revelation,
not natural reason, is the final origin of all knowledge and that the
revelation recorded in the Old Testament, transmitted by the Jews, was
the source of knowledge in other religions and cultures. Humphrey
Prideaux, for example, maintains that Zoroaster borrowed much of his
understanding from the Jews while Edward Stillingfleet attempts to
show that 'the Heathen Mythology' originated from and, in garbled
forms, contained traces of the early history of the world as it is revealed
in the Bible.[104] Theophilus Gale, as has been mentioned, goes even
further. Taking up suggestions by Grotius and others, he attempts to
confirm 'the *Authoritie of the Scriptures*; and so by consequence the *Christian Religion*' by proving the claim of ancient apologists that 'the wisest of

the Heathens stole their choisest Notions and Contemplations' from 'the sacred Oracles' of 'the Scriptures, and Jewish Church'.[105] But whereas apologists like Thomas Burnett may argue that God sent the Jews into Egypt to draw 'that Idolatrous nation . . . to the true Faith, and Worship',[106] their opponents could claim that the borrowing occurred in the opposite direction. Lord Shaftesbury, for instance, infers that 'the manners, opinions, rites, and customs of the Egyptians' in fact 'strongly influenced the Hebrew people'.[107] Chevalier Ramsay presents a further possibility. He accepts that the Jews 'were too long concealed in a corner of the earth, to be reasonably thought the primitive light of the Gentiles', and accounts for the common religious sentiments of all the nations by holding that they are inherited from 'the sublime knowledge of the first men' through the descendants of Noah. In this way he confirms the primacy of the Biblical records while avoiding historically dubious claims about the Jewish people.[108]

In the end, though, the positions of the protagonists, and their views of the Jews, are not straightforwardly derived from their evidence about the Jews but reflect rather the consequences of their judgements about the character of religious truth and, in particular, about the relative status of natural and revealed understanding in religious matters. The treatment of Judaism has special aspects because of its peculiar relationship to Christianity but in the end the character of the arguments about it is determined, as with other religions, by the character of current debates about Christian belief.

V I

The treatment of Islam

Islam receives extensive treatment in seventeenth- and eighteenth-century theology. Partly this is a continuation of a long tradition in Christian apologetics – Aquinas' *Summa Contra Gentiles*, a manual on Christian doctrine for the use of missionaries in Spain, is usually regarded as an early classic in this tradition. Partly it is due to the amount of contact which Christians had with Muslims. Reland mentions the contact made through trade 'at *Constantinople*, upon the Confines of *Hungary* and the *Turkish* Empire, upon the Coasts of *Africa*, in *Syria*, *Persia* and the *East-Indies*'.[1] There was also encounter through conflict. In 1683 Turkish forces were defeated outside Vienna. Turkey's diagnosis as 'the sick man of Europe' was yet to come. Partly, the discussion of Islam is due to the general growth of interest in this period in the cultures, beliefs, customs and religions of people in foreign lands and especially in the supposedly mysterious and exotic East. Above all, though, interest in Islam during this period seems to be aroused by the suspicion that the standard arguments for the truth of the Christian revelation, in some cases at least, use the kind of evidence that can also be found, *prima facie*, in the case of Islam.

Jacob Bryant, for example, describes Islam as the only possible competitor with Christianity while William Paley sees 'the success of Mahometanism' as 'the only event' in the history of humanity that bears comparison with the spread of Christianity.[2] Considerable attention is consequently paid to Islam in order to show that it does not pose a real threat to the rational establishment of the truth of Christianity. At the start of this period 'silver-tongued Smith' apparently considers it important to devote a chapter to 'confuting' Islam as he defends his Puritan Anglican view of Christianity in *Gods Arrow Against Atheists*.[3] At the end Beilby Porteus, the Bishop of London, seeks to protect people from the challenge of Islam. In 1779, when a bill was introduced for the relief of

Protestant dissenters, Porteus supported an amendment aimed at ensuring that the Bill would not extend to 'Mahometans, Deists, Atheists and Pagans'.[4] A generation later his popular apologetic, *A Summary of the Principal Evidences for the Truth and Divine Origin of the Christian Revelation*, includes a comparison of Christ and Mahomet; its author seems to have felt it valuable to protect the young people of his diocese against the claims of Mahomet as well as against the expressions of infidelity that were currently being published.[5]

The knowledge of Islam among theologians in this period is very mixed in quality and in quantity. Robert Jenkin notes that travellers' reports are often contradictory because they present local conditions and opinions as if they obtain generally,[6] while Thomas Chubb even maintains that he has no way of discovering whether the Koran that is available to him is the authentic '*Mahometan* revelation'.[7] One result of this is that some controversialists repeat distortions, errors, misrepresentations and misunderstandings of traditional anti-Muslim lore.[8] Alexander Ross holds that Muslims reverence the sun and moon – although he does deny the identification of Mahomet as the Anti-Christ on exegetical grounds![9] They are accused of hostility to learning[10] and are widely considered to believe all kinds of things 'which none but Madmen and Fools would ever have own'd'.[11] In certain respects, discussions of Islam in this period seem to have embedded some of these false views – such as that the spread of Islam is wholly due to the sword – so deeply that they are still trotted out as obvious truths whenever Islam is discussed.

Other discussions, however, make use of more reliable materials that were becoming available through such works as those of d'Herbelot and Galland in France, Reland in Holland, and Pococke and Ockley in England. Edward Pococke's *Specimen Historiae Arabum* appeared in 1649 and is often referred to. It gives an account of the Arabs, Mahomet and Islam taken from Gregory Abul-Faragius (Abu'l-Faraj), a thirteenth-century Jacobite catholicus, and augmented with notes based on numerous Arabic manuscripts. By using these sources, Pococke attempts to clear Muslims of various false charges. In 1708 and 1718 Simon Ockley produced the two volumes of his *History of the Saracens* in which he uses Arabic sources[12] since, as he puts it, 'a Man might as well undertake to write the History of *France*, for the time, out of our News-papers, as to give an Account of the *Arabians* from Christian Historians'.[13] A composite volume appeared in 1712 which includes translations of a short summary of 'Mahometan Theology' written by a Muslim, a treatise on their rituals written by a convert to Islam, and a life of Mahomet 'extracted chiefly from Mahometan Authors'. It also contains a translation of Reland's refutation of 'several Things falsly charg'd upon the Mahometans' by Christians.[14] Of fundamental importance for British writers is George Sale's translation of the Koran which was published in 1734. The previous translation into English was a rather poor one by Alexander Ross from du Ryer's French translation.[15] Sale's work is all the more valuable because of its 'Preliminary Discourse' and its footnotes to the text, even though they are considerably indebted to Marracci's critical studies of the Koran which had appeared in Padua in 1696 and 1698.[16]

In works such as these, attempts are made to correct widespread misrepresentation of Muslim beliefs and practices. Reland, for example, frequently asserts that his intention is to replace existing errors by a correct account of Islam, 'not as it is disguis'd and cover'd with the Clouds of Detraction and Error, but as it is taught in the *Mahometan* Temples and Schools'.[17] He deals with a great number of misrepresentations and suggests that many of them are due to the zeal of Christian apologists and to their ignorance of Arabic.[18] At the same time he professes that he does not publish the truth about Islam in order to defend it, but so that truth may overcome error. Christian apologists will only be genuinely victorious when they tackle authentic Islam and not some straw men of their invention.[19] Sale similarly is concerned to set the record straight. Accordingly, he corrects mistakes in various works, including Humphrey Prideaux's well-received study, *The True Nature of Imposture, fully displayed in the Life of Mahomet*, a work whose title indicates its attitude and whose target is the rational doubters of the Christian revelation.[20] Again, though, the intention is to help Christian apologists find 'arguments that are proper and cogent'.[21] It is not an attitude that wins universal support.[22] Jenkin suggests that allegedly mistaken charges about Islam probably have some substance in them[23] while Edward Gibbon, himself no known defender of Christianity, comments on one of Sale's criticisms of Prideaux that the former 'is half a Musulman'.[24] This latter comment cannot be reconciled with Sale's own statements about Christianity, his remarks on its effective advocacy and his membership until his death of the S P C K.[25] However, it probably expresses a common response to anyone who is prepared to treat Mahomet with some respect as a man who 'gave his Arabs the best religion he could'.[26]

In spite, then, of Chubb's complaint that no indisputable evidence about Islam is obtainable,[27] opportunities for a more accurate understanding of Islam by Christian apologists improve during the period, especially from the latter part of the seventeenth century. Nevertheless, those apologists are often slow to take much advantage of them. With deep popular prejudice against Muslims and lacking any significant contact with live Muslim thought, there is little pressure on them to stop seeking to defend Christianity by using longstanding misrepresentations of Muslim beliefs and practices. Their major opponents, the critics of belief in revealed doctrines, are similarly not primarily concerned to discover the precise truth about Islam. What they wish to show is that no claim to revelation, whether Christian or Muslim, is tenable. It consequently does not greatly matter to them whether the stories that are entertained about Islam are true or false, so long as they are regarded as true and are detrimental to the claim of that faith to have come from God.[28]

It would be a mistake, however, to consider that the widespread hostility to Islam means that nothing good could be recognised in it.[29] We have already quoted Sale's comment that Mahomet gave the Arabs the best religion that was possible in the circumstances. His 'Preliminary Discourse' notes various commendable qualities in Islam. It established 'the sole worship of the true God' in place of idolatry[30] and inculcates 'moral and divine virtues . . . among which are many excellent things intermixed not unworthy even a Christian's perusal'.[31] Ockley's *History of the Saracens* contains several stories that speak well of Muslim behaviour and faithfulness while Joseph Pitts' experiences among them clearly left him with a favourable impression of their strictness and zeal. On the basis of his own observations he not only repudiates numerous false reports about their faith but also comments approvingly on their practice of it. Richard Simon draws attention to their 'esteem for Prayers, Charity, and other pious Actions' and apparently thinks well of their morality:

> Their Morality consists in doing good, and eschewing Evil: which is the reason why they examine very carefully the Nature of Virtues and Vices; and their Casuists are no less subtile than ours are . . . They are so perswaded that all Actions which are not accompanied with Faith, are Sins, that they maintain that he who denies it, loses the Merit of all his good Works; . . . When they demand any thing of God in Prayer, they are to resign themselves wholly to his Will . . . They recommend nothing so much, as trust and confidence in God . . . They give excellent Precepts for bridling the Passions, and shunning Vice.[32]

Pierre Bayle notes that these remarks provoked some censure. His own view, though, is that if they are justified, Simon ought to be praised because 'we ought not to foment the hatred of evil, by describing it more black and detestable than it really is'.[33]

Most of the criticisms of Richard Simon, though, are the result of his Biblical researches rather than of his descriptions of the religious ways of the Levant. Edward Gibbon creates suspicion of his orthodoxy by his historical researches. When, in *The Decline and Fall of the Roman Empire*, he turns to the rise of Islam, he is basically no better disposed to it than he is to Christianity. Nevertheless he finds in the later faith a number of things to commend. Whereas current Christianity had 'relapsed into a semblance of paganism' with relics, images, the veneration of saints and perplexing doctrines, Mahomet presented a creed that is 'free from suspicion or ambiguity' as it witnesses gloriously 'to the unity of God' and presents 'sublime truths' about his nature.[34] Although Gibbon is unconvinced about the revelatory origin of the Koran, he sees in it a 'simple and rational piety' whose practice still edifies travellers to Turkey and Persia 'in the present decay of religious fervour' at home.[35] For all his faults, and Gibbon is not reticent in drawing attention to them, Mahomet 'breathed among the faithful a spirit of charity and friendship, recommended the practice of social virtues, and checked, by his laws and precepts, the thirst of revenge and the oppression of widows and orphans'.[36] His religious enthusiasm may have combined with his ambition to lead him into 'a mixed and middle state between self-illusion and voluntary fraud' but his genius produced 'one of the most memorable revolutions' in the world.[37]

Christian apologists in this period, however, are not on the whole troubled by the evidence that Muslims and Christians have some articles of belief and moral principles in common. These are attributed either to the insights of natural theology or to borrowing from Jewish and Christian sources. Henry More, for example, comments that the Muslims have been called '*Semichristianos*' since much of their 'Law' comes from Moses and Christ, while Jacob Bryant holds that 'all that it has good and laudable is taken' from Christ.[38] What does bother Christian theologians is the way in which the kind of evidence used in arguments to prove the truth of the Christian revelation may, *mutatis mutandis*, be held to be found also in Islam. Richard Simon points out that Muslims argue that as the coming of Jesus Christ abrogated the Jewish faith, so that of Mahomet marks the proper end of Christianity.[39] Thomas Woolston even adds to the notoriety of his judgements on Christianity by suggesting that the case for Islam is rationally stronger than that for Christianity.[40] Although Woolston's opinion is exceptional, the consequence of the possible parallels between the cases for Christianity and for Islam is that the form of the treatment of Islam by Christian theologians in this period is largely dictated by the nature of five arguments which are put forward to authenticate the Christian revelation. They thereby seek to show that what is sauce for the Christian goose is not, in spite of appearances, also sauce for the Muslim gander! The virulence, though, of the attacks on Islam – Isaac Barrow, for instance, describes it as 'a brood of most lewd and impudent cozenage'[41] – suggests that there is anxiety about the matter. It is not due to fear of Muslim power nor to the expectation of conversions to Islam. As Porteus notes, those who reject Christianity do not do so because they are convinced that Islam is true.[42] The anxiety is due to the worry that, because of the resemblances between the two faiths,[43] reasoning used to reject Islam's case to be God's final revelation can be applied by critics of the Christian faith to argue that its claims to revelation are likewise unacceptable. The primary target of the supposed refutations of Islam by Christian apologists is, generally, not in fact the Muslim faith itself but that diverse group of critics of Christianity often described as the 'deists' and, to a much lesser extent, the Socinian or Unitarian critics of orthodox Christological doctrine.[44]

The most popular argument for the authenticity of the Christian revelation, especially up to the middle of the eighteenth century, is that from miracles. As John Locke puts it, miracles are 'the credentials of a messenger delivering a divine religion'. They authorise his message as coming from God.[45] Christian apologists consequently maintain against Islam that whereas Christ's teaching was backed by what they hold to be undisputable and surpassable miracles, Mahomet provides no such credentials to authenticate his claim to be communicating a divine revelation.[46]

Locke thus dismisses Muslim claims simply on the grounds that 'Mahomet having none to produce, pretends to no miracles for the vouching his mission'.[47] Samuel Clarke and Joseph Butler are equally briefly dismissive: Islam offers 'no publick and uncontestable Miracles' to confirm Mahomet's claims.[48] Others deal with the matter at greater length. Their apologetic concerns give to the issue of miracles an importance which corresponds to later Muslim legends about Mahomet rather than to Koranic teaching and practice.

Some commentators take full advantage of Mahomet's own

acknowledgment that he was no miracle-worker in order to destroy the credibility of his claims for his message.[49] Joseph White argues that Mahomet's own attempts to support his claims are 'weak and unsatisfactory' while as to 'miraculous power, that most infallible and decisive test of divine interposition, he openly disclaimed every pretence; and even boldly denied its necessity'.[50] William Paley similarly quotes several passages from the Koran to show that Mahomet 'expressly disclaims' miraculous powers even though he was aware of 'the value and importance' of such evidence while Jacob Bryant apparently finds it surprising that Mahomet, who could make no appeal to miracles to authenticate his own message, nevertheless presumes to set aside Christ's doctrines although allowing that Christ performed 'evident miracles'.[51] Mahomet's own explanations for not having such power are described as 'laboured and awkward' by Beilby Porteus and as betraying 'weakness and vexation' by Edward Gibbon.[52] Roger Long simply gives Mahomet's own claim that he was instructed through the angel Gabriel to propagate Islam 'by the sword' rather than by miracles like other prophets.[53] It is hardly a position that seems convincing in the age of enlightenment.

Other commentators take up the stories of the miracles that are alleged to have occurred to verify Mahomet's claims. As Richard Simon puts it, 'They who introduce a new Religion, ought to shew some Miracles' to gain credibility and 'therefore the *Mahometans* attribute some to their Legislatour'.[54] The stories that are offered, though, are judged to lack credibility. Henry More repeats some of these stories and remarks that some of them 'are *not possible*' and 'most of them are very *foolish* and *ridiculous*'.[55]

Since one of the criteria of an evidential miracle is that it should be performed in public, stories such as those about the secret visitations of Gabriel and the night journey of Mahomet to heaven are judged to be inadmissible as miraculous credentials.[56] Since there is only Mahomet's 'own Word for them', Charles Leslie describes them as being 'as groundless as the delusions of *Fox* or *Muggleton* among our selves'.[57] Humphrey Prideaux not only rejects these private events as having no evidential value; he further suggests that the stories were deliberately coined by Mahomet in an attempt to meet popular demands for miracles 'to prove his mission'.[58]

Long's 'Life of Mahomet', which was added to the third edition of Ockley's *History of the Saracens*, notes that 'the Mohammedan historians are often very extravagant in their accounts of persons and things that have any relation to their prophet'. After citing four prodigies at the birth of Mahomet, recounted by Abulfeda, 'one of the gravest' of their historians, Long goes on to say that 'some legendary writers' go much further, claiming wonderful things that are 'enough to shock the belief of the most credulous'.[59] Another criterion for evidential miracles, though, requires that the records of them should be clearly connected with the times and places of the alleged events.[60] On the basis of this historical principle, later legends of Mahomet's miracles are dismissed as untrustworthy. Thus William Paley rejects such reports as the 'miraculous stories related of Mahomet by Abulfeda, who wrote his life about six hundred years after his death; or which are found in the legend of Al-Jannabi, who came two hundred years later' on the grounds that they cannot be warrantably connected with the actual incidents of Mahomet's life. Consequently he concludes that 'the whole of Mahomet's authentic history, so far as it was of a nature capable of being known or witnessed by others', does not prove that Mahomet was neither 'an imposter' nor an 'enthusiast'. There are here no 'secure grounds' for following Mahomet's teaching.[61] In using the argument from miracles, Christian apologists ensure that the criteria for authentic miracles can only be satisfactorily met by those miracles which verify their own beliefs.

Suggestions do appear that some of the stories about miracles by Mahomet are not only firmly believed by orthodox Muslims[62] but also may be as well warranted as those believed by some Christians. There are, for example, a number of Roman Catholics 'of very good Sense and Understanding in other things' who nevertheless 'can swallow down all the Legends' of their church even though they seem ridiculous 'to every unprejudic'd Mind'.[63] Such beliefs, though, are not held to justify Muslim claims about Mahomet, but to highlight the credulity and errors of some Christians.[64] As for Mahomet's argument that the Koran itself is a sufficient miracle to prove his authority, this too is rejected as unconvincing. Whatever the greatness of its language and sentiments, there is held to be no reason to regard the Koran as anything more than a human production; indeed, there are many reasons to regard it as not divine. Robert Jenkin, for instance, refers to passages in the Koran to show that it is 'false, absurd, and immoral' and points out that the current text is an edited version of what was left by Mahomet.[65] Joseph White recognises that the style of the Koran and the alleged ignorance of Mahomet may have provided an 'irresistible' argument for its revealed basis 'to an Arab' but he nevertheless maintains that its 'real excellence' is fully explicable by reference 'to natural and visible causes'. Its 'pretensions to a divine original' turn out on examination to be 'haughty', 'arrogant' and 'ill-founded'.[66]

The lack of acceptable miracles is not simply regarded as an unfortunate deficiency. For a number of commentators, Islam's inability to justify itself by one of the marks held to show the authenticity of the Christian revelation, is regarded as a positive indication of the falsity of Islam. The fact that Mahomet had not claimed such credentials is not allowed to save his teaching, nor is the argument, offered eccentrically by Chubb,[67] that God cannot be under any compulsion to provide authenticating miracles for a revelation, allowed to disturb this situation. The accepted argument is this: Mahomet claimed to bring messages from God; divine revelations are backed by miracles – the Bible shows this; Mahomet produced no trustworthy miracles; therefore his claim must be false.[68] It is this argument which gives rise to the frequent references to miracles (or, rather, to the lack of them) in discussions of Islam in this period.

The argument from miracles, however, becomes less prominent as difficulties with it are increasingly, though by no means universally, recognised during the eighteenth century. Christian apologists in consequence tend to lay greater stress on other arguments for the truth of the Christian revelation. As with the case of miracles, some of them also adduce reasons to show that none of these other arguments can be used to verify the Muslim faith.

One of these other arguments for the truth of Christianity is that from prophecy. It is closely related to the argument from miracles and is sometimes treated as a sub-case of that argument. Foretelling future events, however, does not appear to have been as intrinsically problematical for eighteenth-century apologists as claims about alterations in the natural order. For Christian apologetics, the argument from prophecy has two forms.

There is, first, the argument that Jesus' special relationship to God is shown by his ability to foretell future events.[69] It is correspondingly maintained that Mahomet made no prophecies whose later fulfilment proves him to have enjoyed supernatural insights into the future. Henry Smith claims that 'Mahomet was a false Prophet, because he said that within three daies after his death he should ascend into heauen; which was notoriously false'. In order to justify this, Smith cites some tendentiously inaccurate reports of Mahomet's burial.[70] Others argue that while Mahomet was aware of the significance of knowing the future, he avoids risking his credibility by refusing to make specific and clearly falsifiable claims.[71] Humphrey Prideaux, for instance, states that 'Mahomet offer'd at no *Prophecies*, that he might not run the hazard of being confuted by the Event' – in contrast to Christ who 'deliver'd many clear and plain *Prophecies*' which were 'all in their proper time as plainly verify'd by the Completion of them'.[72]

The second form of the argument from prophecy claims that Jesus' status as the Christ is shown by his fulfilment of earlier prophecies about the Messiah. In contrast it is argued that Mahomet's mission cannot be justified as the fulfilment of earlier prophecies. According to Charles Leslie, the Koran acknowledges both the Old and the New Testament but 'it cannot shew that *Mahomet* was foretold either by *Moses* or *Christ*, or by any of the Prophets'. Indeed, it contradicts Christ's announcement 'that he is the last'.[73] Beilby Porteus sums up the position thus: 'The appearance of Mahomet was not foretold by any ancient prophecies, nor was there at the time any expectation of such a person in that part of the world.'[74] Muslim attempts to find predictions of Mahomet's mission in the Bible are dismissed by Prideaux, for example, as the product of interpretations, interpolations and glosses whose 'Absurdity . . . is sufficiently exposed, by barely relating them'.[75] Just as fiercely condemned is the Muslim charge that the Jews and Christians have 'concurred in the atrocious crime of mutilating their scriptures' in order to deprive Mahomet of the testimony that they originally contained. Joseph White describes the charge as an absurdity whose nature makes it difficult to disprove but he gives grounds for holding that the Biblical text never mentioned Mahomet nor alluded to his coming.[76] When Islam is allowed to have been possibly foretold in the Bible, it is to Islam's condemnation. Hugo Grotius sees 'Mahometanism' as foretold by Christ when he warned 'that after his Time there should come some who should falsely say they were sent of God'.[77] Thomas Newton interprets Revelations 9, 1–12 as referring to 'the wicked impostor Mohammed' and the armies of 'swarms of Saracen or Arabian *locusts*'.[78] So far as the argument from prophecy is concerned, then, Mahomet's claims are dismissed on the grounds that they cannot be verified by the tests which Christian apologists use to prove the truth of Christian belief.

Another argument for the truth of Christianity which receives increasing attention in the eighteenth century is that from the character of Jesus. This argument can be caricatured as: either Jesus was what he claimed to be, or he was mad, or he was bad – an impostor; evidence about his character shows that he can be regarded neither as mad nor as bad – an impostor; therefore he must be accepted on his own terms. Another version of the argument finds Jesus' message and status as confirmed by the conformity of his character to them.[79] The growing awareness of other religions, however, means that this argument can provide convincing support for the Christian revelation only if it can also be shown that the founders of other religions were either mad or impostors. For Christian apologetics, Mahomet is clearly the leading rival to Jesus – figures of the Old Testament such as Abraham and Moses are held to have a supporting role to Christ.

One result of this argument for Christianity is a sustained programme of character assassination for Mahomet. With a few exceptions, no serious attempts are made to reconcile the apparent attractiveness and success of Mahomet with the bad character attributed to him.[80] The nearest that most commentators get to such a reconciliation is the suggestion that Mahomet was a rogue who managed to avoid being found out. Henry Smith describes him as 'a fleshly fellow' whose 'filthinesse' has to be exposed; Robert Jenkin as 'lustful, proud, fierce and cruel'; Jacob Bryant as false, treacherous, blasphemous and 'the bane of all happiness'.[81] A few commentators, though, realise that unqualified censure is unlikely to be justified in view of Mahomet's ability to win the devotion of others. His roguery could not have been that apparent and for some was apparently obscured by attractive qualities. George Sale, for example, after mentioning the 'excessive . . . commendations' of Mahomet's virtues in Muslim works, concludes that his success is only explicable if he was a man 'of at least tolerable morals' and not as profligate a wretch 'as he is usually represented'. Sale does not attempt to discover his intentions but does allow that 'a little hypocrisy and saving of appearances, at least, must have been absolutely necessary'.[82] What is more interesting, perhaps, is Joseph White's recognition that to strip Mahomet of the 'qualities and abilities' needed for his success is to make it explicable only as a miracle. Not wanting this conclusion, White allows that the 'impostor' must have 'possessed superior talents' which enabled him 'to deceive his countrymen, to captivate their affections, and to triumph over the external obstacles that opposed him'.[83]

A few writers consider that Mahomet's behaviour was the result of some form of madness. Joshua Toulmin bluntly asserts that '*Mahomet* became so hypocondriac, that he began to talk idly, which terminated in a lunacy'.[84] Others pay particular attention to his revelatory experiences and suggest that they were some form of epileptic fit. Prideaux, for instance, repeats the common charge that Mahomet 'was subject to the Falling Sickness' and pretended, 'whenever the Fit was upon him', that it

was a revelatory trance.[85] Ockley rejects this charge as one of 'those idle
Stories' which Christians tell about Mahomet. Sale agrees.[86] More sympathetic writers treat Mahomet's behaviour as a case of 'enthusiasm'.
Henry More speaks of him as 'an *Enthusiast* amongst rude People' whose
'phrensie' led him to claim that he was the greatest prophet.[87] The author
of *The Life and Actions of Mahomet* compares his convulsions with those
of 'our Quakers at their first appearing, and the late *French* Prophets
among us'.[88] Sale suggests that his desire 'to rescue the world' from
'ignorance and superstition' may well have combined with 'a warm
imagination' to turn him into an enthusiast.[89] In either case, whether
mad or enthusiastic, Mahomet's supposed mental state renders his
claims unattractive to the self-conscious followers of the canon of reason
in an age of enlightenment. However acceptable his message might be
(and we will see that it is largely unacceptable to them), they are likely to
be convinced only by a teacher who was 'always composed, self-
collected and great, assuming no austerity of manners, falling into any
frantic airs' – the character that they attribute to Christ.[90]

Sale, however, whose use of Muslim sources brings him sometimes to
present Mahomet's character in an untypically favourable light, has
reservations about his classification as an enthusiast. He points out that
'the wise conduct and great prudence' with which Mahomet pursued his
aims 'seem inconsistent with the wild notions of a hot-brained religion-
ist'. Furthermore, the 'gravity and circumspection' of his general
behaviour may be compatible either with mental aberration on a specific
issue or with deliberate deception. In the end, therefore, he is unwilling
to try to determine Mahomet's sincerity and intentions.[91] Most Christian apologists are not so reticent. They are prepared without qualifi-
cation to damn Mahomet as an impostor. Prideaux, indeed, uses
Mahomet as a paradigm case for examining the nature of imposture in
order to confute claims by 'Deists' that the Christian gospel is an imposture.[92] He lists seven distinguishing characteristics of imposture and
maintains at length that all of them are instantiated in Islam whereas
'none of them can be charged upon Christianity'.[93] His conclusion is
typical of the period and considerably influences most subsequent descriptions of Mahomet. According to Halyburton, Islam is 'the grossest,
most scandalous and impudent imposture, that ever was obtruded upon
the world'.[94] The author of *The Life and Actions of Mahomet* speaks of the
'pretended Mission' of 'this grand Impostor' while Joseph White
describes him as an 'audacious', successful' and 'artful' impostor.[95]
Indeed, for many Christian commentators Mahomet seems to be linked

with 'impostor' almost as automatically as Jesus is with 'Christ'. Although Mahomet's great cleverness is overcoming opposition and establishing his following are admitted, albeit grudgingly, his claims to be divinely guided are completely rejected.[96]

Sale is prepared to allow that Mahomet's actions can be understood as the result of genuine, if partially mistaken, religious convictions.[97] Most writers about him are not so charitable. They explain his actions as imposture motivated to a great extent, at least, by the desire for power and self-gratification.[98] In *The Life and Actions of Mahomet* it is said that Mahomet, 'being naturally very subtle and crafty, ambitious and aspiring', considered that 'the surest way' to secure 'the Sovereignty over his native City' was 'to institute a new Religion, and feign a Divine Commission'. He accordingly took to religious exercises in order to make his pretences convincing.[99] Unable to envisage Mahomet as anything but an impostor, Prideaux adds to his ambition the motive of being able to have 'as many Women as he pleased to satiate his Lust'. Mahomet embarked upon 'so exceeding difficult and dangerous an Enterprize' as his pretended mission because the material rewards of success would be so great.[100]

The claim that Mahomet is an impostor is justified by circumstantial evidence in several ways. Whereas Christian apologists often point to the lack of education of Jesus and the apostles (apart from Paul) as evidence that their teaching must have been divinely inspired (reflecting the illusion that education is the only source of wisdom), Mahomet's alleged lack of 'a learned education' is not allowed to indicate that his teaching was inspired. Toulmin, for instance, maintains that Mahomet's defects in this respect were 'supplied by the help of *others*; particularly a Christian Monk' and by travels which 'opened to him sources of information'.[101] Again, while the supposed uniqueness and self-evident truth of Jesus' teaching is held to show its divine origin, Mahomet's teaching is dismissed as a mixture of 'absurd opinions, odd stories, and uncouth ceremonies; compounded chiefly of the dregs of Christian Heresies, together with some ingredients of *Judaism* and *Paganism* confusedly jumbled'.[102] The fact that 'Mahomet shows throughout the utmost anxiety to guard against objections' is held against him and interpreted as arising from the fear of being found out as an impostor.[103]

The greatest part of the circumstantial evidence brought against Mahomet's claims, though, consists of assertions of his moral wickedness. The claim that he gave up evil ways when he became a prophet is rejected.[104] In contrast to the sinlessness of Jesus, Mahomet is presented as 'one of the worst characters, in a moral view, that ever disgraced human nature',[105] and it is thus scandalous to think of God using him as his agent.[106] A frequent charge against him concerns his sexual activities – More speaks of him as *insatiably Venereous*.[107] Although it is often recognised that practices were different in Mahomet's place and time,[108] stories about the number of his wives and concubines and his sexual power appear to monogamist Christians as indisputable evidence of his sinful lustfulness – although Gibbon points out that in comparison to Solomon, he was commendably modest![109] He is further accused of fixing the Koran so that he could 'take his full swing . . . without Let or Controul, according as the violent bent of his brutish Appetite this way, should lead him'.[110] It is a much repeated charge. Joseph White presents him as the 'sole master of the oracles of heaven' who 'compelled them to speak that language' which best suited his 'boundless lust' and thereby ensured that he always had 'a satisfactory answer' for those who murmured against his 'sensual immoralities'.[111]

The secrecy of Mahomet's reception of his supposed revelations is regarded as further circumstantial evidence that he was an impostor. According to Porteus, 'Jesus was repeatedly declared to be the Son of God by voices from heaven' which others 'distinctly heard and recorded' while 'no other person ever saw or heard' Mahomet's pretended 'communications with God'.[112] Evidence that Mahomet does not bring a revelation superseding that of Christ is also found in the alleged fact that '*Jesus* was taken up into Heaven, by the Confession of *Mahomet*; but *Mahomet* remains in the Grave'.[113] In such ways, then, Christian apologists judge the actions of Mahomet by their own standards and are unable to entertain seriously the idea that a person of such character could have brought a revelation from God. They have no doubt that he was either an impostor or mad. Nevertheless, in spite of their multisided attacks on Mahomet's creditworthiness, they do occasionally use his views on certain points when they support the Christian case. Charles Leslie refers to the Koran's description of Jesus as the Messiah while John Edwards cites 'the Testimony of that Arch Infidel' when he 'acknowledgeth the Gospel to the Divine and True'.[114]

A fourth argument for the truth of the Christian revelation used in this period is that from the established truth of Jesus' teaching. In some cases its truth is held to be self-evident; in others it is shown by testing the teaching against 'the sanctions of natural religion, and the established opinions of mankind'.[115] In many ways, though, this argument is hardly an 'argument' at all since its conclusions are presupposed in the norms for its judgements. Nevertheless, whether or not it is convincing to non-Christians, the argument is widely used, especially as the more 'objective' arguments from miracle and prophecy come increasingly to be suspected. One way of supporting this argument is by showing that the teachings of rival founders of religions are evidently erroneous. Consequently, as in the case of the argument from the character of Jesus, a number of apologists feel obliged to show that a similar verification cannot be offered for Islam. The result is an assortment of reports about Mahomet's teaching in which it is frequently distorted or misunderstood. Although Joseph White pleads for justice and candour in dealing with the Koran,[116] Richard Baxter is more typical of Christian views when he describes the Koran as being without 'any evidence of solid understanding': it contains 'nothing, but the most nauseous repetition an hundred times over of many simple incoherent speeches, in the dialect of a drunken man'.[117] The extent of the misrepresentations, often repeating long-standing Christian traditions about Islam, can be seen in the few attempts like those of Reland and Sale to put the record straight – or, at least, to present Islam in a less hostile light.[118] These corrections, where they are noticed, reduce the number of unfair charges that might be made (such as that Muslims worship Venus and believe that 'She-Angels' exist) and even indicate some points at which Islamic practice might be an improvement on Christian customs (such as in forbidding worshippers to be dressed in sumptuous clothing and women to worship with men).[119] Nevertheless, there remains considerable scope for Christian apologetics.

It has been noted that one supposed mark of Mahomet's imposture is that he adopted ideas of other religions, resulting in what Henry Smith calls a 'mixt and patched religion'.[120] This borrowing is also used as an argument against the truth of that religion. Not all the ideas that Mahomet adopted, of course, can be condemned as false in themselves since some of them are truths of natural religion and others come from Jewish and Christian sources. Christian apologists, though, are generally so convinced that Christianity is the true and perfect faith that they cannot take seriously a religion that picked out some articles of Christian belief, rejected others, and combined what was selected with items from other (*ipso facto* false) religions and materials of Mahomet's own invention.[121] However, they advance various considerations to show why Mahomet's collection cannot be regarded as intrinsically true.

In the first place, Mahomet's claim that the Koran was divinely communicated to him cannot be plausibly maintained when 'the learned enquirer' discovers that some of its contents have 'a more accessible' and 'probable source' in contemporary materials.[122] The identification of source materials for the Koran in this way undermines its divine status, as does the recognition that its present text is an edited compilation of what survived Mahomet's death as scattered pieces. At a time when modern Biblical criticism is only just beginning, the chequered story of the production of the Koran is widely seen as undermining Muslim claims about its divine authority.[123]

Secondly, much of what is supposed to be revealed in the Koran is redundant. There is very little that is genuinely novel in it and what there is is unimportant or, as with the fanciful descriptions of heaven and hell, ridiculous. Neither in ritual nor in doctrine does the Koran provide any 'improvement of former revelations'.[124] In the third place, the collection of materials in the Koran are condemned as being internally incoherent. Its contents are 'a confus'd and indigested Medley' in which incompatible ideas are conjointly asserted and later instructions may countermand earlier ones.[125] The Muslim doctrine of 'abrogation' which explains these changes as the result of God's decision to revoke what earlier he had commanded is not regarded as theologically reasonable.[126] Joseph White puts the point thus: 'such a conduct, though well accommodated to the shifting policy of a capricious mortal, is totally incompatible with the eternal wisdom of the immutable God.'[127] The inconsistencies are attributed, rather, to Mahomet's attempts to accommodate his ideas to the prejudices of others and to the fanaticism which prevented him from controlling his ideas.[128] Fourthly Mahomet is not merely accused of borrowing ideas, but is further charged with using ideas derived from misunderstandings of the Bible, of Christian doctrines and of the nature of the world. Henry More instances the claims that Mary, the mother of Jesus, is 'the Sister of Moses and Aaron' and that 'God has established the Earth on a Bull's Horn', the shaking of whose head is 'the cause of Earth-quakes'.[129] While the corrupt state of contemporary Christianity in Arabia is allowed to provide at least a partial excuse for these misunderstandings, especially of the Christian doctrine of the Trinity,[130] Mahomet's claim that the Jews and Christians have altered the text of their scriptures is totally rejected.[131] Even if excusable, the presence of these misunderstandings in the Koran is held to undermine any claim to its divine origin and intrinsic truthfulness.[132] Finally, the rationale for Mahomet's teachings as collected in the Koran is held to be whatever will win support for him and not what is the truth. Prideaux is one of many who accuse Mahomet of making 'his *new Religion* . . . go down the easier' with the Arabs by accommodating their preferences. Thus he altered the orientation for praying from Jerusalem to Mecca and retained Arabian traditions concerning the pilgrimage to Mecca.[133] Great play is made with the popular attractiveness of the sensual heaven which Mahomet described. His 'voluptuous paradise' with its robes, palaces, wines and 'seventy-two virgins assigned to each of the faithful' was directed to seizing 'the passions' of his followers.[134] References are made to passages which Mahomet is supposed to have invented as revelations to boost the flagging morale of his followers, to provide him with explanations of his temporal reverses and changes of plan,[135] and to justify his satisfaction of his needs and desires.[136] Investigation of the actual contents of the Koran is thus held to provide clear evidence that the teaching of Mahomet does not have a divine source.

A different line of attack on his teaching seizes on Mahomet's alleged refusal to defend his claims by rational arguments. At a time when the canon of reason largely determines what are acceptable modes of understanding, Mahomet's rejection of this canon, as implied by his refusal to meet its demands, is held to be the result of his having failed to find convincing arguments to verify his claims.[137] This is interpreted as indicating that his teaching cannot be shown to be true and hence, following the canon of reason, that it ought not to be granted assent. Grotius, for example, puts it that just as 'those Goods may justly be suspected, which are imposed upon this Condition, that they must not be looked upon', so Mahomet's teaching is to be suspected because it 'would be believed, without allowing Liberty to enquire into it'.[138] Richard Baxter is another who asks what justification there can be for Mahomet's barbarous suppression of 'all rational enquiry into his doctrine'. In his view, 'the friend of Ignorance is no Friend to Truth'. If the Muslim faith really is from God 'why dare they not soberly prove it to us, and hear what we have to object against it, that Truth by the search may have the Victory [?]'[139] Prideaux supplies the standard answer: it is because Mahomet 'had long been teazed and perplexed' in disputes about his message, becoming 'non-plus'd', confused and embarrassed. Consequently, when he gained power, he banned disputes about his religion on the pain of death.[140] In this respect Islam is compared unfavourably to Christianity, a faith which not only is open to and confirmed by rational investigations but also regards such investigations as a divinely ordained duty.[141] The former, in contrast, is held to secure belief in Mahomet's teaching through the threat of force, not through its manifest truthfulness.[142]

Some writers attack the credibility of Mahomet's teaching on the grounds that it has bad moral results, for instance, that it produces despotism, hostility, hatred to the rest of mankind and ignorance. Alexander Ross presents the 'Religious Orders' of Islam as 'wicked and irreligious', observing various offensive practices,[143] and Joseph White too has much to say on these points.[144] Wherever Islam has been established, people have lost their independence and freedom; their progress in science, invention and the love of learning has been stunted; they have become indolent; they 'must abstain from the innocent enjoyment of the bounties of nature'; their religious precepts are 'adverse to the welfare of humanity' and lead to 'ostentatious hypocrisy, or abject pusillanimity'. In belief, Islam is as 'naturally hurtful' as Christianity is 'naturally beneficial . . . to the intellectual, the social, and the religious character of man'.[145] John Wesley expresses the popular opinion of Muslims when he writes of them as being 'as void of mercy as lions and tygers, as much given up to brutal lusts as bulls or goats: so that they are in truth a disgrace to human nature'. He rejects attempts to give a different character to them as attempts 'to wash the Aethiop white'.[146] As an argument for Christianity and against Islam, though, these references are recognised by some not to be convincing. For one thing, professing Christians are often far from models of good morality; for another there is sound evidence that some Muslims lead morally commendable lives.[147]

The most popular and widely assorted way of attacking the truth of Mahomet's teaching is by displaying its supposed deficiencies and errors. The arguments here do not stop at showing, to the apologist's satisfaction, that a comparison of Christ's teaching with Mahomet's manifests 'the superior excellence' of the former since its precepts are 'pure, excellent and sublime' whereas the latter inculcates 'the weaknesses and idle distinctions of superstition'.[148] They attempt to demonstrate that the Muslim position is contrary to what is held to be correct understanding, whether it be of natural reason or of Christian revelation – or of a combination of them. One form of the argument, therefore, claims that the religious and moral doctrines of Islam are sometimes incompatible with the insights of natural reason. Isaac Barrow, for instance, objects that Islam suffers from a 'multitude of silly ceremonies' which have no obvious value.[149] Hugo Grotius mentions various ways in which God is described in unacceptably anthropomorphic terms,[150] and cites various passages where fabulous tales are presented as historical events.[151] Richard Baxter charges Muslims with having 'doctrines of Polygamy . . . and of murdering men to increase their Kingdoms, and many the like' which are 'contrary to the light of Nature' and so prove that Mahomet's teaching is 'not of God'.[152] The other form of this argument is to show that what Mahomet taught contradicts what is found in the Bible. This, of course, is a strong argument for Christians who accept the Biblical materials as normative but its presuppositions might seem to render it an inappropriate argument to use with Muslims. Joseph White, however, points out that it is legitimate to test the Koran in this way since the Koran reports that Mahomet himself admitted the authority of 'the Law and the Gospel' as 'former revelations'.[153] Mahomet is, for example, thus held to have erred in point of fact when he denied that Jesus died on the cross,[154] and in moral insight in his teachings on marriage, divorce, revenge and warfare against unbelievers.[155]

Since Islam is hardly a live option for seventeenth- and eighteenth-century Britons and since the teaching of Mahomet contains at least a few creditable elements, the deep hostility which is shown to that teaching is interesting. Thomas Hyde, for example, finds value in Islam because it brought Arabians from polytheism to 'the Knowledg and Worship of the *true God*', abolishing idolatry and uniting their faith in the love of God with their moral practice. He thus speaks of that faith as built 'upon the Foundation of true Religion (*the Unity of God*)'. Nevertheless, he is typical of most writers about Islam in this period when he sees what has been erected on that foundation as 'Hay and Stubble . . . which in the Day of Distinction shall not be able to endure the *fiery Trial*'.[156]

Why is there this strong condemnation of Islam? In some cases it may simply reflect a believer's horror at a rival faith. In others it is possibly the result of a long-standing fear of Islam as a little-known and less understood ogre. In many cases, however, it is probably a result of contemporary battles with those ranges of critics of traditional Christian faith popularly labelled as 'deists' and as 'Socinians'. Leibniz evaluates Islam positively as a kind of augmented deism which destroys paganism and prepares the way for Christianity.[157] The self-consciously reasonable believers of this period are not likely to be tempted back to paganism. Some of them, though, may be suspected by Christian apologists of being tempted by some or other form of 'deism' or 'Socinianism' with its stress on the purported re-establishment of the pure, original faith in one God. The uncompromising and rather detailed condemnations of Islam which are sometimes found may then be understandable as indirect attempts by their authors to persuade their contemporaries that a deistic or Socinian type of faith is untenable – so leaving Christianity as the only live option.[158]

The fifth major argument for the truth of Christianity is the argument from its propagation. Often exaggerating the condition and success of early Christianity, apologists point to the spread of that faith through the agency of simple, mostly uneducated and lowly people. William Paley speaks of 'a Galilean peasant, accompanied by a few fishermen' managing to prevail 'against the prejudices, the learning, the hierarchy, of his country; against the ancient religious opinions . . . the wisdom, the authority, of the Roman Empire, in the most polished and enlightened period of its existence'.[159] The apologists then argue that such success can only be explained as the result of divine support. This support is held further to be a way in which God can be seen to endorse the Christian faith as true.

It is a popular argument. One problem, as a number of its advocates appreciate, is that a similar case might be (and in fact has been)[160] advanced for Islam, since the propagation of the Muslim faith was, *prima facie*, as remarkable as that of Christianity. Thus Thomas Stackhouse remarks that 'of all false Religions, the *Mahometan* came nearest to the *Christian* in the swift Manner of its Propagation; for in a small Time it over-ran a great Part of the *Eastern* World'.[161] Indeed, William Robertson claims that 'there is nothing similar in the history of mankind' to the rapidity of Islam's spread.[162] Although this claim may be disputed on historical grounds – Robert Jenkin, for instance, asserts that Christianity has had 'a much larger propagation' than Islam has ever enjoyed,[163] the crux of the argument is seen not to lie in the bare records of success but in the plausibility of maintaining that the success can only be explained as due to divine support. It is with this point in mind that Joseph White approaches the argument. He points out that success on its own provides 'no certain criterion of the truth and divinity of any religious system' for it is obvious that sometimes God permits 'error to prevail in the world'. What is needed by the Christian apologist is some way of showing that Islam's prevalence is thoroughly explicable as due to wholly natural factors while Christianity's spread cannot be so explained.[164] Thus Christian apologists advance natural explanations of Islam's success which interpret the evidence as unfavourably as possible – in contrast to the way in which they put forward a somewhat legendary understanding of the rise of Christianity. In this way they show that Christianity is divinely attested while Islam's success, however extraordinary, 'may easily be accounted for, by reflecting on the Circumstances' which attended its development.[165]

For one thing, it is argued that Islam prospered because it pandered to popular tastes and endorsed popular traditions.[166] That it banned alcohol and gambling and demanded charity and unquestioning obedience[167] is generally ignored, played down or quickly explained away. Thus Humphrey Prideaux explains such rules as designed by Mahomet to prevent dissensions among his people which would impair their effectiveness.[168] Other aspects of Islamic teaching are given far more prominence – in particular, the ways in which it is held to minister to the sensuality of its adherents both in this world and the next. Mahomet is accused of gratifying the Arabs' 'Passions and corrupt Affections which he found them strongly addicted to, especially those of Lust and War'. In this way he made it easier to draw them 'to his Party'.[169] There is far more stress on the way Islam allows 'carnal-minded men' to 'multiply Wives' than on its prohibition of promiscuous conversation between the sexes.[170] What seems especially to offend Christian apologists is the description of the sensual pleasures of Mahomet's heaven. It is a paradise which panders to the flesh.[171] Edward Gibbon amusingly points out in this respect that while this heaven is reportedly open to both the sexes, Mahomet does not specify who meets the needs of 'the female elect', in order to avoid provoking the jealousy of their husbands or disturbing 'their felicity by the suspicion of an everlasting marriage'![172] The reverse of this argument is also offered for it is held that Mahomet scared men from unbelief by the threat of hell as well as lured them by the attractions of paradise.[173] With such a message to proclaim, Islam's success is regarded as unremarkable. As Francis Atterbury puts it, 'a Religion, that gave a full Indulgence to the Ambition, the Lusts, and Cruelty of Mankind, could not fail of gaining Proselytes'.[174]

The success of Islam is naturally explained, secondly, by arguing that, unlike Christianity, it did not have to face the challenge of a viable religion and an educated people. Christian apologists describe the original recipients of Mahomet's message as being on the whole an evil, ignorant and superstitious (or, in some cases, religionless) people,[175] highly vulnerable to conversion to Islam,[176] especially when this religion provided a way of unifying the many conflicting tribal and religious groupings of the inhabitants of Arabia.[177] To such people Mahomet presented an attractive system of belief. Not only did it offer satisfaction for their desires and preserve their cherished traditions, it also recommended itself by its straightforwardness. Its doctrines 'were in general the plainest and most simple that can be imagined' and 'totally disclaimed all those mysteries, at which the pride of human reason is so apt to revolt'.[178] They thus compared well with the tortured sophistications into which Christian theology had developed. Another aspect of this explanation of the rise of Islam is the argument that its early converts had practically no opportunity to become aware of the true character of Christianity, because Islam developed in an area where Christianity had degenerated badly. It had become divided into several sects, some of which professed strange doctrines. Among the reasons which Alexander Ross offers for the establishment of Islam are 'the continual jars, frivolous debates, and needless digladiations' among Christians and 'the wicked and scandalous lives' of the laity and clergy.[179] Joseph White describes how in contemporary Christianity the gospel had been nearly eclipsed by 'the disingenuous arts of sophistry, which industriously perplexed truth', 'a load of idle and superstitious ceremonies' and a 'train of vices and follies' in the increasingly wealthy 'ecclesiastical orders'.[180] It is accordingly argued that the 'rapid and general' success of Islam among the Arabs is partly due to 'the Scandal occasion'd by the fatal Divisions of Christians, by the Proscriptions and the Massacres practis'd upon one another' and to the resulting 'Ignorance . . . as to the Articles of our *Holy Religion*'.[181] Christian apologists, though, have to be cautious here since one of their arguments for the necessity of the Christian revelation is the corrupt state of religion and society at the time of Jesus. The more self-aware of them have to watch that their explanation of the rise of Islam in this respect does not establish evidence by which Muslims could make a similar claim for their revelation.[182]

Some Christian apologists attack Mahomet for the alleged meanness of his background but Edward Gibbon condemns this as 'an unskilful calumny' since he was descended from 'pure and genuine nobility'.[183] Joseph White is a more sympathetic apologist. He puts it that while Mahomet came from 'the most honourable tribe of Arabia', his own inheritance was only 'distress and poverty'.[184] Other apologists, however, prefer to stress the status of Mahomet. They claim that through birth and marriage he attained considerable status in the community and that this is a further factor in explaining his success. In contrast to the lowly status of Jesus and his apostles, Mahomet's early 'influence and advancement' is, according to Toulmin, 'much indebted to the great fortunes and connexions of his wives'.[185] Paley similarly suggests that his wealth, descent and relationship to 'the chiefs of his country' would have helped him secure 'attention and followers'.[186] As for later times, it is held that Islam benefited considerably from the support of rulers. Grotius even suggests that it only continues because of the protection of 'the Civil Power and Authority'.[187]

Above all, though, the spread of Islam is explained as having been through the power of the sword. Christian apologists who argue that the truth of Christianity is proved by its propagation are quite unruffled by the spread of Islam because they are convinced that it gained its adherents by force. The Roman and Persian empires were too weak to stop the Arab armies, and where these armies conquered, they established Islam. John Tillotson neatly expresses the prevailing view: 'As for the Religion of *Mahomet*, it is famously known to have been planted by force at first, and to have been maintained in the World, by the same violent means.'[188] This charge seems to be repeated by Christian apologists nearly every time that Islam is discussed. According to Sale the power of the sword not only explains the progress and establishment of Islam; it also provides 'one of the most convincing proofs that Mohammedism was no other than a human invention'.[189] Muslim claims that their military success shows divine endorsement of their faith[190] are rejected on such grounds as that might is not right and that in any case Muslim armies have sometimes been defeated.[191] There are occasional suggestions that Islam may sometimes have been propagated by persuasion and not by the sword – indeed, the other 'explanations' of the rise of Islam which we have outlined do presuppose this. Thomas Chubb uses his common sense to point out that initially Islam must have gained converts by persuasion before it could raise armies large enough to do it by force. Another author complains that violence alone cannot explain the persistence and extensiveness of conversions to Islam.[192] Alexander Ross points out that Muslims have always been 'very zealous and diligent' in missionary activity.[193] These suggestions, though, are often simply rejected, if not ignored, because they contradict the established Christian conviction that Islam 'diffused it self by rage and terror of arms'.[194] It is in this way, for instance, that Leland replies to Chubb's remarks.[195] For most Christian apologists, this explanation of Islam's spread is not genuinely open to historical falsification. It is too convenient a myth to be questioned since it both justifies Christian condemnation of Islam and supports the claim that the spread of Christianity alone was due to divine action.

In these ways, then, it is maintained that the spread of Islam is explicable without any need to refer to 'the particular and immediate agency of God'.[196] A number of Christian apologists, though, cannot accept the notion that an event as great as the rise of Islam can have occurred apart from God's design. Somewhat paradoxically, they join to their natural explanations of Mahomet's success the claim that God permitted or even sent him to punish Christians for their errors, evils and divisions. Henry Smith sees Islam as one of the scourges by which God whips his people when he is displeased at their wickedness.[197] This 'explanation' is used to understand both why Islam arose in the first place and why it continues to exist in such strength. As Humphrey Prideaux puts it, God in 'his All-wise Providence' allows Islam to continue still as 'a Scourge unto us *Christians*, who having receiv'd so holy and so excellent a Religion . . . will not yet conform our selves to live worthy of it'.[198] In this way, even if the spread of Islam cannot be explained in a wholly natural manner, Christian apologists can reconcile any super-natural activity in it with their claims about God's providential control of events and the truth of Christianity. It does, however, lead to some appearance of inconsistency in their remarks, as when Alexander Ross asserts that Islam arose 'from the voluntary perverseness of Mens hearts, from the Malice and Craft of the Devil, and from the Just Judgments of the Almighty'.[199]

The treatment of Islam in this period is thus to an important extent determined by the nature of current theological arguments. With a few exceptions, Islam is examined in order to show that it is inferior to Christianity and offers no plausible threat to the various proofs of the truth of the Christian revelation. Christian apologists are not interested in establishing and stating the truth about Muslim faith and practice. They use – or abuse – Islam in order to support their own convictions about the perfection of Christianity and to exhort their fellow-believers to a better practice of their faith.[200] In this respect, the case of Islam provides the most developed illustration of the thesis that the treatment of other religions in the theological works of the seventeenth and eight-eenth centuries is orientated by internal apologetic concerns.[201] The result of such an approach, combined with the publication of travellers' stories to satisfy idle but generally uncritical curiosity, has been a deep-seated inability to appreciate other religions as living faiths. As late as 1939 a standard Christian handbook, edited by a scholar of great repute, could dismiss Buddhism as not really a religion and Islam as 'a degener-ate offshoot of Judaism and Christianity' and conclude that we are not faced by a choice between religions but between 'the religion of the Bible or no religion'. The treatment of other religions in the past has left a legacy of theological misunderstanding from which we may not yet be wholly free. One advantage of studying what happened in the past is at least to make us aware of such prejudices.

VII

The uses of 'other religions' for instruction

The treatment of 'other religions' in the seventeenth and eighteenth centuries is not confined to satisfying curiosity about what is unusual and to defending the finality of the Christian faith. Although these two concerns give rise to most of the discussions, other motives are sometimes involved. What is known – or supposed to be known – about non-Christian religions is put to use in various ways, sometimes for instruction and more often for propaganda purposes.

Those wishing to instruct occasionally pretend to a foreign provenance for their material in order to render it more attractive. Others adopt the propaganda technique of guilt by association in attempts to defame their opponents within Christianity. Whereas some of the proponents of natural religion point to alleged common elements in Christianity and other religions as supporting evidence, these controversialists use such evidence for a very different purpose. They suggest parallels between the beliefs and practices of some non-Christian faith and those of a group within Christianity in order to malign the latter. The alleged similarities are presented as justifying the condemnation of the latter as not genuinely Christian. Another use of other religions is to reinforce confidence in the superiority of Christianity by highlighting how its tenets and activities contrast with those of other faiths. The inferiority of the latter is seen as witnessing to the truth of the former – even though in practice it is usually the former's values that are the basis of the judgement of the latter's inferiority! The awareness of other religions is also employed to press the need for Christian unity. There is nothing especially recent about the argument of the ecumenical movement that Christianity will only be effective in converting the world to its gospel when it has overcome its own divisions. 'That they all may be one . . .

that the world may believe' (John 17, 21) is a theme which occasionally appears in discussions of other religions – although the unacknowledged assumption (then as now) generally seems to be that the unity to be achieved should conform to the 'true' Christianity represented by the person making the claim! Finally, to return to the theme of instruction, exegetes sometimes use knowledge gained from the study of other religions in order to gain further insights into Biblical texts.

Some of these 'uses' of other religions are fair and appropriate in terms of the understanding of their time. On other occasions, however, the desire to trounce opponents leads to the abuse of the available inform-ation. When controversialists start to rake up theological mud with which to smear adversaries, respect for accuracy is easily forgotten, though the result can still be fascinating for readers two or three cen-turies later. It reminds us how theological debates can arouse strong passions and distort understanding. Whatever else may characterise the theological debates of the past, they do not lack liveliness – nor plain speaking! We will begin a brief review of these materials, though, in the gentler waters of a literary conceit, by considering how 'other religions' were used for the purposes of instruction.

From *Utopia* to *Erewhon* – which on reflection is not very far – the fascination with things foreign has been employed by writers to make their points more palatable. The tedium of moral instruction has been eased by pretending that it came from an exotic source or by placing it in a story of travel. Furthermore, what at this time might have been offensive and even dangerous to state directly with reference to contem-porary situations could be expressed relatively safely with a knowing wink by putting it in the mouth of a stranger or deriving it from a far country. The more unusual its supposed source, the less likely was it to evoke official action against its real author. In this respect Voltaire's *Letters Concerning the English Nation* (published first in translation in London in 1733 and the following year in French as *Lettres Philosophiques*) were too near home and too direct for the ploy to be successful. Under the guise of approving comments on what he observed in England, Voltaire in effect attacked the church and state as found in France. His book provoked the authorities to such an extent that they had it burned by the hangman as subversive and irreligious. Voltaire had to retire to Lorraine – and sales of the book were considerable! Others, though, managed to enjoy success without hostility by producing more exotic and less contentious collections of letters from fictional travellers to Europe.

Montesquieu's *Persian Letters* enjoyed immediate popularity when they appeared in 1721. First published anonymously in Amsterdam for safety's sake, the work ran through ten editions in a year. The fictitious authors of the letters look quizzically on French customs and beliefs. Sometimes puzzled at what they discover, their rational comments make, with humour, enlightened criticisms of established institutions, including those of religion. They find that the vast number of Biblical commentators are not seeking to accept the doctrines of the Bible but to use it to justify their own ideas.[1] The Koran, though, does not escape criticism from these supposed Muslims; its style is such that it seems to contain 'the language of God and the ideas of men'.[2] As for the differences between religions, they note that the Jews regard both Christians and Muslims as rebellious daughters[3] while from their standpoint Christianity seems to have many of the 'rudiments' of Islam even though Mahomet is not recognised.[4] Their remarks express the Enlightenment's support for toleration and its confidence that if only people would use their understanding, the truth would eventually emerge. It is the truth that in spite of their differences all live 'under the same flag' of a universal faith which transcends the peculiar rules of the individual religions.[5] In the meantime, people best serve God by living as good citizens according to the rules of the society into which they have been born, not by worrying over the ceremonial demands of particular religions but by observing 'the duties of humanity'.[6]

Among other works of this type are Marana's *Letters Writ by a Turkish Spy*, Lord Lyttleton's *Letters from a Persian*, and the Marquis d'Argens' *Chinese Letters*. Voltaire's *L'Ingénu* also uses the fiction of a visitor to Europe. Perhaps the most famous British (or perhaps one should say Irish) use of the genre is Oliver Goldsmith's *Citizen of the World*. The letters, which first appeared twice-weekly in the *Public Ledger* and were collected into a volume in 1762, purport to be the correspondence of 'a Chinese philosopher residing in London'. His reports cast much light on life in that city in the mid-eighteenth century, including people's pretence to know what is genuinely Chinese![7] The lack of attention to religious matters in the letters is probably not untypical of the general attitude among the populace at this time. Opportunity is taken, however, to comment on some issues.

English attitudes towards death are considered to be hypocritical.[8] Conduct in worship and reasons for ecclesiastical preferment receive critical mention in one letter.[9] In another, priestcraft generally is attacked – 'the bonzes, the brachmans and the priests deceive the people' throughout the world as they point out 'the way to heaven' but 'stand still themselves'.[10] Ridicule is held to be the most effective weapon against enthusiasts who, from Fohi 'the idol of China', Zoroaster 'the leader of the Bramins' and Mahomet to contemporary practitioners (Methodists?), are seen as enemies to laughter.[11] None of the 'boasted revelations' of the religions of the world provide the truth about the nature of reality and 'the reasons of our creation',[12] for all are contrary to reason. As for reason itself, the traveller who attempts to leave the state of happy ignorance for *the Land of Certainty*, having had to pass from the guide of 'Demonstration' to that of 'Probability', realises that *The Land of Confidence* is the only region that he can hope to reach. The way there, however, is through the blind use of 'Error': if he tries to see where he is going he falls into *the Ocean of Doubts*. This 'Chinese philosopher', then, has no illusions about the power of reason to reach transcendental truths.[13] Wisdom for him is to seek the mean which gives tranquillity whatever happens.[14] Finally, we may note, he maintains that hardly 'any material difference' obtains between 'a page of our Confucius and of your Tillotson'.[15] The latter died in 1694 as Archbishop of Canterbury. His sermons present a 'reasonable' exposition of the Christian faith and were regarded as models by many divines in the following century. So far as Goldsmith's 'philosopher' can judge, there is apparently no significant conflict between what is involved in the 'reasonable' Christian theism of the one and the 'reasonable' non-theistic morality of the other!

Goldsmith's comments are not especially startling. Through his Chinese sage he presents a mild agnosticism laced with gently humorous reflections on English attitudes. The fiction of a foreign author is not a device intended to avoid official sanctions, for by this time much more radical opinions are openly expressed in England – though there were limits to what the public would tolerate, as both John Wesley and Joseph Priestley experienced. What Goldsmith presents is merely a pleasant – and successful – means of making his urbane comments more attractive by trading on the growing interest in the East.

While, however, the idea of a traveller coming to Europe to comment on its affairs was used as a literary fiction, a great number of travellers went in the opposite direction and reported on what they found as well as about what happened to them. The many published records of voyages of discovery and travellers' tales were popular sources both of amusement and of instruction. From individual works like William Lithgow's *Rare Adventures and Painful Peregrinations* or the *Voyages* of George Anson and James Cook, from collections such as Richard Hakluyt's *Principal*

Navigations, Voyages and Discoveries of the English Nation onwards and from compilations such as Thomas Bankes' *System of Universal Geography*, readers learned, as the last-named advertises on its title-page, about 'the Religion, Laws, Customs, Manners, Genius, Habits, Amusements, and Ceremonies' of the inhabitants of 'the whole world' as well as about the geography, botany, zoology, politics, science and economy of their different countries. So far as religious beliefs and practices are concerned, these ostensibly factual reports only rarely indicate – as in the case of Joseph Pitts' *Faithful Account of the Religion and Manners of the Mahometans* (a record of his captivity in Muslim hands) – that there may be things to commend in other religions. Pitts' record is also unusual in devoting a great deal of attention to religion, which most travellers' tales only mention in passing, being much more concerned with storms, shipwrecks, hardships and sufferings. Where other religions are mentioned, the explorations are generally held to show their worthlessness. Thomas Halyburton provides a typical estimation of the evidence when he asserts that

> Every nation had their own way of worship, and that stuffed with blasphemous, unworthy, ridiculous, ungrounded, impious and horrid rites and usages; of which there are unnumerable accounts, every where to be met with. We can no where in the heathen world find any worship that is not manifestly unworthy of and injurious to the glorious God.[16]

Nevertheless, the worthlessness of what was described did not make it any the less fascinating, rather the contrary. William Lithgow's readers were thus not only provided with comments on the pyramids and crocodiles of Egypt but also told about Muslim practices in Turkey and the mosques of Fez.[17] Writing from a staunchly Protestant viewpoint, he does not exclude other branches of Christianity from his critical observations. He remarks on the 'ridiculous' ceremonies of oriental Christians in Jerusalem and on the 'superstitious profession of Popery' in Ireland.[18] With its tit-bits of interesting information about religion and its generally unsympathetic attitude to beliefs and practices which differ from those of the author, Lithgow's *Rare Adventures* is typical of the genre. It is also not exceptional in the way that its apparently factual account occasionally contains items which preserve false reports, based presumably on hearsay. Lithgow, for example, not only repeats the claim that Mahomet's iron coffin used to hang 'between two adamants' but also says that it has 'of late' been moved from Mecca to Medina 'because the

Turkish pilgrims were often suffocated to death with a fabulous desert in going to Mecca'.[19]

A number of authors exploited this interest in foreign things with success. *The Spectator* and *The Rambler* contain numerous anecdotes supposedly from the East. Various early novels enhanced their appeal by adopting the form of a story of travel or by locating their tale in some distant country. Among the best known of these are Jonathan Swift's *Gulliver's Travels*, Daniel Defoe's *Robinson Crusoe* and *Captain Singleton*, Voltaire's *Zadig* and Samuel Johnson's *Rasselas, Prince of Abissinia*. The religious content of such works is often only incidental but it is not totally absent. Defoe, for instance, as has already been mentioned, portrays his natives as enjoying naturally a measure of religious insight. Indeed, Will Atkins' native wife in effect converts her husband to the Christianity to which he formerly paid only lip-service.[20] *Rasselas* is an exploration of moral truths where the story largely serves as the background for the discussion of ideas. In the course of the story of *Zadig* Voltaire includes an incident in which the hero convinces an Egyptian, an Indian, a Chaldean, a Cathayan, a Greek and a Celt (who was partly drunk and the most angry) that they really are 'all of the same opinion' in religion, for in different forms they all recognise 'a Supreme Being, upon whom form and matter depend'.[21] The theological significance of Zadig's experiences, however, has to wait for an angelic revelation – and it is the sombre message that people must 'submit to the eternal edicts' and not presume to try to comprehend what they should 'adore'.[22] It is a lesson which Voltaire's 'Child of Nature', a Huron, teaches in *L'Ingénu*: 'we are in the power of an eternal Being . . . all the rest is an unfathomable depth of shadows.'[23]

When Swift used the form of the travel story, it was to provide a satirical commentary on the social, moral and political practices of his time. *Gulliver's Travels* appeared in 1726. Some time earlier, in 1699, Fénelon's *Adventures of Télémaque* had been published in The Hague. In the form of a story about the travels of Ulysses' son, it was intended to teach political philosophy to Louis XIV's grandson. From the narrative he was to learn about the evils of absolute power and about the responsibility of a king to his people. Although Louis XIV stopped its initial production in Paris because he judged it liable to corrupt the minds of his descendants, the book sold 'prodigiously'. According to one early report its 'fictions' are 'well contrived, the moral sublime, and the political maxims tending all to the happiness of mankind'.[24] One critic even suggests that its success exceeds that of Homer, Virgil and any other author, sacred or profane. It is perhaps as well that the author of this eulogy is anonymous![25] The genre, though, is a successful one.

In 1717 Andrew Michael Ramsay, a Scot who lived most of his life in France, wrote a laudatory preface for a new edition of *Télémaque*. A decade later, his own version of the genre appeared, *The Travels of Cyrus*.[26] The aim of the work is to provide, under the guise of the story of a series of visits by the youthful Cyrus, 'a philosophical history' on the model of Xenophon.[27] In it, Ramsay attempts to combine in 'a connected system the most beautiful hints of antiquity, in order to unfold the great pinciples of religion' and to show that all nations enjoy some idea of them.[28] At first sight his work may seem to be preaching through its fictions a kind of natural theology, for he announces that he wants to outline the mind's progress in the search for truth by comparing 'the religions, governments and laws of different nations'.[29] In this respect he argues against atheists that 'sense, natural sentiment, and reason' prove the existence of a supreme deity.[30] Indeed, Cyrus' discussions provide him with a religious education whereby he is led 'by a plain and natural chain of ideas'[31] from incipient deterministic atheism[32] through beliefs that resemble deism and Socinianism to what is effectively Christian understanding.[33] While Ramsay thus indicates a pattern of religious education, he also maintains that the final truths to be recognised have in principle always been available to humanity since their original revelation in the patriarchal age. In their transmission 'throughout all nations' since then, except in the case of 'the true religion', these revealed doctrines have been grossly distorted. Nevertheless, traces of them survive. Hence, he states that he wants to show that 'the earliest opinions of the most knowing and civilized nations come nearer the truth than those of latter ages'.[34] On this basis he holds against 'the Deists' that 'the principal doctrines of revealed religion, concerning the states of innocence, corruption and renovation, are as ancient as the world'.[35] Furthermore, in opposition to those who advocate a religious faith based wholly on what human understanding can discover by its own powers, Ramsay asserts that whereas the philosopher may employ 'the powers of reason' both to rebut unbelief and to recognise the limits of reason's competence in religious matters, it is the prophet who gives the final understanding. He presents 'the belief of a supernatural religion' whose doctrines are proved by 'palpable facts' to have been 'divinely revealed'.[36] What Cyrus learns from Zoroaster, Hermes, Pythagoras, Eleazer and others accordingly reaches its climax when Daniel tells him about the future appearance, first in humiliation and then in glory, of 'the

GREAT EMANUEL' who 'will expiate sin, by the sacrifice of himself' and thereby effect what is imperfectly hinted at in the sacrificial practices of the different religions.[37]

Throughout the work, Ramsay treats the fables of the other religions as containing distorted perceptions of true religious understanding. The Egyptians use animals to represent the qualities of Osiris, Isis and Orus and these three themselves express 'three forms of the divinity' of 'the great Ammon' who is 'the unknown God' that is properly the sole object of worship.[38] Their religion is grossly misunderstood when the symbolic nature of its expressions is not appreciated. Phoenician beliefs about Belus, Venus and Adonis are similarly interpreted as telling the story of a fall, the vicarious suffering of the 'son' of God and his resurrection, and the final transformation of all things to the state of perfection.[39] From his travels, then, Cyrus learns 'that all nations were agreed in the doctrine of the three states of the world, the three forms of the Divinity, and a middle God, who by his conflicts and great sufferings was to expiate and exterminate moral evil, and restore innocence and peace to the universe'.[40] This positive appreciation of the proper contents of the beliefs of other religions is combined with a recognition of the normative standing of the Biblical material. At the end of the work Cyrus is said to conclude that

> all the discoveries made by Zoroaster, Hermes, Orpheus and Pythagoras, were but imperfect traces, and chance rays of the tradition from Noah: In Persia, Egypt, Greece, and in all other nations, he had found only obscure, uncertain and loose opinions; but with the Hebrews he had found books, prophecies and miracles, the authority of which was incontestable. Nevertheless, he saw the truth only as through a cloud . . . he waited for the accomplishment of Isaiah's prediction.[41]

Ramsay's readers were presumably expected to realise that the prediction had since been fulfilled and that the salvation-history, which in other religions was described in fables, was perceived in Christianity to have happened in history.

The Travels of Cyrus is not concerned simply to give instruction about ancient beliefs. While the material does provide information about the supposed doctrines of past religions, it is primarily presented as an indirect contribution to contemporary philosophical and theological debates about the nature of religious understanding. Ramsay acknowledges this in the preface when he says that the Magi in Cyrus' time were fallen into a kind of Atheism like that of Spinoza; Zoroaster, Hermes and Pythagoras adored one sole Deity, but they were Deists; Eleazar resembled the Socinians, who are for subjecting Religion to Philosophy; Daniel represents a perfect Christian, and the Hero of this book a young Prince who began to be corrupted by the maxims of irreligion.[42]

Other contemporary theories reflected in the discourses are those of Descartes, Malebranche, Hobbes, Newton and Berkeley, while ideas that were classically to be expressed by Tindal and Butler are also considered. Daniel's response to the problem of evil rejects the 'free will' theodicy offered by Eleazar – and Leibniz – in favour of an assertion of the mysteriousness of God's ways – the response canvassed, for example, by Bayle.[43] The identification of ancient sages with current debates may seem somewhat forced.[44] Nevertheless, Ramsay's work was popular, enjoying over thirty editions. First published in French in 1727 with an English translation the same year, it also appeared in German, Italian, Spanish and Greek. General readers preferred this fictional approach to the more stolid exposition of similar themes in such works as Ralph Cudworth's massive – and unfinished – *True Intellectual System of the Universe*.[45]

Another way in which materials ostensibly about other religions were produced in order to contribute to contemporary religious debates can be seen in Voltaire's *Philosophical Dictionary*. Whereas Pierre Bayle had provided an enormous range of ideas in his *Historical and Critical Dictionary* primarily through articles and remarks on actual figures and movements, Voltaire was happy to invent some of the background for his comments. While he pokes fun at the current interest in the East as a superior source of knowledge – he points out that Chinese doctors 'cure mortal illnesses no better than ours do, and that nature cures minor ailments by herself in China, as it does here',[46] – he also uses that interest to give further liveliness to his sceptical prods at Christianity. The incredibility of the 'theological religion' of a Christianity which affirms the doctrines of the incarnation, the virgin birth and transubstantiation is caricatured by reference to 'a bonze' who 'claims that Fo is a god; that his advent was predicted by fakirs; that he was born of a white elephant; that each bonze can create a Fo by making grimaces'.[47] Disagreements within and between religions are not subject to rational solutions for they are about matters which are not 'obvious truths' when they go beyond the bare acknowledgement of the reality of God and the demand for justice.[48] The study of religions only leads to scepticism about every-thing.[49] The intelligent Arab 'believes' doctrines contrary to common sense because he is threatened with eternal and, worse still, temporal torments.[50] Voltaire even offers a 'Japanese' and a 'Chinese Catechism' to expound his views on authentic religion and on the absurdities of the actual practices of religion.

There is no attempt to disguise the fictional nature of these 'Catech-isms'. The Japanese one refers by easy anagrams to Jews, Papists, Luthe-rans, Anabaptists, Quakers and Deists and the Chinese one to Condé and Brunswick! In the latter, Voltaire's admiration for what he understood to be Confucius' teaching is reflected. A 'disciple of Confucius' presents Voltaire's enlightened deism of the practice of virtue and 'the cult of a single universal God' which is free 'from the chimeras of sophists and the illusions of false prophets'.[51] Voltaire himself, however, was conned in 1760 when he was presented with a copy of a manuscript called the *Ezour Vedam*. This purported to be a Hindu commentary on their scriptures, and gave him a favourable impression of Hinduism, which was later confirmed when he read authentic studies by John Zephaniah Holwell and Alexander Dow. The *Ezour Vedam*, however, was a forgery per-petrated on him by the Jesuits.[52]

In England, the most famous of such inventions is *The Oeconomy of Human Life*. According to its subtitle it is 'Translated from an Indian Manuscript written by an ancient Bramin'. The introduction, in the form of a letter to 'the Earl of [Chesterfield]', gives an elaborate story of how the manuscript was acquired by a Chinese scholar on an embassy to 'Lasa' in 'Thibet'.[53] This scholar translated it into Chinese from its original form 'in the language and character of the ancient Gymno-sophists'[54] and the Earl's correspondent then turned it into English. The latter takes comfort in the fact that his reader cannot compare his version either with the Chinese version or with the original.[55] He also admits that although some of its phrases are peculiarly eastern, its form suggests to some a European origin.[56] This 'Oriental System of Morality' was so successful that it was rapidly followed by a second volume which pur-ported to come from a further manuscript whose 'Antiquity, Charac-ters, and other internal marks' showed it to have the same author.[57] The origin of this work was sufficiently disguised for Rhys Davids, in his inaugural lecture at Manchester in 1904–5, to consider it useful to point out that it expresses neither Brahmin nor Tibetan thought.[58] In fact, although it is still sometimes ascribed to Robert Dodsley who published it, the piece is now generally recognised to have been written by Philip

Dormer Stanhope, the fourth Earl of Chesterfield.

What this small work offers is sensible moral advice in a form that is somewhat reminiscent of the biblical wisdom literature. After an opening invocation calling on the reader to hear the wise and gracious voice of God,[59] the instructions cover the duties of 'man considered as an individual', the 'passions', 'woman', 'consanguinity, or natural relations', 'providence, or the accidental differences of men' – covering such states as being wise and ignorant, rich and poor, master and servants – 'social duties' and, finally, 'religion'. The further volume deals with the nature of man and his infirmities, the 'affections of man, which are hurtful', 'the advantages' which a 'man may acquire over his fellow-creatures' and the 'natural accidents' of adversity, pain, sickness and death. The quality of the teaching can be illustrated by such paragraphs as

> The promises of Hope are sweeter than roses in the bud . . . but the threatnings of Fear are a terror to the heart. Nevertheless let not Hope allure, nor Fear deter thee, from doing that which is right . . .[60]

> Take unto thyself a wife, and obey the ordinance of God . . . and become a faithful member of society. But examine with care, and fix not suddenly; on thy present choice demands the future happiness of thee and thy posterity . . .[61]

> Happy is the man who hath sown in his breast the seeds of benevolence; the produce thereof shall be charity and love . . . He promoteth in his neighbourhood peace and good-will . . .[62]

> Pride and meanness seem incompatible; but man reconcileth contrarieties: he is at once the most miserable and the most arrogant of all creatures . . .[63]

and, finally, from the section on 'Nobility and Honour',

> What good is it to the blind that his parents could see? What benefit is it to the dumb that his grandfather was eloquent? Even so, what is it to the mean that their predecessors were noble?

> A mind disposed to virtue, maketh great the possessor, and, without titles, will raise him above the vulgar . . . The ambitious will always be first in the croud; he presseth forward, he looketh not behind him: more anguish hath he in his soul to see one before him, than joy to leave thousands at a distance.[64]

The whole work is seasoned with pious reflections. The servant is to remember that his position has been appointed him by God – and that it has the advantage of removing from him 'the cares and sollicitudes of life'![65] Both rich and poor are to recognise that 'God dispenseth happiness to them both'.[66] The worshipper is not to try to flatter God nor to challenge God's judgements.[67] Nature is to be studied because it gives reasons to adore its creator.[68] The section on religion only collects together the religious ideas which pervade the whole. What *The Oeconomy of Human Life* teaches are the 'great duties' of 'piety to thy God, and benevolence to thy fellow-creatures'.[69]

The teaching may not be original in content but its morality is sensible – at least, for the culture of eighteenth-century Britain it would have been unexceptionable, whatever modern moralists might make of its acceptance of social divisions as divinely ordained! Rulers and subjects, masters and servants, husbands and wives, parents and children who followed its instructions could reasonably hope to find that they led to a harmonious society. Individuals who applied its precepts to themselves could reasonably hope to face life with equanimity and find satisfaction. What the supposedly mysterious origin of the teaching might have been expected to do was to give to the work an appeal – and even an aura of authority – which would be lacking in a moral tract which straightforwardly stated these precepts. Lord Chesterfield thus used the fascination with the East and the supposed wisdom to be found there as a lure to render his moral instruction more attractive. If the number of editions of the work is any guide, it was a successful 'use' of the interest in other religions.[70]

A further use of the attraction of things foreign which may briefly be mentioned is illustrated by Thomas Wilson's *The Knowledge and Practice of Christianity Made Easy to the Meanest Capacities: or, An Essay Towards an Instruction for the Indians*. This work, which first appeared in 1741 and reached its twentieth edition in 1815, was written, according to its author, as a result of 'a short, but very entertaining Conversation' with General Oglethorpe, the governor of Georgia, about 'the *Condition*, *Temper*, and *Genius*' of the Indians in that territory. Having learnt that they are 'capable of being civilized, and of receiving the Truths of Religion', Thomas Wilson offers an account of the Christian religion 'in Terms suited to the meanest Capacity', aiming to make the saving truths of Christianity 'plain even to the Understanding of an *Indian*' and thereby ostensibly to assist those who seek to convert the heathen.[71] Nevertheless, although the preface discusses the duty of missionary work overseas, what was probably at least as important a motive for the work is indicated when Wilson acknowledges that some items have been included for the instruction of those who live 'among the Professors of Christianity' but who 'are not much better than Heathens'.[72] While, then, the work has the form of a dialogue between an 'Indian' and a 'Missionary', for most of its readers this merely provided an entertaining background for their instruction in the knowledge and practice of Christianity. If taken to heart, its teachings would lead them from 'that sad, but too common Delusion, *of being Christians without Christianity*: – That is, – of *professing* to *obey*' the way of Christ while in fact 'leading *careless* and *unchristian* Lives'.[73] Salvation would be seen to be dependent not only upon 'the Benefits' of the death of Christ but also upon 'Repentance, and a thorough Reformation of Life'.[74] As such it was a very suitable work for 'charitable Persons' to distribute at their own expense among 'poor *Families*, *Children*, and *Servants*' in Britain, whatever use it may have been put to in 'our Plantations in America'.[75] The 1815 edition ends with a note that it has 'lately' been translated into Welsh 'for the Use of the *Ancient Britons*'. Thereby, presumably, it extended its home mission.

A very different use of other religions for instruction is found in a few Christian writers who use their knowledge of foreign beliefs and practices to support and illuminate the contents of the Bible. Alleged parallels to Biblical reports are cited from other religions as confirmation of the trustworthiness of those reports. Edward Stillingfleet, for instance, claims that the 'Heathen *Mythology*' preserves some 'obscure foot-steps, even of that part of Scripture-history which preceeded the Flood' and many more 'Traditions' which give 'broken Fragments' of the Biblical story from Noah onwards.[76] The strength of such arguments, though, depends on the plausibility of claims that persons with different names are identifiable with each other if the stories about them have some resemblances. A number of writers on other religions were happy to undertake this kind of identification, and probably found little difficulty with the procedure because, consciously or, more likely, unconsciously, their thought was prejudiced by Biblical views on the origin and primitive unity of humanity.

Other authors do not seek so much to confirm the historical trustworthiness of the Biblical records by reference to the materials of other religions as to show that there are no serious incompatibilities between them. In doing this they are responding to critics of traditional Christian belief such as Gildon who, for example, points out that Chinese and Indian materials record events which occurred ages before the Biblical date for the creation of the world.[77] Peter Allix replies to such criticisms by various arguments which aim to show that the relationship between the 'Antiquities of *China*' and the Bible is to be seen as that between a 'Tradition' which has suffered much alteration through its transmission and 'an exact Narrative of Matters of Fact drawn up by an Author who knew very well what he writ'.[78] The problem, however, was not as easily solved as Allix may have hoped, especially as it was an age when Christian faith was generally understood to include acceptance of the historical accuracy of the Biblical narratives, including the chronology that could be inferred from them. At the end of the eighteenth century, Sir William Jones still finds it significant to claim that 'the adamantine pillars of our *Christian* faith' cannot be moved 'by the result of any debates on the comparative antiquity of the Hindus'.[79] To support his case he suggests how the Indian Menus may be identified with Adam and Noah.[80] He further finds the Biblical record of the origin of humanity confirmed by his researches into the Hindus, '*Persians*, *Ethiopians*, and *Egyptians*, the *Phenicians*, *Greeks*, and *Tuscans*, the *Scythians* or *Goths*, and *Celts*, the *Chinese*, *Japanese* and *Peruvians*'. His conclusion is that 'they all proceeded from one *central* country' – as the Bible says they did.[81]

A rather different problem is faced by Jacob Bryant: how can the scriptures be true when they report that all humanity is 'derived from Adam or Noah' if it be the case that 'the Negroes are a separate race of men'? His reply is not one of 'Let the Negroes shift for themselves'. He offers a confutation of the objection by showing that differences of hair and complexion 'are not confined to any particular race of men' but depend upon climate and custom.[82] William Whiston had employed a different answer to the problem. He had linked knowledge of the world with that of the Bible by suggesting that 'the different Colours of Mankind' – white, black, olive and copper – together with their 'Peculiarities of Hair and Visage' are the result of God's establishment of distinctions between 'the Children of *Cain* and *Lamech*, and the Children of *Seth*'. According to him, physical causes cannot explain these differences among the descendants of the same parents.[83] In his *Memoirs*, Whiston tackles another problem: what happened to the ten tribes of Israel? On the basis of what he learnt when he lived 'among the *Russes*', he finds it probable that the Tartars are the natural posterity of those Israelites.[84] In varied ways, then, and often with the exercise of imaginative ingenuity, proposals are offered as to how biblical reports may be shown to agree with what is found to be the case in the world.

Much more interesting, though, are the occasional suggestions that knowledge of the beliefs and practices of other religions may help to elucidate the meaning of biblical passages. Both the relative lack of a sense of historical development at this time and the obvious link between the Old Testament and contemporary Jews make it unsurprising that the preface to Bernard Picart's *Ceremonies and Religious Customs of the Various Nations of the Known World* includes the remark that there are various passages in Paul that are better understood when seen in the light of 'the Manners and Customs of the *Jews*' that are currently to be observed.[85] Similarly, David Collyer's *Sacred Interpreter* is following an obvious course when it includes as an appendix 'some Remarks, taken chiefly from modern Travellers of undoubted credit, concerning Palestine, where the Jews lived, and other parts of the Eastern countries, and the present customs of the inhabitants; which illustrate divers passages of the Holy Scriptures'.[86] Among the practices cited are the construction of rock cells for burials (cf. Genesis 42, 29; Matthew 27, 60), slave markets (cf. Genesis 17, 23), giving presents on visits (cf. 1 Samuel 9, 7), the structure of the houses (cf. Deuteronomy 22, 8), the use of 'a thin paste of galls, and calcined copper, to beautify themselves' (cf. Ezekiel 23, 40), divination by arrows (cf. Ezekiel 21, 21), and the incubation of ostrich eggs (cf. Job 39, 14). How Sarah baked bread (cf. Genesis 18, 6 and Hosea 7, 8) is explained by what is currently observed to happen 'in the countries near Mesopotamia'.[87] Such pieces of information may not be very significant religiously but, granted the importance which Christian believers gave to the Bible, they doubtless helped to illuminate puzzling references in the text.

References to materials from further east than Palestine are not common. Matthew Tindal provocatively suggests that 'the plain and simple Maxims' of Confucius 'will help to illustrate the more obscure' sayings of Christ but he does not develop the theme.[88] The straightforward morality of Confucius was presumably more attractive to Tindal's view of reason and the light of nature as our guide than the puzzling rhetoric of some of the dominical commands in the Sermon on the Mount. This view, though, was not widely acceptable. More attractive were attempts like those of Thomas Harmer to illustrate the Bible by illustrations from eastern customs. As well as his general study, *Observations on Divers Passages of Scripture . . . from . . . Books of Voyages and Travels* (1746), he published a commentary on the Song of Solomon whose title claims it to be 'Drawn by the help of Instructions from the East'. Besides other parts of the Bible, his materials are drawn from travels, the *Arabian Nights*, the letters of Lady Mary Wortley Montague and 'an Eastern Song, composed by *Ibrahim*, the great Favourite of Sultan Achmet III' which he quotes in full.[89] He also gives an engraving of 'an East-Indian Vehicle' – in fact an elephant with a howdah – as an illustration of his remarks on Song of Solomon 3, 7.[90] Among the practices to which he refers in his commentary are the use of nuptial crowns by Greek Christians in Egypt, Arab and Turkish marriage customs, ranking among members of a harem, singing on ceremonial occasions, the form of eastern poetry, dress, the use of perfumes, garden kiosks and botany. Although the book ends with a paragraph about the relation between Jews and Christians, Harmer is critical of many of 'the *Prophetical* Interpreters' of the Song of Solomon. Their attempts to see it as a collection of religious allegories can be expressions of whimsical fancies. His interpretation, in contrast, is primarily concerned to draw out 'the Literal Sense' of the poem as a celebration of 'the Nuptials of Solomon'.[91] In this respect there can be little controversy about the legitimacy in principle of using information about eastern customs to discern the meaning of the text, and thus make a positive contribution to instruction and understanding. However, 'other religions' are not only used in such ways in seventeenth- and eighteenth-century works. Sometimes they are 'used' in propaganda as a form of abuse. To instances of this kind we turn our attention in the next chapter.

VIII

The uses of 'other religions' in controversy

In spite of the barbed wit of a Voltaire, most of the fictitious uses of 'other religions' for moral and religious instruction are fairly urbane. They may poke fun or be sententious but their readers would be unlikely to take offence at what is said. The same cannot be claimed for the 'uses' of other religions which are now to be discussed. Priests, Roman Catholics, Socinians, deists and enthusiasts were severally attacked by identifying some of their beliefs and practices, explicitly or implicitly, with what is to be found in 'other' (pagan – and hence false) religions.[1] It is here that mud flies, as odious comparisons and tendentious descriptions are presented. Some are manifestly unfair. Others hurt all the more because they are not so implausible that they can be laughed away. A few may actually be justified. We will start with attacks on priests and priestcraft.

In his *Pansebeia* Alexander Ross presents a favourable view of priesthood. At the end of his survey of 'all religions in the world' he maintains that 'Religion flourisheth and fadeth with the Priests and Ministers thereof; it riseth and falleth, floweth and ebbeth as they do'.[2] Giving examples which range from ancient Rome to contemporary Abyssinia, he finds that the 'chief supporter' of religion everywhere has ever been 'the honour, maintenance, and advancement of the Priesthood'. Since, furthermore, the decline of religion leads to atheism and thence to political anarchy, 'wise States' have always taken care to foster their 'Ministers of Religion'.[3] The acceptance of these conclusions would certainly be to the ministers' benefit, whatever underlying motive Ross may have had for drawing them. Those who consider religion to be intrinsically valuable and those who regard it as useful for society would be inclined to enhance the status and rewards of its official guardians. These, though, are conclusions which a number of critics of religion do not endorse. While some agree that political leaders foster religion for their secular advantage, they do not see this link as genuinely beneficial either to religion or to the state. Even more are critical of the link between religion and the priesthood which results in the practice of religion being dominated by priestly concerns. Rather than regarding the prosperity of the priesthood as coinciding with the flourishing of religion, they consider that the former is often at the expense of the latter.

Those critics who are not hostile to religion as such hold that most, if not all, existing beliefs and practices have been corrupted by priests for their selfish advantage. The recovery of authentic religion will be at the cost of a drastic reformation of priestly influence. Others, much fewer in number, who find little significant value in any form of religion, attack both it and its ministers by arguing that the latter are its only real beneficiaries. Society will be better ordered when priestly impositions are exposed as worthless. Both types of criticism are sometimes made by referring to what occurs – or is alleged to occur – in other religions. Readers, though, are generally left to perceive how what is found elsewhere relates to the current state of Christianity. In these ways references to other religions are used in the anti-clerical propaganda which characterised much radical writing about religion in the seventeenth and, much more, in the eighteenth century.

Herbert of Cherbury, in spite of his reputation, was no enemy of religion.[4] He was a practising theist who believed in divine aid in this life and judgement hereafter. His views on other religions are dominated by his understanding of the universality of divine providence and the general availability of the essential truths of religion. However, he has little that is good to say about the activity of priests. In *De Veritate* he points out that any 'pompous charlatan' may promote a false religion by demanding that no one 'dare to question the sacred authority of priests and preachers of God's word'. His 'Common Notions', recognised by all rational people as the touchstone for what is true, are to be used to uncover the 'deception' of such 'cunning authorities' who declare their 'inventions to be heaven-born'.[5] When he discusses the duty of worship, he allows that priests may be necessary but points out that in practice they 'have often been a crafty and deceitful tribe, prone to avarice, and often ineffective'. They have introduced into religion falsehoods, 'licentious ceremonies and senseless superstitions' with the result that they have 'corrupted, defiled, and prostituted' its pure name.[6] Similar claims appear in *De Religione Laici*: too frequently priests hinder authentic religion by diverting the soul from virtue to ceremonies which provide 'no mean profit' to them.[7] It is in *De Religione Gentilium*, however, that Herbert makes his most extensive attacks on priestcraft.[8] It is largely due to their machinations that the ancient worship of the 'Supreme God' was corrupted.[9] He gives examples of where priests introduced into it practices that 'were not only impious and foolish, but very obscene, fetid and sordid'.[10] Elsewhere he accuses them of using their natural knowledge to pretend to revealed insights and supernatural powers,[11] of introducing sacrifices to 'Convert them to their own use',[12] and of sowing 'Quarrels and Dissentions where-ever they came'.[13] Although he allows that there have been 'exemplary' members of the priesthood,[14] the overwhelming force of his remarks is that religion will be purest when it is freed from their influence. The study of other religions is thus used by Herbert to justify a considerable degree of anti-clericalism in his understanding of religion.

When we turn from the supposed 'father of the English deists'[15] to the so-called deists themselves, it is not surprising that we find similar views. Even though there may be no one doctrine that is held in common by all the supposed deists, they do generally share a critical attitude towards the supposed official directors of religion. Charles Blount, for example, repeats the charge that priests use religion for their own benefit.[16] Although he professes to except Christianity, he sees religions as widely 'tainted with the Interest of the Clergy'. The people were 'seduced' from the rational religion of virtue and piety by the 'crafty and covetous Sacerdotal Order'.[17] Blount not only describes how heathen priests counterfeited miracles,[18] but claims that, having discovered that they stood to gain more from 'the sins and ignorance of the common people, than by their virtue and knowledge', they augmented the number of sins and developed expiatory practices which would enrich them.[19] When they pandered to the interests of the ruling classes, their overriding concern again was their own advantage.[20] Claiming to be the only way to God,[21] priests of the different sects only agreed in their selfishness, whether they be Egyptian, Etruscan, Druid, Brachman, Persian, Celt, Goth or African![22] Anthony Collins defends the necessity of 'free-thinking' on the grounds that the differences between priests are so notorious that they cannot credibly be regarded as guides in matters of religion.[23] He effectively undermines their pretences to authority, for instance, by pointing out how 'throughout the world' they differ about what are the scriptures and about what is their authority. In this respect he refers to 'the Shaster' of the Bramins, the 'Zundavastaw' of 'the Persees', a book written by Sommonocodom which is followed by 'the

Talapoins of Siam', and the 'Alchoran' of the 'Dervizes' as well as to the way in which priests, both Christian and non-Christian, differ over the inspiration and meaning of what they regard as sacred books.[24] Only by 'free-thinking' can people avoid being led astray.[25]

John Toland is similarly critical. In the third of his *Letters to Serena*, for example, he not only alleges that priests in the ancient world developed 'the Heathen Mysterys' in order to 'make their imagin'd Intimacy with Heaven more valu'd, and to get Revenues settled on themselves'.[26] He also accuses them of opposing advances in knowledge that threatened their status[27] and of being in conspiracy with princes to 'preach up' the 'absolute Power' of the latter in return for temporal advantages.[28] Furthermore, he does not think that such practices have ceased. Where they have the authority, clergy still can be found urging people to follow directions that 'always tend to the Increase of their own Glory, Power, and Profit'.[29]

The iconoclastic Conyers Middleton notes at the end of his *Letter from Rome* that the 'corruptions' of Christianity which he had observed in the Church at Rome may have been 'contrived by the *intrigues and avarice of Priests*' who found it advantageous to continue the '*impostures*' which had proved so profitable to their pagan predecessors. Alternatively, the practices may have been foisted on Roman Christianity to render it acceptable to the 'humor' of the people there.[30] Middleton, though, is not concerned to determine which is the correct explanation. His use of other religions is not to attack priestcraft but to attack Roman Catholicism by showing that what is found in Rome is in many ways a survival of the ancient pagan religious life of that city.

In the 'Prefatory Discourse' added to the *Letter from Rome* to defend it against criticisms, Middleton is careful to claim that he is not seeking to attack Christianity itself but 'that System of ceremonies and doctrines, which is peculiar to the *Romish Church*'. His method is to reveal 'by an historical deduction of facts' that its origin lies in pagan Rome.[31] In reply to the critic who claims that some of the practices are borrowed from Jewish usages, he argues that many of the practices cannot claim such ancestry and that in the case of those that can this is no defence since these '*beggerly elements*' were 'wiped away' by the institution of the Christian gospel.[32] He offers a wide-ranging description of ceremonies, stories and customs observed in Rome now for which he knows of parallels in ancient, pre-Christian Rome. He mentions the substitution of the '*Saints*' for '*the old Demigods*',[33] the employment of pagan statues as Christian images, the use in worship of incense, perfume, holy water, lamps and wax candles, the presentation of votive offerings, and flagellation.[34] Stories of miracles copy – with embellishments – pagan reports, to such an extent that 'there is scarce *a Prodigy* in the *old Historians*, or a *Fable* in the *old Poets*, but what is transcribed into *their Legends*, and swallowed by their silly Bigots, as certain and undoubted facts'.[35] By such illustrations Middleton maintains that what is seen 'on every *festival of the Virgin* or other *Romish-Saint*' strongly suggests that in Rome is found 'the genuin remains of *Heathenism*'. Rome is basically 'still the *same Rome*, which *old Numa* first *tamed* and *civilized* by the *arts of religion*'.[36] His conclusion, then, is that the evidence of what happens proves that there is 'an *exact Conformity*, or *Uniformity* rather of *Worship*, between *Popery* and *Paganism*'.[37]

Middleton's polemic is an extended – and learned – example of a popular form of Protestant criticism of Roman Catholicism. In *Leviathan* Thomas Hobbes goes so far as to compare it with 'the *Kingdome of Fairies*'. The papacy is 'no other than the *Ghost* of the deceased *Romane Empire*, sitting crowned upon the grave thereof'. Just as fairies have their 'enchanted Castles', change infants into elves, skim the cream from the milk and have no existence 'but in the Fancies of ignorant people', so the 'Ecclesiastiques' of the papacy have their cathedrals, 'take from young men, the use of Reason', extract 'the Cream of the Land' and have power only as a result of false miracles, traditions and interpretations of the Bible.[38] Others, though, prefer to criticise Roman Catholicism by comparison with actual religions rather than with the subjects of 'old wives' fables'. When Herbert of Cherbury attacks the use of 'External Means' of securing divine pardon on the grounds that in practice it leaves people unconcerned about real repentance and amendment of life,[39] many of his readers would understand his remarks as including an implicit criticism of Roman Catholic practices. Joseph Mede is explicit in his condemnation of the Church of Rome. In its alleged 'Worshipping of Angels, Deifying and Invocating of Saints, Adoring of Reliques, Bowing down to Images and Crosses, &c.' it has produced 'the Apostasy of the latter Times'.[40] After expounding at some length the 'doctrines of demons' prophesied in 1 Timothy 4, 1, Mede presents a 'serious & patheticall Expostulation with the Church of *Rome*'. He calls on this 'Christ-apostaticall Strumpet' to recognise that 'an Husband is more grieved and dishonoured by his Wife's adultery, then if any other women whatsoever . . . should play the harlots'. On this basis he maintains that the 'Prostitute Whore' is not to be found among 'the *Turks, Tartars*, and other *Mahumetans*' nor among 'the *Paynims*' because they do not acknowledge

Christ as their Lord. The real 'Whoredom' occurs in the Roman Church for it is there that 'the Gentiles Theology of Daemons' has been 'revived'.[41] Similar charges from very different theological standpoints are made by John Toland, who sees the veneration of saints and images as gross idolatry,[42] and Theophilus Gale, who devotes a long chapter in *The Court of the Gentiles* to a consideration of 'Pagan Philosophie' as 'the cause of al Antichristianisme' and in particular of that form of it found in popish rites and doctrines.[43] Scholastic divinity and canon law as well as such practices as 'Saint-worship' 'Popish Holy-dayes', wayside crosses, fasts, monasticism and the wearing of surplices are held to be imitations of 'Pagan *Demon-Doctrines* and *Canons*'. What is found in Roman Catholicism 'is but a reviving of the old *Philosophic* . . . *Demon-Dogmas*, *Canons*, and *Traditions*' for 'the whole bodie and spirit of Antichristianisme had its conception and formation in the wombe of Pagan Philosophie' – and as such is nothing but 'Vanitie'.[44]

The attack on Roman Catholicism sometimes employs references to Judaism. Charles Leslie suggests that Jews are scandalised by the idolatry practised 'in the Popish Countries' for they regard it as a sin 'strictly prohibited' in the Bible.[45] Richard Kidder similarly holds that their conversion to Christianity is hindered by their awareness of 'the corrupt Doctrines and Practices' of 'the *Romanists*'. He cites in particular the scandals occasioned by 'the Worship of *Images*, and the Sacrament of the *Altar*', 'the Doctrine of *Transubstantiation*' (for they hold that it certainly cannot be true), the '*Adoration* of the *Host*', and the 'Doctrine of *Purgatory*' as well as such lesser matters as '*Crossing* our selves when it *thunders*, *Christening* of *Bells*' and the celibacy of priests. Here Kidder finds the Jews in the right for these things are part of 'the Roman Church, but not of Christ'.[46]

Other attacks on Roman Catholicism use various comparisons with Islam. Humphrey Prideaux sees Islam and the papacy as the eastern and western forms of the Antichrist in his assault upon Christendom.[47] Benjamin Whichcote points out that the Roman Catholic principle that 'Faith is not [to] be kept with Hereticks' could presumably be adopted by Muslims in their dealings with Christians, and so forth. If this should happen, 'Faith and Truth' would be 'banished the World'.[48] The author of *The Life and Actions of Mahomet* not only points out that the Church of Rome is not alone in honouring 'the Assumption of Virgins', and believing in 'the immaculate Conception, and perpetual Virginity of a Mother': Muslims similarly venerate '*Phatima*'.[49] He also asserts that 'all the Marks' of 'the True Church' claimed by Roman Catholics 'do exactly quadrate to the impious Imposture of *Mahomet*'. What are in mind are such characteristics as extent, duration, success, moral virtues and abstinences. It is inconsistent to accept them as authenticating Roman Catholicism while at the same time rejecting Islam.[50] John Rogers suggests how 'the Romanists Way of proving the Authority of Scripture from the Infallibility of their Church' could be used by Muslims in favour of the Koran. The circular argument would go: 'I believe the *Alchoran* to be true, because the *Mufti*, who is infallible, affirms it to be so: and I believe the *Mufti* to be infallible, because the *Alchoran* says he is so.' Rogers adds, furthermore, that such a Muslim case might be more plausible than the Roman Catholic one in that it might be possible to find 'an Affirmation of the *Mufti*'s Infallibility' in the Koran whereas it is impossible to find the Church of Rome's infallibility declared in the Christian scriptures.[51]

While John Tillotson commends Roman Catholics for their 'Charity and Zeal' in sending missionaries to convert 'Infidel Nations', he qualifies his praise by pointing out that they have been much more interested to convert those 'Parts of the World where Gold and Spices abound' than to go to where there is nothing 'but Frost and Cold'. He further criticises their missionaries in the East for presenting a 'depraved' version of Christianity. In order to avoid scandal they judged it best to conceal from their hearers that part of Christian doctrine which relates to the death of Christ.[52] David Hume, on the other hand, ridicules the Roman doctrine of the real presence by repeating a tale about a Muslim convert who thought he had got rid of God because 'yesterday I eat him'.[53] In the face of such opposite criticisms Roman Catholics could hardly win. References to other religions provided large and various resources for polemics against them. There were also counter-arguments which drew upon the same resources. Some Roman Catholic controversialists reckon Protestants to be, in effect, Muslims on such grounds as that they are notorious 'Enemys to the worshipping of Images, and maintain that all things are infallibly decreed by God'. Other alleged similarities include supposed Protestant claims for Luther's originality and authority, its sectarian divisions, its denial of good works, its permission of divorce and even (with Bucer and Olemdorpius) of a plurality of wives. These are held to have parallels in Islam and so to undermine the Protestant case. Adrian Reland points out that the argument is faulty. The fact that Muslims assert something about the attributes of God is not by itself sufficient reason for denying it to be true.[54] It is a point which the judicious Hooker had made over a century before when he asked 'doth conformity with them that are evil in that which is good, make that thing which is good evil?' The crucial question is the judgement of 'sound reason' about what is 'reasonable, allowable, and good'.[55] Controversialists, though, are not interested in such niceties. They consider that it aids their propaganda to make out that those whom they attack resemble, in some way, those other religions which are, according to their readers, unquestionably false.

The 'enthusiasts' and the 'deists' at opposite ends of the spectrum of Protestant Christianity also occasionally suffer from this form of criticism. Critics suggest detrimental parallels between them and the adherents of other religions. When, for example, Henry More remarks that Mahomet 'seems more orthodox in the grand points of Religion' than the enthusiasts David George and Henry Nicholas – the *begodded Man of Amsterdam*', he is not expressing his approval of the former 'pretended Prophet' but his detestation of the latter pair of 'meal mouth'd Prophets that court the World to follow them by so many mystical Good-morrows, making . . . themselves the only inspired and infallible Lights of the World'.[56] Alexander Ross, in similar vein, not only compares 'the whole rabble of vain, phantastical, or prophane opinions' which currently pester 'this miserable distracted Nation' with the 'old dreams of ancient Hereticks'. He further maintains that if people abandon 'the thread of God's Word presented to us by the Church', they will recreate 'the inextricable *Labyrinth* of erroneous opinions' and 'false religions' which developed in the ancient world after Babel.[57] Humphrey Prideaux attacks the deists not by directly comparing them to Muslims but by using the life of Mahomet as a paradigm case of imposture to show that the deists are wrong in rejecting '*the Gospel of Jesus Christ*' as '*an Imposture*'. He thus attaches to his *Life of Mahomet* an almost equally long 'Letter to the Deists' in which he hopes to convince them that since not 'one Lineament' of the 'filfthy Features' of Mahomet's imposture can be detected in the gospel of Christ, they should believe it as the 'Sacred Truth of *God*'.[58] Such comparisons, though, could be used to criticise as well as to defend the traditional self-understanding of Christianity. While an East Apthorp might see the fortunes of Christianity as displaying 'miraculous protection',[59] Edward Gibbon concluded from the evidence that there was no need to refer to miraculous interventions to explain the propagation of Christianity any more than there was in the case of Islam.[60] Whereas Prideaux sees the 'endless Absurdities' of the various religions in the world as proving the 'Necessity' of a revealed religion,[61] 'A . W .' in *The Oracles of Reason* cites the differences between the self-proclaimed 'Reveal'd Religions', none of which in his judgement can be shown 'to be truer than the rest', as a reason for relying only on the dictates of innate natural religion.[62] Advocates, then as ever, use similar evidence for contrary ends!

So far as developments in Protestant Christianity are concerned, however, the most extensive and virulent use of the propaganda technique of guilt by association is directed against the Socinians or Unitarians.[63] When Edward Gibbon says that Mahomet's followers, 'from India to Morrocco, are distinguished by the name of *Unitarians*',[64] he may be interpreted as making a non-tendentious remark which merely indicates Muslim rejection of pagan polytheism and what they understand as Christian tritheism. Other authors, though, use such terminology with malicious intent – that is, to besmirch Unitarian notions by linking them with the errors of other religions, especially Islam. John Edwards, for example, casts his net wide when he says of the 'pernicious' theology of the Socinians that

> it is a Fardle of mix'd and disagreeing Notions, it is a Nest of Heterodoxies, a Galimafrey of Old and New Errors, a Medley of Heresies taken from *Ebion* and *Cerinthus*, the *Sabellians*, *Samosatenians*, *Arians*, *Photinians*, *Macedonians*, who corrupted the doctrine of the *Holy Trinity*. They joyn with *Jews*, *Pagans* and *Mahometans* in disowning and denying this Great Mystery of Religion.[65]

A few pages later, though, Edwards concentrates his attack on an alleged connection between Socinianism and Islam. He describes Socinians as followers of Servetus who, among other errors, 'declar'd his approbation of the *Alcoran*' and regarded it as 'reconcileable with the New Testament, if the doctrine of the *Trinity* were laid aside'. Other Socinians are alleged to maintain that Mahomet only intended to restore the true Christian belief in the unity of God and that the doctrine of the Trinity ought to be given up since it prevents the conversion of Muslims.[66] Sale's rejoinder to the last claim – that it expresses 'a fond conceit of the Socinians' to think that their doctrines are more amenable to Muslims[67] – is largely beside the point where anti-Unitarian propaganda is at work. The critics are not concerned to debate how a convincing case for Christianity might be presented to Muslims. Their aim is simpler. They want to tar the opponents of Trinitarian doctrine by implying that their thoughts and sympathies warrant describing them as Muslims. It is a theme which is taken up by several defenders of Trinitarian Christianity.

Charles Leslie opens his *Socinian Controversy* by printing a letter from 'our Unitarians' to the Moroccan ambassador to Charles II, which he had acquired with difficulty.[68] The two authors describe themselves to Ameth Ben Ameth as 'your nearest fellow champions' for the truth of belief in 'one supreme God' who 'hath rais'd your Mahomet' to be 'a scourge on those idolizing Christians'. While in their 'duty of love' the authors wish to show the Muslims the 'weak places' in their religion ('contradictions' which were 'foisted' into the papers that composed the Koran after Mahomet's death), they conclude their list of their predecessors in opposing the error of Trinitarianism with 'you *Mahometans*, who also consent with us' in monotheistic belief and worship.[69] Both in *The Socinian Controversy* and in *The Truth of Christianity Demonstrated* Leslie follows up these comments to accuse the Socinians 'now among us' of being 'much more *Mahometans* than Christians' on the grounds that they 'agree almost wholly' with Mahomet's doctrine even though they have some reservations about his person.[70] Their views on Christ and the Bible go no further than those of the Koran and in some respects not as far.[71] They are not Christians but 'scouts amongst us for *Mahomet*'[72] even though they generally will not own him to be of their 'Party' for fear of being stoned by 'the People' who 'have all a great aversion to *Mahomet*'.[73]

The author of *Historical and Critical Reflections upon Mahometanism and Socinianism* declares that his treatise is intended to 'frighten' the Socinians 'back to *true Religion*' by showing them how closely their opinions – and those of their predecessors – resemble the doctrines of Mahomet.[74] He does not condemn Islam in all respects – he recognises, for instance, that its teaching on alms and usury is an example to Christians,[75] – but he is primarily concerned to indicate the parallels between Islam and Socinianism. Both are 'proud to be call'd Unitarians',[76] refuse to accept the 'plain Texts of the *New Testament*',[77] deny the redeeming death of Christ,[78] attack Christianity[79] and trust human reason[80] in similar ways, and accept polygamy.[81] The Socinians are further held not only to have cited the Koran as an authority and to have regarded it 'in the Infancy of their Sect . . . as one of the Classick Books of their Religion',[82] but are accused, in the person of Adam Neuser, of trying to incite the Emperor of the Turks to 'reduce the idolatrous Christians to the Knowledg of one only God' at the same time as aggrandising his empire.[83] In beliefs about creation, providence and predestination, the Unitarians are judged to be 'at a greater distance from the Truth than the *Mussulmen*'.[84] Basically, though, the differences between them are 'imperceptible'. Only 'worldly Interests' can explain why Socinians generally do not acknowledge themselves to be Muslims.[85] In a letter to the author of these *Historical and Critical Reflections* Leibnitz points out that the actions of 'Renegadoes' like Neuser should not be held against the Socinians and that some of these '*Anti-Trinitarians*' lead 'very good moral Lives'.[86] He admits that the Socinians have to be allowed to 'come very near the *Mahometans*' in their doctrines and in some respects 'push their Temerity further' as when they 'weaken even natural Theology, in denying God the Prescience of future Contingencies, and disputing against the Immortality of the Soul'.[87] The parallels between the two, however, apparently do not greatly disturb Leibnitz since, in spite of his favourable remarks about Trinitarian doctrine, he regards Islam as 'a kind of Deism' which could, in principle, serve to prepare the pagan world for the reception of Christianity, especially if the prejudicial items which it has added to natural religion were removed from it.[88]

Attacks on the 'hydra of Socinianism' for being hardly different from Islam in its views on 'the unfathomable mystery of our *redemption*'[89] continue to the end of our period. In the notes appended to his Bampton Lectures for 1784, Joseph White recognises that contemporary Socinians abhor any association of their tenets with those of Mahomet. Nevertheless, he asserts that 'to the eye of reason' the similarity of their views on the person and work of Christ is 'clear and apparent'.[90] They reject Trinitarian doctrine because it cannot be reduced to the level of human comprehension[91] and they use the same hermeneutical methods to pervert or evade the 'plain and obvious meaning' of the scriptures.[92] There were, of course, some replies to these attempts to malign the Socinians. On the one hand, critical deists who reject particularly Christian doctrines can profess to find no fault in Muslim rejection of Trinitarian ideas. Bolingbroke, for example, observes that it is the introduction of this doctrine into Christianity which gives Muslims 'reason to say that the revelation which Mahomet published was necessary to establish the unity of the Supreme Being'.[93] On the other hand, Unitarians who wish to establish their position as authentically Christian are concerned to reject the odious claim that their doctrines resemble those of Islam. Thus Joshua Toulmin, who sees Christ as bringing 'a divine attestation' of his teaching as declared in the Bible but who rejects Trinitarian notions as human misunderstanding,[94] replies to White that Unitarian notions of God as one can be associated with Christ and Moses 'on the same principle and with equal justice' that they can be linked with Mahomet. He protests that it is thus improper for Unitarians to be 'ignominiously ranked with Mahometans' because they affirm the Biblical doctrine of the unity of God 'whole and uncorrupted, in all its simplicity'.[95] As for the charge that they deny the significance of the death of Christ, he quotes from Socinus to justify his claim that their view of Christ cannot be associated with that of Islam.[96] Such protests, however, came from the injured party, and probably had little effect in countering this propaganda. It is easier to make dirt stick than to wash it off – and, with rare exceptions, for the controversialists of the seventeenth and eighteenth centuries the description 'Mahometan' was dirt.[97]

A much more wide-ranging controversialist use of other religions than those discussed so far is to confirm Christian belief in general. As has been indicated throughout this study, especially in the chapter on 'Pride and prejudice', various authors point to what they regard as the faults of other religions to show by comparison the superiority of Christianity. It is on this basis that Alexander Ross, for example, defends his study of all religions. Against those who argue that 'the world is pestered with too many Sects' and that errors should not be given publicity, he replies that while 'Truth' may be 'comely in it self', it is 'yet more lovely, when compared with falsehood'. By the detection of the darkness in other religions, we become aware of 'the excellency of the light' in Christianity.[98] This excellency, in the judgement of many, is both humanly recognised and divinely confirmed by the spread of Christianity. Only so, according to Laurence Echard, could 'the Assistance and Support of twelve poor Persons . . . without Learning, without Forces, without Reputation or Authority in the World' and using methods 'contrary to all human Policy, and human Imagination' have brought Christianity to have 'in a few Years out-stretch'd the Bounds of the *Roman* Empire' and spread 'like Flashes of Lightning to the utmost Limits of the Universe'.[99] It managed to do this, furthermore, while opposed by the stratagems of the Devil. In practice, though, arguments from the supposed historical fact of the propagation of Christianity used the evidence in two inconsistent ways. On the one hand, in spite of attempts such as that of Edward Gibbon to show that the establishment of Christianity does not demand supernatural explanation,[100] many Christian apologists throughout the period are convinced otherwise. They argue that the pagan faith was so strong that it could not have been 'shaken by any *human* power inferiour to its own'.[101] On the other hand, they also seek to maintain that by comparison with the beliefs of other religions, those of Christianity are so obviously superior that there can be no question of their truth. If this latter argument be convincing, though, it is not easy to accept that people are so intellectually blind that divine aid is required for them to recognise the truth once it is revealed to them.[102] The success of one argument undermines the other.

As has also been mentioned in earlier chapters, Christian apologists often support their case by comparing Christ with the leading figures of other religions in ways which are highly favourable to the former. Henry More, for instance, presents an extended comparison between Christ and Apollonius Tyaneus in order 'that the *Gravity and Divinity of the one*, and the *Ridiculousness and the Carnality of the other* may the better be discerned'.[103] The miracles of the latter are 'either *frivolous* or *exorbitant*', his life 'nothing else but a lofty Strutting on the Stage of the Earth', and his alleged resurrection 'a whiffling Business . . . and a mere Piece of Magical Ostentation.'[104] By contrast, Christ's excellency becomes clear. Consequently, even if the story of Apollonius were to turn out to be historically accurate, it 'falls infinitely short of the Truth of the *Divine Life* manifested in Christ'.[105] Comparisons with Moses, Mahomet, Socrates and Confucius are held to be no less supportive of Christian claims.

A different apologetic use of other religions is found in claims made by some that other faiths in fact contain materials which testify to the truth of Christian beliefs. George Stanhope takes up a perennial Christian argument when he maintains that what the Jews either accept 'or in conformity to their own Principles, ought to admit' should remove any impediment to their becoming Christians.[106] Samuel Horsley seeks to prove that 'the Gentile world in the darkest ages was possessed of explicit written prophecies of Christ' by reference to 'the oracles of the Cumaean Sibyl' and to records of the same prophecies being 'extant . . . in various parts of the world'. These prophecies were, in his view, fragments which had survived from 'the patriarchal ages' through 'the corrupt remains of the ancient priesthood of Noah's universal church'.[107] Sir William Jones points to the 'great similarity' between the religions of widely scattered parts of the world as indicating an original 'general union' of the 'inhabitants of the primitive world' and so as confirming Moses' accounts of that time.[108] John Edwards cites Mahomet, 'that Arch Infidel', as witnessing to Christ and acknowledging 'the *Gospel* to be Divine and True'.[109] Even the doctrine of the Trinity is held to have the support of pagan testimonies. Ralph Cudworth finds in Mithraism 'a manifest Indication of a *Higher Mystery, viz. a Trinity* in the *Persian Theology*'. Other examples are located in 'the *Arcane Theology* of the *Egyptians*', in the philosophies of the Pythagorean and Platonic schools, and among the Samothracians.[110] Andrew Ramsay augments the list with instances from

China.[111] Whatever the source of these notions – whether they originated with a revelation to the Hebrews[112] or express 'an ancient universal
tradition',[113] they show the error of 'the Deists, the Socinians, the
Unitarians and the Freethinkers' in asserting that Trinitarian doctrine is
'a modern fiction'.[114]

In various ways, then, the supremacy of Christianity is held by its
defenders to be confirmed by the examination of other religions. There
are critics, though, who argue differently. They point to evidence that
challenges rather than supports aspects of the traditional self-understanding of Christianity. On the one hand, George Fox uses Biblical
reports about people outside the Judaeo-Christian dispensation to maintain that God acts among and is known by people who have 'neither
written Law nor Gospel'. Both '*Protestants* and *Papists*' err in claiming
that God can only be known through the scriptures.[115] On the other
hand – and much less rare – are the rationalist critics of Christianity who
cite the beliefs and practices of other religions to cast doubt on all actual
religions and especially on Christianity. Conyers Middleton finds pagan
miracles as well attested as any that 'Papists' can produce.[116] Bolingbroke asserts that 'the superstitions of ignorant ages' and 'fantastical
knowledge' have produced 'some as extravagant opinions among Christians' as can be found among Muslims and pagans.[117] His conclusion is
that the only way to avoid such errors is to submit the Christian – or any
other – gospel to the examination of reason.[118] The evidence of actual
religions shows that 'natural religion, unmixed and uncorrupted' is
much superior to 'artificial theology and superstition' both in its
reasonableness and in its effects.[119] Occasionally, criticisms of Christianity do not stop at suggesting that in some respects it shares the faults
found in other religions, and go on positively to commend some other
religions. Boulainvilliers thus describes Islam as a religion 'stript of all
controversy, and . . . proposing no mystery to offer violence to reason'.
It is the product of 'long and deep meditation upon the nature of things,
upon the state and condition of the nations of the world at that time, and
upon the reconcilement of the objects of religion with reason'.[120]
Although his English translator claims that Boulainvilliers was opposed
to popery, not to Christianity, he nevertheless sees in his presentation of
Islam qualities of 'integrity, temperance, benevolence, and liberality'
which Christians would do well to learn from '*Saracens*, *Turks*, and
Mahometans'.[121] John Zephaniah Holwell describes 'the original divine
institutes of Bramah' as 'simple and sublime, comprehending the whole
compass of all that is' while Alexander Dow similarly suggests that

Hindu polytheism is to be understood as the symbolical representation of 'the unity, eternity, omniscience and omnipotence of God'.[122] The origin of this religion, furthermore, predates Moses.[123]

A far more widespread attitude is that found in Humphrey Prideaux's writings. He closes the 'Letter to the Deists' appended to his *Life of Mahomet* by urging them to compare 'that Holy *Christian Religion* which we profess' with 'all the other *Religions* that are in the World'. He is convinced that a thorough consideration will show Christianity to be 'vastly above them all, the worthiest of God for him to give unto us, and the worthiest of us to observe'.[124] While the East in particular had a certain mystery and fascination, only a few considered that its religious doctrines and practices could do anything but enhance the standing of Christianity. As for the rest of the world, descriptions of its religions provided a contrast to reinforce the sense of Christianity's supremacy.

A very occasional use of other religions is in support of arguments urging Christian unity. The divisions of the Church are held to weaken its resistance against attack. Thus Alexander Ross not only reminds Christians that pagans' zeal shows up their lukewarmness,[125] but calls on them to remember that they are 'the sheep of one fold', 'a little flock beset with many Wolves, of *Jews*, *Turks*, *Pagans*, *Atheists*'. They should, therefore, seek unity in order to render themselves 'formidable' to their foes.[126] Indeed he considers that God has permitted Muslim power to continue in order to bring Christians 'to stick close together against the common Enemy' as well as to threaten them with 'this Whip' should they need correcting by it in the future as they had in the past.[127]

Others see the disunity of the Church as an obstacle to the conversion of the adherents of other faiths. Charles Leslie's hostility as a non-juror to Latitudinarian attitudes in the Church combines with his concern for the conversion of the Jews in his protest against 'the various Sects which are tolerated, and own'd as Churches'. The Jews, in his judgement, will never be convinced that the Church has inherited the 'promises and privileges' granted initially to them until it shows itself to have a 'monarchical' form of government. At this point, though, Leslie has to tread carefully. While wanting an episcopal structure for the Church, as an Anglican he cannot accept Roman claims for the supremacy of the Bishop of Rome over all the churches. He thus has to claim that the 'one catholick Church' is to consist of many independent national churches each 'under her own Bishop'![128] At the end of the eighteenth century the founders of the London Missionary Society heard George Burder quote a prediction that Christian co-operation in missionary work will lead to increasing contact between members of the denominations involved. This will in turn result in the decline of 'party spirit' and growth in love and unity.[129] A decade later, Andrew Fuller claims that this has indeed occurred among missionaries in India: 'the sending out of missions to the heathen' has produced 'a communication of sentiment, and a unity of action'.[130] Both 'experience and fact' testify that differences of opinion among the missionaries are not allowed 'to furnish any stumbling-block to the natives'. They seek conversion to Christ, not denominational aggrandisement – and in any case the British empire is vast enough for the denominations, if they so wish, to operate in separate areas without fear of interfering with each other![131] The relationship between missionary activity and attitudes to other religions is, however, the topic of the next chapter.

IX

Missionary activity and
'Other religions'

No survey of seventeenth- and eighteenth-century attitudes towards 'other religions' would be complete without some mention of missionary activity. A Corporation for the Propagation of the Gospel in New England was set up in 1649, but much more significant was the establishment of the Society for Promoting Christian Knowledge in 1698 and the Society for the Propagation of the Gospel in Foreign Parts in 1701. Among the aims of the S P C K was to disperse 'at home and abroad, Bibles and tracts of religion'. The S P G was intended to develop the work overseas by sending Anglican clergymen and schoolmasters to minister to the British settlers and to evangelise among non-Christians. Although the non-Anglican colonists had generally taken with them their own forms of church government and ministry, the size of the problem facing the Church of England is indicated by the claim that when the S P G was founded there were only about fifty clergymen in the thirteen colonies, most of them being in Virginia and Maryland. Throughout the century the S P G's missionaries worked mainly among Europeans but some ministered to the American Indians and a few to the negroes as well.

It was not, however, until late in the eighteenth century that a concern to evangelise throughout the world was more widely organised. In 1784 Thomas Coke published his *Plan of the Society for the Establishment of Missions amongst the Heathen* and his *Address to the Pious and Benevolent*. He appealed for both money and people to work among the heathen in India and Africa as well as in rural Ireland, Wales and north-western Scotland. John Wesley considered the plan to be impractical, preferring to concentrate on developing work in America. Having consecrated Coke as 'Superintendent', he sent him with two others to the Methodist movement in America. Three years later, while attempting to reach Nova Scotia with three missionaries, Coke's ship was obliged because of the weather to bear off to the West Indies. The four landed on Antigua and made contact with the Methodist movement that had developed there, predominantly among the negroes. After visits to other islands, Coke returned to England to urge Wesley and the Conference of British Methodism to accept responsibility for work in the West Indies.[1] He succeeded, but it was not until 1813 that the Wesleyan Methodist Missionary Society was formed – in the year in which Coke persuaded the conference to send missionaries to the Cape, Ceylon (now Sri Lanka) and Java. Meanwhile, largely as a result of the efforts of William Carey, the Baptist Missionary Society had been established in 1792 with Andrew Fuller as its secretary. The following year Carey sailed to India as its first missionary, and in five years had translated the New Testament into Bengali and visited two hundred villages. In 1795 'Evangelical Ministers and Lay Brethren of all denominations' gathered in London to form the Missionary Society (later known as the London Missionary Society) with the object of 'promoting the great work of introducing the Gospel and its ordinances, to Heathen and other unenlightened countries'.[2] Originally, as one of the preachers at its inaugural meetings was happy to proclaim, 'here are Episcopalians, Methodists, Presbyterians, and Independents, all united in one society . . . assembled with one accord to attend the funeral of *bigotry*' and to 'join to diffuse Christianity, and not their own particular sects.'[3] Eventually, though, the society became almost exclusively supported by Congregationalists. In 1799 evangelical Anglicans started the Society for Missions in Africa and the East, later known as the Church Missionary Society, while five years later the British and Foreign Bible Society was founded.

Nevertheless, even though the nineteenth century was the great age of missionary activity, there are a number of comments on the reasons for and the methods of such activity to be found in the religious writings of the earlier period covered by this survey. They provide further illuminating insights into its attitudes towards other religions. Most of these comments come from self-consciously Christian theologians. The advocates of natural religion and natural theology were generally more interested in questioning Christian doctrines than in proclaiming their own understanding overseas.[4] Anthony Collins, though, does take an opportunity in his *Discourse of Free-Thinking* to argue that if the S P G is to 'hope to have any effect on *infidel Nations*', it should first acquaint them with 'their *duty* to *think freely*' both about their inherited notions of

God and religion and about those brought to them by the missionaries. Only so will it act consistently in seeking converts through 'no other *arms* but reason and evidence'.[5] In this way, Collins turns the principle on which missionary activity professes to be based into another way of justifying the legitimacy of the critical approach to religious beliefs! Those advocating missionary work would not have found this argument congenial – they sought converts, not free-thinkers – but on the other hand, his argument was annoyingly plausible.

Surveys of the religions of the world such as Alexander Ross' *Pansebeia* make clear the great extent of the other religions. Throughout the period considered in this survey, however, most of the expressions of concern for missionary work concentrate on the need to minister to British traders and the colonists in America, their negro slaves and the native peoples in their neighbourhood. Thomas Secker's sermon before the SPG in 1740, for instance, points out that while the purpose of the society is to 'carry on' Christ's work of 'directing Mankind to present and future Happiness', it is primarily established 'for the Support of Christianity in our Colonies and Factories abroad, then for the Propagation of it amongst the Heathens intermixed with them, and bordering upon them'.[6] John Wesley speaks of the world as his parish in order to justify his right to preach anywhere, but when it comes to world missions, his view is more circumspect and practical. In a sermon on 'The General Spread of the Gospel', for example, he points out that Brerewood had calculated that only a sixth of the world are 'so much as nominally Christians' and that the figure should now probably be revised downwards because of discoveries since then. Nevertheless, while he looks forward to the time when God's messengers will cover the earth, he also considers that up to the present God has 'permitted' a different state of affairs to obtain, implying that the evangelisation of heathen nations is for the future rather than a present duty. As he looks to the development of his own movement, he sees it spreading through the rest of North America and Europe before being 'gradually diffused' among Christians elsewhere in the world. Only after it has thus revived Christianity will the conversion of Muslims and heathens become possible.[7]

William Carey, however, sought to bring home to people the extent of the field for evangelism overseas and the duty of Christians to work in it. In the third section of his *Enquiry into the Obligations of Christians to Use Means for the Conversion of the Heathen* he produces a statistical survey of the size, population and religion of the countries of Europe, Asia, Africa and America.[8] He calculates that of the 731 million people in the world, 420 million 'are still in pagan darkness', 131 million are Muslims and seven million are Jews. A 'vast proportion of the sons of Adam' are thus 'in the most deplorable state', only having what knowledge of God is available from 'the works of nature' and in some cases being 'as destitute of civilization, as they are of true religion'.[9] He also suggests that the so-called Christians of 'the greek and arminian churches, in all the mahometan countries' need conversion since 'they are, if possible, more ignorant and vicious than the mahometans themselves'. Papists are similarly criticised, nor do Protestants, of all types, escape for they too show 'many errors, and much looseness of conduct'.[10] Christians are thus summoned to show equal zeal with members of trading companies in facing risk, hardship and anxiety in order to extend their interest:[11] 'Pity therefore, humanity, and much more Christianity, call loudly for every possible exertion to introduce the gospel' amongst those who have 'no Bible, no written language, (which many of them have not) no ministers, no good civil government, nor any of those advantages which we have'.[12] It is an appeal whose basic ideas became familiar in the churches in the nineteenth and first half of the twentieth century.

The main reason offered for missionary activity was then as it generally ever has been in Christianity, a concern to preach the Christian gospel of salvation to those who have not yet received it. In spite of the difficulties involved, Secker reminds the S P G that both 'the natural Dictate of Piety and Virtue' and 'the express Command of our blessed Lord' require Christians to ensure 'the Offer of Instruction to Heathens' that salvation may come to them.[13] The religious side of this appeal was put by George Burder in his sermon at the inaugural meetings of The Missionary Society:

> I stand up as the advocate of thousands, of millions of souls, perishing for lack of knowledge. I stand up to plead the cause of Christ, too, too long neglected by us all – to plead the cause of the poor benighted heathen – to lay before you their miserable state – to convey to your ears and hearts the cry of their wretchedness – O that it may penetrate your souls – 'Come over – Come over, and help us.'[14]

In the following sermon Samuel Greatheed emphasised the moral obligation of missionary work: the duty to love one's neighbour 'is *applicable to the whole human race*'. Philanthropy must exceed the power of the sun by enlightening and warming 'both hemispheres at once' in preaching the Christian gospel throughout the globe – even in 'the continents and islands at our antipodes' since 'the adventurous wings of navigation . . . have assured us' that they are 'filled with fellow-men'![15]

East Apthorp indicates two variations on this theme when he suggests that 'the conversion of the heathens, Jews, and mohammedans' is essential for 'the amplitude and felicity of the Church' and that the 'influence of the pure Gospel' might be a fitting return to 'the untutored Indian . . . for that ill-omened opulence which they have showered on us'.[16] The need for missionary work is also defended on the grounds that only so can the light of religious truth dispel the darkness of heathen superstition. In this respect, what are regarded as the evident errors and unjustifiable practices of other religions provide reasons for sending missionaries to their adherents.[17] Andrew Fuller uses such an argument in his *Apology for the late Christian Missions to India* in the early years of the nineteenth century in reply to those who deny the need for such interference because of the supposed 'excellence of the religious and moral doctrines of the Hindoos'.[18] He asserts that while the 'Hindoos' may acknowledge one God, in practice they appear to worship 'certain subordinate powers', principally 'B I R M H A, the creator of all; V I S H-N O O, the preserver of all; and S E E B, the destroyer of all', although a great number of others are also worshipped. The fact that Seeb receives the most extensive recognition shows that their worship is 'chiefly the effect of superstitious *fears*'. The 'foulest vices' are ascribed to their deities while the 'one Supreme God' is held responsible for 'all the evil' which the people commit, thereby absolving them of all moral accountability. The beliefs and practices of the Hindus are thus in many crucial respects erroneous, puerile and immoral.[19] Opposition to missionary work can consequently be condemned as a further example of Socinian opposition to the light of authentic Christianity.[20]

Fuller's remarks are in response to attempts to stifle missionary work in India, inspired by the fear that it will upset the natives and so disturb the profits of the East India Company. There were also religious objections raised against such activity which its advocates needed to rebut. In reply to those who maintain that 'the Deity delights in the variety of religions which have appeared' Joseph White argues both that the human love of variety is not to be ascribed to God and that proper appreciation of the divine will acting in human morality shows that those with better understanding ought to communicate it to those with inferior views.[21] As for the objection that religious beliefs are indifferent so long as people practise 'good morality', he rejoins that religion cannot be satisfactorily divided from morality. They influence each other 'with an intense and incessant force' and neither can be complete without the other.[22] Another objection is that no religion can finally be proved to be true and therefore it is wrong for adherents of one to seek to interfere with the beliefs and practices of those of another. Here White rejects the premise. Because some religions which are believed in are false, it does not follow that none can be true.[23] In fact, in his judgement, Christians have a duty to instruct 'the ignorant and the mistaken' with their 'juster notions of religion'.[24] They are not, furthermore, to seek to avoid the task by claiming that their teaching would be 'imperfectly understood, or grossly misconceived'. On the one hand, the intellectual state of Muslims would allow them to be successfully instructed 'in the sublimer doctrines of Christianity'. On the other, savages might be persuaded through their 'kind of instinctive propensity to believe in those things which are extraordinary'. The propagation of the gospel would neither debase it nor show it to be ineffective.[25]

Another religious objection to missionary work is faced by David Bogue in his inaugural sermon to The Missionary Society. It is the assertion that it is not yet time to embark on the conversion of the heathen 'because the Millenium is still at the distance of some hundred years'. His retort is that while there are differences of opinion about the time and character of the millenium when all nations shall have 'received the gospel', there should be no dispute that God enjoins Christians 'as a duty' to preach the Gospel to all. The rate of its success is God's concern: theirs is to undertake it without delay.[26] Just as Englishmen 'are diffusing the blessings of civil freedom over the remotest branches of the empire' so, according to White in 1784, as Christians they should also be making attempts 'to emancipate them from the chains of superstition'.[27]

Religious reasons, however, are not the only motives advanced for engaging in missionary activity. Another kind of argument claims that it will have beneficial moral effects.[28] Not only will the spread of Christianity replace error by truth, but it will also replace evil by good, both among colonists whose declining morals are frequently a cause of worry, and among the heathen. Secker is confident that there is 'abundant Proof' that 'the bare Profession and outward Appearance' of Christianity 'must have some right Influence: and the Body of a People cannot go the utmost Lengths in Wickedness, whilst that Appearance subsists'. He defends the moral value of religious instruction and Sunday observance on the grounds that it not only offers people 'Refreshment' but also 'greatly tends to civilize them also, by uniting Neighbourhoods in formed Assemblies . . . with Hearts disengaged from selfish Attentions, and open to friendly Regards'.[29]

These concerns for morality overseas are not entirely disinterested. Secker, for example, points out that moral goodness will have material value for his hearers in London. If people overseas are 'dishonest and profligate; every single Person here, who hath Concerns with them, will be in Danger of suffering by it. If they consume their Wealth and their Time in Vices and Follies; their Trade will be gained over, from Them and Us, by our Rivals and Adversaries'.[30] Preaching the gospel to 'the poor Negroes' not only will make 'Amends' for 'the Servitude and hard Labour, which they undergo'. It will also 'compose and soften their vindictive and sullen Spirits'. They will become better workers and less prone to rebellion as they are brought to accept 'the Scripture' that 'far from making any Alteration in Civil Rights, expressly directs, that *every Man abide in the Condition wherein he is called*' and serve his master faithfully.[31] As for the American Indians, the gospel will make them happier and recompense them for having 'yielded up to us a considerable Part of their Country' and receiving in return 'Diseases and Vices' from us. It will also make them 'a Friend and Ally . . . against the remaining Heathen and a much more dangerous Neighbour' (i.e. the French in Canada!).[32] Towards the end of the century Coke and Moore, in their *Life of John Wesley*, testify to the good effects of Christian work among the negro slaves on Antigua: military law due to fear of insurrection was 'now become a mere form' and 'candid men among the planters acknowledge that the religious negroes are the best servants'.[33] A few years later Fuller, rejected any such appeals to self-interest as a way of justifying Christian missions.[34] Nevertheless, he countered the charge that missions disturbed British security in India with the claim that they will produce political benefits for its government[35] by establishing Christian morals and civic virtues in place of Hindu and Muslim immorality.[36] He quotes a missionary in India, Mr Marsham, as claiming that the British government would find its interests advanced by the presence of missionaries since in each of them 'it would have a friend' whose 'influence and capacity of rendering service would be constantly increasing'. Each missionary would acquire a 'train of pious, peaceable, loyal, and faithful disciples' and, as a messenger of peace and love, 'would endear to the inhabitants the very nation' to which he belonged.[37] Fuller himself does not merely consider that the government ought to tolerate missionary work,[38] but suggests that British conquests may be part of a divine plan to aid the spread of the gospel.[39]

Missionary activity is thus defended on the grounds that it will prosper trade and the flag as well as because it will provide religious, moral and intellectual enlightenment for the ignorant and depraved. Appeals for support, consequently, are not only directed at believers, but are also made in terms which the City and Whitehall can appreciate![40] Secker even suggests that missionaries are important if the American colonists are to be kept loyal to the British crown: 'if the Ties of a Religion, binding Men so strongly to *be subject for Conscience Sake*, are loosened from off their Minds . . . it will much facilitate their becoming Adversaries themselves. And we shall well deserve their revolting from Us, if we take no Care of their obeying God.'[41] The missionary activity of the soundly Anglican S P G will have the added benefit of hindering 'Corruptions of Christianity' and the 'pernicious Errors' of other denominations from spreading there. This denominational prejudice is defended on theological and on secular grounds. In the latter case it is argued that Anglican teaching will preserve 'the Safety of all Governments' by preventing the actions of enthusiasts like the Quakers in Pennsylvania who have forbidden all contributions 'to the publick Defence against Enemies'.[42]

Those who considered that missionaries ought to be sent had no doubts about their right to proselytise in other countries.[43] Henry More points out, though, that the right should be recognised to be in principle universal. Any people who recognise that '*Liberty of Religion*' is a '*common and natural Right*' should be allowed to send representatives of their persuasion into neighbouring states in order to try to convince their inhabitants of 'the Errrours' of their religion. These representatives should 'act above-board' by declaring themselves to the local authorities and by arguing with 'prudent Insinuations' and 'demonstrative Reasons'. Nevertheless, while the general acceptance of this principle would be of greater advantage to Christianity since it is 'incomparably more demonstrable to Rational Spirits than any Religion ever extant in the World', More considers that it is '*hugely unpracticable*' because of the '*general Perverseness and Corruption of Men*'.[44] Anthony Collins, though, uses the same principle to argue provokingly that members of the Church of England who support the S P G ought therefore to accept that the King of Siam had the right, if he so desired, 'to send us a *pack* of his *Talapoins*' to attempt to convert us to the faith established in his land![45]

It was not, however, questions about the right to go nor the danger that missionaries of other faiths might claim the reciprocal right to preach in Britain (for no other faith was generally regarded as a serious candidate for belief) but practical difficulties which caused some to hesitate over the propriety of supporting missionary work, especially if it were intended to venture beyond the confines of European settlements. Such doubters wondered if the problems facing the missionaries would be so great that their efforts would be doomed to fail and, whatever their sympathies, therefore questioned if such work was a justifiable use of resources. Their doubts echoed problems which missionary advocates had to overcome in theory and the missionaries themselves in practice. Among the impediments which William Carey foresees are distance, the uncivilised and barbarous ways of life of those among whom the missionaries would have to live, the danger of being killed, the difficulties of 'procuring the necessaries of life' and the need to learn strange languages. He does not see them as insuperable problems. Developments in navigation, willingness to face 'inconveniences for the good of others', the likelihood that the missionaries will not be molested if they act prudently,[46] readiness to rough it and fend for themselves, and patience to study the language meet these questions. Having piety, courage, forbearance and 'undoubted orthodoxy', the missionaries will apparently be equipped if they are further provided with 'clothing, a few knives, powder and shot, fishing-tackle, and the articles of husbandry'.[47] Among other objections are the opposition likely to be raised by the authorities, the previous lack of success in work among the heathen, the expected hardships and the difficulty of finding volunteers of the right calibre.[48] David Bogue, however, raises these difficulties in order to answer them.[49] What is needed is money and volunteers, and he is confident that they will be found. In spite of discouragements that may arise, he looks forward to the time when 'Idolatrous Pagans' will be 'changed into Christians' and 'Churches formed of worshippers of stocks and stones'.[50]

The views of theologians, preachers and missionary advocates on the means to be used to convert non-Christians give further insights into the understanding – or rather lack of understanding – of other religions which informed the attitudes towards them in the seventeenth and eighteenth centuries. Alexander Ross points out 'violence must be avoided; for faith cometh by perswasion, not by compulsion'.[51] He was writing of attempts to convert the Jews in Europe but the point he was making was generally accepted. When, however, missionary societies instruct their missionaries to respect idolatrous practices, even if they seem evil, and to debate with the heathen in an atmosphere of love and reason,[52] it is not because they consider the heathen religions worthy of respect in their own right but because they realise that any other approach would be detrimental to their work. With such an approach, some are optimistic enough to believe that it would not be difficult to gain converts. George Berkeley holds, for example, that those who are involved in propagating the gospel have the advantages of 'power against weakness, civility against barbarism, knowledge against ignorance'. They are thus in a much stronger position than the first apostles of Christianity.[53] East Apthorp, in the safe haven of the chapel of Lincoln's Inn, claims that the character and situation of the peoples of the East 'are predisposing circumstances very favourable to their illumination by the Christian Faith'.[54] William Carey asserts that while the 'poor heathens' may be 'barbarous', they seem 'as capable of knowledge as we are'. Furthermore in 'many places' they have been found to have 'uncommon genius and tractableness'.[55] It is the view of the receptiveness to the Christian gospel which is found in Will Atkins' native wife.[56] Unfortunately, this latter description is fiction and the previous claims reflect expectations rather than experiences.

In practice, while other religions are held to be undoubtedly false, their adherents are generally found to be resistant to conversion to Christianity. In part this may be blamed on the bad example of so-called Christian settlers. John Wesley suggests that the missionaries will succeed only when Christians live according to their faith:

> The Malabarian Heathen will have no more room to say, 'Christian man take my wife. Christian man much drunk: Christian man kill man! *Devil-Christian!* Me no Christian.' Rather . . . the holy lives of the Christians will be an argument they will not know how to resist. . . .[57]

Unfortunately it is not an argument that is currently available. William Robertson also points out that even when Christians do what seems to them unobjectionable, they may cause offence to the adherents of other faiths. By eating 'the flesh of that animal which the Hindoos deem sacred' and drinking 'intoxicating liquors' Christians are seen as being on 'a level with the Pariars, the most contemptible and odious race of men'. The fundamental difficulty, though, is that non-Christians are not easily persuaded by the Christian message. The numbers of converts are relatively few.[58] William Paley even finds a defence of the miraculous character of the spread of early Christianity by comparing its achievements with the lack of success in contemporary Christian missions. Although modern missionaries may be credited with as much zeal, piety and sanctity as the first apostles and with more education and learning, although the gospel retains its 'intrinsic excellence', although missionaries come from a country which is regarded with 'deference' by those to whom they go, although the heathen faiths which they combat are basically the same as those confronting the early Church, and although the missionary today has the advantages of facing other faiths rather than general disbelief, the result of missionary activity is to show 'the feebleness and inadequacy of human means'. Whether it be the Baptists and Anglicans in India or the Moravians in Greenland, the complaint is often the same. Converts are hard to secure.[59]

East Apthorp responds to the problem by taking responsibility for lack of success out of human hands. He suggests that such a faith as the Christian which 'disclaims all force, and rests on persuasion only, and at the same time aspires to universality, can only justify its claim by MIRACLES'. Where it has become established, it is not through 'human *counsels*' and 'artifice' but by means that are 'miraculous and divine'.[60] About a century earlier, John Tillotson had claimed that since purely human efforts would be unlikely to succeed, he believed that missionaries to heathen lands would, like the first apostles of Christianity, enjoy the divine credentials of miraculous powers. While such means are not needed to convince people who have been 'brought up in the Christian Religion', he thinks 'it still very credible, that if Persons of sincere Minds did go to preach the pure Christian Religion, free from . . . Errors and Superstitions . . . to infidel Nations, that God would still enable such Persons to work Miracles, without which there would be little or no Probability of Success'.[61] He has to admit, though, that to date there are reports of only 'very few Miracles', if any, from such situations[62] and consequently he wonders if an alternative method might be through divine action whereby 'some powerful Prince, of great Reputation for his Wisdom and Virtue' is brought over to Christianity. He suspects, however, that this latter eventuality is as likely to result in the Prince's overthrow as in the successful establishment of Christianity in his realm![63] Conyers Middleton some time later considered Roman Catholic claims that their missionaries in the East did have miraculous powers but judges that these reports are not credible. His conclusion is that no missionaries, whatever their denomination, have been able to work a single miracle to confirm their mission.[64] Whatever Tillotson (and Grotius before him) might have regarded as necessary or proper in such cases, experience shows that the deity does not act according to such human expectations.[65]

For many Christian apologists, however, their faith is so self-evidently true that the most effective means of propagating it is simply that of teaching its tenets and, even more importantly, of displaying its moral holiness in practice. The obstacle created by the immoral behaviour of many so-called Christians has already been mentioned.[66] It is a common refrain. Matthew Tindal even quotes Bishop Richard Kidder's remark that if a person were to choose his religion 'by the Lives of those who profess it; perhaps, Christianity wou'd be the last Religion he would choose'.[67] Richard Baxter could validly retort to such views that Christianity ought not to be condemned for the behaviour of those who are not 'true genuine' Christians,[68] but it is widely appreciated that so far as the adherents of other faiths are concerned, deeds will be more influential than words. It is when 'the *Christian dogs*' become real Christians in practice that, as John Wesley puts it, the heathen may be expected 'to consider and embrace their doctrine'.[69]

As for establishing the credibility of Christian doctrine, George Berkeley is not worried by the lack of the gift of miracles, for contemporary apologists have 'other advantages'. Unlike the first apostles, they can point to 'the benefit of Christ's religion' which 'whole nations' have experienced. Furthermore, they have their 'ordinary faculties' and secular riches to employ in the work.[70] The gospel is to be presented, according to Thomas Secker, in the same form overseas as at home. First, the hearers must be reminded of the law of God that they may 'see their Need of Repentance and Pardon' and then be offered 'the Gospel of Christ' which they 'will gladly receive' because it is 'infinitely preferable to what they have believed hitherto'. The 'superior Knowledge, and good Lives' of the missionaries and their converts, aided by 'the Grace of God', will afford sufficient 'rational Motives of Assent, especially to Persons capable of no further Information'.[71] The importance of translating the Bible, and especially the New Testament, is stressed by East Apthorp. Once it is available in the vernacular, its inspired nature is such that it may be expected to find its way 'directly to the heart', conquering 'unbelief by a more than human energy'.[72] In various ways, then, Christian apologists show their confidence in the unquestionable excellence of their beliefs by assuming that they basically only need to be proclaimed in order to be accepted.[73] Thomas Stackhouse was so confident that he approved of the idea that Jews should be 'obliged' to listen to sermons and to engage in debates about Christianity![74]

In a preface to his translation of the Koran, George Sale adopts Kidder's rules for such debates, rules which most of those who were confident in the superiority of Christian doctrine would have been happy to accept. First, compulsion is to be avoided; secondly, doctrines which are 'against common sense' must be avoided (Sale cites the worship of images and the doctrine of transubstantiation as examples of doctrines which Muslims are not fools enough to accept); thirdly, weak arguments must not be used but only ones that are 'proper and cogent'; and fourthly, no article of the Christian faith must be surrendered in order to prevail with them.[75] The naive assurance that lies behind many Christian attitudes to other religions is seen in Joseph White's conviction that such an approach is likely to lead Muslims 'by an easy transition' into 'a full belief of the doctrines of Christianity'.[76] As Middleton remarks about miracles, theoretical expectations and actual practice do not always coincide!

A final comment on attitudes to 'other religions' in this period is provided by the issue of slavery. East Apthorp protests that 'the system of African slavery' presents 'a powerful obstacle to the humane business of conversion'. He hints that perhaps it ought to be abolished rather than merely have its horrors mitigated – as some 'distinguished prelate' had suggested.[77] Earlier in the eighteenth century, George Berkeley and Thomas Secker had not been so troubled. For the former, the scandal is that the slaves continue as heathens while under Christian masters whereas they would become 'better slaves' and their masters better Christians if they were baptised.[78] Secker similarly maintains that conversion would make them more satisfactory as slaves and might fittingly 'procure the poor Wretches themselves a little more kind Usage'.[79] He considers that the slaves' condition 'cannot well be worse than it would have been at home' and, like Berkeley, is anxious to point out that conversion did not entitle slaves to manumission.[80] In Thomas Wilson's view, sincere attempts to convert the slaves to Christianity are likely to be the only way of justifying *'the Trade of* BUYING, TRANSPORTING, *and* SELLING *them as Beasts of Burden'*.[81] Among the owners of slaves was the SPG. In a sermon to the Society in 1783 Beilby Porteus urged it to seek to produce on its plantation a model society of *'truly Christian* Negroes' who are not only civilised in their manners and diligent in their service[82] but who also look to 'a better and a happier country, where all tears shall be wiped from their eyes, and where sorrow and *slavery* shall be no more'.[83] While, though, the society is to lead the way in converting their slaves and in alleviating their miseries,[84] it is not called to free them. To be fair to Porteus, though, it should be noted that when the act abolishing the slave trade was passed in 1807, he was thankful that at last there was an end 'to the most inhuman and execrable traffic that ever disgraced the Christian world'.[85] At the same time he judged that it was imprudent, even if benevolent, to attempt the further step of emancipating the slaves in the British colonies.[86]

These views on missionary work bring to a conclusion this survey of attitudes to 'other religions' in the seventeenth and eighteenth centuries. While a few respected the qualities found in other faiths, most looked on them with self-conscious superiority, interpreting them in terms of current Christian debates and using them to justify their own convictions. It was from this mixed, often mistaken and sometimes distorting background that the modern study of world religions was eventually to emerge. The prevalent attitude in Britain in the age of reason and of enlightenment to 'other religions' is perhaps to be summed up in three verses by Isaac Watts. They come from his 'Praise for Birth and Education in a Christian Land', one of the *Divine Songs for Children*:

'Tis to thy sovereign grace I owe
That I was born on British ground,
Where streams of heav'nly mercy flow,
And words of sweet salvation sound.

I would not change my native land
For rich Peru, with all her gold;
A nobler prize lies in my hand,
Than East or Western Indies hold.

How do I pity those that dwell
Where ignorance and darkness reigns?
They know no heav'n, they fear no hell,
Those endless joys, those endless pains.[87]

READINGS
Extracts from texts
illustrating attitudes to 'other religions'
in the seventeenth and
eighteenth centuries

I

General views on religion

These two extracts give contrasting views of the nature of the religions to be found in the world. The first comes from a piece of Christian apologetic, but shows more appreciation of non-Christian faiths than is common at this time, while also expressing the conviction that Christianity is the perfect religion. The second expresses views on the origin of religion which resemble those classically given in David Hume's *Natural History of Religion* and then, with reference to Indian thought, describes the kinds of improvements in belief that come from developments in rational thought and their application to religion.

(i) A survey of the world's religions

Richard Baxter (1615–91) was a Puritan divine renowned both for his piety and for his scholarship. Love of moderation led him, while ministering at Kidderminster during the Civil War, to seek to secure co-operation between Presbyterian, Episcopalian and Independent ministers in fulfilling their office. While a chaplain to the parliamentary army he sought to counter sectarian and republican tendencies. After the Restoration his hopes for a scheme whereby moderate dissenters like himself could remain in the Church of England were disappointed, and after the ejectment of 1662 he suffered some persecution until the Revolution of 1688. He was a prolific writer. His most famous work, *The Saints' Everlasting Rest*, is a devotional classic. Having both strong convictions and wide sympathies, he believed in the power of persuasion and considered everyone to be amenable to reasonable arguments. *The Reasons of the Christian Religion* is an apologetic work which deals with both natural and revealed religion, presenting Christianity as the climax of religious understanding. The following extract comes from early in the second part of the work where Baxter considers 'supernatural revelation' and the perfection of Christianity. This passage shows his willingness to recognise goodness and truth wherever it is present in other religions, as well as his convictions about Christianity, in the course of a brief survey of the world's religions as commonly categorised at this time.

Of the several Religions which are in the world

Having finished my enquiries into the state and book of Nature, I found it my duty to enquire what *other men* thought in the world, and what were the reasons of their several beliefs, that if they knew more than I had discovered (by what means soever) I might become partaker of it.

§1. *And first I find that all the world, except those called Heathens, are conscious of the necessity of supernatural Revelation; yea, the Heathens themselves have some common apprehension of it.*

§2. *Four sorts of Religions I find only considerable upon earth: The meer Naturalists, called commonly Heathens and Idolaters: the Jews: the Mahometans: and the Christians. The Heathens by their Oracles, Augures and Aruspices, confess the necessity of some supernatural light; and the very Religion of all the rest consisteth in it.*

§3. *As for the Heathens, I find this much good among them: That some of them have had a very great care of their Souls: and many have used exceeding industry in seeking after knowledge, especially in the mysteries of the works of God; and some of them have bent their minds higher to know God, and the invisible worlds: That they commonly thought that there is a Life of Retribution after death . . .* And the Christians ever since have made great use of their Writings in their Schools; especially of *Aristotle*'s and *Plato*'s with their followers.

§4. *And I find that the Idolatry of the wisest of them was not so foolish as that of the Vulgar; but they thought that the Universe was one animated world, and that the Universal Soul was the only Absolute Sovereign God, whom they described much like as Christians do: and that the Sun, and Stars, and Earth, and each particular Orb, was an individual Animal, part of the Universal world, and besides the Universal, had each one a subordinate particular Soul, which they worshipped as a subordinate particular Deity, as some Christians do the Angels. And their Images they set up for such representations, by which they thought these gods delighted to be remembred, and instrumentally to exercise their virtues for the help of earthly mortals.*

§5. *I find that except these Philosophers, and very few more, the generality of the*

Heathens were and are foolish Idolaters, and ignorant, sensual brutish men.

At this day through the world, they are that sort of men that are likest unto Beasts, except some few at *Siam*, *China*, the *Indian Bannians*, the *Japonians*, the Ethnick *Persians*, and a few more. The greatest deformity of Nature is among them: the least of sound knowledge, true policy, civility and piety is among them. Abominable wickedness doth no where so much abound. So that if the doctrin and judgment of these may be judged of by the effect, it is most insufficient to heal the diseased world, and reduce man to holiness, sobriety and honesty.

§6. *I find that those few among the Heathens who attain to more knowledge in the things which concern man's duty and happiness than the rest, do commonly destroy all again by the mixture of some dotages and impious conceits.*

The *Literati* in *China* excel in many things, but besides abundance of ignorance in Philosophy, they destroy all by denying the immortality of the Soul, and affirming rewards and punishments to be only in this life, or but a little longer. At least, none but the Souls of the good (say some of them) survive: and though they confess One God, they give him no solemn worship. Their Sect called *Sciequia* or *Sciacca*, is very clear for *the Unity of the Godhead, the joys of Heaven, and the torments of Hell*, with some umbrage of the *Trinity*, &c. But they blot all with the *Pythagorean* fopperies, affirming these Souls which were in joy or misery, after a certain space to be sent again into Bodies, and so to continue through frequent changes to eternity: to say nothing of the wickedness of their lives. Their third Sect called *Lauru* is not worth the naming, as being composed of fopperies; and sorceries, and impostures. All the *Japonian* Sects also make the *world to be eternal*, and *Souls to be perpetuated through infinite transmigrations*. The *Siamenses*, who seem the best of all, and nearest to Christians, have many fopperies, and worship the Devil for *fear*, as they do God for love. The *Indian Bramenes*, or *Bannians*, also have the *Pythagorean* errors, and place their piety in redeeming Bruits, because they have Souls which sometimes were humane. The *Persians* dispersed in *India*, who confess *God, and Heaven, and Hell*, yet think that these are but of a thousand years duration. And it is above a thousand years since they believed, that the world should continue but a thousand years, and then Souls be realeased from Hell, and a new world made.

§7. *Their great darkness and uncertainties appear by the innumerable sects and differences which are among them; which are incomparably more numerous, than all that are found in all parties in the world besides.*

I need not tell you of the 288 Sects or Opinions *de summo bono*, which *Varro* said was in his days . . . In *Japan*, the twelve Sects, have their subdivisions. In *China*, the three general Sects, have so many subdivisions . . . It were endless to speak of all the Sects in *Africa* and *America*; to say nothing of the beastly part of them in *Brasil*, the *Cape of good hope*, that is, *Soldania*, and the Islands of Cannibals, who know no God, (nor Government, nor Civility some of them.) They are not only of as many minds as countries, but of a multitude of sects in one and the same country.

§8. *I find not my self called or enabled to judge all these people as to their final state, but only to say, that if any of them have a holy heart and life, in the true love of God, they shall be saved; but without this, no form of Religion will save any man, be it never so right.*

§9. *But I find it to be my duty to love them for all the good which is in them, and all that is true and good in their Religion, I will embrace: and because it is so defective, to look further, and try what I can learn from others.*

There is so much lovely in a *Cato, Cicero, Seneca, Antonine, Epictetus, Plutarch, &c.* in the Religions of *Siam*, in the dispersed *Persian* Ethnicks in *India*, in the *Bramans*, or *Bannians* of *India*, in the *Bonzii* of *Japan*, and divers others in *China* and else-where, that it obligeth us not only to love them benevolently, but with much *complacence*. And as I will learn from *Nature it self* what I can do, so also from these *Students* of Nature. I will take up nothing meerly on their trust, nor reject any doctrine meerly because it is theirs; but all that is true and good in the Religions, as far as I can discern it, shall be part of mine; and because I find them so dark and bad, I will betake me for further information to those that trust *supernatural Revelation*; which are the *Jews, Mahumetans* and the *Christians* . . .

§10. *As to the Religion of the Jews, I need not say much of it by it self; the Positive part of their doctrine being confessed by the Christians and Mahumetans, to be of Divine Revelation; and the negative part, (their denying of Christ) is to be tryed, in the tryall of Christianity* . . .

§11. *In the Religion of the Mahumetans I finde much good, viz. A Confession of one only God, and most of the Natural parts of Religion; a vehement opposition to all Idolatry; A testimony to the Veracity of Moses, and of Christ; that Christ is the Word of God, and a great Prophet, and the Writings of the Apostles true: All this therefore where Christianity is approved, must be embraced.*

And there is no doubt but God hath made use of *Mahumet* as a great Scourge to the Idolaters of the World; as well as to the Christians who had abused their sacred priviledges and blessings: Wheresoever his Religion doth prevail, he casteth down Images, and filleth mens mindes with a hatred of Idols, and all conceit of multitude of Gods, and bringeth men to worship one God alone, and doth that by the sword in this, which the preaching of the Gospel hath not done in many obstinate Nations of Idolaters.

§12. *But withall I finde a Man exalted as the chief of Prophets, without any such proof as a wise man should be moved with; and an Alcoran written by him below the rates of common Reason, being a Rhapsody of Nonsence and Confusion; and many false and impious doctrines introduced; and a tyrannical Empire and Religion twisted, and both erected, propagated, and maintained, by irrational tyrannical means; All which discharge my reason from the entertainment of this Religion.*

1. That *Mahomet* was so great (or any) Prophet, is neither confirmed by any true credible Miracle, nor by any eminency of Wisdom or Holiness, in which he excelled other men; nor any thing also which Reason can judge to be a Divine attestation. The contrary is sufficiently apparent in the irrationality of his *Alcoran*: There is no true Learning nor excellency in it, but such as might be expected among men of the more incult wits, and barbarous education: There is nothing delivered methodically or rationally, with any evidence of solid understanding . . .

2. And who can think it any probable sign that he is the Prophet of truth, whose Kingdom is of this World, erected by the Sword; who barbarously suppresseth all rational enquiry into his doctrine, and all disputes against it, all true Learning and rational helps, to advance and improve the Intellect of man: and who teacheth men to fight and kill for their Religion . . .

3. Moreover, they have doctrines of Polygamy, and of a sensual kinde of Heaven, and of murdering men to increase their Kingdoms, and many the like, which being contrary to the light of Nature, and unto certain common Truths, do prove that the Prophet and his doctrine are not of God.

4. And his full attestation to *Moses* and Christ as true Prophets of God, doth prove himself a false Prophet who so much contradicteth them, and rageth against Christians as a blood-thirsty Enemy, when he hath given so full a testimony to Christ.

From Richard Baxter, *The Reasons of the Christian Religion* (London, by R. White for Fran. Titon, 1667), pp. 198–204.

(ii) The origin of religion and rational belief

William Robertson (1721–93) was a Presbyterian minister who led the 'moderate party' in the General Assembly for many years. He was regarded as one of the most eloquent Scottish preachers of his day. He was also a member of the 'Select Society', a debating club in Edinburgh whose other members included Adam Smith and David Hume. His literary fame is the result of various historical works, most notably his *History of Scotland* (1759) and his *History of Charles V* (1769). The following passage comes from his *Historical Disquisition concerning the Knowledge which the Ancients had of India* (1791), a work which he hoped would improve the reputation and the treatment of Indians. The extract is from the sixth section in the appendix, which deals with the religious tenets and practices of the ancient Indians. After describing how religion originated in attempts by primitive people to make sense of their world by personifying its mysterious forces as divinities (a theory which closely parallels that offered by his friend Hume), Robertson uses the example of India to indicate how religious thought may be improved, even though the result is not perfect, by developments in the understanding of nature and hence of God as its ground.

We may observe, that, in every country, the received mythology, or system of superstitious belief, with all the rites and ceremonies which it prescribes is formed in the infancy of society, in rude and barbarous times. True religion is as different from superstition in its origin, as in its nature. The former is the offspring of reason cherished by science, and attains to its highest perfection in ages of light and improvement. Ignorance and fear give birth to the latter, and it is always in the darkest periods that it acquires the greatest vigour . . . The idea of creation is so familiar, wherever the mind is enlarged by science, and illuminated by revelation, that we seldom reflect how profound and abstruse the idea is, or consider what progress man must have made in observation and research, before he could arrive at any distinct knowledge of this elementary principle in religion. But even in its rude state, the human mind, formed for religion, opens to the reception of ideas, which are destined, when corrected and refined, to be the great source of consolation amidst the calamities of life . . . When they behold events to which they are not accustomed, they search for the causes of them with eager curiosity. Their understanding is often unable to discover these, but imagination, a more forward and ardent faculty of the mind, decides without hesitation. It ascribes the extraordinary occurrences in nature to the influence of invisible beings, and supposes the thunder, the hurricane, and the earthquake, to be the immediate effect of their agency. Alarmed by these natural evils, and exposed, at the same time, to many dangers and disasters, which are unavoidable in the early and uncivilized state of society, men have recourse for protection to power superior to what is human, and the first rites or practices which bear any resemblance to acts of religion have it for their object to avert evils which they suffer or dread . . .

Without descending farther into detail, or attempting to enumerate that infinite multitude of deities to which the fancy or the fears of men have allotted the direction of the several departments in nature, we may recognise a striking uniformity of features in the systems of superstition established throughout every part of the earth. The less men have advanced beyond the state of savage life, and the more slender their acquaintance with the operations of nature, the fewer were their deities in number, and the more compendious was their theological creed; but as their mind gradually opened, and their knowledge continued to extend, the objects of their veneration multiplied, and the articles of their faith became more numerous. This took place remarkably among the Greeks in Europe, and the Indians in Asia, the two people, in those great divisions of the earth, who were the most early civilized, and to whom, for that reason, I shall confine all my observations . . . What is supposed to be performed by the power of Jupiter, of Neptune, of Æolus, of Mars, of Venus, according to the mythology of the West, is ascribed in the East to the agency of Agnée, the god of fire; Varoon, the god of oceans; Vayoo, the god of wind; Cama, the god of love; and a variety of other divinities.

The ignorance and credulity of men having thus peopled the heavens with imaginary beings, they ascribed to them such qualities and actions as they deemed suitable to their character and functions . . . Men ascribe to the beings whom they have deified, such actions as they themselves admire and celebrate. The qualities of the gods who are the objects of adoration, are copied from those of the worshippers who bow down before them; and thus many of the imperfections peculiar to men have found admittance into heaven . . . (pp. 312–17).

In India as well as in Greece, it was by cultivating science that men were first led to examine and to entertain doubts with respect to the established systems of superstition . . . In Greece there was not any distinct race or order set apart for performing the functions of religion, or to serve as hereditary and interested guardians of its tenets and institutions. But in India the Brahmins were born the ministers of religion, and they had an exclusive right of presiding in all the numerous rites of worship which superstition prescribed as necessary to avert the wrath of Heaven, or to render it propitious. These distinctions and privileges secured to them a wonderful ascendant over their countrymen; and every consideration that can influence the human mind, the honour, the interest, the power of their order, called upon them to support the tenets, and to maintain the institutions and rites, with which the preservation of this ascendant was so intimately connected.

But as the most eminent persons of the cast devoted their lives to the cultivation of science, the progress which they made in all the branches of it . . . was great, and enabled them to form such a just idea of the system of nature, and of the power, wisdom, and goodness displayed in the formation and government of it, as elevated their minds above the popular superstition, and led them to acknowledge and reverence one Supreme Being, "the Creator of all things (to use their own expressions), and from whom all things proceed."

This is the idea which Abul Fazel, who examined the opinions of the Brahmins with the greatest attention and candour, gives of their theology. "They all," says he, "believe in the unity of the Godhead, and although they hold images in high veneration, it is only because they represent celestial beings, and prevent their thoughts from wandering." The sentiments of the most intelligent Europeans who have visited India, coincide perfectly with his, in respect to this point . . . The Pundits, who translated the Code of Gentoo Laws, declare, "that it was the Supreme Being, who, by his power, formed all creatures of the animal, vegetable, and material world, from the four elements of fire, water, air, and earth, to be an ornament to the magazine of creation; and whose comprehensive benevolence selected man, the center of knowledge, to have dominion and authority over the rest; and, having bestowed upon this favourite object judgment and understanding, gave him supremacy over the corners of the world." . . .

The principal design of the Baghvat-Geeta, an episode in the Mahabarat, a poem of the highest antiquity, and of the greatest authority in India, seems to have been to establish the doctrine of the unity of the Godhead, and from a just view of the divine nature, to deduce an idea of what worship will be most acceptable to a perfect Being. In it, admidst much obscure metaphysical discussion, some ornaments of fancy unsuited to our taste, and some thoughts elevated to a tract of sublimity into which our habits of judgment will find it difficult to pursue them, we find descriptions of the Supreme Being entitled to equal praise with those of the Greek philosophers which I have celebrated. Of these I shall now produce one which I formerly mentioned, and refer my readers for others to the work itself: "O mighty Being," says Arjoon, "who art the prime Creator, eternal God of Gods, the World's Mansion. Thou are the incorruptible Being, distinct from all things transient. Thou art before all Gods, the ancient *Pooroosh* (i.e. vital soul), and the Supreme Supporter of the universe. Thou knowest all things, and art worthy to be known; thou art the Supreme Mansion, and by thee, O infinite Form, the universe was spread abroad. – Reverence be unto thee before and behind; reverence be unto thee on all sides; O thou who art all in all. Infinite is thy power and thy glory. – Thou art the father of all things, animate and inanimate. Thou art the wise instructor of the whole, worthy to be adored . . . " A description of the Supreme Being is given in one of the sacred books of the Hindoos, from which it is evident what were the general sentiments of the learned Brahmins concerning the divine nature and perfections: "As God is immaterial, he is above all conception; as he is invisible, he can have no form; but from what we behold of his works we may conclude, that he is eternal, omnipotent, knowing all things, and present every where."

To men capable of forming such ideas of the Deity, the public service in the Pagodas must have appeared to be an idolatrous worship of images, by a superstitious multiplication of frivolous or immoral rites; and they must have seen that it was only by sanctity of heart, and purity of manners, men could hope to gain the approbation of a Being perfect in goodness. This truth Veias labours to inculcate in the Mahabarat, but with the prudent reserve, and artful precautions, natural to a Brahmin, studious neither to offend his country-men, nor to diminish the influence of his own order . . .

But so unable are the limited powers of the human mind to form an adequate idea of the perfections and operations of the Supreme Being, that in all the theories concerning them, of the most eminent philosophers in the most enlightened nations, we find a lamentable mixture of ignorance and error. From these the Brahmins were not more exempt than the sages of other countries. As they held that the system of nature was not only origi-nally arranged by the power and wisdom of God, but that every event which happened was brought about by his immediate interposition, and as they could not comprehend how a being could act in any place unless where it was present, they supposed the Deity to be a vivifying principle diffused through the whole creation, an universal soul that animated each part of it. Every intelligent nature, particularly the souls of men, they conceived to be por-tions separated from this great spirit, to which, after fulfilling their destiny on earth, and attaining a proper degree of purity, they would be again re-united. In order to efface the stains with which a soul, during its residence on earth, has been defiled, by the indulgence of sensual and corrupt appetites, they taught that it must pass, in a long succession of transmigrations, through the bodies of different animals, until, by what it suffers and what it learns in the various forms of its existence, it shall be so thoroughly refined from all pollution as to be rendered meet for being absorbed into the divine essence, and returns like a drop into that unbounded ocean from which it originally issued. These doctrines of the Brahmins, concerning the Deity, as the soul which pervades all nature, giving activity and vigour to every part of it, as well as the final re-union of all intelligent creatures to their primaeval source, coincide perfectly with the tenets of the Stoical Schools.

From William Robertson, *An Historical Disquisition concerning The Know-ledge which the Ancients had of India* (London, A. Strahan and T. Cadell; Edinburgh, E. Balfour, 1791), pp. 312–17, 324–31.

II

The question of natural religion

The following readings provide examples of some of the views on the possibility and value of natural religion advanced in the seventeenth and eighteenth centuries. The passage from Herbert of Cherbury illustrates his view of natural religion as what all people fundamentally acknowledge to be true, even though the practice of religion has often been corrupted by priestcraft. Robert South, in contrast, sees such religious understanding as having been immediately available to Adam before his Fall but as having been lost to humanity by that event. Samuel Clarke has considerable confidence in the power of reason to bring people to a knowledge of the truths of natural religion. In the passage quoted, however, we see how he considers this knowledge to be limited. It needs to be supplemented by revelation if people are to be sure of having a saving faith. The final extract is from Philip Skelton, who has little confidence in the light of reason. He cites the evil practices of pagan religions to ridicule claims that reason is the way to true religion. (On the need for revelation, cf. also Barrow, IV (ii), and on the unsatisfactoriness of natural religion, cf. also Burder, VIII (ii).)

(i) Universal religion

Edward Herbert, first Baron Herbert of Cherbury (1583?–1648) was a gentleman soldier, diplomat, poet, historian, philosopher and theologian. His *De Veritate (On Truth)*, first published in 1624, may fairly claim to be the first purely metaphysical treatise by an English author. In it Herbert combines epistemological, psychological and methodological considerations in attempting to determine the character of true understanding. Among his doctrines is that of the 'common notions' – initially latent principles which become explicit when aroused by appropriate experiences, which are universally acknowledged to be true, and which provide the foundations of all true understanding. He suggests that there are five common notions for religion, which provide the only proper basis for judgements about what is true in matters of religion and revelation. In *De Religione Gentilium (On the Religion of the World)* he seeks to show that the actual evidence of religious beliefs and practices agrees with his view that the common notions of religion are universally acknowledged. While largely concerned with ancient Greek and Roman religion and dependent to some extent on *De Theologia Gentili* by Gerardus Vossius, Herbert's study is one of the earliest works in the modern study of comparative religion. His manuscript was sent to Vossius in 1645 but publication was delayed until 1663. The following extracts are taken from the English translation made by William Lewis and published in 1705. As they indicate, Herbert was motivated by a concern to find some way of understanding salvation which coheres with the universality of divine providence, in contrast to the widespread view in Christianity that only by means of that faith would people secure salvation. The extracts also include his brief summary of the five common notions of religion, examples of his way of interpreting the evidence of other religions to fit his theory and, finally, the tests which he considers ought to be met by claims to revelations from God. His sympathetic attitude to other religions does not blind him to the evils present in them but he maintains that evidence which appears to contradict his thesis can be dismissed as being due either to misunderstanding of the terms involved or to priestly perversions of the true understanding for selfish interests. The work overall indicates the largeness of Herbert's sympathies and his attempt to understand the relations between God and humanity in a way that does justice to the universality of the former and the diversity of the latter. It shows him to be a liberal theologian who accepted the canon of reason for deciding about religious beliefs and practices and whose sympathies extended beyond the confines of Christianity's traditional exclusiveness. (For Herbert on the corruption of religion by priestcraft, cf. VII (i).)

The Occasion of the whole Work

When, for a long time I had employ'd my most serious Thoughts, in considering whether any common Means for the obtaining Eternal Salvation, were so proposed to all Mankind, that from thence we might necessarily conclude and infer the Certainty of an *Universal Divine Providence*, I met with many Doubts and Difficulties, not easie to be solv'd. I found, that very

many Fathers of the Church had not only a mean and contemptible Opinion
of the antient divulged Religion of the Heathens, but also absolutely and
entirely condemn'd it. The Divines of this last Age also pronounce as severe a
Sentence against all those that are without their *Pale*; so that according to their
Opinions, the far greatest part of Mankind must be inevitably sentenced to
Eternal Punishment.

This appearing to me too rigid and severe to be consistent with the
Attributes of the *Most Great and Good GOD*, I began to consult the Writings
of the Heathens themselves. But when, by their own Histories, I found their
Gods were often not only meer Men, but also some of the most vile; and
when I had observ'd that their Religious Worship, Rites and Ceremonies,
were ridiculous and extravagant, I was very much inclin'd to be of the
common Opinion against them. But then again, when I consider'd that this
was altogether incompatible with the Dignity of an *Universal Divine Providence*, I began to make a diligent Enquiry, whether they meant the same by
GOD as we now do.

Now by GOD we understand a Perfect, Immense, and Eternal Being;
and I found, that with them it sometimes signified Nature, or a certain
Imperfect, Finite, and Transitory Power; so that not only Heaven, the
Planets, Stars, Etherial and Aerial Spirits; but those Men also who had
deserved well of Mankind in general, or their own Country in particular,
were unanimously translated into the Number of their Deities. Their
Emperours also (some of whom were the worst of Men) were deified in their
life-time; and even the *Fever*, *Fear*, and *Paleness* were esteem'd Gods and
Goddesses by them; so that they ascribed Divine Honour to whatsoever was
above the common Rank of Mankind, or exceeded the Apprehension of the
Vulgar: But still it is very evident, that where-ever we find the Attributes of
Summus, Optimus, Maximus; Most Supreme, Most Good, and Most Great,
they meant the same GOD and common Father with us. So that the
Homonomy of the Word being explained, the Doubts that arise by compar-
ing our GOD with theirs, will soon be cleared.

But yet neither their Religious Worship or Rites, could ever make me have
an ill Opinion of the Common People, they being the Invention of the Priests
only; wherefore this Crime ought solely to be imputed to their Great Men,
and not to the Populace, who were only passive in the matter. I suppose none
will deny but that Priests have introduced Superstition and Idolatry, as well
as sown Quarrels and Dissentions where-ever they came: This inclin'd me
not to make so rash and peremptory a Determination, concerning the Future
State of the Laity, as some Divines have done; they being only culpable, for
totally devoting and subjecting themselves to the Authority of their Priests.
Their great Defection from the Pure Worship of the *Supreme God* being justly
to be attributed to the Sacerdotal Order, put me upon the Enquiry, whether
amongst those Heaps of Ethnical Superstitions, a Thread of Truth might be

found, by the assistance of which it was possible for them to extricate themselves out of that *Labyrinth* of Error, in which they were involv'd.

Upon this, Five undeniable Propositions presently occur'd; which not only we, but all Mankind in general, must needs acknowledge:

I. *That there is one Supreme God.*
II. *That he ought to be worshipped.*
III. *That Vertue and Piety are the chief Parts of Divine Worship.*
IV. *That we ought to be sorry for our Sins, and repent of them.*
V. *That Divine Goodness doth dispense Rewards and Punishments both in this Life, and after it . . .*

And seeing that Nature or Common Providence, did supply us here with all things that were necessary and convenient for Food and Raiment; I could not conceive how the same God, either could or would, leave any Man quite destitute (either by Nature or Grace) of the Means of obtaining a more Happy State; and tho the Heathens did not make so good use of them as they might have done, yet the *Most Good and Great G O D*, was not in the least to be charged with their Miscarriage.

I know it is a generally receiv'd Opinion, That Common Providence doth not afford sufficient Means, without the Concurrence of Grace and Particular Providence: But my Design is to make it evident, That an *Universal Providence* is extended to all Mankind. Now forasmuch as the Heathens (as the Holy Scriptures testifie, and Learned Divines acknowledge) worshipped the same God as we do; had the same abhorrence of Sin; believed Rewards and Punishment after this Life; I cannot but think, that after they had led a Good Life, they were made Partakers of the Fulness of that Divine Grace; especially in regard they knew the most rational and perspicuous Parts of the True Divine Worship.

I pretend not to defend the Gross of the Heathen Religion, which I always esteemed foolish, incongruous, and absurd; but only propose those Truths which shined in the midst of their greatest Obscurity. Now when they mixt Superstitions and Fictions with them, and had polluted their Souls with such Crimes as no Repentance could sufficiently purge and expiate, their Destruction was justly owing to themselves; but let Glory be to the *Great G O D* for ever . . . (pp. 1–7).

Of the Worship of the Sun, and his several Names

Not only Holy Scripture, but also *Homer*, *Hesiod*, and the Antient Historians inform us, that the Adoration of the *Sun* was both very Antient and Universal; for it being the general Opinion, that the *Supreme God* had made the Heavens the place of his Residence, (immortal things being most suitable to Immortality) the *Heathens* could not observe any thing there so conspicuous, or which seem'd to them more worthy of Worship and Adoration.

Thus, not only in great Dangers and Difficulties, but in their Prosperity also, they devoutly lifted up their Eyes and Hands towards the Heavens; thither they directed their Prayers, not knowing from whence else any good thing could proceed.

Then they began to think it very incongruous that G O D, who required religious Worship to be paid him by all, should conceal himself from them. For this reason most of the *Heathens* esteem'd the *Sun* to be a G O D, and though not the *Supreme*, yet the very next to him, and his most noble and excellent Representative; although others were of opinion, That the whole *World*, being full of G O D, was the most exact *Image* of him. Those who worshipp'd the *Sun* instead of the *Supreme God* himself, did like those, who, when they come to the Court of some great Monarch, take the first person they see in a rich Habit for the King, and pay him that Respect that is due only to Majesty it self.

The *Inca* of *Peru* was much more in the right, who being askt, whether he acknowledg'd any other *Deity*, Superiour to the *Sun*? answer'd, *I do not esteem the* Sun *to be the* Supreme *G O D, but his Minister only, who being carried round the Earth, doth perform his Will and Pleasure*. A very ingenious Answer. For how could that be esteemed *Supreme* by which all sublunary things would be consumed and reduced to ashes, if it were permitted to act without any restraint. The *Sun* was only a kind of sensible Representation of the *Supreme God* under which consideration only the most Wise amongst the *Heathens* worshipped him; knowing very well that G O D himself could not be discerned in any one thing; Universal Nature it self being insufficient to represent him according to his excellent Dignity . . . (pp. 32 f).

Of the SUPREAM GOD

Having given an account of the *Oeconomical* constitution of the *Celestial* Body, according to the Doctrine of the *Heathens*; it remains that I explain what Head it was that presided over them, that at last we may come to speak of those things, for which, according to their own Principles, we ascend, and have admittance into *Heaven*. Now it is clear beyond all dispute, that this only can be, that *S U P R E A M G O D, who is, and will be, to all Eternity*. For tho' the *Heathens* did often dispute, concerning some Attributes or Properties of *God*, as I shall shew hereafter, yet I am of Opinion, that neither the Learned nor Ignorant did ever question, that there *always was*, and now is, one *Supream God*. But, whether that God had an Eternal Principle from himself, but so that the *World* was Coeternal with him; or whether he preceeded it in Order, Dignity and Power; but not in time, and Fashion'd and Form'd this *Mundane* Matter, in the Shape and Figure we behold it in; or Created the very Matter it self at first, and out of it it made the *World*, is a thing much controverted by the Antients. Those that own *God* to be an Eternal Principle, and yet deny his being the Maker of the *World*, have very jejune Sentiments concerning him; for no Person can be so absurd to imagine, that the *World* was produc'd without any cause (be it whatsoever it will) or can pretend to find a more excellent than the *Supream God* himself. The second Opinion, that the *Supream God* did not only form the *World* out of the *Chaos* at the beginning, but is continually so doing; ridiculously implying this sluggish lump of Matter of which the *World* is compos'd to be equally Eternal, confounding the Cause with the Effect . . . (pp. 255 f).

If it should be objected, That such diversity of things as are in the Universe, proceeding from so many different Causes, necessarily implies Plurality of *Gods*; for there would be too much business for only one, and it would be impossible for him to perform so many things of such quite different Natures; and that the World could not have been made so perfect and compleat, but it would have been very defective.

To this I answer: The more indifferent the Instrument is, the more doth the *Musician* shew his Skill to make such melodious Harmony with dissonant and different Strings; but yet the Instrument that performs those things, was not made in a hurry, but with deliberate Consideration.

In short, the more, not only Diversity, but Contrariety and Repugnancy there is in the Nature of things, it sends us the sooner to some one *Supream God* or Deity, that regulates and keeps all things in such an agreeable *Decorum* . . . (pp. 206 f).

Of the most Sound parts of the Religion *of the* Heathens

Many Reverend and Learned *Divines* of this present Age do assert that the *Heathens* worshipped the same *Supream G O D* as we do. But the difference was that the *Adoration* they paid unto him was Erroneous and Idolatrous; and they also affirm that it is equally as sinful to worship the true *God* after a false Manner as to worship a false *God* after the true Manner. This is not to be understood that they were of Opinion the *Heathens* rejected the *Mind, Virtue, Faith, Piety*, and the other parts of true Religion: But that they intermixed Superstitious, Prophane, Barbarous Rites with them. Nor did they ever deny but that *Virtue, Faith, Hope* and *Love* were in themselves the Rule of worshiping *God* . . . (p. 297).

Before I treated of such *Heathenish* Rites which may admit of a very favourable Interpretation; I thought fit to declare my Dislike of them, tho' not of the End for which they were instituted; for they were very instrumental in reclaiming the Vulgar; and I would desire any *Priest* that now condemns them, to tell me what fitter Methods he could have found out.

I therefore begin with Expiations, Lustrations, and other Solemn Rites, which were supposed to be Effectual for the *Purgation* of the *Soul*. For having discoursed of those *Virtues* by which the Antients believed they obtained Heaven, it will be very necessary to subjoin that which reduces those that have deviated from the true Path, into the right Way, and cures them of their Errors: and this the Antients thought was done by *Expiations* and *Lustrations*; without which they did not believe they were freed from either the Crime or Punishment. They had the same Notions of their Sins and Vices as we have; and they esteemed all Sin and Vice to proceed either from Anger, which being stirred up and enraged, grew into Malice and Fury; from Concupiscence and depraved Desires, exerting themselves in various Manners; the Society of wicked Persons; Imprudence or Ignorance of what was Evil. For which the *Heathens*, especially the Philosophers, applied these Remedies.

1. To restrain the Impetuosity of all evil *Affections*.

2. To wash away those Stains of Sin which had defiled their Conscience, and for which they felt a penitential Compunction; and by the Assistance of the Priest made Expiation, and purified their Souls.

3. To refrain from and avoid all evil and debaucht Company and Conversation.

4. To make a strict and diligent Enquiry into what Good it was they ought to embrace, and what Evil was to be shun'd and avoided.

5. To correct and curb those vitious Propensions which proceeded from humane Frailty.

6. To make frequent and fervent Supplications, by devout Forms, according to the Direction of their Priests, to render the *Gods* Propitious to them . . .

There was nothing delivered in the Theological, or Philosophical Schools of the *Gentiles* by the antient Writers both of *Greece* and *Rome*, but what tended to make Men live well and happy, and to guard and preserve them from all Evil. For all impious Persons after this Life should suffer Eternal Punishments; especially those who had render'd their Vices Habitual and Natural to them . . . For they did think that Man, considered simply and in his own Nature, was neither Good nor Evil; but that he was inclinable both Ways, according to his Education; and that Vice and Sin were not so radicated in Man, but that they might be totally weeded out and destroyed . . . (pp. 314–16).

Tho' the *Heathens* may bring such Arguments, and many more, of their Virtue, Piety and Antiquity of their *Hierarchy*, and that it became very Eminent and Conspicuous; tho' they produce their *Sacred Books*, full of Prophecies, which proceeded from those who were Inspired with a Divine and Prophetick Spirit, by which they prove their Communion to have been very Antient and Common: and altho' they make it appear that they used the same Means (especially as much as the Rule of Right Reason could direct) as we now do, and by that Means endeavoured to obtain a Celestial Life. It will still be impossible for them to acquit themselves of the Suspicion of *Idolatry*, or even from the Practice of it; (for they gave great occasion to the People to fall into very gross Errors, who had not a right Notion of their *Symbolical* Worship) and that their Histories were not Fabulous, their Rites ridiculous, and in short, that all Virtue and Piety was not Restored and Adorned by the *Christian Church*.

But it will require a further Enquiry to discover what was Good and Bad in their religion. Every one will readily acknowledge that these Five Articles are *Orthodox* and *Catholick*; tho' some will not allow them to be sufficient to procure Eternal Happiness. Those of this Opinion seem to me to pronounce a bold, rash and severe Sentence, in regard the Divine Judgments are not to be penetrated into with meer Reason; also I shall not presume to assert that they are altogether sufficient: the Opinion of those who judge more tenderly and reverently concerning *G O D*'s Judgments, seems to me the most probable, whilst Man does all that is in his Power; for it is not in him to repose an entire Faith and Assurance in the Truth of Traditions, especially when they are controverted, nor can any Man by the Assistance of Common and Right Reason, add another to our Five Articles; which will render Men more Sincere and Pious, and more promote the Publick Peace and Tranquillity. I very well know, That many Doctrines were spread abroad every where, by which Sinners were encourag'd with the Hopes of Pardon, which afforded great Solace and Consolation: But it is much to be feared, that unless they were cautiously and justly explain'd, they might prove very mischievous; for considering that Pardon for Sin was obtain'd on such easy terms, they would soon Relapse, and fall into greater Abominations: for whilst they could depend on attaining *Heaven* by Auxiliary Assistance, they would generally omit and neglect what was to be perform'd on their own Parts. The *Priests* will answer, that Virtue and Repentance were both enjoin'd and imply'd. Tho' this be granted, common Experience tells us, Men have been more prone to endeavour to procure Eternal Happiness by External Means, than from Virtue and Internal Penitence.

If more be required to compleat the Religious Worship of *G O D*, than what is contain'd in the aforemention'd Five Articles, the *Priests* of the former and present Ages will tenaciously assert it is contain'd in some *Oracle* deliver'd by Divine Inspiration, or commanded by the *Word* of *G O D*. But, with Submission to such Great Men, one of the *Laity* amongst the *Heathens* would answer, That these things are requisite, to prove the Truth of an *Oracle*; or what is the *Word* of *G O D*.

(1.) That it may be prov'd, beyond all Contradiction, that the *Supream* *G O D*, did use to speak with an Articulate Voice, and deliver *Oracles*.

(2.) That the *Priest* who heard that *Oracle*, was certainly assur'd that it proceeded from the *Supream* G O D, and not from a Good or Evil Angel; and that he was not in a Trance or Delirious, or between Sleep and Awake at the same time.

(3.) That it may evidently appear, that *Oracle* or *Word* was faithfully recited and delivered to the People; or, where occasion requir'd, written and recorded, and transmitted to Posterity from the *Autography* of their *Priests*; so that if any things should happen to be added, diminish'd or alter'd, it might be corrected by its Authority.

(4.) That it may be manifest to all, That the Doctrine which has its Original from the *Oracle*, or the *Word* of G O D, has such an intimate regard to Posterity; that it was absolutely necessary it should become an Article of Faith, especially seeing most things of this Nature were coin'd in the Mint of a single Evidence. When the *Priests* have perform'd this, the *Lay Heathen* will readily submit to their Injunctions.

From Edward, Lord Herbert of Cherbury, *The Antient Religion of the Gentiles, and Causes of their Errors Consider'd*, translated by William Lewis (London, J. Nutt, 1705), pp. 1–7, 32–3, 255 f, 260–1, 297, 314–16, 364–6. (Herbert of Cherbury's *De Religione Gentilium* was first published in Amsterdam in 1663, edited by Isaac Vossius. The manuscript had been sent to his father, Gerard Vossius, in 1645.)

(ii) *Natural religious understanding lost by the fall of Adam*

Robert South (1634–1716) was educated at Westminster School and Christ Church, Oxford. Although for a time sympathetic to Presbyterian views, he was ordained in the Church of England in 1658. In 1660 he became public orator at Oxford and domestic chaplain to Lord Clarendon, in 1663 prebendary of Westminster and in 1667 chaplain to the Duke of York. In 1663, although opposed by some who saw him as a time-server, he received the D D at Oxford. He was appointed a canon of Christ Church in 1670 and rector of Islip in 1678. He ridiculed the Royal Society in an oration in 1669 and joined in the Socinian controversies in the 1690s, accusing William Sherlock (the Dean of St Paul's) of tritheism. Many of his sermons, which were witty, popular and somewhat outspoken, were first published separately and then by South in a six-volume collection from 1679 to 1715. A seventh volume appeared in 1717 and five more in 1744. In the following extract from one of his sermons, he expresses the view that before the Fall Adam, having been created in the image of God, enjoyed immediate, pure and perfect insight into the nature of things, including moral and religious understanding. Because of the Fall, however, such insight has been lost to humanity. Its religion has become largely a matter of degenerate and ridiculous forms of idolatry. The Christian religion is God's means for remedying the effects of the Fall. In this way, South expresses the view that whereas in principle humanity might naturally apprehend what it ought to believe and practice, in fact its fallen status means that no such perception is so available to it.

There are some general Maxims and Notions in the Mind of Man, which are the Rules of Discourse, and the Basis of all Philosophy. As, that *the same Thing cannot at the same Time be, and not be*; That the Whole is bigger than a Part; That two *Dimensions severally equal to a third, must also be equal to one another*. *Aristotle*, indeed, affirms the Mind to be at first a meer *Rasa tabula*; and that these Notions are not ingenite, and imprinted by the Finger of Nature, but by the latter and more languid Impressions of Sense; being only the Reports of Observation, and the Result of some many repeated Experiments.

But to this I answer two Things.

1. That these Notions are universal; and what is universal must needs proceed from some universal, constant Principle, the same in all Particulars, which here can be nothing else but humane Nature.

2. These cannot be infused by Observation, because they are the Rules by which Men take their first Apprehensions and Observations of Things, and therefore in Order of Nature must needs precede them: As the Being of the Rule must be before its Application to the thing directed by it. From whence it follows, that these were Notions, not descending from us, but born with us; not our Off-spring, but our Brethren: and (as I may so say) such as we were taught without the Help of a Teacher.

Now it was *Adam*'s Happiness in the State of Innocence to have these clear and unsullied. He came into the World a Philosopher, which sufficiently appeared by his Writing the Nature of Things upon their Names; he could view Essences in themselves, and read Forms without the Comment of their respective Properties: he could see Consequents yet dormant in their Principles, and Effects yet unborn, and in the Womb of their Causes: his Understanding could almost pierce into future Contingents, his Conjectures improving even to Prophecy, or the Certainties of Prediction; till his Fall he was ignorant of nothing but of Sin; or at least it rested in the Notion, without the Smart of the Experiment. Could any Difficulty have been proposed, the

Resolution would have been as early as the Proposal; it could not have had time to settle into Doubt . . . This is the Doom of fallen Man, to labour in the Fire, to seek Truth *in profundo*, to exhaust his Time and impair his Health, and perhaps to spin out his Days, and himself into one pitiful, controverted Conclusion. There was then no Poring, no Struggling with Memory, no Straining for Invention. His Faculties were quick and expedite . . . An *Aristotle* was but the Rubbish of an *Adam*, and *Athens* but the Rudiments of Paradise.

The Image of God was no less resplendent in that which we call Man's Practical Understanding; namely, that Store-house of the Soul, in which are treasured up the Rules of Action and the Seeds of Morality. Where, we must observe, that many, who deny all connate Notions in the speculative Intellect, do yet admit them in this. Now of this sort are these Maxims; *That God is to be worshipped*. That *Parents are to be honoured*. That *a Man's Word is to be kept*, and the like; which, being of universal Influence, as to the Regulation of the Behaviour and Converse of Mankind, are the Ground of all Vertue and Civility, and the Foundation of Religion.

It was the Privilege of *Adam* Innocent, to have these Notions also firm and untainted, to carry his Monitor in his Bosom, his Law in his Heart, and to have such a Conscience, as might be its own Casuist: and certainly those Actions must needs be regular, where there is an Identity between the Rule and the Faculty. His own Mind taught him a due Dependance upon God, and chalked out to him the just Proportions and Measures of Behaviour to his Fellow-Creatures. He had no Catechism but the Creation, needed no Study but Reflexion, read no Book, but the Volume of the World, and that too, not for Rules to work by, but for Objects to work upon. Reason was his Tutor, and First Principles his *magna Moralia*. The Decalogue of Moses was but a Transcript, not an Original. All the Laws of Nations, and wise Decrees of States, the Statutes of Solon, and the twelve Tables, were but a Paraphrase upon this standing Rectitude of Nature, this fruitful Principle of Justice, that was ready to run out, and enlarge itself into suitable Determinations, upon all emergent Objects and Occasions. Justice then was neither blind to discern, nor lame to execute. It was not subject to be imposed upon by a deluded Fancy, nor yet to be bribed by a glozing Appetite, for an *Utile* or *Jucundum* to turn the Balance to a false and dishonest Sentence. In all its Directions of the inferior Faculties, it conveyed its Suggestions with Clearness and enjoyned them with Power; it had the Passions in perfect Subjection . . . (pp. 52–7).

Now the Use of this Point might be various, but at present it shall be only this; to remind us of the irreparable Loss that we sustained in our first Parents, to shew us of how fair a Portion *Adam* disinherited his whole Posterity by one single Prevarication. Take the Picture of a Man in the Greenness and Vivacity of his Youth, and in the latter Date and Declensions of his drooping Years, and you will scarce know it to belong to the same Person: There would be more Art to discern, than at first to draw it. The same and greater is the Difference between Man innocent and fallen . . . The Light within us is become Darkness; and the Understanding, that should be Eyes to the blind Faculty of the Will, is blind itself, and so brings all the Inconveniences that attend a blind Follower under the Conduct of a blind Guide. He that would have a clear, ocular Demonstration of this, let him reflect upon that numerous Litter of strange, sensless, absurd Opinions, that crawl about the World, to the Disgrace of Reason, and the unanswerable Reproach of a broken Intellect.

The two great Perfections, that both adorn and exercise Man's Understanding, are *Philosophy* and *Religion*: for the first of these; take it even amongst the Professors of it, where it most flourished, and we shall find the very first Notions of common Sense debauched by them. For there have been such, as have asserted, *That there is no such Thing in the World as Motion; That Contradictions may be true.* There has not been wanting one, that has denied *Snow to be white* . . . But then for Religion; what prodigious, monstrous, mishapen Births has the Reason of faln Man produced! It is now almost Six Thousand Years, that far the greatest Part of the World has had no other Religion but Idolatry: And Idolatry certainly is the first-born of Folly, the great and leading Paradox; Nay, the very Abridgment and Sum-total of all Absurdities. For is it not strange, that a rational Man should worship an Ox, nay, the Image an Ox? that he should fawn upon his Dog? bow himself before a Cat? adore Leeks and Garlick, and shed penitential Tears at the Smell of a deified Onion? Yet so did the *Ægyptians*, once the famed Masters of all Arts and Learning . . . Briefly, so great is the Change, so deplorable the Degradation of our Nature, that, whereas before, we bore the Image of God, we now retain only the Image of Men.

In the last place, we learn from hence the Excellency of Christian Religion, in that it is the great and only Means that God has sanctified and designed to repair the Breaches of Humanity, to set faln Man upon his Legs again, to clarify his Reason, to rectify his Will, and to compose and regulate his Affections. The whole Business of our Redemption is, in short, only to rub over the defaced Copy of the Creation, to reprint God's Image upon the Soul, and (as it were) to set forth Nature in a second, and a fairer Edition.

From Robert South, 'Man was created in God's image', a Sermon preached at St Paul's on 9 November 1662, in *Twelve Sermons Preached upon Several Occasions* (London, by G. James for Jonah Bowyer, third edition, 1715), pp. 52–7, 72–5.

(iii) The limits of natural religion

Samuel Clarke (1675–1729) was one of the most learned people in Britain in the generation after Locke. Educated at Gonville and Caius College, Cambridge, he initially came to notice for his understanding of Newton's theories. Later in life, in 1715 and 1716, he defended some of Newton's ideas in correspondence with Leibniz. His Boyle Lectures for 1704 and 1705 established his reputation as a metaphysician and theologian. In them he seeks to prove both the existence and attributes of God by *a priori* reasoning, the autonomy of morality and the nature of moral obligation, the necessity of revelation and the truth of the Christian revelation. The arguments are in the form of demonstrations of twenty-seven propositions intended to be 'as near Mathematical' as possible. Their rational bias, however, made certain self-consciously orthodox divines suspicious of his views. Their doubts were confirmed in 1712 when he published *The Scripture-Doctrine of the Trinity*, which stirred up great controversy and led Clarke to be accused of Arianism. Having been appointed rector of St James's, Westminster, in 1709, questions about his orthodoxy prevented him receiving episcopal preferment. He is probably to be summed up as a rational Christian who sought to establish the reasonableness of Christian belief. The following extract, from the second series of his Boyle Lectures, is part of his argument for the necessity of revelation. While he has argued earlier that reason can provide knowledge of the existence and attributes of God and of moral duty, he does not consider that the resultant natural religion can provide all that is involved in a saving faith. Though it is good as far as it goes, natural religion needs to be supplemented by divine revelation. The passage given here illustrates how Clarke understands the inadequacy of natural understanding alone for a living faith.

. . . And indeed, for many Reasons, it was altogether *impossible*, that the Teaching of the Philosophers should ever be able to reform Mankind, and recover them out of their very degenerate and corrupt Estate, with any considerably great and universal Success.

1. In the first place, Because the *Number* of those, who have in earnest set themselves about this excellent Work, have been *exceeding Few*. Philosophers indeed, that called themselves so, there were enough in every place, and in every Age. But those who truly made it their business to improve their Reason to the height; to free themselves from the Superstition which overwhelmed the whole World; to search out the Obligations of Morality, and the Will of God their Creator; to obey it sincerely themselves, as far as they

could discover it by the Light of Nature; and to encourage and exhort others to do the like: were but a *very few Names*. The Doctrine of far the greatest part of the Philosophers, consisted plainly in nothing but Words, and Subtilty, and Strife, and empty Contention; and did not at all amend even their own Manners; much less was fitted to reform the World . . .

2. Those *few* extraordinary Men of the Philosophers, who did indeed in good measure sincerely Obey the Laws of natural Religion Themselves, and make it their chief Business to instruct and exhort Others to do the same; were yet *Themselves intirely ignorant* of some Doctrines absolutely necessary to the bringing about this great End, of the Reformation and Recovery of Mankind.

In general: Having no knowledge of the whole Scheme, Order, and State of things, the Method of God's governing the World, his Design in Creating Mankind, the original Dignity of Humane Nature, the Ground and Circumstances of Mens present corrupt Condition, the Manner of the Divine Interposition necessary to their recovery, and the Glorious End to which God intended finally to conduct them: Having no knowledge (I say) of all This; their whole Attempt to discover the Truth of Things, and to instruct Others therein, was like wandering in the wide Sea, without knowing whither they were to go, or which way they were to take, or having any Guide to conduct them. And accordingly the Wisest of them were never backward to confess their own ignorance and great blindness: *That* Truth was hid from them, as it were in an unfathomable Depth . . . *That* the very first and most necessary thing of all, the Nature and Attributes of God himself, were, notwithstanding all the general Helps of Reason, very difficult to them to find out in particular, and still more difficult to explain; it being much more easy to say what God *was not*, than what he *was*: And finally, *that* the Method of instructing Men effectually, and making them truly Wise and Good, was a thing very obscure and dark, and difficult to be found out . . .

More particularly: The *Manner*, in which *God* might be *acceptably worshipped*, these Men were entirely and unavoidably ignorant of. That God *ought to be worshipped*; is, in *general*, as evident and plain from the Light of Nature, as any thing can be: But in *what particular Manner*, and with *what kind of Service* he will be worshipped, cannot be certainly discovered by bare Reason. Obedience to the Obligations of Nature, and Imitation of the Moral Attributes of God; the wisest Philosophers easily knew, was undoubtedly the *most acceptable* Service to God. But some *external Adoration* seemed also to be necessary; and *how* this was to be performed, they could not with any certainty discover. Accordingly even the very best of them complied therefore generally with the outward Religion of their Country, and advised Others to do the same; and so, notwithstanding all their wise Discourses, they fell lamentably into the practice of the most foolish Idolatry . . . *Cicero*, the greatest and best Philosopher that *Rome* or perhaps any other Nation every produced, allowed

Men to continue the Idolatry of their Ancestors; advised them to conform themselves to the superstitious Religion of their Country, in offering such Sacrifices to different Gods, as were by Law established; and disapproves and finds fault with the *Persian* Magi, for burning the Temples of the *Grecian* Gods, and asserting that the whole Universe was God's Temple. In all which, he fondly contradicts himself, by inexcusably complying with all Practices of those Men, whom in many of his Writings he largely and excellently proves to be extremely Foolish upon account of those very Practices . . .

But *still more particularly*: That which of all other things, these best and wisest of the Philosophers were most absolutely and unavoidably ignorant of; and yet which, of all other things, was of the greatest Importance for *Sinful* Men to know; was *The Method, by which such as have erred from the right way, and have offended God, may yet again restore themselves to the Favour of God, and to the Hopes of Happiness*. From the consideration of the Goodness and Mercifulness of God, the Philosophers did indeed *very reasonably hope*, that God would show himself placable to Sinners, and might be some way reconciled: But when we come to enquire more particularly, *what Propitiation* he will accept, and in *what Manner* this reconciliation must be made; here Nature stops, and expects with impatience the aid of some particular Revelation. That God will receive returning Sinners, and accept of Repentance instead of perfect Obedience, *They* cannot *certainly know*, to whom he had not declared that he *will* do so. For though this be the most *probable* and *only* means of reconciliation, that Nature suggests; yet whether this will be alone sufficient; or whether God will not require something further, for the Vindication of his Justice, and of the Honour and Dignity of his Laws and Government, and for the expressing more effectually his Indignation against Sin, before he will restore Men to the Privileges they have forfeited; they cannot be satisfactorily assured. For it cannot positively be proved from any of God's Attributes, that he is *absolutely obliged* to pardon all Creatures all their Sins at all times, barely and immediately upon their Repenting. There arises therefore from Nature no *Sufficient* Comfort to Sinners, but anxious and endless Sollicitude about the Means of appeasing the Deity. Hence those divers way of Sacrificing, and numberless Superstitions, which over-spread the Face of the Heathen World, but were so little satisfactory to the wiser part of Mankind, even in those times of darkness . . .

3. Some other Doctrines absolutely necessary likewise to the bringing about this great End of the Reformation of Mankind; though there was indeed so much proof and evidence of the Truth of them to be drawn from Reason, as that the best Philosophers could not by any means be *intirely ignorant* of them; yet so much *doubtfulness, uncertainty*, and *unsteddiness*, was there in the Thoughts and Assertions of these Philosophers concerning them, as could not but very much diminish their proper Effect and Influence upon the Hearts and Lives of Men. I instance in the *Immortality of the Soul*, the

Certainty of a Future State, and *the Rewards and Punishments to be distributed in a life to come*. The Arguments, which may be drawn from Reason and from the Nature of things, for the Proof of these great Truths; seem really . . . to come very little short of strict Demonstration: And Accordingly the wisest Philosophers . . . did indeed sometimes seem to have reasoned themselves into a firm Belief of them, and to have been fully convinced of their Certainty and Reality; even so far as to apply them to excellent purposes and uses of Life. But then on the other hand, a Man cannot without some pity and concern of Mind observe, how strangely at other times the weight of the same Arguments seem to have slipt (as it were) out of their Minds; and with what wonderful *Diffidence, Wavering* and *Unsteddiness*, they discourse about the same Things.

From Samuel Clarke, *A Discourse Concerning the Being and Attributes of G O D, The Obligations of Natural Religion, and the Truth and Certainty of the Christian Revelation* (London, John and Paul Knapton, eighth edition, 1732), pp. 288–97. (The material was originally given as the Boyle Lectures for 1704 and 1705.)

(iv) The darkness of the light of nature revealed by pagan religions

Philip Skelton (1707–87) was a student at Trinity College, Dublin and a schoolmaster at Dundalk before being ordained into the Church of Ireland. After being curate at Drummilly and at Monaghan, he was appointed in 1750 to the parish of Templecarn, whose inhabitants are said to have been ignorant of even the most basic Christian ideas. In 1759 he moved to Devenish and then in 1766 to Fintona. He was a diligent pastor and having been brought up in great poverty, showed concern for the poor throughout his ministry. Twice he sold his library to find funds to help people in times of distress. Besides work attacking the Socinians and Bishop Hoadley's views on the Lord's Supper, his most famous book is *Ophiomaches, or Deism Revealed* which was published in 1748 by Andrew Millar on the recommendation of David Hume. The piece is in the form of eight conversations between two deists, a clergyman and a layman. In it Skelton particularly attacks the views of Collins, Toland, Chubb and Shaftesbury. The following extract is an attack on those deists who argue that reason makes the true religion evident to everyone. Skelton ridicules this claim by pointing to what in practice is to be found in pagan religions. Their immoralities and cruelties show the radical inadequacy of 'natural light' in religious matters.

. . . be so good as to shew us, from what history you please, an instance of any one nation under the sun, that emerged from absolute atheism or idolatry, into the knowledge or adoration of the one true God, without the assistance of revelation. The *Americans*, the *Africans*, the *Tartars*, and the ingenious *Chinese*, have had time enough, one would think, to find out the true and right idea of God, which you say is more evident to all mankind, than any idea of sense; and yet, after above five thousand years improvement upon their innate ideas of God, and the full exercise of reason, which you exalt, and almost deify, they have at this day got no farther in their progress towards the true religion, than to the worship of stocks, stones, and devils. How many thousand years must be allowed to these nations, to reason themselves into the true religion . . .? The Christian religion, it seems, came too late into the world, to be true; but natural religion, tho' not yet arrived, is recommended sufficiently by its truth, antiquity, and universality. What the lights of nature and reason could do to investigate the knowledge of God, is best seen by what they have really done. We cannot argue more convincingly on any foundation, than that of known and incontestable facts. Give me leave therefore to be particular in exposing the theology of the Pagans from the records of their own writers. All the nations of the earth, that were left to themselves, fell, some sooner, and others later, into gross idolatry. At first they worshiped the luminaries of Heaven, and then their departed Kings and benefactors, for gods. Then they made images for them, and in a little time terminated the greater part of their adoration in those wooden representatives of their dead deities. It was not long after these first-fruits of nature, till they added to the catalogue of their gods, the most barbarous oppressors, the vilest impostors, the lewdest prostitutes, and the most infamous adulterers, murderers, and parricides, the earth ever groaned under. Such deities were to be worshiped with suitable rites and sacrifices. The *Salii* and *Corybantes*, priests of *Mars* and *Cybele*, performed the ceremonies of those deities with frantic dances, and outrageous fits of madness. In the rites of *Bacchus*, not only the priests, but all the people, men, women, and children, having their faces smeared with the lees of wine, and being half-drunk, ran about the fields, and through the woods, in a most horrible fit of distraction, howling like wild beasts, and frisking from place to place with such ridiculous and immodest gesticulations, as nothing but the strong possession of some demon could have prompted them to. It was, no doubt on't, a most rational kind of religion, that could have put the antient men, the discreet matrons, and the modest virgins, on such wild extravagancies. The sight of such a ceremony was, I must own, wonderfully decent and solemn and its tendency highly edifying and virtuous. Much the same sort of strikings and howlings were used in the ceremonies of many other heathen gods; and in those of *Baal* they were accompanied with a custom most shocking and unnatural. The priests, as they capered about the altar, gashed their flesh with knives and lancets, and ran into furious fits of distraction. The most solemn act of worship, performed to the *Syrian Baal* by his ordinary devotees, was to break wind, and ease themselves, at the foot of his image. The religious rites performed in honour of *Venus* in *Cyprus*, and at *Aphac* on Mount *Libanus*, consisted in lewdness of the grossest kinds. The young people of both sexes crouded from all parts to those sinks of pollution, and, filling the groves and temples with their shameless practices, committed whoredom by thousands, out of pure devotion. All the *Babylonian* women were obliged to prostitute themselves once in their lives, at the temple of *Venus* or *Mylitta*, to the first man that asked them; and the money earned by this extraordinary act of devotion, be it more or less, was always esteemed sacred. The nocturnal mysteries at *Rome* were not carried to such enormous excesses; but they were nevertheless very scandalous meetings, and gave occasion to all sorts of debaucheries. The devils, however, whom nature had chosen for her gods, were not contented with drunkenness and lewdness; they must be worshiped with murder too, and that of the most shocking sort. Human sacrifices were offered up almost in all the heathen countries; and, to make them the more acceptable to their good-natured gods, the parents burned their own children alive to *Baal*, *Moloch*, and many other of their deities. Here in *Britain*, and in *Gaul*, it was a common practice to surround a man with a kind of wicker-work, and burn him to death, in honour of their gods. The *Scythians* sacrificed to *Mars* one in every hundred of the captives taken in war. The *Peruvians*, in their sacrifices, had a custom of tying a living man to a stake, and pulling the flesh off his bones by small pieces, which they broiled and eat in his sight, believing they did him the greatest honour in treating him after this manner. The *Carthaginians*, in times of public calamity, not only burnt alive the children of the best families to *Saturn*, and that by hundreds, but sometimes sacrificed themselves in the same manner in great numbers. Oracles, astrology, soothsaying, superstition, magic, &c. over-ran the whole heathen world, and presided over the very councils of the wisest states . . . Such were the bright rays of natural light! Such the blessed effects in Pagan countries to this day, of following the wise dictates of nature! . . . *Le Compte* and *Duhald* assure us, the *Chinese*, after offering largely to their gods, and being disappointed of their assistance, sometimes sue them for damages, and obtain decrees against them from the Mandarins. This ingenious people, when their houses are on fire, to the imminent peril of their wooden gods, hold them to the flames, in hopes of an effect, that might be more rationally expected from a small vessel of water. A religion, so highly respected, must, no doubt on't, have excellent effects upon the morality of its professors, and powerfully enforce the laws of society.

From [Philip Skelton], *Deism Revealed Or, The Attack on Christianity Candidly Reviewed* (London, A. Millar, second edition, 1751), I, pp. 76–9.

III

The Jews

The following passages illustrate some of the ways in which the Jewish faith was described and understood in the seventeenth and eighteenth centuries. The extract from Barrow is a typical expression of Christian apologetic which claims that Judaism, while originally founded on a divine revelation, has now been superseded. Bayle's article illustrates the difficulty facing a Jew who wanted to let reason govern his religious position while the passage by Leslie is an example of issues that were raised from the Christian side in controversies with Jews and matters which the latter might raise in reply. The final extract is from Picart's monumental work on world religions. It illustrates the type of information which a sympathetic approach led to being circulated about the Jews – most of it, in fact, coming from a Jewish source.

(i) The imperfection of the Jewish religion

Isaac Barrow (1630–77) was an eminent mathematician, classicist and theologian. Having been a student and then a fellow of Trinity College, Cambridge, he was appointed Master of Trinity in 1673. He had previously been made Professor of Greek in 1660 and then, in 1663, the first Lucasian Professor of Mathematics at Cambridge. He resigned this latter post in 1669 in favour of his pupil, Isaac Newton, both because he saw that Newton was the greater mathematician and because he wanted more time for his theological studies. He was a successful, if lengthy, preacher – Charles II complained of his 'unfairness' in so exhausting every topic in his sermons that there was nothing left for anyone else! His sermons and his theological writings were regarded as reasonable, balanced and perceptive. The following extract is taken from one of a series of sermons on the Apostles' Creed. In it he argues that, while the Jewish religion is the product of a divine revelation, it does not present a serious challenge to the excellency and final authority of the Christian religion. His case, which includes some derogatory comments on the character of the Jews, is that the revelation which established the Jewish religion was restricted in its scope, incomplete and temporary. Implicitly it is being contrasted with the universality, completeness and permanent validity of the revelation on which Christianity is founded. Barrow claims that the situation of the Jews since their dispersion provides empirical confirmation of this view of their religion. He also attempts to clear God's reputation from any suggestion that the imperfection of the revelation to the Jews reflects poorly on him as the revealer. In this last respect Barrow shows that he does not share Herbert of Cherbury's conviction that God must be thought of and act consistently as a universal providence. (For Barrow on Islam, cf. IV (ii).)

> The *Jewish* Religion, we acknowledge, had its birth from the revelation and appointment of God; its truth and goodness we do not call in question; but yet looking into it, we shall find it in many respects defective, and wanting the conditions due to such a revelation as we require. For it was not universal; (neither being directed to, nor fitted for the nature and needs of mankind;) it was not full and complete, it was not designed to be of perpetual obligation, or use.
>
> 1. *First*, I say, this *Revelation* was not general; not directed to, or intended for to instruct and oblige mankind; it self expressly affirms so much: the whole tenour and frame thereof shews it; so do all the circumstances of its rise and progress. That it was intended peculiarly for that small Nation, possessing a very inconsiderable portion of the earth; distinguished, and indeed, as it were, concealed from the rest of mankind both on purpose, and in effect; for it so remained for many Ages, (till the *Macedonian* first, and afterward the *Roman* conquests opened the world and disclosed them) hid in a solitary obscurity; even so far as to escape the observation of the most inquisitive surveyours of the earth, the most curious searchers into the customs of all people (as of *Herodotus* for instance, who nicely describing the places and manners of the People all about them, could not discern them, and takes no notice of them, although for their peculiar manners otherwise most remarkable, and deserving his mention) appears by express passages in their Law and holy writings: *He sheweth his word unto Jacob, his statutes and his judgments unto Israel; He hath not dealt so with any nation; and his judgments they have not known them* . . . God transacted with that people singly and separately from all other; taking them (on purpose) as it were, into a corner, at a good distance and beyond hearing of others, that he might there signify alone to them his pleasure, peculiarly concerning them. Yea to this purpose, of maintaining a

distance and distinction from the rest of mankind, divers of their laws were appointed . . .

I may also hereto add; that as the laws and rites of this Religion were designed only for this People, as they did only agree to their circumstances; so they were only suted to their inclinations, and their capacities; their inclinations, which were very stubborn and perverse; their capacities, which were very low and gross, as their own Prophets do upon many occasions affirm and complain; being dissentaneous and repugnant to the common humour and *genius* of mankind . . . By which and many other like considerations obvious enough may appear that this dispensation was not (either according to its nature, or in its design) general, or such as respected the main body of mankind, but rather very particular and restrained; designedly restrained to the oblation and use of one place or people, if compared to the world of men, inconsiderably narrow and small; the fewest of all people God himself says they were. That in fine, this constitution had only the nature of a municipal law, imposing burthens, and indulging privileges upon one City or Territory; not of a common civil sanction, established for the obligation, use and benefit of the whole Commonwealth or Empire subject to the Almighty King.

'Tis not therefore in reason to be taken for such a Revelation, as we argued needful for us, and to be expected from him, *who* (as the *Psalmist*, as reason, as experience tells us) *is good to all* . . .

2. Farther; As this Revelation was particular, so was it also partial; as God did not by it speak his mind to all, so he did not therein speak out all his mind . . . Surveying first, I say, the directive part, we may observe, both a redundancy in things circumstantial or exteriour, and a defectiveness in things substantial and interiour: there be ritual institutions in vast number very nicely described, and strongly pressed; The observation of times and places, the distinction of meats and of habits, (*touch not, taste not, handle not*) corporeal cleansings and purgations; modalities of exteriour performance in sacrifices and oblations . . . we see with extreme punctuality prescribed and enjoined, some of them under very heavy penalties (of utter extermination and excision.) While moral duties (duties of justice and charity, yea of temperance and sobriety it self,) and spiritual devotions (so exceedingly more agreeable to rational nature, and which could not but be much more pleasing to God) were more sparingly delivered in precept, less clearly explained, not so fully urged with rational inducements; nor, in a due proportion guarded with rewards. Many things were plainly permitted, or tacitly connived at (as *polygamy*, and *divorce*; some kinds of retaliation, cursing, revenge; some degrees of uncharitableness) which even natural reason dislikes, or condemns. So faulty was that dispensation as to the part thereof directive of life; and it was no less in that part, which promotes and secures good practice, by applying fit excitements to obedience, and fit restraints from disobedience;

rightly managing those great instruments of springs of humane activity, natural courage, hope and fear . . . Indeed as to evident discovery concerning the immortality of man's soul, or the future state (so material a point of Religion, of so grand moment and influence upon practice) even the *Gentile* Theology (assisted by ancient common Tradition) seems to have out-gone the *Jewish*, grounding upon their revealed law; the *Pagan* Priests more expressly taught, more frequently inculcated arguments drawn from thence, than the *Hebrew* Prophets; a plain instance and argument of the imperfection of this Religion . . .

Neither in discoursing thus do we lay any misbeseeming imputation upon God, the Author of that Religion; the making so imperfect a Revelation no-wise being disagreeable to his wisdom, his goodness, or his justice. As for a time he might with-hold the declaration of his mind to all mankind, so might he (upon the same or like grounds of wise counsel) forbear to declare some part thereof to that People: no special reason appears that could oblige, that might induce him not to be reserved as well in part to these few men, as in whole to those, all the rest of men . . .

I add; That through all course of times their manners have not procured in a manner from any men any good-will, or respect; but indeed the common dislike, contempt and hatred of men: they have always (since well known and observed in the world) been reputed a sort of people not only above all men vain and superstitious, addicted to fond conceits and fabulous stories, but extremely proud and arrogant, churlish and soure, ill-natured and false-hearted toward all men; not good or kind, yea not so much as just or true toward any but themselves . . . Now the tree, which hath always bore such fruits (so unsavoury, so unwholesome) we have no reason to admire, to esteem excellent and perfect: It might *be good* for those times, when men willingly did feed on acorns, on crabs, on bramble-berries; but cannot so well serve now, when higher improvements of reason, when philosophy and learning by a general influence upon the world have prepared the palates of men to relish, their stomachs to digest more delicious and more wholesome fare. But I

3. Proceed to shew the third defect, which I at first observed, in this Religion, that it was not designed for perpetual obligation and use: (As it was particular in respect of the persons to whom it was directed, whom it obliged; as it was partial and incomplete in its frame, so it was, according to its design, temporary and mutable.) This conclusion we might infer from what hath been said concerning the narrow extent, and concerning the intrinsick imperfection thereof; for supposing a new general and perfect revelation made to mankind, . . . that would naturally swallow and void those which are particular and imperfect . . . Nothing in nature, or in providence, that is scant or defectuous, can be stable and lasting. Thus, I say, is this a conclusion, a consequence of those which preceded; but we have another more convincing

sort of evidence to prove it by (most valid *ad homines*) even by many pregnant intimations; yea many express remonstrances and predictions, that God did intend in due time to introduce a great change in affairs of this kind . . . In fine, that he would dispense a general full revelation of his mind and will, of his grace and favour to mankind; such as should not be consistent with that particular and partial law, such as implies a disannulling thereof for obligation, and disabling it for use. The holy writings of that people acquaint us, that God intended *to raise up another Prophet* (for extraordinariness and eminency) . . .

Thus doth God's design concerning the abolition of this Religion appear by verbal testimonies; the same we see also declared by real effects: his providence hath made good his word, he hath not only disobliged men from that Religion, but hath manifestly discountenanced it; yea hath disabled even the most obstinate adherents in opinion and will thereto, from the practice and excercise thereof, according to its primitive rules and prescriptions. Long is it (for above fifteen hundred years) since they, exiled from their ancient country and scattered over the world, have wanted a place whither to resort, wherein to perform those most weighty parts of worship and service to God, oblation of sacrifices, incense and tithes: Their Tribes being confounded, the distinction of priesthood and people seems taken away; all the mysterious emblems of God's special presence, all the tokens of God's favour and endearment to them are embezel'd and quite lost; nothing is left substantial or solemn in their Religion, which if they would they could put in practice: all that they retain of their ancient institution is the observation of some petty formalities, in matters of less importance; which also they have so blended and corrupted with impure mixtures of their own device and forgery, (false and impious opinions, ridiculous and uncouth ceremonies, idle and absurd stories) that we may justly suppose genuine *Judaism* no where to be found; that it cannot be, nor is intended any where practised.

So that what reason shewed fit to be, what God hath declared should be, that experience doth attest to be done; the cessation and abolition of that way of Religion, both as to obligation and use.

From Isaac Barrow, *The Works* (published by John Tillotson, London, printed for James Round, Jacob Tonson and William Taylor, third edition, 1716), I I, pp. 157–67. (The first edition of *The Works* was in four volumes and appeared 1683–7.)

(ii) The trials of a convert and the dangers of using reason in religion

Pierre Bayle (1647–1706) was the son of a provincial Huguenot minister who went over to Roman Catholicism in 1669 after being beaten in an argument about the nature of the church by a priest. He soon became scandalised, however, by Roman Catholic practices of worship and in the following year returned to Protestantism. After a time in Geneva, where he became a keen Cartesian, in 1675 he was appointed Professor of Philosophy in the Protestant Academy at Sedan. When this academy was suppressed in 1681, he went to Rotterdam where a chair in philosophy and history was created for him and where he spent the rest of his life. His critical views and support for universal toleration, however, evoked hostility among influential French Protestants and his chair was suppressed in 1693. He is generally described as a sceptical writer whose large and famous *Dictionnaire historique et critique* (1695–7) not only shows his encyclopedic knowledge but also provided considerable material for the attacks on Christianity made in the following century by the so-called deists and philosophes. It is arguable, however, that he is rather to be understood as a profoundly religious believer who deeply distrusted attempts to reconcile rationality and religious faith. His criticisms are thus to be interpreted as provocative challenges to the prevailing assumption that religious faith is only tenable if its beliefs and practices can be shown to be reasonable. In the following passage from the *Dictionary* he tells the story of Acosta, a Portuguese Jew who found satisfaction neither in Roman Catholicism, in which he was educated, nor in Judaism, and who committed suicide in 1647. Acosta's troubles, arising from his problems in trying to find a faith that was rationally acceptable, reflect Bayle's own experiences to some extent. The passage, though, casts light on the situation facing Jewish converts at this time, as well as being an example of the way in which reports about other religions can be used in controversy – here to show how attempts to govern faith by reason, whatever the faith, can render life unpleasant.

ACOSTA (URIEL) a Portugeze Gentleman, was born at Oporto about the close of the sixteenth Century. He was brought up in the Romish religion, of which his father was a sincere Professor, although descended from one of those Jewish families which had been violently constrained to submit to the ceremony of baptism. He also had an education suitable to his birth, and was instructed in a variety of sciences, the last of which was the Law. He had received very happy dispositions from Nature, and Religion had made so deep an impression on his mind, that he ardently desired to practise all the injunctions of the church . . . However, as the Popish doctrines would never suffer his mind to be at rest, and that he yet resolved to profess some Religion or other, he applied himself to the study of Moses and the Prophets, which gave him more satisfaction than the Gospel, and at last he was persuaded the Jewish Religion was the true one; but, as it would be impossible for him to profess it in Portugal, he resolved to leave it. Accordingly he . . . embarked for Amsterdam with his mother and brothers, whom he had dared to instruct in the Jewish principles, and which they indeed had pretty well imbibed. Immediately after their arrival in the last mentioned city, they made themselves members of the synagogue, and were circumcised according to the usual custom; and thereupon Acosta changed his name of Gabriel for that of Uriel. He had been but a few days among the Jews, before he perceived that their morals and rites were not conformable to the laws of Moses, upon which occasion it was impossible for him to be silent. However, the chiefs of the synagogue gave him to understand, that he must observe exactly their tenets and customs, and that he would be excommunicated in case he deviated ever so little from them. But Acosta was not terrified at this menace, and thought it would be beneath a man, who had left his native country, and the affluence he enjoyed in it purely for the sake of liberty of conscience, to submit to a set of Rabbis, who were not invested with a judiciary power; and that it would argue either want of courage or piety, in case he should betray his sentiments on such an occasion as this; and therefore he went on. Upon this he was excommunicated, which had such an effect, that his own brothers, whom he had instructed in the Jewish Religion, did not dare to speak to, or even salute him, whenever they met him in the streets. Acosta being under these circumstances, writ a book in his own justification, wherein he shewed, that the rites and traditions of the Pharisees, clash directly with the writings of Moses. He had scarce begun this work, when he embraced the opinion of the Sadduces, having wrought himself to a strong persuasion, that the rewards and punishments of the old law, relate to this life only; and that chiefly, because Moses does not any where mention, either the joys of paradise or the torments of hell. His adversaries rejoiced greatly to hear he had imbibed the opinion abovementioned, foreseeing that this would be a good handle, whereby to justify (in the minds of the Christians) the proceedings of the synagogue against him, &c. Hence it was, that even before his work was printed, they published a book upon the immortality of the soul, written by a Physician, who used all the arguments he could think of, to make Acosta pass for an Atheist. Children were even spirited up to insult him in the streets, and to throw stones at his house; but all this did not prevent his writing a treatise against the Physician, in which he did his utmost to invalidate the doctrine of the soul's immortality. The Jews had recourse to the Magistrates of Amsterdam, and impeached him as a man who sapped the foundations both of the Jewish and Christian Religions; whereupon he was thrown into prison, but was bailed about eight or ten days after; however, all the copies of his work were confiscated, and he was obliged to pay a fine of three hundred florins. Acosta nevertheless did not stop here, for time and experience made him carry matters much farther. He examined whether the law of Moses came from God, and imagined he had found solid reasons to convince himself that it was merely of human invention; but instead of drawing the following consequence from it, *I therefore ought not to return to the communion of the Jewish church*, he put the following question to himself, *Why should I persist in abstaining from it all my life time, exposed to so many inconveniencies; especially as I am in a strange country whose language I am ignorant of? Will it not be better for me to play the ape among apes?* Having weighed these matters, he returned again to the Jewish church, fifteen years after his excommunication, and retracting what he had written, subscribed every thing as they directed. Some days after he was impeached by a nephew of his, a young lad, that lived in the house with him, who had perceived, that his uncle did not observe the laws of the synagogue, either with respect to eating, or other points . . . upon which the Jews resolved to turn him out of their communion. Words could never express the insults with which he was afterwards loaded, or the injurious treatment he met with from his relations. Having spent seven years in this melancholy condition, he resolved to declare that he was ready to submit to the sentence of the synagogue . . . and was forced to undergo, in its utmost rigour, the penance which had at first been proposed to him. These are the particulars I have extracted . . . from a little piece written by Acosta . . . It is believed that he drew it up a few days before his death, after having determined to lay violent hands upon himself, which strange resolution he executed a little after he had failed in his attempt to kill his principal enemy. For the moment that the pistol with which he intended to shoot him, as he past by his house, missed fire, he shut the door and shot himself with another pistol. This happened at Amsterdam, but the year is not exactly known. Here is an example which favours those that condemn the liberty of philosophizing on religious subjects, the principal stress of whose argument lies in this, that it leads insensibly to Atheism or Deism . . .

Footnote: 'That it leads insensibly to Atheism or Deism': Acosta serves as an example to these people. He refused to comply with the decisions of the catholic church, because he did not find them consistent with reason; and he embraced the Jewish religion, because he found it more conformable to the knowledge he had acquired. He afterwards rejected a numberless multitude of Jewish traditions, because he judged they were not contained in the holy scripture; he even denied the immortality of the soul, upon pretence that it is not mentioned in the law of God; and lastly, he denied the Divinity of the books of Moses, because he thought that the religion of nature was not conformable to the ordinances of that Legislator. Had he lived six or seven years longer, he possibly would have denied the religion of nature, because his wretched reason would have suggested a great number of difficulties in the hypothesis concerning the providence and free will, of the eternal and necessary Being. Be this as it will every one who makes use of his reason, stands in need of God's assistance; for without this, it is a guide that leads us astray: and we may compare Philosophy to powders, which are of so corrosive a nature, that they not only eat away the proud flesh of a wound, but the sound also; rot the bones, and pierce to the very marrow. Philosophy refutes errors at first, but in case she is not stopp'd there, she attacks truths; and if suffered to grow head-strong, she goes such lengths, that she loses herself, and does not know where to fix. This must be imputed either to the weakness of the mind of man, or to the ill use he makes of his pretended strength. Happily, or rather by the wise dispensation of providence, few men are capable of falling into this abuse.

From the article 'Acosta' in P. Bayle, *A General Dictionary, Historical and Critical*, translated and augmented by J. P. Bernard, T. Birch, J. Lockman and others (London, J. Roberts and P. Vaillant, 1734), I, pp. 212–15.

(iii) Why Jews object to becoming Christians

Charles Leslie (1650–1722), after studying law at Trinity College, Dublin and the Temple, was ordained in the Anglican Church in 1680. In 1686 he became chancellor of Connor but was deprived as a non-juror after the Revolution and moved to London. From 1713 he belonged to the Court of the Pretender although he retained his strong anti-Roman Catholic views. He returned to Ireland the year before his death. Leslie was a vigorous and voluminous controversialist who accused Whig divines such as Burnet and Tillotson of Socinianism, attacked the Quakers for their doctrine of the inner light as showing 'blasphemous pride' and, most famously of all, opposed the deists in his *Short and Easy Method with the Deists*. In this work he sought to demonstrate the 'certainty of the Christian religion', primarily by reference to the alleged sound historical evidence of Christ's miracles. This work appeared in 1698 and he then produced, on similar lines, a refutation of the Jews by proving Jesus to be the Messiah. In the following extract from the latter work, he accuses the

Jews of tampering with the evidence which would show that Jesus Christ is the Messiah, of erroneously prefering outward ceremonies to truly spiritual worship and of abandoning their former views. He finally considers some Jewish objections to Christianity and uses them, implicitly, to criticise Roman Catholic practices and Latitudinarian toleration in Protestantism.

Therefore I would here enquire a little into some of those most visible causes which have all this time, and do still harden the *Jews* in their obstinacy, against the receiving the Doctrine of *Christ*.

And some of these are on the *Jews* side, and some on the Christians.

I. First for the *Jews*. They have since *Christ* came quite altered their own Doctrine and Topicks from whence they us'd to argue before, on purpose to avoid the plain proofs thence drawn for our *Jesus* being the *Messiah*. To instance in a few:

1. There are great presumptions, that they have alter'd and corrupted the very Text of their own Scriptures of the Old Testament, in those places which speak of the *Messiah*, which gave the marks of him, and pointed out the time of his coming. However this they cannot deny, that whether by the loss of the Vowels in the *Hebrew* Tongue, or from whatever cause, that Language is now render'd so uncertain, beyond any other in the World, as that one word bears many different significations, insomuch that every Text almost will afford perpetual jangling: Which has made some of your most learned *Rabbies* complain that your Scriptures are become, in the Words of the Prophet . . . as a *Book seal'd up* to you: And that the true sense of them will not be known till the coming of the *Messiah*, who will restore the Vowels and right Knowledge of the *Hebrew* Tongue.

It is long since the *Hebrew* has ceas'd to be the vulgar Language of your Nation, and consequently to be well understood by the *Jews* themselves, who now learn it at Schools, as other Men do . . . This occasion'd that the *Greek* Translation of the seventy was publickly read in the *Jewish* Synagogues many years before the coming of *Christ*.

This Translation they thought to have been divinely inspir'd, and made great boasts of it; as you may read in *Josephus*, and many other of your Authors: And it continu'd in this reputation with you, and was read in your Synagogues till *Christ* came, and for about an hundred years after: Then you rejected it because of the plain proofs that were brought out of it for our *Jesus* being the *Messiah*; and set up the spurious *Greek* Translation of *Aquila*, who was an Heathen, a Christian and a *Jew*, which he then made when the *Hebrew* Tongue was so greatly decay'd from that Purity which it confessedly retain'd when your seventy Priests made that famous Translation for *Ptolemy* King of *Ægypt*, about three hundred years before *Christ*: And was never question'd by any of you, but held in the highest veneration all that time, till after the coming of our Saviour, because of the flagrant testimonies it bore to him . . .

2. As the *Jews* have thus manifestly stood out against the conviction of the holy Scriptures, by inventing and using these Arts to corrupt them, at least to hide and obscure their true meaning; so have they for the same reason, *viz.* in prejudice to our *Messiah*, alter'd their former principles and notions, which they had received by Tradition from their Fathers. Thus finding that the notion of the [Logos], or *Word of God* . . . led directly to the Divinity of our Saviour, and all that is said of him in the Gospel, [the Jews presently forsook their own principles, and as early as *Justin Martyr* began to deny them . . .

3. The *Jews* finding that the mystical and primary sense of their Law did refer to the *Messiah*, and was most exactly and particularly fulfill'd and compleated in our Saviour; rather than be convinc'd by this, they have now (as the learned *Jew* that disputed with *Limborch*) deny'd that the Law was typical, or referred to any more perfect State: The contrary of which is plainly intimated, *Exod.* xxv. 40. From whence our Apostle convincingly argues, *Heb.* viii. 5. But the *Jews* now will have no Type in the Law, or the Office of the *Messiah* to extend beyond temporal Conquests, to any spiritual or heavenly Acquisitions; sticking in the bare Letter of the Law . . .

Your *Cabala* makes your outward Law but the *cortex* or shell of the hidden Mysteries that are contained it.

Yet you are now grown to that violent prejudice against this (tho' you would stick to your *Cabala* too, and think it divinely inspir'd) because it leads directly upon Christianity, that your learned *Jew* has set up this Principle . . . *That the outward Worship, as such, is more perfect than the internal*, And therefore, *That the outward Worship is not less grateful to God than the internal*. These are the Titles of his Chapters. And the end of setting up these desperate Positions is, to obviate the christian Argument, That the inward and spiritual Worship is chiefly regarded by God: and consequently the inward and spiritual meaning of the Law is much preferable to the Letter and outward observances . . .

4. The modern *Jews* have, since *Christ*'s time, gone away from the constant Tradition of their Fathers before *Christ* came, *viz.* That the *Messiah* wou'd shew himself to the World, and vouch his Commission by Miracles . . . And this contrivance discovers plainly their guilt, that it is not conviction which they want, but that they are resolv'd not to be convinc'd.

5. They have not only departed from the Traditions of their Fathers; but they have invented new and strange conceits, of which their Fathers, before *Christ* came, never dreamt. As of two *Messiah*'s, the one a suffering, the other a triumphing *Messiah*: To answer these two states of suffering and triumphing, which were foretold of the *Messiah*; and both fulfill'd in our blessed Saviour. To avoid which, the *Jews*, since his time, have invented these two *Messiah*'s . . . You can shew no footstep of any such Doctrine amongst the *Jews* before *Christ* came. And it shews the distress your latter *Rabbies* were

driven to, when they cou'd find no shift, but so groundless and foolish an Invention: Which is of a piece with your other fulsome and ridiculous Legends . . . of the *Messiah*'s sitting these one thousand six hundred years amongst the *Lepers* at the Gates of *Rome*. That he is in Paradise, but ty'd in a Womans Hair that he cannot come . . .

I I. I come now to other Obstacles, which lie on the *Christians* side.

First, The learned *Jew* that disputes with *Limborch*, complains of the great scandal given to the *Jews* in the Popish Countries.

1. By the Idolatry which they see practis'd there. They cannot bear to see the great God painted like an Old Man in their Churches and Mass-Books, in their Shops and Houses, and publickly sold by allowance: This they take to be the sin so strictly prohibited, *Deut*. iv. 15, 16. in the many other Scriptures. Besides their worshipping of Saints, Angels, *&c* . . .

2. There is another strange sort of Impediment, which the *Jews* have met with in Popish Countries; that is, That if any of them turn'd Christians, they forfeited all their Estates, on pretence that they or their Ancestors had got them by Usury. Of this several good Men in the Church of *Rome* have complain'd . . . How it is at this day at *Rome*, in *Spain*, *Portugal*, and other Popish Countries, I cannot tell . . .

Secondly, I come now to the reformed Churches, where the *Jews* meet with neither of the fore-mentioned impediments . . .

1. But there is another sort of impediment which they meet with there, that is, the various Sects which are tolerated, and own'd as Churches, tho' most opposite and contradictory to one another. This goes violently athwart the fixed and stated principle of the *Segullah* or *Peculium*, which God deliver'd to the *Jews* from the beginning, and implies the true notion of a Church, as being a *Peculium* or select Society, gather'd from amongst the rest of Mankind; under Governors and Laws, with promises and privileges of their own, peculiar to themselves, and independent of all others upon the Earth. Now the *Jews* cannot think this *Segullah* transferred to a christian Church, where there is no notion of any *Segullah* at all; or such a lame one, as admits and excludes no body. A Park without Pales! Which reduces the Church from a Society to a Sect . . . without any principle of Unity. A Church without a Bishop! A Body without a Head! This *Latitudinarian* no-principle is so perfectly adverse to the receiv'd notions of the *Jews* all along, that they can as easily believe no Faith as no Church . . .

2. Let me add, that you will be here free from another great scandal which you have met with more frequently in *Holland*, that is, *Socinianism*, to which some that oppos'd you there, made too near approaches. And if they had converted you, it had not been to Christianity; but rather to Idolatry, in paying divine honours and adoration to *Christ*, while they suppose him but a Creature . . . This vast prejudice you will likewise avoid in the Church of *England*, where these *Socinian* Heresies, on both sides, are detested and

exploded.

If you take scandal that such differences shou'd be amongst those who call themselves Christians, remember that your *Sadducees* deny'd the *Resurrection*, and *both Angels and Spirits*; which takes away the future State of Heaven. And this you now believe, and make it a great Article of your Creed; and say, that it was always the faith of the Jews; therefore you cannot object it against us, that there shou'd be divisions, even in fundamental points, and Schisms amongst us; since there has been the same amongst your selves, your *Samaritans*, *Saducees*, &c. And you will not think that this hurts the truth, to those who hold it.

From Charles Leslie, *A Short and Easy Method with the Jews, Wherein the Certainty of the Christian Religion is Demonstrated*, in *The Theological Works of the Reverend Mr. Charles Leslie* (London, W. Bowyer, 1721), I, pp. 76–85. (*A Short and Easy Method With the Jews* first appeared in 1698.)

(iv) Jewish customs and beliefs today

Bernard Picart (1673–1733) was a French designer and engraver. Coming from a Protestant family, he settled in Amsterdam in 1710, supplying plates and engravings to printers and booksellers on a variety of subjects. His monumental series of eleven large folio volumes on *Cérémonies et Coutumes Religieuses de Tous les Peuples du Monde* (*The ceremonies and religious customs of all the peoples of the world*) appeared between 1723 and 1743. Picart supplied the drawings, while the text describing the ceremonies, customs and beliefs of the different religions was mainly compiled from works by a number of authors including Henri, Comte de Boulainvilliers, Adrian Reland and Richard Simon. An English translation of the work was published in seven volumes in London, 1733–9, and an abridged version in one volume in 1741. The following extract comes from the abridgement. The section on the Jews is interesting not only because of its extensive coverage of Jewish beliefs and practices but also because it treats Judaism as a current faith rather than primarily as a religion of people of Old Testament and Apostolic times. It is largely dependent on the writings of Leon of Modena (1571–1648), a Jewish scholar whose family had gone to Italy after the expulsion of the Jews from France. The following passages on current Jewish customs and thought are only a small sample of a wide-ranging description which covers such topics as Jewish kitchen furniture, views on sleeping and dreaming, ablutions, synagogues, schools, rites, tithes, language, contracts, Sabbath observance and other festivals, treatment of women, children and slaves, heretics, and notions about death and beyond.

Concerning their Houses

I. When any *Jew* builds a House, he is obliged to leave some Part of it incompleat, pursuant to the Directions of the Rabbi's on this Topick, that he may the better remember the present Desolation of *Jerusalem* and the Temple; and in order to testify his unfeigned Sorrow, he must express himself in these Words of the Psalmist: *If I forget thee, O Jerusalem, may my Right Hand forget her Cunning.* Or, if he builds, he must leave at least a Cubit square of the Wall free from Lime, and write thereon in large Capitals those Words of the Psalmist just mentioned; or these, *Zecher la Chaban*, which signifies *a Memorial of Desolation*.

II. At the Doors of their Houses, Chambers, and all Places of publick Resort, they fix up against the Wall, at the Right Hand of the Entrance, a Reed, or any other Pipe, with a Parchment in it prepared for that purpose, whereon are written after a very correct Manner, these Words from *Deuteronomy*; *Hear, O Israel, the Lord our God is one Lord, &c.* as far as these other Words, *and thou shalt write them upon the Posts of thy House, and on thy Gates.* Then leaving a small Blank on the Parchment, these Words are continued; *And it shall come to pass, if ye shall hearken diligently unto my Commandments, &c.* as far as these Words, *and thou shalt write them upon the Door-Posts of thine House, and upon thy Gates.* This Parchment is rolled up, and enclosed within the Reed, and at the Bottom is written the Name *Sciaddai*. And whenever the *Jews* come in or go out, they touch this Place very devoutly; then kiss that Finger which touched it; and this is what they call *Mezuza*.

III. They have neither Picture, Image, nor Statue; neither will they permit any such Representations in their Houses, much less in their Synagogues, and other Places, set apart for divine Worship; conformable to that negative Commandment in the XXth of *Exodus*, and in several other Places of the Old Testament, which expressly saith, *thou shalt not make unto thee any graven Image.* But in *Italy* there are abundance of *Jews*, who have both Portraits and History Pieces in their Houses. They avoid however having any *Relievos*, especially those where the Bodies are compleat . . . (pp. 12 f).

Concerning their Charity to the Poor

I. Notwithstanding the *Jews* lie more open and exposed than any other Nation to injuries and Insults; and although but few of them are rich, and such as are, have little in their Possession that can properly be called Riches; yet those few supply the Necessities of their numerous Poor, and succour and relieve them at all Times, and on all Occasions; so that it must be allowed that the *Jews* are very indulgent to their Poor.

II. In all Cities of any Repute the Poor go on the Eve of the Sabbath, and other solemn Feasts, to the Houses of such as are most rich and substantial; and every House-keeper relieves them according to his Ability. Besides, the *Parnassim*, or *Memunin*, who are proper Persons appointed for that Purpose, send them Money constantly every Week, but chiefly to such Poor as are ashamed to beg, and to Widows and other old or infirm People, who are not able to make their personal Application.

III. A Fund is likewise raised for the Poor out of the charitable Contributions which are put into the Box of the Synagogue; and out of the Money which is collected by the Priests in the Time of their divine Service.

IV. When there is a Necessity to bestow a larger Charity than ordinary, either to one of the Poor, or on Account of the Marriage of a young Woman, the Redemption of a Slave, the Rulers of the Synagogue direct the Reader to go round the Congregation, who, as he passes by them, still names the Persons to whom he speaks; saying, God bless *N.* who will bestow such or such a Sum towards such a Charity. As the *Jews* do not touch any Money on the Sabbath, and as this Collection is generally made on that Day, such Persons as are then charitably disposed, oblige themselves on their Words to give such a Sum to the Reader upon that Account; and this verbal Promise is called *Nedavia*, i.e. *Liberality*; which they always discharge before the Week is at an End.

V. There are also in all populous Cities several Assemblies or Clubs, who are very beneficent to their Poor: Some assist the Sick, others bury the Dead; that Society which collects the small Alms, are generally called *Ghemilud Hassadim*; that which undertakes the Redemption of Slaves, *Pidion Suevim*; and they who employ themselves about the Marriage of the young women are called *Hassibetuloth* . . . (p. 18).

Concerning Trade

I. Every Man is obliged, both by their written and their oral Law, to be true to his Word, and not over-reach or defraud any Person whatever, *Jew* or Stranger, and in all their Dealings to comply with the Rules of Commerce prescribed in several Places of the Scripture, and particularly *Leviticus*, xix. 33. &c.

II. Some have ungenerously asserted, that the *Jews* are under an Obligation to cheat the Christians, whenever it is in their Power, but this is mere Scandal and Ill-Nature, and only charged upon them to render them Objects of Contempt. So far is this Aspersion from being true and just, that several Rabbi's have written against it; and even our Master *Bachii* hath composed a Treatise in his Book *Cad Achema*, Letter *Ghimel Ghezela*, where he lays down this Proposition, That it is a much greater Crime to defraud a Person who is not a *Jew*, than one who is; because the Action in the first Place is wicked in itself, and because the Scandal is the greater: For which Reason such a Practice is called *Chillul Ascem*, or *a Prophanation of the Name of God*, which is a Sin of the most heinous Nature.

III. It is very probable, however, that as they are reduced to a deplorable Condition, by being dispersed all over the Earth, and almost every where debarr'd from the Privilege of holding any Lands, and deprived of all the certain Ways of Commerce, or advancing their Stock, their Souls have been corrupted, and have degenerated from the primitive Integrity of the *Israelites* . . . (p. 20).

Of the Theology of the Jews

The whole *Jewish* Creed is comprised in thirteen Articles, called by them the fundamental Principles of their Religion; and in this they follow *R. Moses*, Son of *Maimon*, who digested these Principles into Order; the first of which relates to the Existence of the supreme Being; the second to his Unity; the third to his Spirituality, and the absolute Impossibility of his being Corporeal; the fourth to his Eternity, a Perfection peculiar to himself alone; the fifth to the Service and Adoration due to him alone; the sixth to Prophecy, *viz.* that there have been Prophets, and may be more amongst the *Hebrews*; the seventh to the peculiar Prophecy of *Moses*, which was above the Degree of Prophecy communicated to the rest of the Prophets: the eighth absolutely determines that the Law of *Moses* came not from himself, but that God was the sole Author of it; and was graciously pleased likewise afterwards to expound it: the ninth specifies, that this Law is immutable, and that no Person whatever is permitted to add to, or diminish it: the tenth establishes God's Providence, and his peculiar Regard and Affection for all his Creatures: the eleventh implies, that God will be the sure Rewarder of all those who observe the Precepts of the Law, and the severe Punisher of all those who dare to transgress it: The twelfth specifies, that the Messiah will come, and that altho' the Time thereof may be prolonged, and must not be determined, it ought however to be depended on as absolutely certain: the thirteenth and last relates to the Resurrection of the Dead. These thirteen fundamental Principles of the *Jewish* Religion distinguish them from all other Nations, as the sole Favourites of the Almighty, and his true Children, to whom he promised the Inheritance; and for this Reason they account all such as deny these Principles, abominably wicked and deserving Death itself. The *Jews* therefore would doubtless be much to be feared even at this Day, were they invested with Power . . .

What the *Jewish* Doctors say in their Writings relating to Angels, is not always to be taken in the literal Sense, it being little else but Allegories and

Fables invented at Pleasure by such People as made a wrong Use of their vacant Hours, and of the easy Credulity of the illiterate Vulgar: not to mention the Introduction of their Names for the Solution of some Difficulty or other, as the antient Poets brought in their Gods on the like Occasions. These very Doctors were the Projectors of the *Cabalistick* Art, which is a chimerical Science, without the least Foundation: And therefore such *Jews* as apply themselves to it are for the most part Enthusiasts, and so possessed with their own divine Fancies, as to imagine that by the Assistance of this Art they are able to work Miracles at their Pleasure . . . The *Jews*, particularly those of *Poland*, and some other Places in the North, are in this respect so super-stitious, that in case any of them are accidentally condemned to Death, they have recourse to this practical *Cabala*; but we do not find it has proved of any great Advantage to them, except in the historical Dissertations which they have published relating to the Miracles performed by it; nay sometimes it unluckily falls out that their Judges, being ignorant of the Vanity of that Science, pass Sentence on them, and punish them as Conjurors . . .

From Bernard Picart, *The Ceremonies and Religious Customs of the Various Nations of the Known World*, with additions and remarks omitted by the French Author, Faithfully Abridg'd from the French Original (London, 1741), pp. 13–44.

I V

Islam

The following passages indicate some of the different ways in which Islam was treated in this period. Most of the comments were basically hostile, attempting in one way or other to refute any claim to divine origin and authority. These approaches are illustrated by the passages from Smith, Barrow and Prideaux. Others, though, seek to correct erroneous reports about Islam and to present it in a more favourable light. Reland and Boulainvilliers provide examples of this less common attitude. The piece from Pitts gives a first-hand account of how a captured seaman was forced to become a Muslim. (For other remarks about Islam, cf. I (i) and VII (ii).)

(i) Seven reasons why Islam is false

Henry Smith (1550?–91) was a Puritan divine. While basically in sympathy with the Church of England, conscientious scruples over subscription made him unwilling to accept parochial charge. He therefore served as a 'Lecturer', first at Husbands Bosworth and then, from 1587, at St Clement Danes without Temple Bar in London. His preaching brought him such fame that he was known as 'silver-tongued Smith'. Because of ill-health he resigned his lectureship and returned to Husbands Bosworth in 1590. A collection of his sermons was edited by him but not published until after his death, and soon passed through several editions. The following passage comes from a small work, *Gods Arrow Against Atheists*, which first appeared in 1593 with his sermons. In it he not only attacks Muslims but other opponents of the Christianity of the Church of England, from atheists, infidels throughout the world, and Roman Catholics, to Brownists and Barrowists. His conclusion is that 'the Church of England is the true Church of God from which it is utterly unlawfull to make a separation' (p. 96). The following extract shows how he explains away the rise of Islam and gives his reasons for asserting 'the vanitie of the Turkes religion'. The material is not always edifying but it indicates how Mahomet and Islam were often presented at this time. The reference in the third point is presumably to the legend repeated earlier in the chapter of how Mahomet's corpse was first left until it stank in the hope that he would rise and then was placed in an 'yron coffin' which was suspended in the air in the Temple because of 'mightie Load-stones' that had been placed on the roof of the Temple.

This *Mahomet* while hee liued, vsed the companie of Christians, Iewes, and Infidels . . . And to the end his law might be the more fauoured, hee borrowed something of euery Sect. Satan furnished him with three instruments, as helpes to bring his mischieuous intent about. The first was a Iew, a great Astronomer and a Magician, who opened to him at large the Iewish follies: the second, one *Iohn* of Antioch: the third, one *Sergius* a Monk, both abominable heretickes. Euery one plaid his part . . . The Christians haue Sonday for their Sabbath, the Iewes Saterday, and *Mahomet* Friday, to dissent from the Hebrewes and Christians: or, as *Antonius* writeth in the honour of *Venus* the Goddesse of Arabia, thereby the rather to winne that countrie people: and thus it pleased him to deuise a Religion mixt of all these, to the ende hee might haue of all religions some to build vp his kingdome. And indeed *Mahomet* tooke the aduantage of the time: for that time was a time of dissension among Princes, and of diuision amongst those which called themselues Christians. *Heraclius* the Emperor, and *Chosdroes* King of Persia were at deadly enmitie, one warring against another. The Scythian nation were of neither side, but at last against both, raising a power of themselues, hauing *Mahomet* there ring-leader. The Church was troubled with diuers sects & heresies, as with Nestorians, Iacobites, Monothelites, &c. And then was there contention amongst the Bishops, who should haue the proud title of vniuersall Bishop. God was highly displeased with this wickednesse, and suffered Nations to rise as a rod or scourge to whip his people: for where the hedge is broken, there it is easie for the beasts of the field to enter and spoyle. Now the vanity and falsehood of this religion may be proued thus.

1. First, by the newnes of it: for it is but of late yeeres begun, and there was neuer any prophecie that did allow of such a Prophet, or of the doctrine of such a one. And therefore he cometh in his own name, and so consequently not to be receiued.

2. Secondly, hee did no miracle at his comming, and therefore no reason that any should beleeue in him. Hee spake vnto the Saracens of himselfe: . . . I am not sent vnto you with miracles & signes. There was no diuine power shewed in all his practise.

3. Thirdly, it is manifest that *Mahomet* was a false Prophet, because he said that within three daies after his death he should ascend into heauen; which was notoriously false, as before appeareth.

4. Fourthly, the religion of *Mahomet* is fleshly, consisting in naturall delights and corporall pleasures, which shew that man, and not the diuine spirit of God, is the author thereof: for it is permitted the Saracens by that his law to haue foure wiues (though these be of nigh kinne) yea fiue, marrying them virgins, and to take besides as many of them which they haue bought and taken captiues, as their abilitie will serue to maintaine. The paradise likewise promised to his followers is this, namely they shall haue garments of silke; with all sorts of colours, bracelets of gold and Amber, parlours and banquetti..g houses vpon floods and riuers, vessels of gold and siluer, Angels seruing them, bringing in gold, milke, siluer, wine, lodgings furnished, cushions, pillowes, and downe beds, most beautiful women to accompanie them, maidens & virgins with twinckling eyes . . . and to bee short, whatsoeuer the flesh shall desire to eate. Thus fleshly people haue a fleshly religion, and a fleshly paradise to inhabite. But like Prophet, like people, and like religion: for *Mahomet* himselfe was such a flleshly fellow, as that though modest eares are loth to heare, yet because the filthinesse of this Prophet may not be concealed, I must vtter it: Hee committed buggery with an Asse; *Bonsinius* writeth it: Againe, hee committed adulterie with another mans wife, that vpon displeasure was from her husband: and when he perceiued the murmure of the people, hee fained that hee had receiued a paper from heauen, wherein it was permitted him so to doe, to the end he might beget Prophets and worthie men . . .

5. *Mahomets* law is a tyrannicall law: for hee made it death to dispute of it, and if any man speak against it (saith he) . . . Let him be traiterously put to death . . . Moreouer, hee wrote in the Arabian tongue, and taught his followers, that his religion . . . Began by the sword, is holden by the sword, and is finished or ended in the sword. Which sheweth that the sword and arme of flesh is all the author and protector that his religion hath . . .

6. As *Mahomets* religion is defended by force of sword and fraud . . . so likewise did it begin, as by the force of sword, so likewise by notable fraude, and was established through wiles, deceit, subtiltie, and lyes. For first hee hauing the falling sicknes, perswaded his wife and others, that it was the power of God, and the presence of the Angell *Gabriel* that caused him to fall down . . . He made the Saracens beleeue, that before God made the world, there was written in the Throne of God, *There is no God, but the God of Mahomet.* When he had framed his Alcoran, and bound it vp faire, he caused secretly a wilde Asse to bee taken, and the booke to be bound about his necke, and as he preached vnto the people, vpon a sudden he stood amazed, as if some great secrecy were reuealed to him from aboue, and brake out and told the people; *Behold God hath sent you a lawe from Heaven: goe to such a desert, there*

ye shall find an Asse, and a booke tyed about his necke. The people ran in great haste, they found it so as he had said, they take the Asse, they bring the book, they honor the Prophet . . .

7. *Mahomets* religion is no true religion, but a meere deuice of his owne, and of three others his false conspirators: for he hath patched together his Alcoran of the doctrine of Heathens, Indians and Arabians, of superstitious Iewes, of Rechabits, of false Christians & heretickes, . . . of illusions, and inuentions of their owne: and lastly, (for further credit) he borrowed some out of the old and new Testament. But God will not thus be serued . . . Satan being coniured to deliuer the truth of the Alcoran of *Mahomet*, said, that therin were comprised twelue thousand lyes, and the rest was truth: by al likelihood very little. And therefore I conclude, that there is no euidence to proue *Mahomet* a true Prophet, many to prooue him to be a false Prophet, & blasphemous, & presumptuous, & his religion to be a wicked, carnall, absurd, and false religion, proceeding from a proud spirit, and humane, subtile, and corrupt inuention, & euen from the diuell, the craftie father of lies, a murtherer, and mankiller from the beginning. And so much hereof may suffice.

From Henry Smith, *Gods Arrow Against Atheists* (London, imprinted by G.M. for Edward Brewster, and Robert Bird, 1628) pp. 46–52.

(ii) *The circumstances of Islam's rise show it not to be from God*

For Isaac Barrow (1630–77) see III (i) *supra*. In the following passage from a series of sermons on the Apostles' Creed, Barrow asserts 'the Impiety and Imposture of Paganism and Mahometanism'. After declaring that paganism is the product of either human or devilish invention and shows the need for revelation, he turns to Islam. His argument against it is that the circumstances of its origin and spread show that it cannot reasonably be regarded as the result of God's initiative and that Islam confirms this by refusing to submit itself to the canon of reason. To develop his case, Barrow compares the character, composition and situation of the birth of Islam with that of Christianity. Whereas the latter is said to have appeared at a most suitable time for the propagation of a message from God and was communicated by persons of exemplary character in an appropriate way, Islam is held to be stained by the immorality of its founders, to present a compilation of errors and to have appeared at a most unpropitious time for the spread of heavenly truth. It is thus, according to Barrow, obvious that Islam cannot be accepted as being divine. This form of argument, incidentally, has been used at times against Christianity when it has been queried how credible it is to hold that God chose Palestine and the Jews as the location of his revealing and redeeming activity – an argument whose first form is presumably Nathanael's 'Can any good come from Nazareth?' (John 1, 45) Presupposed in Barrow's remarks are not only somewhat distorted reports about the rise of Islam but also a firm conviction that God's actions must be eminently reasonable – and recognisable as such.

. . . *Paganism* did not proceed from divine Revelation, but from Humane invention or suggestion Diabolical.

I shall only adjoin, that the considering this case of *Heathens* may be of good use, (and to that use indeed St. *Paul* hath largely applied it) in confirming what we before urged, The great need of some full and plain Revelation to the world of God's mind, in order to God's glory and man's good; as also it is of singular use (which also the same *Apostle* frequently did put it to) by the contemplation thereof to discover our great obligations to bless and thank God for his great mercy in revealing his heavenly truth to us, from whence we are freed from errours and mischiefs so deplorable; which otherwise from humane infirmity, and the Devil's malice, we should easily (and in a manner necessarily) have incurred.

That Pretence was ancienter in standing: but there hath even since Christianity started up another, (*Mahometanism*) which if not upon other accounts, yet in respect to its age, and to the port it bears in the world, demands some consideration; for it hath continued a long time, and hath vastly over-spread the earth: neither is it more formidable in its looks, than peremptory in its words; vaunting it self to be no less than a complete, a general, an ultimate declaration of God's pleasure, cancelling and voiding all others that have gone before. But examining both the substance and circumstances thereof, considering the quality of the instruments by whom, of the times when it was introduced; of the places where, of the people who first, or afterward did receive it; the manner of its rise, progress and continuance; as also the matter it teaches or injoins; we shall not find stamped on it the genuine characters of a divine original and authority; but have great reason to deem it a brood of most lewd and impudent cozenage. In times of great disturbance and confusion, when barbarous nations, like torrents, did overflow the world, and turned all things upside down; in times of general corruption and disorder in mens minds and manners, when even among Christians ignorance and superstition, dissension and uncharitableness, impiety and iniquity, did greatly prevail; in a very blind and obscure corner of the earth, among a crew of wild thieves and runnagates (such have those *Arabians* been always famed and known to be) this *Sect* had its birth and fosterage; among those fierce and savage over-runners of the world it got its growth and stature; into this sort of people (being indeed in its constitution well accomodated to their humour and *genius*) it was partly insinuated by jugling tricks, partly driven by seditious violence; the first Author hereof being a person, according to the description given of him in their own Legends, of no honest or honourable qualities, but having all the marks of an Impostour; rebellious and perfidious, inhumane and cruel, lewd and lascivious, of a base education, of a fraudulent and turbulent disposition, of a vicious life, pretending to enthusiasms, and working of wonders; but these such as were both in their nature absurd and incredible, and for their use vain and unprofitable: at such a season, and in such a soil, by such means and by such a person (abetted by Associates like himself, whom his arts, or their interests had inveagled to join with him) was this Religion first planted; and for its propagation it had that great advantage of falling in the way of barbarous people, void of learning and civility, and not prepossessed with other notions, or any sense of Religion; who thence (as mankind is naturally susceptive of religious impressions) were capable and apt to admit any Religion first offering it self, especially one so gross as this was, so agreeable to their furious humours and lusts. Afterward being furnished with such Champions, it diffused it self by rage and terror of arms; convincing mens minds only by the sword, and using no other arguments but blows. Upon the same grounds of ignorance and force, it still subsists; neither offering for, nor taking against it self any reason; refusing all examination, and upon extreme penalties forbidding any dispute about its truth; being indeed so far (whether out of judgment or fatal instinct) wise, as conscious to its self, or foreboding, that the letting in of a little light, and a moderate liberty of discussing its pretences, would easily overthrow it. Now that Divine wisdom should chuse those black and boisterous times to publish his will, is, as if the King should purposely order his Proclamations to be made in a tempestuous night, when no man scarce dared to stir out, nor any man could well see what was done, or hear what was said; much fitter surely to that purpose were a serene and calm day; a time of general civility and peace, like that of *Augustus Caesar*. That the declaration of God's mind should issue from the desarts of Arabia (that den of robbers) is as if the King should cause his Edicts to be set up in the blindest and dirtiest nook of the Suburbs; the Market-cross surely, or the Exchange (the place of most general and ordinary concourse) such as, in respect to the world, was the flourishing Empire of *Rome*, were more convenient, and wisely chosen for that purpose: that passing over the more gentle and tractable part of his people, a Prince should send his laws to a rabble of *Banditti*; should pick out for his messenger a most dissolute Varlet, attended with a crew of desperate ruffians, resolved to buffet and rifle all they met; were an odd way of proceeding: To communicate his pleasure unto the better and more orderly sort of people (such as were the subjects of that well governed Empire) by persons of good meaning, mild disposition, and innocent behaviour, (such as were the *Apostles* of our Lord) in a quiet and gentle manner (such as these only used) would surely better become a worthy Prince: Thus even the exteriour circumstances of *Mahome-tanism* (both absolutely and in comparison) belonging to its rise, its growth, its continuance (so full of indecency, of iniquity, of inhumanity) ground strong presumptions against its divinity; or rather plainly deminstrate, that it could not proceed from God, whose truth cannot need such instruments, or such courses to maintain it, whose goodness certainly abhors them. But farther, if we look into the matter and inward frame thereof, we shall find it a mass of absurd opinions, odd stories, and uncouth ceremonies; compounded chiefly of the dregs of Christian Heresies, together with some ingredients of *Judaism* and *Paganism* confusedly jumbled, or unskilfully tempered together. From Christian Heresies it seems to have derived its negative Doctrines, opposite to Christianity; as for instance, when allowing Christ much respect, it yet denies his being the Son of God, and that he did really suffer; rejecting his true story, it affixes false ones upon him: as also some positive ones; for example, that unreasonable opinion, so much mis-beseeming God, that God hath a body (*Mahomet* forsooth once touched his hand, and felt it very cold) might be drawn from the *Anthropomorphites*; that Doctrine concerning the fatal determination of all events (so prejudicial to all religion, subverting the foundations of justice between God and man, man's free choice in serving God, God's free disposal of rewards sutable to mens actions) they probably borrowed from the *Manichees*, a Sect that much obtained in those *Eastern* parts. The *Jew* contributed his ceremonies of Circumcision and frequent purgations by washing, his abstinence from swines flesh, his allowance of polygamy and divorce: I might add, that perhaps from him they filcht that proud, inhumane, and uncivil humour of monopolizing divine favour and good-will to themselves . . .

> *From* Isaac Barrow, *The Works* (published by John Tillotson, London, printed for James Round, Jacob Tonson and William Taylor, third edition, 1716), II, pp. 154–5. (The first edition of *The Works* was in four volumes and appeared 1683–7.)

(iii) *Mahomet's revelations and the production of the Koran*

Humphrey Prideaux (1648–1724) was a student of Christ Church, Oxford and Busby's Hebrew lecturer there. He left the college in 1686 when James II made a Roman Catholic its dean and went to Norwich, of which he had been a canon since 1681 and where he became dean in 1702. He was involved in controversies with Roman Catholics and welcomed the revolution of 1688. In the following year, he supported plans to change the Prayer Book to make it more acceptable to dissenters. In 1691 he was offered but declined the Hebrew Chair at Oxford which had become vacant on the death of Edward Pococke. Prideaux's literary fame rests on two works, *The Life of Mahomet* (1697) and *The Old and New Testament Connected in the History of the Jews* (two volumes, 1716–18). Of both works it is said that when the manuscript was offered to a bookseller, he declined it on the grounds that he 'could wish there were a little more humour in it'! *The Life of Mahomet* is in fact an attack upon the 'deists'. It uses the alleged evidence of Mahomet's career to argue that they are unjustified in rejecting Christianity as an imposture by showing, in contrast, what the character of such an imposture would be like as exemplified in the case of Mahomet. In the following passage from the work – of which the tenth edition appeared in 1808 – Prideaux discusses the character of Mahomet's revelations and how the Koran was compiled from them, as well as Mahomet's attempt to meet the challenge to authenticate his claims by miracles through the story of the night ride to heaven. The first extract also includes an attack on the Socinians and the final one lists what Prideaux sees as the distinguishing marks of an imposture – marks which he regards as evident in the case of Mahomet and Islam and absent in that of Christ and Christianity. The material is a good example of how reports about other religions were in fact used – or abused – to make points in debates within Christianity.

He [*sc.* Mahomet] did not pretend to deliver to them any new *Religion*, but to revive the old one, which *God* first gave unto *Adam*; and when lost in the corruption of the Old World, restored it again by Revelation to *Abraham*, who taught it his Son *Ismael* their Forefather; and that he, when he first planted himself in *Arabia*, instructed Men in the same *Religion* which he had received from *Abraham*; but their Posterity afterwards corrupted it into *Idolatry*, and that *God* had now sent him to destroy this *Idolatry*, and again restore the *Religion* of *Ismael* their Forefather . . .

He allowed both the *Old and the New Testament*, and that *Moses* and *Jesus Christ* were *Prophets* sent from God; but that the *Jews* and *Christians* had corrupted these holy Writings, and that he was sent to purge them from those Corruptions, and restore the *Law of God* to that purity in which it was first deliver'd; and therefore most of those Passages which he takes out of the *Old and New Testament*, are related otherwise by him in his *Alcoran*, than we have them in those *Sacred Books*. And in this certainly he acted much wiser than our *Socinians*, who with him denying the *Holy Trinity* and the *Divinity of our Saviour*, yet still allow the *holy Scriptures*, as now in our hands, to be genuine and uncorrupted, with which their Doctrine is in the most manifest manner totally inconsistent. If they had with this their *Master* denied the *Scriptures* which we now have, as well as the *Trinity*, and the *Divinity* of our *Saviour*, which are so evidently proved by them, and forged others in their stead, they might have made their impious *Hypothesis* look much more plausible, than now it can possibly appear to be.

He pretended to receive all his *Revelations* from the *Angel Gabriel*, and that he was sent from *God* on purpose to deliver them unto him. And whereas he was subject to the *Falling Sickness*, whenever the Fit was upon him, he pretended it to be a *Trance*, and that the *Angel Gabriel* was come from *God* with some new *Revelations* unto him . . .

His pretended *Revelations* he put into several *Chapters*, the Collection of which make up his *Alcoran*, which is the *Bible* of the *Mahometans*. The Original of this Book he taught them was laid up in the *Archives of Heaven*, and that the *Angel Gabriel* brought him the Copy of it Chapter by Chapter, according as occasion required they should be published to the People. Part of these he published at *Mecca*, before his flight from thence; and the other part at *Medina*, which he did after this manner. When he had forged a new *Chapter*, which he intended to publish, he first dictated it to his *Secretary*, and then delivered the written Paper to be read to his *Followers* till they had learnt it by heart; which being done, he had the Paper brought to him again, which he laid up in a *Chest*, which he called the *Chest of his Apostleship*. This he did, I suppose, in imitation of the *Ark* or holy *Chest* among the *Jews*, in which the Authentick Copy of their *Law* was reposited. This *Chest* he left in the keeping of *Haphsa*, one of his Wives, and out of it, after his death, was the *Alcoran* compiled, in the same manner as *Homer's Rhapsodies* were out of the loose *Poems* of that *Poet*. *Abu Beker*, who succeeded the *Impostor*, first made the Collection . . . having recourse to *Haphsa*'s Chest, partly out of the Papers which he found there, and partly out of the Memory of those who had learnt them by heart, when the *Impostor* first delivered them unto them, composed the Book. For several of those Papers being lost, and others so defaced as not to be read, he was forced to take in the assistance of those who pretended to remember what the *Impostor* had taught them, to make up the matter, and under this pretence made use of their advice to frame the Book, as he thought would best answer his purpose. When the Work was compleated, he caused the Original to be laid up in the same Chest, out of which he had compiled it, which he still continued in the keeping of *Haphsa*, and then delivered out Copies of it among his Followers. But the Book had not been long published, but so many various Readings were got into the Copies and so many Absurdities discovered in the Book it self, that when *Othman* came to be

Caliph, he found it necessary to call it in again to be licked into a better shape; and therefore having commanded all to bring in their Copies under the pretence of correcting them by the Original in the keeping of *Haphsa*, he caused them all to be burnt, and then published that *Alcoran* a-new model'd by him, which we have, . . . This was done in the 32d year of the *Hegira*, Ann. 652. twenty one years after the death of the *Impostor*; after which time the Book underwent no other Correction . . . (pp. 16–20).

In the twelfth Year of his pretended Mission, is placed the *Mesra*, that is, his famous Night-journey from *Mecca* to *Jerusalem*, and from thence to *Heaven*, of which he tells us in the 17th Chapter of his *Alcoran*. For the People calling on him for Miracles to prove his Mission, and he being able to work none, to salve the matter, he invents this Story of his Journey to *Heaven*; which must be acknowledged to have Miracle enough in it, by all those who have Faith to believe it . . . On his relating this *Extravagant Fiction* to the People the next Morning after he pretended the thing hapned, it was received by them as it deserved, with a *general hoot*; some laughed at the ridiculousness of the Story, and others taking indignation at it, cryed out shame upon him for telling them such *an abominable Lye*, and by way of reproach, bid him ascend up to *Heaven* by day-light there immediately before them all, that they might see it with their Eyes, and then they would believe him. And even of his *Disciples*, a great many were so ashamed of him for this Story, that they left him thereon; and more would have followed their Example, but that *Abu Beker* came in to put a stop to the defection, by vouching the truth of all that Mahomet had related, and professed his firm belief to the whole of it . . .

The *Imposture* was never in greater danger of being totally blasted, than by this *ridiculous Fable*, such a stumbling-block did it lay even before those of his own Party, and therefore he needed to interpose the utmost of his Art to support the Credit of it; for which purpose he not only got his Friend *Abu Beker* to be a Voucher to it; but also brings in *God* himself in two places of his *Alcoran* beari[n]g witness thereto, that is, in the Chapter of *the Children of Israel*, and in the Chapter of *the Star* . . . But how ridiculous soever the Story may appear, *Mahomet* had his Design therein, beyond barely telling such a miraculous Adventure of himself to the People . . . For could he once make it believed among his *Followers*, that he had there such a Converse with *God* as *Moses* had with him in the *Mount*, and was there fully instructed by him in the knowledge of all Divine Truths, as this Story pretends he was, he thought he should therein have a sufficient Foundation to build this pretence upon, and might by a just consequence from it, claim the whole which he aimed at; and he was not mistaken herein. For how ridiculous soever the thing at first appeared, yet in the result he carried his Point, and obtained all that by the Project, which he proposed to himself from it. For the whole of it at length going down with those who had swallowed the rest of his *Imposture*, from that time all his Sayings became looked on as Sacred Truths brought down from *Heaven*, and every word which at any time dropped from so enlightned a Person (as this Story supposeth him to be) as well as every Action which he did, any way relating to his *Religion*, were all carefully observed by them; which being after his death all collected together from the Memoirs of those who conversed with him, make up those Volumes of *Traditions* from him, which they call the *Sonnah*, which are with the *Mahometans* the same in respect of the *Alcoran*, that the *Oral Law* among the *Jews* is in respect of the *Written* . . . (pp. 46, 55–9).

In all these Instances I have mentioned, it appears how much he made his Imposture serve his Lust. And indeed almost the whole of his *Alcoran* was in like manner framed to answer some purpose or other of his, according as occasion required. If any new thing were to be put on foot, any Objection against him or his Religion to be answered, any Difficulty to be solved, any Discontent among his People to be quieted, any Offence to be removed, or any thing else done for the Interest of his Designs, his constant recourse was to the Angel *Gabriel* for a new *Revelation*; and out comes some addition to his *Alcoran* to serve his turn herein. So that the most of it was made on such like occasions, to influence his Party to what he intended. And all his *Commentators* thus far acknowledge it, that they are on every Chapter very particular in assigning for what Causes and for whose sakes it was sent down from Heaven unto them. But hereby it came to pass that abundance of Contradictions got into this Book. For as the Interest and Design of the *Impostor* varied, so was he forced to make his pretended *Revelations* vary also; which is a thing so well known to those of his *Sect*, that they all acknowledge it; and therefore where the Contradictions are such, as they cannot salve them, there they will have one of the contradicting places to be revoked. And they reckon in the whole *Alcoran*, above an hundred and fifty verses which are thus *revoked*; which is the best shift they can make to solve the Contradictions and Inconsistencies of it. But thereby they do exceedingly betray the Unsteadiness and Inconstancy of him that was the Author of it. (pp. 131 f)

From the appended *A Discourse for the Vindicating of Christianity from the Charge of Imposture. Offer'd, By Way of Letter, to the Consideration of the Deists of the Present Age.*

Gentlemen,
If I am not mistaken, the Reason you give for your Renouncing that Religion ye were Baptized into, and is the Religion of the Country in which ye were born, is, *That the Gospel of Jesus Christ is an Imposture:* An Assertion that I tremble to repeat . . . Now the *Marks* and *Characters* which I look on to be inseparable from every such *Imposture*, are these following: 1. That it must always have for its end some carnal Interest. 2. That it can have none but wicked Men for the Authors of it. 3. That both these must necessarily appear

in the very Contexture of the *Imposture* it self. 4. That it can never be so fram'd, but that it must contain some palpable Falsities, which will discover the Falsity of all the rest. 5. That where-ever it is first propagated, it must be done by Craft and Fraud. 6. That when entrusted with many Conspirators, it can never be long conceal'd. And, 7. That it can never be establish'd, unless back'd with Force and Violence. That all these must belong to every *Imposture*, and all particularly did so to *Mahometanism*; and that none of them can be charged upon *Christianity*, is what I shall now proceed to shew you . . .

> From Humphrey Prideaux, *The True Nature of Imposture Fully Display'd in the Life of Mahomet. With A Discourse annex'd for the Vindicating of Christianity from this Charge, Offered to the Consideration of the Deists of the Present Age* (London, E. Curll, J. Hooke, and T. Caldecott, sixth edition, 1716), pp. 16–20; 46, 55–9; 131 f; 141, 144. (The first edition was published in 1697.)

(iv) Conversion to Islam

Joseph Pitts (1663–1735) came from Exeter. In 1678 he sailed as an apprentice in a merchant ship to the West Indies and Newfoundland. On the return voyage the ship was captured off the Spanish coast by Algerine pirates. Pitts was taken to Algiers and sold to a merchant. In 1680 he was bought by another master from whom he tried, with the aid of the English consul, to buy his freedom but he failed to raise the hundred pounds that was demanded. In this situation force was used to compel him to become a Muslim. He was then sold to a third master, Eumer, who treated him well, took him on pilgrimage to Mecca and, while in Mecca, gave him his 'letter of freedom'. He stayed as a paid servant with him until 1693 when he managed to escape with the support of the English consul at Smyrna. On landing in England he was impressed into the navy but managed to secure his release, returning to Exeter in 1694 where he is recorded as still living in 1731. In 1704 he published his *Faithful Account of the Religion and Manners of the Mahometans* which not only reports his adventures but provides one of the earliest records by an Englishman of the pilgrimage to Mecca. Although Pitts protests his unwillingness to become a Muslim, his description of that faith is interestingly sympathetic and he was confessedly impressed with many aspects of its adherents' devotion to it. The following extract is from his account of his conversion. Although his profession of faith was extracted from him by force, he does indicate in other comments that those who compelled him saw his conversion as a meritorious act. He also indicates in this extract the ceremonies that attended a voluntary conversion to Islam.

His younger Brother would be frequently (behind his Back, and sometimes before his Face) perswading me to turn *Mahometan*, and to gain me, made me large Offers; but I little regarded them. And I can truly appeal to Almighty God, that it was not out of Choice, or Inclination, or Perswasion, or any Temporal Advantage, that I became a *Mahometan*, for I abhorred the Thoughts of such an *Apostasy* . . .

But finding all these Methods to be ineffectual to the End they drove at, the two Brothers consulted together, and resolv'd upon *Cruelty*, and *Violence*, to see what that would do. Accordingly, on a certain Day, when my *Patroon*'s Barber came to trim him, I being there to give Attendance, my *Patroon* bid me kneel down before him; which I did: He then ordered the Barber to cut off my Hair with his Scissars; but I mistrusting somewhat of their Design, struggled with them; but by stronger Force my Hair was cut off, and then the Barber went about to shave my Head, my *Patroon* all the while holding my Hands. I kept shaking my Head, and he kept striking me in the Face. After my Head, with much ado, was shaved, my *Patroon* would have me take off my Clothes, and put on the *Turkish* Habit. I told him plainly I would not: Whereupon I was forthwith hal'd away to another Tent, in which we kept our Provision; where were two Men, *viz.* the *Cook*, and the *Steward*; one of which held me, while the other stript me, and put on me the *Turkish* Garb. I all this while kept crying, and told my *Patroon*, that although he had chang'd my *Habit*, yet he could never change my *Heart*. The Night following, before he lay down to sleep, he call'd me, and bid me kneel down by his Bed-side, and then used Entreaties that I would gratify him in renouncing my *Religion*. I told him it was against my *Conscience*, and withal, desired him to sell me, and buy another Boy, who perhaps might more easily be won; but as for my part, I was afraid I should be everlastingly damn'd, if I complied with his Request. He told me, he would pawn his Soul for mine, and many other *importunate* Expressions did he use. At length I desired him to let me go to bed, and I would pray to God, and if I found any better Reasons suggested to my mind than what I then had, to turn, by the next Morning, I did not know what I might do; but if I continued in the same mind I was, I desired him to say no more to me on that Subject. This he agreed to, and so I went to Bed. But (whatever ail'd him) having not Patience to stay till the Morning for my Answer, he awoke me in the Night, and ask'd me what my Sentiments now were. I told him they were the same as before. Then he took me by the Right-hand, and endeavoured to make me hold up the Fore-finger, as they usually do when they speak those Words, viz. *La Allah ellallah, Mohammed Resul Allah* (which initiates them *Turks* (as I have related before) but I did with all my might bend it down, so that he saw nothing was to be done with me without *Violence*; upon which he presently call'd two of his Servants, and commanded them to tie up my Feet with a Rope to the Post of the Tent; and when they had so done, he with a great Cudgel fell a beating of me upon my bare Feet: And being a very strong Man, and full of Passion, his blows fell heavy indeed; and the more he beat me, the more chafed and enraged he was) and declared, that, in short, if I would not turn, he would beat me to Death. I roar'd out to feel the Pain of his cruel Strokes; but the more I cry'd the more furiously he laid on; and to stop the Noise of my crying, would stamp with his Feet on my Mouth; at which I beg'd him to dispatch me out of the way; but he continued beating me. After I had endured this merciless Usage so long, till I was ready to faint and die under it, and saw him as mad and implacable as ever, I beg'd him to forbear, and I would turn. And breathing a while, but still hanging by the Feet, he urg'd me again to speak the Words. Very unwilling I was, and held him in suspense a while; and at length told him, that I could not speak them. At which he was more enrag'd than before, and fell at me again in a most barbarous manner. After I had received a great many Blows a second time, I beseech'd him again to hold his Hand, and gave him fresh hopes of my turning *Mahometan*; and after I had taken a little more Breath, I told him as before, I could not do what he desired. And thus I held him in suspense three, or four times; but at last, seeing his Cruelty towards me insatiable, unless I turn'd through *Terrour* I did it, and spake the Words as usual, holding up the Fore-finger of my Right-hand: And presently I was had away to a Fire, and care was taken to heal my Feet, (for they were so beaten, that I was not able to go upon them for several Days) and so I was put to Bed.

All the Ceremony that any Person who turns *Mahometan*, by *Compulsion*, useth, is only holding up the Fore-finger of the Right-hand, and pronouncing the Words before-mentioned. But when any Person *voluntarily* turns from his Religion to the *Mahometan*, there is a great deal of *Formality* used. Many there are who so turn, out of Choice, without any Terrour or Severity shown them. Sometimes in a mad, or drunken Humour; sometimes to avoid the Punishment due . . .

Now when any Person so turns *Mahometan*, he goes to the Court, where the *Dey*, and *Divan*, (*i.e.* his Council) sits, and there declares his willingness to be a *Mahometan*; upon which he is immediately accepted, without demanding of him any Reason for his so doing. After which, the *Apostate* is to get on Horse-back, on a stately Steed, with a rich Saddle, and fine Trappings: He is also richly habited, and hath a *Tur*bant on his Head, (but to be sure, not of a green Colour; for none durst wear their *Turbants* of that Colour, but such as are of *Mahomet's Blood*) but nothing of this is to be call'd his own; only there is given him about two or three yards of Broad-Cloth, which is laid before him on the Saddle. The Horse, with him on his Back, is led all round the City; and he carries an Arrow in his Right-hand, holding it straight up, and thereby supporting the Fore-finger of his Right-hand, which he holds up against it. This he doth all the while he is riding round the City; which he is several Hours in doing . . . The *Apostate* is attended with Drums, and other Musick, and twenty or thirty *Verkil Harges*, or *Stewards* . . . These march in Order on each side of the Horse, with naked Swords in their Hands, intimating thereby (as I was inform'd) that if he should repent, and shew the least Inclination of *Retracting* what he had declared before the *Dey* and the *Divan*, he deserv'd to be cut in Pieces; and the *Vekil Harges* would accordingly do it. There are likewise two Persons who stand one on each side of the Street, as he marcheth thorow, to gather what People are pleas'd to give, by way of Encouragement to the New *Convert* . . . And within a few Days the *Sennet Gee* of the Town, *i.e.* the *Circumciser*, comes and performs the Ceremony of *Circumcision*, and then he is a *Turk* to all Intents and Purposes. It is reported by some, that when any thus *voluntarily* turns *Mahometan*, he throws a Dart at the Picture of *Jesus Christ*, in token of his disowning him as the *Saviour* of the World, and preferring *Mahomet* to him: But there is no such Usage; and they who relate such things deceive the World.

From Joseph Pitts, *A Faithful Account of the Religion and Manners of the Mahometans* (London, printed for T. Longman and R. Hett, fourth edition, 1738), pp. 192–9. (The first edition appeared in 1704.)

(v) What Muslims believe and what they do not believe

Adrian Reland (1676–1746) – also spelt Relandus, Relant, Reelant and Reeland – was a Dutch orientalist who was a student at Utrecht and Leyden and then taught at Harderwijk before becoming professor of oriental languages and ecclesiastical archaeology at Utrecht. He produced important works on the archaeology of Palestine – *Antiquitates Sacrae Veterum Hebraeorum* (1708 – *The sacred antiquities of the ancient Hebrews*) and *Palestina ex Monumentis Veteribus Illustrata* (1714 – *Palestine illustrated from the ancient monuments*) – the latter work enjoying for well over a century a high reputation among students of that area. The following extracts come from a translation of his *De Religione Moham-medica, Libri duo* (1705, second edition 1717) which is contained in *Four Treatises Concerning the Doctrine, Discipline and Worship of the Mahometans*, published in London in 1712. In the first of his two 'books', Reland gives a translation of an Arabic manuscript entitled 'A Short System of the

Mahometan Theology' together with explanatory notes on items in the text. After giving the outline printed in the following extract, the work continues with a short commentary on the six points 'required' of an Muslim together with instructions about ritual washing, praying, alms-giving, fasting and the pilgrimage to Mecca. The second of the 'books' is Reland's exposure of a number of things which he holds to be 'falsly charg'd upon the *Mahometans*'. It contains thirty-nine sections. Among those not included in the following extracts are discussions which range from claims about Muslim beliefs on providence, she-angels and the salvation of all the devils to their views on keeping promises with infidels, the status of dogs and the literacy of Mahomet. The material indicates the extent to which Islam was commonly misrepresented at this time as well as illustrating the attempt by scholars like Pococke, d'Her-belot and Ockley as well as Reland, to secure a more accurate and even a sympathetic understanding of that faith.

Book I

In the Name of the most Merciful God
Praise and Glory be to God, who hath brought us to the Faith, and appointed that Portion, whereby an Entry is prepar'd into the Heavenly Paradise; and put a Veil between us, and an eternal abiding in Flames. And may the Favour of God and Peace be towards *Mahomet*, the best of Men, the Captain, who leads his Followers in the strait way; and to his Kindred, and most glorious Associates, be perpetual and ever-growing Peace throughout all Ages.

Here begins the Description of Faith, and the Explanation of it. Know then that Faith is the first of the Foundations of *Islamism*, as the Prophet *Mahomet* hath declar'd; with whom may God be well-pleas'd, and give him all manner of Salvation.

Islamism stands upon five Foundations: The first of which is Confession of God, that there is none but that true God, and *Mahomet* his Ambassador. The second is a stated Observation of Prayers. The third is Giving of Alms. The fourth is the Fast of the Month *Ramadini*. The fifth is the Pilgrimage to *Mecca*, to be undertaken by everyone who is able to perform that Journy. Now that Confession is what we call Faith.

We must know therefore, that the first thing requir'd of a Man duly qualify'd, is, that he believe in God. 2. His Angels. 3. His Books. 4. His Prophets. 5. The Last Day. 6. The Decree of God concerning Good and Evil.

Now Faith consists in this, that a Person be persuaded of the Truth of these things in his Mind; but Confession of the Tongue takes in the Demonstration of it by outward Signs. (pp. 19–21)

[The remainder of Book I is an exposition of these points.]

Book II

SECT. I.

Treating of several Things falsly charg'd upon the Mahometans

From the time that the *Mahometan* Doctrine poison'd almost the whole Earth
with its Infection and Contagion, there were a great many who endeavour'd
to put a stop to a growing Evil, and confute a most abominable Religion:
Which, as it was very necessary (lest an Error, subverting the Foundations of
the whole Christian Religion, should take root in the Minds of the Ignorant,
as it did in *Asia* at the Time when *Mahomet* arose) so it was no less difficult.
For an exact Knowledg of the *Arabick* Tongue (in which the Impostor
deliver'd his Religion, and without the help of which 'tis scarce possible to
enter into the Mysterys of *Mahometanism*) was necessary. But the greatest part
of those who meddled in this Affair, had not the least knowledg of that
Language. For which Cause they pretended, in their Writings, that things
were most certainly believ'd, and asserted by the *Mahometans*, which they
never dreamt of, and which none but Madmen and Fools would ever have
own'd. We may add, that the imprudent Zeal of some puny *Greeks* ascrib'd
many things to them, which the *Mahometans* themselves detest; as it is
customary for ill-natur'd Men, who explain the Opinions of the adverse
Party. Wherefore I have propos'd in this Book, to examine some Opinions
which are unjustly attributed to the *Mahometans*; and in some places to
discover the ground of the Mistake, lest those who give credit to all things
that are commonly said of the *Mahometans*, should be entertain'd with Lyes.

SECT. II.

Whether the Mahometans *believe that every one may be sav'd in his own
Religion*

In the first place I shall take notice of their gross Mistake, who write, That the
Mahometans assert, that every Man may be sav'd in his own Religion, and
obtain eternal Salvation, provided he lives piously . . . The Ground of the
Mistake lies in the Text of the *Alcoran*, which I shall exactly translate word for
word. *Surat.* 2. *vers.* 59. 'Verily those who believe, both *Jews* and *Nazarens*
(i.e. *Christians*) and *Zabians* (i.e. *Gentiles* in *Arabia*, or *Ishmaelites*) whosoever
of these believe in God and the last Day, and do good Works, have their
Reward with their Lord; and no fear shall come upon them, neither shall they
be affected with Sorrow.' *Mahomet* means this: That the way to Salvation is
shut up from no Man, and that there is hope for Pardon to every one, who
will be converted to his Religion; and whether he is *Jew*, or *Christian*, or
Gentile, so he believes in God and in his last Day (i.e. provided he embrace the
Mahometan Religion, which is Faith in God alone, since both *Jews*, and
Christians, and *Zabians*, as he thinks, worship more Gods than one) he may

be sav'd . . . What can be more clear? To believe in God, is not merely to believe that God is, but to give an Assent to all the Principles of the *Mahometan* Religion. And then, what is it *to do good Works*, according to *Mahomet*'s Mind, other than observing Lustrations, Prayers, Alms, and Fasts? And can a *Christian*, or a *Jew* do these in their Religion? . . . (pp. 47–50).

SECT. III.

Whether they believe God to be Corporeal

It is no less a Calumny, *That the Mahometans* believe God to be corporeal. And yet Pope *Pius* the Second wrote so in a Letter to *Morbisanus*, tho he is reckon'd very honest and candid by those of his own Party: But this is a matter of Fact, and not of Right; and many Papists confess, that the Pope may be deceiv'd in matters of Fact . . . This Mistake hath sprung from the ambiguous signification of a word we translate *Sphere*, which also signifies *Eternal*; and in this sense it is rightly affirmed of God . . . I don't think I need be at much pains to prove, that the *Mahometans* believe God to be a Spirit, which nobody can be ignorant of, that has look'd into the genuine Volumes of the *Arabian* Divines . . . (p. 52 f).

SECT. IV.

Whether God is the Author of Evil

The *Mahometans* believe God to be the Author of Evil, if we trust *Cedrenus* . . . *Euthymius Zigabenus*, in *Panopl. Dogmat.* insisting upon the same Calumny, endeavours to demonstrate what he advances upon this Head, out of the *Alcoran*; Teaching that God is the Author of all Evil, as well as of all Good, he says, 'Whom God directs, he is led into the right Way; whom he leads into Error, he is deserted.'

I confess this is written in the *Alcoran*; but can we from thence infer, by a just Consequence, but God is the Author of Evil? In my Opinion, we cannot. This way of speaking denotes, that the Providence of God is conversant about both Good and Evil: And the Holy Scriptures make use of the same way of speaking, when God is said to *create Evil*, Isa. 45. 7. Amos 3. 6. *and to cause Men to wander from the right way of Salvation, and to harden them* . . . The *Mahometans* always extol the Holiness of God, remove every Defect from him, say that God directs Evil by his Providence, but does not please himself in it; they never pronounce him to be the Author of Evil: And therefore they are unjustly charg'd with this Opinion; with which all who maintain the absolute Providence of God, and his independent Right in all things, are wont to be charg'd. (pp. 55 f).

SECT. V.

Whether they worship Venus

It is false that the *Mahometans* worship *Venus*, and yet this is said in the

Anathema's, by which a *Mahometan* converted to the Christian Faith, was wont to curse the *Mahometan* Faith . . . (p. 57).

SECT. VIII.

Whether they believe that God prays for Mahomet

There are many who also upbraid the *Mahometans* with a very foolish Opinion, as if they believ'd that God prays for *Mahomet* . . . The Original of this Mistake, as of many others, lies in the abominable *Latin* Version of the *Alcoran* by *Rob. Retenens.* and *Herman. Dalmata*, and which *Bibliander* publish'd in the year 1550. In *Surat. 33. ver.* 56. we read in their Translation of this Place, *God and the Angels pray for the Prophet.* But pray whom should God pray to for him? The true sense of the words is this: "Verily, God and his Angels favour *Mahomet* . . . (p. 61 f).

SECT. XI.

Whether they believe that Sins are taken away by frequent Washing of the Body

Some write that the *Mahometans* think, the Pollutions and Sins of the Soul are done away by frequent Washings of the Body, and that they take great care about the Purification of the Body, but neglect the Purity and Holiness of the Soul . . . The *Mahometans* are not quite so mad, but expect the Purification of their Soul, and the blotting out of their Sins, only from God and his Grace . . . (p. 64 f).

SECT. XII.

Whether they believe the Devils to be the Friends of God and of Mahomet

Johannes Andreas (who had himself been a *Mahometan*, which renders his Ignorance unpardonable) in *Confus. Sect. Mahometan.* writes, that the Alcoran says, 'The Devils were made the Friends of Men, God and *Mahomet*;' . . . The Text he cites is found in *Surat.* 72. which from the Argument is call'd the Chapter of *Genii.* It is said there, that some *Genii* hearing the *Alcoran* read, approv'd the Doctrine contain'd in it, and said, *We also believe one God.* But, good Sir, this is told of *Genii*, not of Devils . . . (p. 66).

SECT. XV.

Whether the Devils hear

It is written in *Azoara* XXXVI. of the *Alcoran* (that is, in the *Arabic* Text, *Surat* XXVI. *v.* 212. for the Sections in the *Latin* Version differ from those in the *Arabic* Text) That the Devils do not hear: and hence *Mahomet* argues, that the Devils did not compose the *Alcoran*, if we believe him who put the Marginal Arguments to *Rob. Retenens. Latin* Version, where in the very Text it is written, *They are far remov'd from hearing*: and the Annotator crys out, *The*

Devils did not compose the Alcoran, *because they do not hear.* This Man must certainly have been a Conjurer! Indeed we read in the *Arabic* Text, *That they are Strangers to Obedience, and do not obey God's Command.* He might have learnt that from the preceding Verse, where they are said *to be disobedient to God.* There is nothing there, strictly speaking, about Hearing; nor about the *Alcoran*'s being compos'd by the Devils. But this Version is so full of Blunders, that he who would correct them, would be oblig'd to write a Volume of equal bulk with the Version it self. And yet 'tis chiefly from this, that the Christian World has had its accounts of the *Mahometan* Religion. (pp. 71 f).

SECT. XVIII.

Whether Women are to enter into Paradise

There are some who say, that the *Mahometans* believ'd, that Women shall not enter into the Heavenly Paradise: That certainly there will be charming Maids in Heaven, but different from those that have liv'd in this World . . . But *Mahomet* was not so hard-hearted towards the Women, as to exclude them from Heaven . . . When I discours'd upon this Head with our *Sike*, who told me he had been several times consulted upon this Affair, both in *Italy* and elsewhere; we wonder'd that a Doctrine so absurd, and supported by no Authority, should everywhere be attributed to the *Mahometans* . . . (pp. 77f).

From: *Of the Mahometan Religion, Two Books. The Former of which is A Short System of the Mahometan Theology, Translated from an Arabick Manuscript, and Illustrated with Notes. The latter examines into some Things falsely charg'd upon the Mahometans.* Done into English from the Latin of Adrian Reeland (London, 1712), pp. 19–21, 47–78.
(This work is part of *Four Treatises Concerning the Doctrine, Discipline and Worship of the Mahometans* (London, printed by J. Darby for B. Lintot and E. Sanger, 1712), pp. 1–102.)

(vi) Cultural relativity and the reasonableness of Islam

Henri, Comte de Boulainvilliers (1658–1722) served in the army until 1697. He wrote several works on French politics which were published posthumously. In them he defends aristocracy, attacking both absolute monarchy and popular government and claiming that a feudal form of government is the best. His *Vie de Mahomet* came out in 1730, the English translation from which the following extracts are taken appearing the following year. Although Boulainvilliers admits that he does not know Arabic (cf. p. 7), his work shows considerable sympathy for Mahomet and Islam, arguing that this faith can only be properly appreciated when it is seen in terms of its own cultural background. Mahomet is regarded, furthermore, as one who largely sought to restore recognition of the universal 'antient truths' of religion which had been forgotten by the people (cf. pp. 176, 187) and his teaching is held to be commendably reasonable on the whole. In such respects Islam is implicitly presented as having significant similarities to current 'deist' views of religious belief. Boulainvilliers also points out that Christian apologists, like Prideaux, who seek to discredit the character and behaviour of Mahomet, cannot escape having great difficulty in finding any convincing explanation of the success of Islam other than that it was divinely prospered! Boulainvilliers died before finishing the work. The final section of the English version contains a completion of Mahomet's life by the translator. This continuation is dependent on the works of Prideaux and Maracci among others, and is noticeably in the style of that anti-Muslim polemic which Boulainvilliers was, with others such as Herbelot, Pococke, Reland and Ockley, seeking to counteract. In the continuation Mahomet is described, for example, as a 'celebrated impostor', a 'crafty' and 'artful' prophet who 'pretended a revelation from Heaven' to defend the honour of one of his wives and whose wars were more like 'the ravages of thieves than military expeditions'. In this respect the continuation is a reminder that the kind of approach which Boulainvilliers advocates in the following extracts was far from widely accepted.

. . . *Mahomet* established a system of religion, not only fitted to the understandings of his countrymen, agreeable to their sentiments, and the reigning customs of the country, but also adapted in such a manner to the common ideas of all mankind, that in less than forty years it drew into its opinions more than half the world; so that it seem'd as if 'twas only necessary that the doctrine should be clearly understood, in order to subdue the minds of men to its reception. 'Tis also necessary to attend to the choice of the means employ'd by this new legislator to intoxicate nations with the same enthusiasm with which himself was transported. Means, which represent him perfectly acquainted with the character of those on whom he rely'd for the execution of his mighty enterprize under his own conduct, or for the carrying it on after his death; but which more particularly respect that talent of persuasion which he possess'd; by which he arrived at a power, not of bringing the vulgar only into a religion inexplicably mysterious, yet apt to strike the imagination; but also, the sublimest heroes of the age, for valour, generosity, wisdom, and moderation; (heroes in spirit and understanding, as well as disposition of heart!) and convinced them all; in the most untempting manner, and the most contrary to self-esteem, by imposing upon them the necessity of believing every thing that he should please to declare to them; and this without being warranted by any miracles, or juggling pretence, to any, or any gift that could be thought supernatural. I acknowledge 'tis difficult to think without amazement on such a force of human eloquence, breaking forth without any thing mild or softening, but accompany'd with an offensive arrogance, that defyed both men and angels to compose any thing equal to that which he deliver'd to the world . . . (pp. 136 f).

. . . To judge from our general constitution, it should seem that our thoughts and our opinions ought to be always alike, in all nations. We have all but one way of acquiring knowledge, which is the perception of objects, joyn'd with a faculty every mind is endued with, of comparing its ideas, of dividing them, and compounding them at pleasure. Again, forasmuch as objects are nearly the same in all parts of the world, and the natural appetites are the consequences of the common organization of mankind, from hence there should result a like sensation from the presence of the same objects in all men; were it not still more true, that all sensation being no more than a passive affection of the perceptive substance, it can never become an active universal power, whose effect we may suppose to be constantly alike. Hence it comes to pass, that we find the same object does not always make the same impression upon our ownselves; and that we are differently affected according to the disposition we are in: not to mention our uncertainty of the perceptions of others who may have quite different ideas from ours, of colours, sounds and tastes, and yet agree with us in their way of expressing them. It follows from all this, that our personal ideas, commonly, have neither relation nor connection, with those of other people, only so far as we have them from imitation: which alone happens in communities, where the use of the same language occasions our adopting reciprocally passions and sentiments which we should never have felt, if we had been deprived of examples . . . Nevertheless it appears from this observation, that the notions removed or separated by the diversity of language are not exposed to this reciprocal imitation of ideas, dispositions, and passions: so that having only the first common perceptions, they are respectively ignorant of the conclusions that each may draw from them; which conclusions, variously combined and compounded, produce sensations, manners, and customs as different as their several habits, or the lines of their countenance . . .

Return we now to our assertion, that every nation has its customs, consecrated by use; and that they are independant of the notions, and different practices, that other people have upon the same subject. So that each of them, being persuaded they adhered to the best consequences they could draw from the principles they knew, have settled that religion, those political laws, and that form of government, which are peculiar to them. And thus the *Chinese*, within a certain extent of knowledge; the *Arabians*, in another; and the *Christians* according to the perfect light of revelation; every one of them, on their part, could not draw better conclusions from their premises than those which they have followed. This reason should determine us, Ist, to respect mutually the customs of every country. 2dly, to desire the instruction of those who err in the sincerity of their hearts. 3dly, to pity those over whom the power of prejudice prevails above the brightness of that light they might obtain. 4thly, not to invent false principles to slander events that are contrary to our notions, and which we would not have to be true. 5thly, to acknowledge, as to *Mahomet* himself, that whoever could project such mighty schemes, and execute them so successfully, as well in religion as politicks, could never be a person despicable for his natural defects. Common sense leads us to judge on the contrary, that if he was an impostor he must have possess'd still more superior qualities to enable him to impose upon his contemporaries, to draw them into his sentiments, and to captivate them; and that his fraud has always had the appearance of truth, at least, with respect to those that he seduced. Whereas by divesting him arbitrarily of those abilities which might naturally conduce to his successes, solely to gratify a disposition to hatred, which 'tis true, every Christian might justly conceive against the greatest enemy to his religion, (tho' at the bottom those qualities or talents in no wise affect Christianity, since it only concerns a dead man, who has been so, above a thousand years) yet it must be acknowledg'd that such a revenge reduces our reasoning to an absurdity. Since if the fortune of this personage was not the effect of natural means, the success could be only from G O D; whom the impious will accuse of having led half the world into an error, and destroy'd violently his own revelation. (pp. 172–9).

This is the manner in which *Mahomet* wrought up his scheme, and the system of a religion stript of all controversy, and which proposing no mystery to offer violence to reason, confined the imaginations of men to be satisfied with a plain invariable worship, notwithstanding the fiery passions, and blind zeal that so often transported them beyond themselves. A system, that cannot be attributed to the suggestion of some ignorant Monk, or some whimsical impostor, who actually pitched upon a man, full of vices and natural imperfections, that they were afterwards obliged to disguise with all kinds of artifices, in order to make him their Prophet; but which seems to have been the result of long and deep meditation upon the nature of things, upon the state and condition of the nations of the world at that time, and upon the reconcilement of the objects of religion with reason, which must always try the things presented to the understanding. (pp. 223 f).

. . . I reject two opinions, upon which our controversy with the musulmen has turned, unto this day. The first is, 'that there is not any rational inducement in all that they believe or practise; insomuch that common sense must be discarded in order to embrace their system.' The second is, 'That *Mahomet* was so coarse and barbarous an impostor, that he is not a man, who does not or cannot perceive plainly his cheat and corruption.' Against these principles I maintain. First, That setting aside Christianity, which enlightens us vastly beyond what *Mahomet* was desirous of conceiving or knowing, there would not have been a more plausible system of doctrine than his, more agreeable to the light of reason, more comfortable to the righteous, or more terrible to wilful and careless sinners; and that in the exercise of the worship he has establish'd, we manifestly discover the cause of that unconquerable affection the *Mahometans* bear to their religion: an attachment of the heart, which our missionaries have greatly experienc'd; who are oblig'd to confess the little progress they make among them. Secondly, I maintain, that *Mahomet*, the impostor, was neither coarse nor barbarous; that he conducted his enterprize with all the art, all the delicacy, all the resolution, intrepidity, and extensive views, that *Alexander* or *Caesar* had been capable of, in his circumstances. 'Tis true his manners were more simple than theirs; he knew less than those two heroes, of avarice, interest, luxury, and prodigality: in the room of which he employ'd religion as the means of his exploits. He did not more enslave his country; on the contrary, he only desir'd to govern it, in order to make it the mistress of the world, and its various riches; of which, both he, and his first successours made so disinterested a use, that in this respect they must compel the admiration of their greatest enemies. (pp. 243 f).

. . . *Mahomet*, in preaching morality, had no doubtful or suspected truth besides to press upon his auditors, excepting the doctrine of the resurrection, little credible to carnal men. The unity and supreme power of G O D were not truths of that kind; they were demonstrated by mere human reason. Wherefore the *Arabians* had no right, and still less had the *Christians*, to require miracles from a man who constantly declared and protested that he had no other power than to persuade those who would calmly listen unto him, or to conquer those by force of arms who resisted the force of his *reasons*, with respect to which, he dared to defy men and angels to enter the lists with him. (pp. 249 f).

But since we have mention'd the theology of this new Prophet, 'tis proper to observe farther, that this was the time wherein he must have published the settlement of *three* capital points, which 'tis of importance to declare in this place.

The *first* was, to believe the *truth*, that is, the existence and unity of G O D, exclusive of every other Being that can be imagined to partake, or modify, his power and will: this he rejected, under the general term of *association*, as the lowest and most unworthy notion that could be formed of the deity.

The *second* was, to believe that G O D, the universal Creator, is intelligent, potent, and just, for rewarding the vertue of the pious, and punishing the iniquity of the wicked; not only in this life, but even after death; since all men shall rise again, and appear before him, to receive the most equitable judgment that he shall then pronounce upon their actions.

The *third* was, to believe that G O D, commiserating men who perish for want of instruction, which might recover them from vice, and lead them to the knowledge of the truth, hath in these last times, especially and personally raised up *Mahomet* to be his *Prophet* and *Messenger*; from whom they were to learn the means of pleasing him, and of arriving at the recompense of the righteous, and of escaping the punishment of the impenitent. This was the whole of this pretended Prophet's theology. And even afterwards, he does not seem to have extended it farther, except in relation to the Angels, and the construction of heaven, of which he talks very grossly and idly. As to the particular precepts of his morality, both positive and negative, which composed his new law, 'tis very probable that he only resolved upon them one after another, according as occasion offer'd for their establishment.

From [Henri,] Count of Boulainvilliers, *The Life of Mahomet*, translated from the French original (London, W. Hinchliffe, 1731), pp. 136 f, 172–9, 223 f, 243 f, 249 f, and 293–5.

V

Religions of Africa, America and the East

The following passages have been chosen to illustrate how actual religions other than Christianity, Judaism and Islam are understood and treated in this period. None of these religions were generally regarded as significant options for belief and for most of them the available evidence was slight, patchy and of very varied quality. Although the descriptions often betray the pride and prejudices of those providing them, the final extract from Sir William Jones is a reminder that at least towards the end of the period a different attitude – one of appreciative evaluation – was not totally unknown.

(i) Brief views of religions in Africa and America

Alexander Ross (1590–1654) was born in Aberdeen and seems to have entered King's College there in 1604. Around 1616 he became schoolmaster at the Free School at Southampton and by 1622 had been appointed a chaplain to Charles I through the influence of Laud. In 1642 the King appointed him vicar of Carisbrooke. He died at Bramshill, where he was living with Sir Andrew Henley, to whom he left his books. Ross wrote on many topics but his favourite subjects were theological, philosophical and historical. He produced a continuation of Sir Walter Raleigh's *History of the World* but it was not well received. His attempts to debate with such writers as Sir Thomas Browne, Sir Kenelm Digby and Thomas Hobbes were often marred by scurrility in his arguments. In 1649 his translation of André du Ryer's French version of the Koran was published with, at the end, 'A Needful Caveat or Admonition' by Ross. The *Pansebeia* appeared in 1653 and was often reprinted. It uses a question and answer form and attempts to live up to its title of being 'A View of All Religions in the World' – at least of the world, ancient and modern, as then known. Nearly two-thirds of it, though, deal with the divisions and heresies of Christianity. The following extracts come from the 'Third Section' in which Ross describes the religions of Africa and America. They indicate the kind of information that was generally available on these religions, much of it coming from travellers' observations.

Q. *What is the Religion of* Angola *and* Congo?

A. In *Angola* they are all Heathens. In the midst of their Towns they worship Wooden Idols resembling Negroes, at whose feet are heaps of Elephants Teeth, on which are set up the Skulls of their Enemies killed in the Wars. They believe they are never sick but when their Idol is angry with them; therefore they please him by pouring at his feet the Wine of Palms. They use to wash and paint and new cloath their dead, and bury with him meat, drink, and some of his goods, at whose grave they shed the blood of Goats. They are much addicted to divination by birds; and their Priests are in such esteem, that they think life and death, plenty and famine are in their power. In the Kingdom of *Congo* they worship some monstrous creatures instead of God. But they were converted to Christianity by the *Portugueze*, *Anno* 1490. At the City of *Banza*, afterwards called S. *Saviour's*, was erected a Cathedral Church for the Bishop, who was there received by the King in great magnificence. This Church had 28 Canon Residents. All their Idols of Beasts, Birds, Trees, and Herbs, with their Conjuring Characters were burned . . .

Q. *What Religion do the Northern Neighbours of* Congo *profess?*

A. In *Loango* under the Line, they worship Idols and are Circumcised. Every Tradesman appeaseth his God with such things as belong to his Trade: the Husbandman with Corn, the Weaver with Cloth, &c. At the death of their Friends they kill Goats, to the honour of their Idols, and make divers Feasts in memorial of the dead. They will rather die than touch any meat which is prohibited by their Priests. At *Kenga* the Sea-port of *Loango*, there is an Idol kept by an old Woman, which is once a year honoured with great solemnity and feasting. There is another Idol at *Morumba* Thirty Leagues Northward, where Boys are Sworn to Serve this God and are initiated with hard diet, ten days silence, abstinence from certain Meats, and a cut in their Shoulder, the blood of which is sprinkled at the Idols feet. Their Trials of life and death, are in the presence of this Idol. At *Anzichi* they are Circumcised, worship the Sun and Moon, and each Man his particular Idol. In some of these neighbouring Coutreys the People are Man-eaters, and worship the Devil, to whom, when they offer sacrifice, they continue from morning till night, using Charming Vociferations, dancing and piping . . .

Q. *Of What Religion are the Islands about* Africa?

A. In some of them are Mahumetans, in some Christians, but in most Heathens. In *Socotera*, an Island near the mouth of the Red-Sea, whence we have our best *Aloes*, they are *Jacobites*, and are governed by their *Abuna* or Priest. They much reverence the Cross. They have Altars in their Churches, which they enter not, but stand in the Porch. In the *Madagascar*, or the great Island of St. *Lawrence*, there are many Mahumetans upon the Coast, but more Idolaters within the Land, who acknowledge one Creator, and are Circumcised; but use neither to pray nor keep holy-day. They punish Adultery and Theft with death. In the Isle of St. *Thomas*, under the Line, are Christians and Moors. In divers Islands are no People at all, in the *Canaries* are Christians; before they were Idolaters, and had many Wives, whom they first prostituted to their Magistrates, and this uncivil civility they used to strangers instead of Hospitality. They bury the dead by setting them upright against a Wall, with a staff in their hand; and if he was a great Man, a Vessel of Milk by him. *Madera* is also possessed by Christians, and so be the other Islands on this hither part of the *African* Coast . . .

Q. *What Religion was professed among the* Americans?

A. Before the *Spaniards* came thither, they were all Pagans; who as they were distinguished into divers Nations, so they worshipped divers gods, after divers manners; but they did generally acknowledge the Sun and Moon for the chief gods. In *Canada* they worshipped the Devil, before the *French* came thither, and in most places there as yet they worship him; who, when he is offended with them, flings dust in their eyes. The Men Marry two or three Wives, who, after the death of their Husbands never Marry again, but go still after in Black, and besmear their Faces with Coal-dust and Grease; they do first expose their Daughters to any that will lie with them, and then give them in Marriage. They believe that after death their Souls ascend into the Stars, and go down with them under the Horizon into a Paradise of Pleasure. They believe also that God stuck a multitude of Arrows in the Beginning into the Ground, and of these sprung up Men and Women. They have divers ridiculous opinions of God, as that he once drank much Tobacco, and then gave the Pipe to their Governour, with a command that he should keep it carefully, and so doing he should want nothing; but he lost the Pipe, and so fell into want and misery. Such senseless conceits have these people, who as they are savage in their carriage, so in their understanding they are little better than beasts. They use to sing the Devils praises, to dance about fires, which they make to his honour, and leap over them. They bemoan the dead a great while, and bring presents to the Grave. Many of these ignorant Souls were Converted to Christ by the Industry of the Jesuites, *Anno* 1637, and 1638 . . .

Q. *What is the Religion of* Virginia?

A. Before the *English* planted Christianity there, they worshipped the Devil, and many Idols, as yet they do in many places there. They believe many gods, but one principally who made the rest; and that all creatures were made of Water, and the Woman before the Man, who by the help of one of the gods conceived and bore Children. They are Anthropomorphites, giving to their gods the forms of Men, whom they worship with Praying, singing, and offerings. They hold the Souls Immortality, rewards and punishments after this life, the one in Heaven, the other in a burning pit towards the West. The Priests are distinguished from other People by Garments of Skins, and their hair cut like a Comb on their Crowns. They carry their gods about with them, and ask Counsel of them. Much of their devotion consisteth in howling and dancing about fires, with Rattles, or Gourd, or Pumpion rindes in their hands, beating the ground with stones, and offering of Tobacco, Deer-suet, and Blood on the Stone Altars. They undertake no matters of consequence without advice of their Priests, the chief whereof is adorned with Feathers and Weasels Tails, and his Face painted as ugly as the Devils. They bury their Kings (after their bodies are burned and dryed) in white skins, within arches and mats, with their wealth at their feet, and by the Body is placed the Devil's Image. The Women express their sorrow with black paint, and yellings for Twenty four hours. None but the King and Priest may enter these houses, where the Images of Devils and their Kings are kept. Instead of saying Grace at Meat, they fling the first bit into the Fire; and when they will appease a Storm, they cast Tobacco into the Water. Sometimes they sacrifice children to the Devil . . .

Q. *What is the Religion of* Florida?

A. Their chief Deities are the Sun, and Moon, which they honour with dances and songs. Once a year they offer to the Sun a Harts Hide stuffed with Herbs, hanging Garlands of fruits about his Horns, so presenting this gift towards the East, they pray the Sun to make their Land produce the same fruits again. But to their Kings, they use to sacrifice their first-born Males. Much of their Devotion, like the rest of barbarous Savages, consisting in singing, dancing, howling, feasting, and cutting off their own skins. Adultery in the Woman is punished with whipping. In some parts of this Country the next of Kin is permitted to cut the Adulteresses Throat, and the Woman to cut the Adulterers. In some parts also of the Country they worship the

Devil; who, when he appears and complains of Thirst, humane blood is shed to quench his thirst. When a King is buried, the Cup wherein he used to drink, is still set upon his Grave, and round about the same are stuck many Arrows; the People weep and fast three days together; the Neighbour Kings his Friends cut off half their hair. Women are hired, who for six months howl for him three times a day. This honour the King and Priest have, that they are buried in their houses, and burned with their houses and goods . . .

Q. *Of what Religion are the Nations by* West-Virginia *and* Florida?

A. Few of them are yet known, but such as by Navigation are found upon the Sea-coasts, and some Islands conquered by the *Spaniards*, are worshippers of the Sun, and Water: because the Sun by his heat, and the Water by its moisture produce all things; therefore when they eat, drink, or sacrifice, they use to throw up in the air, towards the Sun, some part of their Food. The *Spaniards* took advantage of this Superstition, and made these People believe they were Messengers sent thither to them from the Sun; whereupon they submitted, holding it impious to reject the Messengers, which their chief god had sent them. They worship also here Idols, and in some places the Devil, and observe the same Superstitious Ceremonies in the burial of their Dead, that their Neighbours do . . . (pp. 72–6).

Q. *What Religion did the people of* Peru *profess*?

A. Their chief god was *Wiracocha*, by whom they understood the maker of all things; next to him they worshipped the Sun, and the Thunder after him: the Images of these three they never touched with their bare hands: they worshipped also the Stars, Earth, Sea, Rainbow, Rivers, Fountains and Trees. They adored also wild beasts, that they might not hurt them; and in sign of their devotion, when they travelled, they left in the cross ways, and dangerous places, old shooes, feathers, and if they had nothing else, stones. They worshipped the Sun, by pulling off the hairs from their Eye-brows: when they fear, they touch the Earth, and look up to the Sun. They worshipped also the dead bodies of their Emperours, and indeed every thing they either affected or feared. They have some glimring knowledge of the beginning of the world, of *Noah*'s flood, and they believe the end of the world, which still they fear when the Sun is eclipsed, which they think to be the Moons husband: they held their Priests in such esteem, that no great matter was undertaken by Prince or People without their advice. None had access to the Idols but they, and then only when they are clothed in white, and prostrate on the ground. In sacrificing they abstain from Women; and some out of Zeal would put out their own eyes. They used to consult with the Devil, to whom they sacrificed men, and dedicated boys in their Temples for *Sodomy*. They had also their Temples richly adorned with Gold and Silver, and their Monastries for Priests and Sorcerers. Their Nuns were so strictly kept, that it was death to be deflowered: after fourteen years of age they were taken out of the Monastry, either to serve their Idols (and such must be Virgins still) or else to serve as Wives and Concubines to the *Ingua*, or Emperor. They are very frequent and strict in their confessions, and chearfully undertake what penance is enjoyned them. But the *Ingua* confesseth only to the Sun: after confession they all wash in baths, leaving their sins in the water. They used to sacrifice Vegetables, Animals, and Men, chiefly Children, for the health or prosperity of their *Ingua*, and for victory in War: In some places they eat their men-sacrifices, in others they only dried and preserved them in silver Coffins; they annoint with blood the faces of their Idols, and doors of their Temples, or rather slaughter-houses . . .

> From Alexander Ross, *Pansebeia: Or, A View of All Religions in the World: With the several Church-Governments, from the Creation, till these Times* . . . Sixth Edition, Enlarged and Perfected (London, M. Gillyflower and W. Freeman, 1696), pp. 72–6, 82 f.

(ii) Siamese religious beliefs and the story of Sommonocodom

For Charles Leslie (1650–1722) see III (iii) *supra*. In *The Short and Easy Method with the Deists Vindicated* (1710), Leslie refers to the claim by a critic of his earlier work that the story of 'Sommonocodom now worshipped in *Siam*' meets the four marks of 'the truth of Facts' which Leslie had advanced as the basis of his defence of the reports of Christ's miracles and so of the truth of Christianity. In reply to this charge, Leslie appends a letter from a friend whom he had asked to check on the information about Sommonocodom to which his critic had referred. The following passage is taken from this letter, dated 21 September 1710. The author explicitly provides the stories of the kite-flying and of the stride from Ceylon to Siam in order to show that the story of Sommonocodom is 'ridiculous to a superlative degree' and could not meet Leslie's tests of authentic historical reports. Leslie's own summary of the significance of his friend's letter is that it shows that any comparison with the case of Christ is mistaken since the Siamese neither regard Sommonocodom as 'the founder of their Religion' nor have concerning him anything better than 'sensless stories . . . without the appearance of truth or any foundation'. While the letter itself suggests, furthermore, how beliefs on virtue, the transmigration of souls and nibbana ('Nireupan') might be appreciated, it also indicates the shortage of reliable information which could be culled from the reports of European visitors both about the Buddha and about Buddhist faith and practice.

> . . . *Sommonocodom* once flying Paper Kite (an exercise not altogether unknown in *England*) found the height and inequality of certain Trees to be a great obstacle to his pleasure, upon which he commanded the tops of those Trees to fall even; they instantly obey'd: Flying of Kites has been ever since a solemn diversion among the *Siamese*, I mean those of the greatest authority and distinction; and to favour them in it, the Trees continue still even. Another time *Sommonocodom* being upon an expedition that requir'd haste, took a stride from the Isle of *Ceylon* to the Kingdom of *Siam*, which are not above twelve hundred miles asunder, nor much less if our Maps are not very defective: To prove the truth of this, they shew us the Print of both his Feet; that which is to be seen in *Ceylon*, is still on the top of a high Mountain; that of *Siam* is on a Rock, now almost even with the plain, tho' a Mountain once as high as the other, having sunk under the mighty weight of the Deity. 'Tis indeed remarkable, that this Print of the Foot does not shew it to have been above four or five times bigger than one of ours, which disproportion to so large a step, would be a sufficient ground to one of our christian Philosophers to question the truth of the fact; and even in *Siam*, where the greatest Wits are less scrupulous, there were those alive in 1688, who affirm'd that Monument not to be of above ninety years standing; yet the King and all his Subjects, Clergy and Laity, paid it extraordinary veneration. Such instances as these may serve for a taste of the *Indian* penetration and judgment in matters of Religion; and yet they are much of the same pitch in what relates to Arts and Sciences: Their Histories are all either barren, or fill'd up with adventures too gross to find a place in our Romances; Truth, Reason, and Nature, are what they mind least, they think sticking close to any of them to be a mark of a servile Genius, that wants fertility and invention; their roving Imagination is continually employ'd in quest of wonders, and when they have done, they will assert with the greatest air of conviction, the most extravagant absurdities. Thus one of the chief Ministers of the King of *Siam*, being sent by his Master to congratulate Monsieur *Chaumont*, the *French* Ambassadour, upon his arrival on their Coasts, he presently claim'd acquaintance with him, putting him very seriously in mind how above a thousand years before he had been sent by the then King of *France* to conclude an alliance with the Crown of *Siam*: The *Mandarin* did in this complement allude to the transmigration of Souls, the first Principle of their Religion, which being universally believed, gives every one who pleases an opportunity of relating whatever comes uppermost of the various accidents which have befallen him in all the Bodies

he has passed through, and you may easily guess it would be very hard to disprove him; but indeed they are generally too well bred to offer at it, and as ready to believe the wildest chimera's of others, as they are to vent their own . . .

These general observations of the genius and temper of the People may not be improper; but to speak a little more particularly of *Sommonocodom* and his worship. Shou'd any *Talapoin* go about to persuade me to adore him, I shou'd desire some more satisfactory evidence of the truth of that Doctrine, than they usually give. The Language in which it is preserv'd is different from the vulgar Tongue, but they cannot inform us whether it ever was a living Language, nor where, nor when they learnt it, the few Books they have, bear neither date nor name: They are in the same uncertainty as to their civil Laws and Government; *Siam* and *Laos* a neighbouring Kingdom, derive their origin mutually from one another. Neither do their most authentick writings agree on the chief circumstances of the birth, life, and death of their *Messiah*. Sometimes they make him Son to a King of *Ceylon* by his lawful Queen call'd *Mania* or *Maria*, and tell you that he had a thousand Brothers, not born after the usual manner, but all sprung out of the impurities which accompany'd his birth. At another time they will have him born of a Virgin who lived a retir'd life in an impenetrable Forest, was during her prayers impregnated by the beams of the Sun, and afterwards deliver'd without pain. They agree as little about the place, which some say was on the banks of a great lake between *Siam* and *Camboya*, others in the Isle of *Ceylon*. After his birth the fortune-tellers were consulted by his Father King *Taousout*, to know what the fate of his Son wou'd be: They told him that he wou'd be Emperour of the whole Universe, or if he chose to abandon the World and become a *Talapoin*, he shou'd at last arrive to the *Nireupan* or soveraign degree of felicity, And here I must observe . . . That *Sommonocodom* is not pretended to be the founder of the *Siamese* Religion, or the institutor of their Ascetick Orders. They hold the one and the other to be as ancient as the World, that is eternal. For they have not so much as the notion of the first and supreme being which we call God, and worship as the Creatour and Soveraign Lord of all things. Their Scheme in short is this: There is a continual transmigration of Souls from one Body into another, beast, fish, or man indifferently. The Soul that behaves it self well in one station, meets its reward by being plac'd next time in a better, and sin is punish'd after the same method; yet all this is not suppos'd to happen thro' the will and direction of any over-ruling providence, but to proceed from a fatal necessity, or rather from the nature and essence of virtue and vice, as the flame ascends, and the Loadstone attracts Iron. But when a Soul after the revolution of many ages, has in all its various habitations, perform'd its part so well, as to have acquir'd a fix'd and unalterable habit of virtue, it becomes *Nireupan*, that is, 'tis freed from the troubles of this World, and discharg'd from all farther attendance upon matter, and thenceforward enjoys an eternal rest, without care or concern for what passes among Men. Of these perfect Souls they reckon in all but four, of which *Sommonocodom* was the last, who notwithstanding his incapacity of doing good or hurt, is still, say they, to be worshipp'd, till another, whom they daily expect, appears. Such were the Gods whom *Epicurus* allow'd, that he might avoid the scandalous name of Atheist, and whom he wou'd have to be ador'd for no other reason than the excellency of their own nature. And 'twas perhaps from these *Indians* that the *Stoicks* borrow'd their notion of Virtue being its own reward, tho by their way of explaining it, they made it yet more absurd. To return to our story; *Sommonocodom* resolv'd to become a *Talapoin*, in which pious undertaking he had for Companions ten thousand Young Men, all Princes, all of his own kindred. One of his first acts of heroick Virtue, was to pluck out both his Eyes, and then kill his Wife and two Children, to satisfy the hunger of some of his Disciples. How to reconcile this action with their one Law (which not content to condemn Murther as the greatest of crimes, looks upon all killing, even of a Beast, to be extremely sinful) may perhaps be somewhat difficult: But this was not the only Blood he shed, for being transform'd into a Monkey, he kill'd a strange Monster, that was coming to devour a whole City; but this cost him dear as we shall afterwards find. Seeing himself violently persecuted by his wicked Brother or Kinsman *Thevetar* (for Authors are not agreed how nearly they stood related) he began to examine his conscience, that he might discover what he had done to deserve such ill usage; for 'tis in *Siam* a fundamental Doctrine, that every action good or bad, must necessarily meet with a proportionable reward: And he remembred that being once in his Cups, he had thrown a small stone at a *Talapoin*, and given him a slight wound, for which he had been punish'd during four hundred ninety nine Generations, and had besides lain a considerable time in Hell. I believe you may by this time be tir'd with such a rhapsody of nonsense, and therefore I shall come to a conclusion of *Sommonocodom*'s life. His death is related in two different manners: Some tell you that having liv'd to his eighty second year, he died of the Colick, which he got by eating of Swine's flesh, and this was a judgment upon him, for his Monkey trick in killing the Monster mention'd before, the Soul of that Monster having been since transferr'd into that very Swine: Others say he kill'd himself, and charitably distributed his own flesh amongst a parcel of ravenous Beasts. It is not I think, our business to examine which Tradition is the best grounded, and for the Siamese they never quarrel about the matter. Let the manner be what it will, they place it five hundred and fourty four years before the birth of our Saviour, and from thence pretend to number their years. But Monsieur *La Loubere*, an Author of great credit, who concludes upon very good grounds that there never was any such Man in *rerum natura*, and Monsieur *Cassani* the famous Astronomer, are both of opinion, that this can only be an arbitrary Epoch deriv'd from some remarkable

Conjunction of the Planets which happen'd at that time, and might have been reckon'd a proper beginning for Astronomical Calculations.

From 'The Letter about Sommonocodom' appended to *A Vindication of the Short and Easy Method with the Deists* by Charles Leslie and printed in *The Theological Works of the Reverend Mr. Charles Leslie* (London, W. Bowyer, 1721), I, pp. 131–3.

(iii) *Ritual sacrifices and priesthood in Mexico*

For Bernard Picart (1673–1733) see I I I (iv) *supra*. The following extract is part of the description of Mexican religion and is based on reports of what the Conquistadors found in the country and on later works like *Historia de la Conquista de Méjico* by Antonio de Solís (1684). It is a good example of the way in which some treatments of other religions draw out what their readers would see as the horrible aspects of their practices and thereby, explicitly or implicitly, highlight the superiority of the religious beliefs and practices entertained by the author and his readers. As well as giving the outlines of the sacrificial procedures, penances, priesthood and finishing school for young ladies described in the following extract, the material also covers the Aztec view of the gods, the forms of their idols, the structure of their temples, the nature of their festivals, their calendar, and the rites that attended their coronations, marriages, births and deaths. Not only do the descriptions at times betray the Christian (and Roman Catholic) viewpoint from which these matters are apprehended by the terms which are used, there is also an interesting aside early in the piece where it is suggested that the Mexicans may be connected with the lost tribes of Israel. After briefly noting how the Mexicans related their coming to Mexico, it is pointed out that there are certain parallels between this story and that of the Isralites' entrance into Canaan. It is then said to be possible that the Mexicans, who originally came from the north of Asia, might have had among them some of the 'Posterity of the antient Jews' who were dispersed after the destruction of Israel!

Their Sacrifices and Penance

As it would be no easy Matter to find any Species of Idolatry among the Antients as extensive as that of the *Mexicans*, it would be full as difficult to meet with any Sacrifices so barbarous and inhuman as theirs; not that we are ignorant they were practised by the Antients, since we have given Instances of it: But 'tis certain that nothing can be compar'd to this inexecrable Worship, unless it be that of the *Carthaginians* and the *Canaanites* from whom they are descended. The bloody Sacrifices of the *Mexicans* were performed in this Manner: The Victims designed for Sacrifice were led to the Charnel-House, which, rises like a kind of Platform or Terrass, supported by several Trunks of Trees. The Victims, who were closely guarded by some *Mexican* Soldiers, waited at the Foot of the Terrass till such Time as they should be put to Death; and to heighten their Distress, a great Number of skulls hanging on the Poles which went from Tree to Tree, were continually presenting themselves to their Sight; these were the Skulls of such as had been sacrificed before them. A Priest holding in his Hand an Idol made of Wheat, Maiz, and Honey, drew near to these unhappy Wretches, and presenting it to each of them, cry'd out at the same Time, *There is your God*. This done they withdrew, going off on the other Side of the Terrass, when the Victims were immediately brought upon it; this being, as we have already observ'd, the Place appointed for the Sacrifice. Here it was that six Ministers of the Idols slaughter'd these Victims. After having tore out their Hearts, they threw the Bodies down the Stair-Case from the Top of the Terrass to the Bottom. We are assured that all those who had taken any of these unhappy Wretches in War, used to divide them among themselves, and eat them. They never sacrific'd less than forty or fifty of these Victims at a Time; and those Nations who either bordered on, or were tributary to the *Mexicans*, imitated them in this bloody Worship. The famous *Ferdinand Cortez* relates, that the Inhabitants of *Mechoacan* first protested they would abandon a Worship which was as injurious to the Deity as unworthy of Humanity. We must not omit that those Priests who sacrific'd Men, were distinguished by the Title of *Ministers of sacred Things*; and that this Employment was the highest Dignity of the Priesthood. To the High-Priest alone belong'd the Privilege and Honour of ripping up the Victim's Stomach; and this he perform'd so very dextrously, as, upon any other Occasion, would have raised the Wonder and Admiration of the Spectators. It is true, indeed, that as the Stone on which the Victim was laid, was very sharp and pointed, his Body, which rested altogether upon the Loins, made the Dexterity of the Priest less surprising.

It was a Custom among them on certain Festivals, to dress a Man in the bloody Skin, just reeking from the Body of one of their Victims. A *Spanish* Author assures us, that even their Kings and Grandees did not think it derogatory to their Honour to disguise themselves in this Manner, when the Captive sacrificed was a Person of Distinction. Be that as it will, the disguised Person used to run up and down the Streets, and Places of publick Resort of the City, to beg the Charity of all those he met with, and to beat such as refused. This bloody Kind of Masquerade continued till such Time as the

Skin-Coat began to stink. The Money that was collected in this devout Ramble, was employ'd in pious Uses.

Another religious Ceremony, which indeed does not seem altogether so barbarous as the former, was the Duel of the Victim; if we may give this Name to the Liberty he was allow'd of defending himself against the Priest who was to sacrifice him. The Captive, whose Feet were tied to a Stone, parried the Instrument with which the Priest struck at him, and even attack'd him. If he had the good Fortune to gain the better of the Priest, he was released, and look'd upon as a brave Man; but if the Priest came off Conqueror, he first kill'd him, then flea'd off his Skin, and, as we are told, had his Limbs dressed and serv'd up in one of those they call'd their religious Meals.

It was always their Custom, before they sat down to eat, to offer to the Sun and to the Earth, the First-Fruits of their Meats and Drink, as also of their Corn, Fruits and Flowers. They had other religious Customs, infinitely more absurd than the foregoing, tho' the Principle from which they flow'd, was not altogether to be condemned; which was the laying themselves under a Necessity of doing certain Things, not excepting the most unseemly, for the Love of their Gods: For they not only eat, drank, carried weighty Burdens, anointed and besmear'd themselves out of Love to them, but even stoop'd to the vilest Offices purely to do them Honour.

Their Penance was at last as severe as that of other Religions. The Priests, as Mediators between the Gods and Men, offer'd up Victims for Sinners, and also took upon themselves the Iniquities of the People. When this solemn Penance was to be undertaken, it was their Custom to meet together at Midnight in the Temple of the Idol, when one of them used to call the People together to their Devotions with a Kind of Horn, while another was incensing the Idol. Then one of the Ministers of the false Gods began the Penance, consisting in a small Effusion of Blood which he drew from the Ancle, by pricking it with a *Manghey* Thorn or a Stone-Lancet. After this he rubb'd his Temples and Ears with this Blood, then went and wash'd himself in a certain Water, which from that Circumstance was call'd *The Water of Blood*. 'Twas their Custom, the better to testify the Merit and Truth of this wonderful Penance, to shew to the People the Instrument which had been made use of on that Occasion. The other Punishments which their Priests inflicted on themselves before *Tescalipuca*, or the God who presided over Penance and Afflictions, were to whip one another with Thongs of *Manghey* in great Knots, and to strike one another with great Stones, *&c.*

Their Priests, Discipline, &c.

The High-Priest wore on his Head a Crown of beautiful Feathers of various Colours, with golden Pendants, enriched with Emeralds, at his Ears, and a small blue Tube, like to that of the God of Penance, ran through his Lip. He was clothed with a Scarlet Robe, or rather Mantle. The Vestments of their Priests were frequently chang'd according to the different Seasons or Festivals.

The Priests used to incense four Times a Day the God whose Ministers they were: But at Midnight the principal Ministers of the Temple rose to perform the nocturnal Office, *viz.* to sound a Trumpet and Horn for a long Time together, and to play on certain Instruments accompanied with Voices, which together celebrated the Praises of the Idol. After this, the Priest, whose Turn it was, took the Thurible, saluted the Idol and incensed it, himself being clothed in a black Mantle. In fine, after the Incensing was over, they all went together into a Chapel, where they practised all those rigorous Penances.

These Priests used to observe a very rigorous Fast; they fasted for five, six, and even ten Days together, which they commonly did when the Time of their solemn Festivals drew nigh. During these Fasts, such of them as were married, used to abstain from all Commerce with Women. Their Chastity would undoubtedly have been glorious, had it been built on a reasonable Foundation; but that Confidence, or rather Principle of Presumption, which prevails so much over those who desire that Applause for things of Form which they cannot merit by a solid Virtue, sullied all the Glory of this forced Continency . . .

All these Priests were possess'd of great Revenues, and received the Oblations which the People made to the Idols, which brought them in immense Sums, particularly at the Time of their grand Festivals . . .

They had an Order of Vestals, who were clothed in White, and call'd by the Name of *Daughters of Penance.* These were admitted into the Order at twelve or thirteen Years of Age, and were oblig'd to have their Heads shav'd, at a certain Season excepted, during which they were suffer'd to let their Hair grow. These Nuns were under the Direction of an Abbess, whose Office was to keep the Temples clean, and they also dressed the sacred Meats which were presented to the Idols, and which afterwards served as Food to their Ministers. They were employ'd also in making Carpets and such like Ornaments for the Temples and the Idols. They rose at Midnight to administer to the Gods, and to exercise certain Austerities which the Rules of their Order obliged them to observe. Above all, they were bound to preserve their Chastity unsullied, the Violation of which was punished with Death. This Continence was not indeed to be perpetual, since, as they were sent to the Convent only to fulfil some Vow which their Parents had made to the Gods, they were allow'd to marry after a certain Term of Years. 'Tis even probable that this Abbess or Matron might, properly speaking, superintend a kind of Nursery in which the young Ladies of Quality were educated, since they were never taken from under her Care, but only when their Parents intended to settle them in the World.

From Bernard Picart, *The Ceremonies and Religious Customs of the Various Nations of the Known World*, with additions and remarks omitted by the French Author, Faithfully Abridg'd from the French Original (London, 1741), pp. 317–18.

(iv) The idolatries of China, India, Japan, Siam and Tibet

Thomas Stackhouse (1677–1752) entered St John's College, Cambridge, in 1694, but the degree of 'A.M.' which is mentioned on the title page of his books seems to have come from residence abroad and not from a British university. In 1701 he became headmaster to Hexham Grammar School and in 1704, after ordination, curate at Shepperton. From 1713 he was minister of the English church in Amsterdam and from 1731 curate at Finchley. He suffered from poverty and in 1722 published a work (originally anonymous) on the unfortunate position of 'the inferiour clergy in and about London'. Edmund Gibson, the Bishop of London, presented him to the living of Benham in 1733 but Stackhouse did not give up his house in London and seems to have worked for publishers there. He published his sermons, memoirs of Atterbury, two pieces criticising Woolston and the *Compleat Body of Divinity* from which the following passage is taken. The 'Compleat Body' may not contain everything but its size – 979 folio pages – indicates that it was a serious attempt to live up to its title! It covers arguments for the being of God and for divine revelation, the doctrines of creation, providence and predestination, the major events in history up to the time of Christ, the sacraments of grace, salvation, Christology, *post mortem* states and Christian morality. The extract given below comes from a chapter in which Stackhouse considers 'The State of Religion, and of the Idolatry, and Polytheism of the Heathen World'. His footnotes show that his material is derived from a few works of history, geography and travel. The term 'Banians' strictly refers to Hindu traders, especially from the area of Gujerat, but he uses it here, as was common, for Indian Hindus generally.

The *Chinese*, in general, worship the *Supreme* God, the King of Heaven and Earth, or rather the *Eternal Mind*, which (as they imagine) animates the whole Creation; but him they suppose to govern the Universe by a *Vicegerent*, whom they call *Laocon-Tzanty*; by the *Sun*, which they account an eternal Spirit; and by another Divinity, named *Chansay*, whom they suppose to have Dominion over all *sublunary* Things. To these Spirits, and the three principal Ministers employed under them, together with the Heavens, and all the heavenly Host, the Souls of their Ancestors, and of such as have been the Authors of any notable Invention, they present Oblations, and religious Worship; only with this Distinction, that the *King* alone sacrifices to *celestial* Bodies, the Sun and Stars, &c. the *Lords* and *Grandees* to *terrestrial*, to the Mountains and Lakes, &c. the *Gentlemen* and *Officers*, to the four Seasons of the Year, &c. and the *Commonalty* to their Houshold-Gods, and tutelar Angels. In their Temples, they have three remarkable Idols set up for the publick Use: *The Image of Immortality*, which they worship in the Form of a monstrous fat Man, sitting cross-legg'd, with his Breast open, and an huge prominent Belly: *The Image of Pleasure*, about twenty Foot high; and between these, another large Image, of thirty Foot, gilded all over, and adorned with a Crown, and rich Apparel, to which they pay a particular Adoration, and call it the great King *Kang*. Lesser Images are *innumerable*, not only in the Temples, but in the Streets, and other publick Places. Every one has his *Jos*, or Houshold-God, but they sometimes use them very coarsely; for if they have prayed to them any considerable Time, and find no Effect of their Prayers, they not only upbraid them with Neglect, but very often drag them through all the Kennels of the Streets: However, if in the mean Time, they happen to obtain what they asked, they set the Idol in its Place again, fall down before and adore it, excusing their *ignominious* Usage of it, and (to make it more *propitious* for the future) they wash, and paint, and gild it over afresh. They consecrate Temples to *Daemons*, who (as they fancy) are confined within Statues; and have, particularly, a *little Island* dedicated to the Devil, where they sacrifice solemnly to him, under the Name of *Camassono*, and where the *Vessels*, which pass by, make an Offering to him of whatever they have on board, and throw it into the Sea, to prevent his Anger.

The *Banians* believe, that there is but one *Supreme* God, whom they call *Parabrama*, which, in their Language, signifies *absolutely perfect*, existing from himself, and free from all Corruption: But then they say, that he has committed to *Brama* the Care of all Things concerning *Religion*; to *Wistnow*, another of his Sons, the Care of Men's *Rights* and *Necessities*; and to a third, the Power over the *Elements* and *human* Bodies. These three they represent by an Image with three Heads, rising out of one Trunk, and make their Addresses to them, as the chief Dispensers of divine Favours. But because they imagine, that God created the *Devil*, on Purpose to punish, and to do Mischief to Mankind, they therefore worship him likewise, and have their Temples filled with the Representations of him, in Statues of all Kinds of Metals and Materials. The *Figure*, under which they usually represent him, is dreadful to behold. Out of its *Head* (which is adorned with a triple Crown, in the Fashion of a *Tiara*) grow four Horns; out of its *Mouth* come two large *Teeth*, like the Tusk of a wild Boar; and its *Chin* is set out with a great ugly *Beard*. Under its Naval, between its two Thighs, comes out another Head, more ghastly than the former, having two Horns upon it, and from its Mouth thrusting out a filthy Tongue; and (as an Addition to all this Ghastliness) instead of Feet, it has *Paws*, and behind it a long Cow's Tail. This Figure they set upon a Table of Stone, which serves instead of an *Altar*; on the Right-hand of which, stands a *Trough*, full of Water, wherein those, that intend to do their Devotions, wash and purify themselves; and, on the Left, a *Box* or *Chest*, for the Reception of such Offerings, as they are minded to make to the *Braman*, or Priest of the Place, that is in waiting.

The *Japanese*, though they acknowledge a Supreme Being, which dwells in the highest *Heaven*; yet admit of several other inferior Gods, whom they place among the *Stars*; though, it must be owned, they do not much worship and adore them. What they chiefly worship and invoke are the Gods, whom they suppose to have the sovereign Command of their Country, and the chief Direction of its Produce, its Elements, its Animals, &c. and who, by Virtue of their Power, can more immediately affect their present Condition, to make them either miserable or happy, in this Life, and, by their Assistance and Intercession, obtain Rewards for them, proportionable to their Deeds, in that which is to come. Of these Gods of their own Country, they make mention of two Successions; the first, they say, was that of the *seven great Celestial Spirits*, who lived in the most ancient Times of the *Sun*, long before the Existence of Men and Heaven, and inhabited the *Japanese* World (the only Country, in their Opinion, then existing) many Millions of Years. The seventh and last of these *Celestial* Spirits, whose Name (as they fable) was *Isanagi*, begot of his divine Consort, *Isamani*, a second Succession of Divinities, called *the Succession of the five Terrestrial Deities*, who lived, and governed the Country of *Japan* a long while, and of whose Adventures, and *Knight-Errantries*, their Defeats of Giants, Dragons, and other Monsters, they tell many ridiculous Stories. But besides these invisible Deities, which they call by the Names of *Sin* and *Cami*, signifying *Souls* or *Spirits*, they have an infinite Number of *Pagods*; and, among these, one of a prodigious Size, in a stately Temple at *Meaco*, and other at *Tencheda*, no less famous for other extraordinary Qualities, have the principal Esteem and Adoration. Their Temples, which are curiously carved and gilt, and dedicated some to the *Devil*, and others to Apes, Rivers, and Fishes, have many frightful Figures in them, and in that dedicated to *Chamis*, one of the Heads of their *Sects*, they have as many Idols, as there are Days in the Year.

The *Siamese* believe, that there is One God, who created the Universe; but, at the same Time, they are persuaded, that he has under him several other Gods, by whom he governs the World. The God, whom they worship with the highest Devotion, they call *Sommona Codom*, and of him they tell this

Romantick Story; – that he, being the King of *Ceylon*, bestowed all his Estate in Charity, and even killed his Wife and Children, and gave them to the *Talapoins*, *i.e.* the Priests of the Place, to feed upon; that, before he entered into Bliss, he had acquired a prodigious Strength, and was able to work Miracles; could enlarge his Body to what Size he pleased, and then reduce it to so small a Point, as almost to be invisible; that he had two principal Disciples, *Pra Molga*, and *Pra Scarabout*; that *Pra Molga*, at the Request of the evil *Genii*, overturned the Earth, and took Hell-fire in the Hollow of his Hand, with a Design to extinguish it; but, finding himself not able to do it, he begged the Assistance of *Sommona Codom*, who, apprehending, that Men would abound in Wickedness, if the Dread of the Punishment were once removed, refused to grant it him. This, and Abundance more of the like Nature, the deluded People believe, and accordingly, place the Image of this their *Favourite* Deity, with his two Disciples, on the same Altar, and behind him several other Statues, representing the Officers of his Court, to whom they address their Vows and Supplications. They are of Opinion, that the Dead have Power to assist or torment the Living; and are therefore very careful and magnificent about their Burials. The Priests are hired to sing in the Room, on Pretence of teaching the Souls of the Deceased (which they suppose to stand about the Chamber) the Road to Heaven; and, as they believe themselves commonly tormented by their Apparitions, they carry Provisions to their Tombs, in order to appease them, and give Alms to the Priests, as esteeming Charity the best Ransom for the Sins of the Deceased . . .

From the Idolatry of the *Eastern* Nations, we proceed to that of the *Tartars*, (a People now subject to the Empire of *China*) who are said to acknowledge One God, the Maker of all Things, and the Author of all worldly Blessings and Punishments; but yet, instead of addressing him, they have a Kind of *inferior* Deity, called *Itoga*, whom they believe to be the God of the Earth, and him they worship with the greatest Solemnity, though their Adoration generally terminates in secular Advantages. They worship likewise the Sun and Moon, as the Authors of all the noble Productions of the Earth; and, though they do not believe that there is an *Hell*, yet they are persuaded there are *Devils*, and evil Spirits, which afflict and torment People in this Life; and therefore endeavour to *appease* them with rich Presents, and costly Sacrifices. One Sort of Idolatry, peculiar to this Nation, especially to those who live in the *Eastern* Parts of it, is, their worshipping a *living Man*, whom they call *Lama*, and to whom they pay such a superstitious Veneration, that the greatest Lords esteem themselves happy, if they can, by rich Presents, obtain some of his *Excrements* dried, which they put into a golden Box, and wear about their Neck, as a certain Preservative against Calamities of all Sorts. In a secret Part of his Palace, bedecked with Gold, Silver, and precious Stones, and illuminated with costly Lamps, the Man is shewn, sitting upon a stately Throne, and dressed in Robes excessively rich, to receive the Adorations of those, who come from all Parts to prostrate themselves before him, and humbly kiss his Feet. They call him the *Eternal Father*; and, that he may be thought *immortal*, and, in some Measure, answer his Name, his Priests take care to have one in Readiness, as like him as possible, to set up in his Stead, as soon as he dies; and burying the Corps privately, carry on the *Imposture* to a Miracle, and make his Votaries believe, that he really lives for ever.

From Thomas Stackhouse, *A Compleat Body of Speculative and Practical Divinity*, Third Edition, revised, corrected and improv'd by the author (London, T. Cox, 1743), pp. 525–8.

(v) Zoroaster

For Thomas Stackhouse (1677–1752) see V (iv) *supra*. Stackhouse's *New History of the Holy Bible* is his greatest work. It initially appeared in sections and was finally published in two massive folio volumes in 1737. It was illustrated by numerous plates which were changed in later editions – the 1760 edition from which the following extract is quoted has a note saying that its 104 engravings cost over £800 to produce and its text covers 1650 pages! The passage on Zoroaster is part of a Dissertation covering 'Profane History' in the centuries before Christ which closes the Old Testament part of the work. This dissertation deals briefly with 'some *extraordinary* and remarkable Events' in the Persian, Grecian, and Roman Empires' which are not included in the exposition of the Biblical history.

Stackhouse's references indicate that the sources for his remarks on Zoroaster are basically Thomas Hyde's *Religio Veterum Persarum* (1700) and Humphrey Prideaux's *Old and New Testament Connected* (1714–16) – indeed various sentences seem to have been lifted nearly verbatim from Prideaux's text! The treatment of Zoroaster not only shows the kind of information that was available about him but also illustrates how any parallels between Jewish and Christian ideas and practices and those found in 'other religions' are often held at this time to be the result of borrowing by the latter from the former. This accords with the view that the superiority of Christianity (and its Jewish antecedents) is confirmed by the originality of its contents – although in such cases as the one here it is the principle which determines the interpretation of the evidence rather than the evidence which confirms the principle!

At what Time this *Zoroastres* (or *Zardusht*, as the *Persians* call him) liv'd, there is a wide Difference both among the *Greek* and *Oriental* Writers; since some of them will have it, that he liv'd many years before the *Flood*, others in the Days of *Abraham*, and others again not before the Reign of *Darius*, the Son of *Hystaspes* . . .

If then we suppose that *Zoroastres* was the first Author of the Worship of Fire, we must acknowledge him more antient than *Moses*; but if we look upon him only as the *Reformer*, or *Restorer* of it, (tho' we cannot tell the precise Time when he flourish'd) it must not be long after the *Magians* fell into Disgrace, and may therefore very properly be thought to be in the Reign of *Darius Hystaspes*.

He was a Man of mean and obscure Parentage;* by Birth and Education very probably a *Jew*, and (as some suppose) a Servant to the Prophet *Daniel*; because he was certainly a Man of great Learning, and thoroughly acquainted with the Books of *Moses*. As soon as he took upon him the *prophetic* Office, he retir'd into a Cave, and there liv'd a long Time as a *Recluse*, pretending to be abstracted from all worldly Considerations, and to be given wholly to Prayers and Divine Meditations. In this Retirement he compos'd the Book,† wherein all his pretended Revelations are contain'd. The first Part of it consists of a Liturgy, which the *Magians*, in all their *Oratories* and *Fire-Temples*, make use of to this Day. The Rest is an historical Account of the Life, Actions, and Prophesies of its Author, the several Articles and Branches of his Superstition, together with Rules and Exhortations to Morality, wherein he is very pressing and exact, except his allowing of Incest; and the Whole being interspers'd with several Things taken out of the *Old Testament*, abundantly shews that his Original was from the *Jews*.

Upon leaving his Retirement, he went into *India* among the *Brachmans*, where having learn'd all their Knowledge in Mathematicks, Astronomy, and Natural Philosophy, he came back, and taught his Disciples these Sciences, which gain'd them so great a Reputation, that, for many Years after, a *learned Man*, and a *Magian* became equivalent Terms. Nay, he pretended, that, once upon a Time, he was taken up into Heaven to be instructed in those Doctrines, which he was to deliver unto Men; and there he heard God speak out of the Midst of a great and bright Flame of Fire; and for this Reason he taught his Followers, that Fire was the truest *Representation* of the Divine Presence, and the Sun (as the most perfect Fire) the more immediate *Throne* of his Glory; that, of the Fire, from whence God spake, he upon his Return brought some with him, and plac'd it on the Altar of the first *Fire-Temple* which he erected; from whence (as they say) it was propagated to all the rest; and this is the Reason, they give, for keeping it so carefully, and treating it with so much Superstition.

Having thus qualify'd himself to be a Prophet, he made his first Appearance in *Media*, in the City of *Ziz* say some, or in *Ecbatana*, (now *Tauris*) according to others; where the principal Doctrines that he profess'd (as a Refinement upon what the old *Magians* maintain'd) were these, – 'That there was one supreme Being, independent, and self-existing from all Eternity; that, under him there were two Angels, one the Angel of *Light*, who is the Author and Director of all *Good*, and the other the Angel of *Darkness*, who is the Author and Director of all *Evil*, and that these two, out of the Mixture of Light and Darkness, made all Things; that they are in perpetual Struggle with each other, and that where the Angel of Light prevails, there the most is Good, where the Angel of Darkness, there the most is Evil; that this Struggle shall continue unto the End of the World, when there shall be a general Resurrection, a Day of Judgment, and a Retribution to every one according to his Works; and that after this, the Angel of Darkness and his Disciples shall go into a World of their own, where they shall suffer, in everlasting Darkness, the Punishments of their evil Deeds; and the Angels of Light and his Disciples shall go also into a World of their own, where they shall receive, in everlasting Light, the Reward due unto their good Deeds, whereupon they shall remain separated for ever, and Light and Darkness are to be no more mix'd together to all Eternity.' And all this the Remainder of that Sect (which is now in *Persia* and *India*) do, after so many Ages, still hold without any Variation, even to this Day.

After *Zoroastres* had acted the Part of a Prophet in *Media*, and there settled all Things according to his Intentions, he remov'd from thence into *Bactria*, the most *Eastern* Province of *Persia*, and there settling in the City of *Balch* (which lies on the River *Oxus*, in the Confines of *Persia*) under the Protection of *Hystaspes* the Father of *Darius*, he soon spread his Imposture thro' all that Province with Success. From *Bactria* he went next to the Royal Court at *Susa*, where he manag'd his Pretensions with so much Address and Insinuation, that he made *Darius* likewise a Proselyte, and, from his Example, drew over the Courtiers, Nobility, and great Men of that City into the same Profession: But when, upon his Return into *Balch*, he attempted the like upon *Agarsp*, King of the *Oriental Scythians*, and a zealous *Sabian*, and pretended an Authority from *Darius* to that Purpose, the *Scythian* Prince resented it with such Indignation, that he invaded *Bactria* with an Army, and, having there defeated the Forces, that oppos'd him, slew *Zoroastres*, with all the Priests of his *Patriarchal* Church, amounting to the Number of eighty Persons, and demolish'd all the Fire-Temples in the Province: but, it was not long before *Darius* fell upon him, and reveng'd the Injury.

[*Footnotes*]

⋆ To this Purpose we may observe, that most of his *Reformations* in the old Religion of the *Magians* are taken either from the ancient Writings, or the ancient Usages of the *Jews*. For, whereas *Moses* heard God speak to him out of a *Flame of Fire* in the *Bush*; *Zoroastres* pretended, that he in like

Manner heard God speak to him, at the Time when he was taken up into Heaven. Whereas the *Jews* had a visible *Shechinah* of the Divine Presence among them, resting over the *Mercy-Seat* in the *Holy of Holies*, unto which they turn'd themselves, when they pray'd; *Zoroastres* taught his Disciples, that in the *Sun*, and in the sacred Fires in their Temples, God more especially dwelt, and therefore he oblig'd them to offer up all their Prayers with their Faces turn'd to both of these. Whereas the *Jews* had a sacred Fire, which came down from Heaven upon their Altar of Burnt-Offerings, which, as long as *Solomon*'s Temple stood, was preserv'd with the utmost Care from extinguishing; *Zoroastres* pretended, that, when he was in Heaven, he brought some of that *holy Fire* out of which God spake unto him, and therefore he enjoin'd, that it should be kept with diligent Care, and that all the Fires, on the Altars of new-erected *Fire-Temples*, should at first be lighted only from thence: And whereas the *Jews* were very nice in using no Wood on the Altar of their Temple, but what was reputed *clean*, and had it therefore all bark'd, and examin'd, before it was laid on, and, when it was laid on, allow'd of no Bellows to blow it, but left it to kindle and flame out of itself; *Zoroastres* ordain'd his Followers, in Relation to the sacred Fire of their Temples, to observe both these Particulars, commanding them to bark all their Wood, and use no other Means for the kindling it up into a Flame, but the pouring Oil, and leaving it to the Blasts of the open Air: And that he should, in so many singular and unobvious Things, imitate the *Jewish* Religion in the *Scheme* of his *Reformation*, it can hardly be imagin'd, without supposing, that at first he had his Education in it; nor is it improbable, that if (as some think) he was the Disciple of *Daniel*, his seeing that great and good Man arrive to such an Height of Dignity, by being a *true* Prophet of God, might put him upon the Thoughts of being a *false* one, in Hopes that, if he acted his Part well, he might obtain to himself the like Advancement . . .

† This book is called *Zendavesta*, and by Contraction *Zend*, which signifies a *Fire-Kindler*, such as a Tinder-Box is with us; and this fantastical Name the Impostor gave it, because, as he pretended, all that would read this Book, and meditate thereon, might from thence kindle in their Hearts the Fire of all true Love for God, and his holy Religion.

From Thomas Stackhouse, *A New History of the Holy Bible, from the Beginning of the World, to the Establishment of Christianity* (London, J. Hinton, 1760), II, pp. 1176–78.

(vi) Confucius compared with Christ

Joshua Toulmin (1740–1815) was a dissenting historian and biographer. Although trained in an Independent academy, he did not share its strict Calvinism. In 1761 he became minister of the Presbyterian church in Colyton. Difficulties arose over his refusal to baptise infants, and in 1764 he became the minister of a General Baptist church in Taunton. He stayed there for thirty-eight years although around 1770 he adopted Socinian views. He helped to found the Western Unitarian Society and in 1794 received the degree of DD from Harvard on Priestley's recommendation. He agreed with Priestley on doctrinal matters except over determinism. In 1791 Toulmin's liberal views in politics led to some threats against his person and his property. From 1804 he was minister to the New Meeting in Birmingham. His various publications include several biographies, among which is a notable one of Faustus Socinus, and theological works defending Baptist and Unitarian views. The following extract comes from a work in which he argues for the excellency of Christ both by examining his character and teaching and by comparing him with Mahomet, Socrates and Confucius. The extract is an example of how founders of other religions were compared with Christ in order to show the superiority of the latter. It is interesting because of the sympathetic way that it appreciates Confucius – in some ways he comes over rather like an intelligent English gentleman of good family – and also because its high evaluation of Christ is a reminder that the Christological difficulties of eighteenth-century Unitarianism did not arise from doubts about the deeds and instruction of Christ.

> *Confucius* came from a noble family; his mother being a woman of illustrious birth, and his father, besides having held the first and chief offices of the empire, was descended from one of the Emperors. Though the dignity of his· descent communicated no real merit to his character; yet it must be allowed to have been favourable to the reception and influence of his instructions, as well as to the pursuit of knowledge, and to the cultivation of his powers. Rank gives superior advantages, and commands respect. But, if we see a person, like *Jesus* of *Nazareth*, communicating lustre to his descent, instead of receiving glory from it; and, without the culture of education, displaying a wisdom surpassing that of the schools, is there not more to admire in such a character? . . . (pp. 224 f).
>
> It would be very uncandid and unfair to withhold from the *Christian Teacher* the praise due to the purity, sublimity, and perfection of his doctrine and morals. Indeed, the excellence of the Precepts he delivered, commands

the applause of every reflecting mind. With the considerate and impartial, can it fail of producing an *higher* effect? We read of the morals of *Confucius*, and we admire the *man*: we study those of *Christ*, and we revere the *Prophet*. It is an acknowledged point, that the principles of the *former* were the result of enquiry and study: from the education and condition of the *latter*, we are naturally led, since no *human* sources of his doctrine appear, to resolve it into *divine* communications . . .

Confucius did not exhibit the divine placability to sinners, nor announce the forgiveness of the penitent. *Christ* came preaching repentance, and published the glad tidings of pardon and favour.

Confucius laid down, as the leading principle of *his* philosophy, acting according to *reason*. *Christ* referred every rule of conduct to the will of his *Father in heaven*. *Religion* was the spirit, which pervaded the system of one: *Human wisdom* was the chief principle, the ultimate criterion of the laws of the other. *Confucius* seemed to aim at little else than establishing the influence of a refined system of *Policy*, and the precepts of social conduct. *Christ* began with the *heart*, with poverty and meekness of spirit, and with purity of soul: and H E addresses his sanctions to the secret views of the mind, leading the thoughts forward to a distant recompence.

Confucius no where taught the doctrine of a future state: *Christ* called on men to "lay up treasures in heaven," and had "the words of eternal life." How insinuating, how weighty the precepts of *Christ*, when accompanied with *these* motives!

The principles of *Confucius* were diffused through various treatises; those of our *Lord* comprehended in a small compass; and, with an admirable union of majesty and simplicity, conveyed in a few familiar discourses, or striking parables. The philosophy of the *former* was a very mixt kind; and his collections, from the ancient laws, took a wide scope, embracing the principles of Logic, Rhetoric, and Politics, as well as of Morality. Though this variety of instruction may do honour to the extent of his enquiries, and the comprehension of his mind; yet the moral and spiritual doctrine of *Christ* appears with greater *simplicity*, and addresses the mind with greater *force*, as it is *less complex*, and of more universal importance, having *only the moral improvement* of mankind for its object. In a word, *Christ* shines with a singular and superior glory as the Preacher of *Righteousness*, and the true Way to *eternal Life* . . . (pp. 230–33).

The signal part of *Confucius's* character, was his zeal and self-denial in the prosecution of the great and benevolent scheme which he pursued. His whole delight was in teaching, and conciliating the attention of men to his doctrine. Such was the ardor with which he followed after virtue himself, and with which he laboured to promote the practice of it, that his real efforts fell short of his wishes; and he frequently blamed himself for not being assiduous enough in instructing others, or not being sufficiently vigilant and active in improving his own character, we must applaud this zeal and ardor.

But can we pass a righteous judgment on characters, unless we yield the like tribute of praise to *him*, whose meat and drink it was to do the will of him that sent him? Let it be remembered, how *Jesus* spent his days in journies, labours, and preaching, and *his* nights in devotion . . .

Confucius is celebrated for the self-denial he practised, as well as the activity he exerted. That he might be free from all incumbrances and connexions, which would impede his efforts to propogate his Philosophy, he divorced his wife, whom he had married at the age of nineteen. The celibacy of our Lord, had undoubtedly the same general design. The matrimonial connexion would not have been perfectly compatible with the unsettled life to which his public ministry called him, nor with the singular character he was to support. But his self-denial, in foregoing the innocent delights of this union, redounded to the honour of his virtue . . .

Confucius rose by his merit to public dignities: He filled various high employments, and was advanced to the rank of Minister of State. But his greatest aim being the public good, and the propagation of his doctrine, when he saw that he could not accomplish his end, but was frustrated in his hopes, he withdrew from the posts he filled, relinquished his honours, left the Court, exiled himself from his native country, travelled through other kingdoms, to find minds more disposed to relish and pursue his maxims, and by the neglect of his interest reduced himself to extreme poverty. A noble sacrifice this to the cause of reforming a corrupt State, and of amending mankind.

Let the Christian set against it the disinterested zeal of *his Master*; who, while the foxes have holes, and the birds of the air have nests, had not where to lay his head: who was indebted to the liberality of others for the supply of his common wants . . .

Confucius left the world with the sentiments of despondency. A few days before his death, he told his disciples with tears, that he was overcome with grief at the sight of the disorders which prevailed in the empire. The reflexion so grievously afflicted him, that he presently languished: and seven days before his death, after having testified his regret and trouble at seeing that his maxims and instructions were not observed, he dolorously subjoined, seeing that things go thus, "nothing more remains than to die." He had no sooner said these words, but he fell into a lethargy, which ended in his death.

Contrast this language and these emotions with the sentiments and views which *Christ* expressed on the reception of *his* labours . . . Here the benevolence of *Jesus* appears, free from the chagrin of disappointment, from which partly the tears of the *Chinese* seem to have flowed.

Our *divine Master*, while H E wept for his country, was possessed with the most comprehensive, elevating views of the operation of his doctrine and the future spread of his cause . . .

The mind of *Jesus* looks forward. H E doth not give up all as lost, because he had been rejected, and was about to suffer death. H E looks beyond his sufferings, and he anticipates the reception of his doctrine in the world . . . (pp. 234–40).

Confucius, having discoursed of the perfection of reason and virtue, used these remarkable words: "We must wait for the coming of this *perfectly holy man*; and then we may hope, that, having such a Guide and Teacher, virtue, which is of such an excellent nature, will be brought into practice and be performed by men."

A little after, *Confucius* is related to say of the Emperor, who ruled according to the law of reason and example of the God of Heaven, "that such a one need not doubt but his virtue will be approved *by that holy person who is expected to come upon earth.*"

And according to a tradition universally received amongst the Chinese, *Confucius* was often heard to say, that in the West *the Holy One* will appear.

All these expressions seem to be presages, which this wise and good man had concerning the coming of *Christ*, the H O L Y   O N E   O F   G O D, to deliver to mankind a perfect rule of religion and virtue. And his saying that his appearance would be in *the West*, seems to point out *Judea*, the most western country of *Asia*, in respect to *China*. And as there is no absurdity in supposing that such virtuous and religious heathens as *Confucius* was, might be inspired with a foreknowledge of the coming of the Saviour of the World: so, whenever God shall raise up Preachers of true Christianity amongst the people of *China*, they may be led to see and be convinced, that *Christ* is the *Holy One*, and that *divine Teacher* whom their own *Prophet* so many ages before had taught them to expect: and this may be the means of their conversion to the *Christian* Faith.

From Joshua Toulmin, *Dissertations on the Internal Evidences and Excellence of Christianity: and on the Character of Christ, compared with that of some other celebrated Founders of Religion or Philosophy* (London, J. Johnson, 1785), pp. 224–43.

(vii) Indian insights into philosophy and morality

Sir William Jones (1746–94) was a student at Harrow school, where he taught himself some Arabic and Hebrew, and at University College, Oxford, where he studied Persian, Arabic, Chinese and several European languages. He became a fellow of the college in 1764. He produced works on oriental literature but turned to the law for financial reasons. Called to the bar in 1774, he became a commissioner in bankruptcy two years later. In 1783 he was knighted on his appointment as a judge of the Supreme Court at what was then known as Fort William and now as Calcutta. In January 1784 he founded the Asiatic Society of Bengal and remained its president until his death. It was instituted to enquire into the natural and civil history, the antiquities, arts, sciences and literature of Asia. Its journal, *Asiatick Researches*, was an important medium for disseminating in Europe the results of serious investigations into these matters. Its early volumes contain the annual Anniversary Discourses which Jones gave to the society. Jones himself was a classical scholar and historian of ability, and could write authoritatively on astronomy, philology, botany and music as well as being a pioneer in the European study of Sanskrit. He published various works on Hindu and Muslim law, Arabic and Persian poetry, and parts of the Vedas. The following passage is part of his last Anniversary Discourse when he spoke to thirty-six members of the Society on 'The Philosophy of the Asiaticks'. In this extract he shows that he does not share the view that the supremacy of Christianity requires its tradition to be the original of all insights. He considers, rather, that various philosophical insights were grasped initially in India and perhaps later adopted by Greek thinkers. Furthermore, modern idealist (and perhaps materialist) views were anticipated in ancient Indian thought. The basic truths of morality were also independently perceived in different parts of the East and missionaries are warned not to pretend otherwise. Such pretence is not necessary to the truth of their message and their hearers will be able to expose its falsehood. (*Cf.* also Robertson, I (ii) for further remarks on Indian thought.)

. . . the oldest head of a sect, whose entire work is preserved, was (according to some authors) C A P I L A; not the divine personage, a reputed grandson of B R A H M A', to whom C R I ' S H N A compares himself in the *Gitá*, but a sage of his name, who invented the *Sánc'hya*, or *Numeral*, philosophy, which C R I ' S H N A himself appears to impugn in his conversation with A R J U N A, and which, as far as I can recollect it from a few original texts, resembled in part the metaphysicks of P Y T H A G O R A S, and in part the theology of Z E N O: his doctrines were enforced and illustrated, with some additions, by the venerable P A T A N - J A L I, who has also left us a fine comment on the grammatical rules of P A ' N I N I, which are more obscure, without a gloss, than the darkest oracle; and here by the way let me add, that I refer to metaphysicks the curious and important science of *universal grammar*, on which many subtil disquisitions may be found interspersed in the particular grammars of the ancient *Hindus*, and in those of the more modern *Arabs*. The next founder, I believe, of a philosophical school was G O ' T A M A, if, indeed, he was not the most ancient of all; for his wife A H A L Y ' A was, according to *Indian* legends, restored to a human shape by the great R A ' M A; and a sage of his name, whom we have no reason to suppose a different personage, is frequently mentioned in the *Véda* itself; to his rational doctrines those of C A N A ' D A were in general conformable; and the philosophy of them both is usually called *Nyáya*, or *logical*, a title aptly bestowed; for it seems to be a system of metaphysicks and logick better accomodated than any other anciently known in *India*, to the natural reason and common sense of mankind; admitting the actual existence of *material substance* in the popular acceptation of the word *matter*, and comprising not only a body of sublime dialecticks, but an artificial method of reasoning, with distinct names for the three parts of a proposition, and even for those of a regular syllogism. Here I cannot refrain from introducing a singular tradition, which prevailed, according to the well-informed author of the *Dabistán*, in the *Panjáb* and in several *Persian* provinces, that, 'among other *Indian* curiosities, which C A L L I S T H E N E S transmitted to his uncle, was *a technical system of logick*, which the *Bráhmens* had communicated to the inquisitive *Greek*,' and which the *Mohammedan* writer supposes to have been the groundwork of the famous *Aristotelean* method: if this be true, it is one of the most interesting facts, that I have met with in *Asia*; and if it be false, it is very extraordinary, that such a story should have been fabricated either by the candid M O H S A N I *Fánì*; or by the simple *Pársís Pandits*, with whom he had conversed; but, not having had leisure to study the *Nyáya Sástra*, I can only assure you, that I have frequently seen perfect syllogisms in the philosophical writings of the *Bráhmens*, and have often heard them used in their verbal controversies. Whatever might have been the merit or age of G O ' T A M A, yet the most celebrated *Indian* school is that . . . founded by V Y A ' S A, and supported in most respects by his pupil J A I M I N I, whose dissent on a few points is mentioned by his master with respectful moderation: their several systems are frequently distinguished by the names of the first and second *Mímánsá*, a word, which, like *Nyáya*, denotes the operations and conclusions of reason; but the tract of V Y A ' S A has in general the appellation of *Védánta*, or the scope and end of the *Véda*, on the texts of which, as they were understood by the philosopher, who collected them, his doctrines are principally grounded. The fundamental tenet of the *Védántí* school, to which in a more modern age the incomparable S A N C A R A was a firm and illustrious adherent, consisted, not in denying the existence of matter, that is, of solidity, impenetrability, and extended figure (to deny which would be lunacy), but, in correcting the popular notion of it, and in contending, that it has no essence independent of mental perception, that existence and perceptibility are convertible terms, that external appearances and sensations are illusory, and would vanish into nothing, if the divine energy, which alone sustains them, were suspended but for a moment; an opinion which E P I C H A R M U S and P L A T O seem to have adopted, and which has been maintained in the present century with great elegance, but with little publick applause; partly because it has been misunderstood, and partly because it has been misapplied by the false reasoning of some unpopular writers, who are said to have disbelieved in the moral attributes of G O D, whose omnipresence, wisdom, and goodness are the basis of the *Indian* philosophy: I have not sufficient evidence on the subject to profess a belief in the doctrine of the *Védánta*, which human reason alone could, perhaps, neither fully demonstrate, nor fully disprove; but it is manifest, that nothing can be farther removed from impiety than a system wholly built on the purest devotion; and the inexpressible difficulty, which any man, who shall make the attempt, will assuredly find in giving a satisfactory definition of *material substance*, must induce us to deliberate with coolness, before we censure the learned and pious restorer of the ancient *Véda*; though we cannot but admit, that, if the common opinions of mankind *be* the criterion of philosophical truth, we must adhere to the system of G O ' T A M A, which the *Bráhmens* of this province almost universally follow.

If the metaphysicks of the *Védántís* be wild and erroneous, the pupils of B U D D H A have run, it is asserted, into an error diametrically opposite; for they are charged with denying the existence of pure spirit, and with believing nothing absolutely and really to exist but *material substance*; a heavy accusation which ought only to have been made on positive and incontestable proof, especially by the orthodox *Bráhmens*, who, as B U D D H A dissented from their ancestors in regard to *bloody sacrifices*, which the *Véda* certainly prescribes, may not unjustly be suspected of low and interested malignity. Though I cannot credit the charge, yet I am unable to prove it entirely false, having only read a few pages of a *Saugata* book, which Captain K I R K - P A T R I C K had lately the kindness to give me; but it begins, like other *Hindu* books, with the word *O'm*, which we know to be a symbol of the divine attributes: then follows, indeed, a mysterious hymn to the Goddess of Nature, by the name of *Áryá*, but with several other titles, which the *Bráhmens* themselves continually bestow on their *Dévì*; now the *Bráhmens*, who have no idea, that any such personage exists as D È ' V Ì, or the *Goddess*, and only mean to express allegorically the *power* of G O D, exerted in creating, preserving and renovating this universe, we cannot with justice infer, that the dissenters admit no deity but *visible nature*: the *Pandit*, who now attends me, and who told Mr. W I L K I N S, that the *Saugatas* were atheists, would not have attempted to resist the decisive evidence of the contrary, which appears in the very instrument, on which he was consulted, if his understanding had not been blinded by the intolerant zeal of a mercenary priesthood. A literal version of the book just mentioned (if any studious man had learning and industry equal to the task) would be an inestimable treasure . . .

T H A T both ethicks and abstract law might be reduced to the *method of science*, cannot surely be doubted; but, although such a method would be of infinite use in a system of universal, or even of national, jurisprudence, yet the *principles* of morality are so few, so luminous, and so ready to present themselves on every occasion, that the practical utility of a scientifical arrangement, in a treatise on ethicks, may very justly be questioned. The moralists of the east have in general chosen to deliver their precepts in short sententious maxims, to illustrate them by sprightly comparisons, or to inculcate them in the very ancient form of agreeable apologues: there are, indeed, both in *Arabick* and *Persian*, philosophical tracts on ethicks written with sound ratiocination and elegant perspicuity: but in every part of this eastern world, from *Pekin* to *Damascus*, the popular teachers of moral wisdom have immemorially been poets, and there would be no end of enumerating their works, which are still extant in the five principal languages of *Asia*. Our divine religion, the truth of which (if any history be true) is abundantly proved by historical evidence, has no need of such aids, as many are willing to give it, by asserting, that the wisest men of this world were ignorant of the two great maxims, that *we must act in respect of others, as we should wish them to act in respect of ourselves*, and that, *instead of returning evil for evil, we should confer benefits even on those who injure us*; but the first rule is implied in a speech of L Y S I A S, and expressed in distinct phrases by T H A L E S and P I T - T A C U S; and I have even seen it word for word in the original of C O N - F U C I U S, which I carefully compared with the *Latin* translation. It has been usual with zealous men, to ridicule and abuse all those, who dare on this point to quote the *Chinese* philosopher; but, instead of supporting their cause, they would shake it, if it could be shaken, by their uncandid asperity; for they ought to remember, that one great end of revelation, as it is most expressly declared, was not to instruct the wise and few, but the many and unenlightened. If the conversation, therefore, of the *Pandits* and *Maulavis* in this country shall ever be attempted by protestant missionaries, they must beware of asserting, while they teach the gospel of truth, what those *Pandits* and *Maulavis* would know to be false: the former would cite the beautiful *A'ryá* couplet, which was written at least three centuries before our era, and which pronounces the duty of a good man, even in the most of his destruction, to consist *not only in forgiving, but even in a desire of benefiting, his destroyer, as the* Sandal-*tree, in the instant of its overthrow, sheds perfume on the axe, which fells it*; and the latter would triumph in repeating the verse of S A D Ì, who represents *a return of good for good as a slight reciprocity*, but says to the virtuous man, 'Confer benefits on him, who has injured thee,' using an *Arabick* sentence, and a maxim apparently of the ancient *Arabs*. Nor would the *Muselmans* fail to recite four distichs of H A ' F I Z, who has illustrated that maxim with fanciful but elegant allusions;

Learn from yon orient shell to love thy foe,
And store with pearls the hand, that brings thee wo:
Free, like yon rock, from base vindictive pride,
Imblaze with gems the wrist, that rends thy side:
Mark, where yon tree rewards the stony show'r
With fruit nectareous, or the balmy flow'r:
All nature calls aloud: 'Shall man do less
Than heal the smiter, and the railer bless?'

Now there is not a shadow of reason for believing, that the poet of *Shiraz* had borrowed this doctrine from the *Christians*; but, as the cause of *Christianity* could never be promoted by falsehood or errour, so it will never be obstructed by candour and veracity; for the lessons of C O N F U C I U S and C H A N A C Y A, of S A D Ĩ and H A ' F I Z, are unknown even at this day to millions of *Chinese* and *Hindus, Persians* and other *Mahommedans*, who toil for their daily support; nor, were they known ever so perfectly, would they have a divine sanction with the multitude; so that, in order to enlighten the minds of the ignorant, and to enforce the obedience of the perverse, it is evidently *a priori*, that a revealed religion was necessary in the great system of providence: but my principal motive for introducing this topick, was to give you a specimen of that ancient oriental morality, which is comprised in an infinite number of *Persian, Arabick*, and *Sanscrit* compositions.

From 'The Philosophy of the Asiaticks', the eleventh anniversary discourse delivered to the Asiatick Society on 20 February 1794 and printed in *The Works of Sir William Jones* (London, G. G. and J. Robinson, and R. H. Evans, 1799), I, pp. 163–9.

VI

Discovery and instruction

The following passages provide examples, first, of how the thoughts and practices of the East were used for instruction and, then, of how those thoughts and practices were discovered. Of the first pair of passages, one is from a fictitious work which pretends that it gives a translation of an ancient Eastern manuscript recently brought to light, while the other is an example of how Eastern customs might be used to illuminate Biblical allusions. The other extract is an example of a travellers report about what had been observed of religious customs in the places visited. These extracts indicate the kind of material which many of the attempts to understand 'other religions' had to use as evidence.

(i) Wisdom from the East

Philip Dormer Stanhope, fourth Earl of Chesterfield (1694–1773), entered the House of Commons in 1715 but then had to retire to France after making a maiden speech since he was still under age! He was elected again in 1722 but defeated in elections the following year. On the death of his father in 1726 he entered the Lords. From 1728 to 1732 he was ambassador to The Hague. He married a natural daughter of George I for financial and political reasons but largely neglected her. In 1742 he was involved in the defeat of Sir Robert Walpole's ministry and in the next few years he served for short periods as Lord Lieutenant of Ireland and then as Secretary of State for the North. After 1748 he was not directly involved in politics to any great extent. He wrote a great deal on political and social matters in the *World*. After his death his *Letters* to his natural son, Philip, were published and enjoyed popularity. *The Oeconomy of Human Life* was published anonymously and at first was ascribed to Robert Dodsley, its publisher, but it is now recognised to be by the Earl of Chesterfield. The first two extracts quoted below are part of the prefatory material in which 'an English Gentleman residing in China' tells how the Chinese Emperor appoints an ambassador to go to Tibet to seek ancient manuscripts there and then about an ancient manuscript which the ambassador is supposed to have found there. The remaining extracts are from the correspondent's translation into English of the ambassador's Chinese version of this manuscript. They show what might pass at the time as the style and content of Eastern wisdom. In fact the material is reminiscent of the Psalms and Proverbs. The views on women and servants will probably raise hackles in this egalitarian and androgynous age but the religious instruction expresses a safely pious theism!

> Adjoining to China on the west, is the large country of Thibet, called by some Barantola: in a province of this country, named Lasa, resides the grand Lama, or high-priest of these idolaters; who is reverenc'd, and even ador'd as a god, by most of the neighbouring nations. The high opinion which is entertained of his sacred character induces prodigious numbers of religious people to resort to Lasa, to pay their homage to him, and to give him presents, in order to receive his blessing. His residence is in a most magnificent pagod, or temple, built on the top of the mountain Poutala. The foot of this mountain, and even the whole district of Lasa, is inhabited by an incredible number of Lamas, of different ranks and orders, several of whom have very grand pagods erected to their honour, in which they receive a kind of inferior worship. The whole country, like Italy, abounds with priests; and they entirely subsist of the great number of rich presents, which are sent them from the utmost extent of Tartary, from the empire of the great Mogul, and from almost all parts of the Indies. When the grand Lama receives the adorations of the people, he is rais'd on a magnificent altar, and sits cross-legg'd upon a splendid cushion: his worshippers prostrate themselves before him in the humblest and most abject manner; but he returns not the least sign of respect, nor ever speaks, even to the greatest princes; he only lays his hand upon their heads, and they are fully perswaded that they receive from thence a full forgiveness of all their sins. They are likewise so extravagant as to imagine, that he knows all things, even the secrets of the heart: and his particular disciples, being a select number of about two hundred of the most eminent Lamas, have the address to make the people believe he is immortal; and that whenever he appears to die, he only changes his abode, and animates a new body.
>
> The learned in China have long been of opinion, that in the archives of this grand temple, some very ancient books have for many ages been conceal'd: and the present emperor [sc. of China], who is very curious in searching after

the writings of antiquity, became at length so fully convinced of the probability of this opinion, that he determined to try whether any discovery of this sort could be made. To this end, his first care was to find out a person eminently skilful in the ancient languages and characters. He at length pitch'd upon one of the *Han-lins*, or doctors of the first order, whose name was *Cao-tsou*, a man about fifty years of age, of a grave and noble aspect, of great eloquence, and who, by an accidental friendship with a certain learned Lama, who had resided many years at Peking, was become entirely master of the language, which the Lamas of Thibet use among themselves . . . (pp. vi–x).

But the most ancient piece he hath discover'd, and which none of the Lamas for many ages had been able to interpret or understand, is a small system of morality, written in the language and character of the ancient Gymnosophists or Bramins; but by what particular person, or in what time, he does not pretend to determine. This piece, however, he wholly translated; though, as he himself confesses, with an utter incapacity of reaching, in the Chinese language, the strength and sublimity of the original. The judgments and opinions of the Bonzees, and the learned doctors, are very much divided concerning it. Those who admire it the most highly, are very fond of attributing it to Confucius, their own great philosopher; and get over the difficulty of its being written in the language and character of the ancient Bramins, by supposing this to be only a translation, and that the original work of Confucius is lost. Some will have it to be the insitututes of *Lao Kiun*, another Chinese philosopher, contemporary with Confucius, and founder of the sect of *Tao-sseë* . . . There are others who, from some particular marks and sentiments which they find in it, suppose it to be written by the Bramin *Dandamis*, whose famous letter to Alexander the great is recorded by the European Writers . . . (pp. xiv–xvi).

Anger

As the whirlwind in its fury teareth up trees, and deformeth the face of nature; or as an earth-quake in its convulsions overturneth whole cities: so the rage of an angry man throweth mischief around him; danger and destruction wait on his hand.

But consider, and forget not, thine own weakness; so shalt thou pardon the failings of others . . . (p. 36).

Woman

Give ear, fair daughter of love, to the instructions of prudence, and let the precepts of truth sink deep in thine heart . . . Remember thou are made man's reasonable companion, not the slave of his passion; the end of thy being is not merely to gratify his loose desire, but to assist him in the toils of life, to sooth him with thy tenderness, and recompense his care with soft endearments.

Who is she that winneth the heart of man, that subdueth him to love, and reigneth in his breast?

Lo! yonder she walketh in maiden sweetness; with innocence in her mind, and modesty on her cheek.

Her hand seeketh employment, her foot delighteth not in gadding abroad . . . (pp. 45 f).

Masters and servants

Repine not, O man, at the state of servitude: it is the appointment of God, and hath many advantages, it removeth thee from the cares and sollicitudes of life.

The honour of a servant is his fidelity; his highest virtues are submission and obedience.

Be patient therefore under the reproofs of thy master; and when he rebuketh thee, answer not again: the silence of thy resignation shall not be forgotten . . .

And thou who art a master, be just to thy servant; if thou expectest from him fidelity; and reasonable in thy commands, if thou expectest a ready obedience . . . (pp. 69 f).

Religion

There is but one God, the author, the creator, the governor of the world; almighty, eternal, and incomprehensible.

The sun is not God, tho' his noblest image; he enlighteneth the world with his brightness, his warmth giveth life to the products of the earth; admire him as the creature, the instrument of God, but worship him not.

To the One who is supreme, most wise, and beneficent, and to him alone, belong worship, adoration, thanks-giving, and praise.

Who hath stretched forth the heavens with his hand; who hath described with his finger the courses of the stars.

Who setteth bounds to the ocean, which it cannot pass; and saith unto the stormy winds, Be ye still.

Who shaketh the earth, and the nations tremble; who darteth his lightnings, and the wicked are dismay'd.

Who calleth forth worlds, by the word of his mouth; who smiteth with his arm, and they sink into nothing.

'O reverence the majesty of the Omnipotent; and tempt not his anger, lest thou be destroy'd.'

The providence of God is over all his works; he ruleth and directeth with infinite wisdom.

He hath instituted laws for the government of the world: he hath wonderfully varied them in all beings; and each, by its nature, conformeth to his will.

In the depths of his mind he revolveth all knowledge; the secrets of futurity lie open before him.

The thoughts of thy heart are naked to his view; he knoweth thy determinations before they are made.

With respect to his prescience there is nothing contingent; with respect to his providence there is nothing accidental.

Wonderful he is in all his ways; his counsels are inscrutable; the manner of his knowledge transcendeth thy conception.

'Pay, therefore, to his wisdom all honour and veneration; and bow down thyself in humble and submissive obedience, to his supreme direction.' . . .

The creatures of his hand declare his goodness, and all their enjoyments speak his praise: he cloatheth them with beauty, he supporteth them with food, he preserveth them with pleasure from generation to generation . . .

But thee, O man, he hath distinguish'd with peculiar favour; and exalted thy station above all creatures.

He hath endow'd thee with reason, to maintain thy dominion; he hath fitted thee with language, to improve by society; and exalted thy mind with the powers of meditation, to contemplate and adore his inimitable perfections.

And in the laws he hath ordained as the rule of thy life, so kindly hath he suited thy duty to thy nature, that obedience to his Precepts is happiness to thyself . . .

The Lord is just and righteous; and will judge the earth with equity and truth . . .

The high and the low, the rich and the poor, the wise and the ignorant, when the soul hath shaken off the cumbrous shackles of this mortal life; shall equally receive from the sentence of God, a just and everlasting retribution, according to their works . . .

This is the true O E C O N O M Y of H U M A N L I F E.

From [The Earl of Chesterfield], *The Oeconomy of Human Life*, Translated from an *Indian* Manuscript, written by an ancient B R A M I N, to which is prefixed An Account of the Manner in which the said M A N U - S C R I P T was discover'd in A L E T T E R from an *English* Gentleman, now residing in *China*, to the Earl of ★★★★ (London, R. Dodsley and M. Cooper, seventh edition, 1751), pp. vi–x, xiv–vi, 36, 45–6, 69–70, 91–6.

(ii) Local light on Solomon's song

Thomas Harmer (1714–88) was educated for the Independent ministry at Fund Academy in Moorfields. Although he was elected pastor of an

Independent church at Wattisfield in 1733, it was not until the following
year, when he came of age, that he was ordained. His liberal sympathies,
evangelical endeavours and studiousness combined to give him considerable influence among the nonconformists of the eastern counties.
He wrote various pieces on their churches in Norfolk and Suffolk as well
as exegetical works which illustrated Biblical passages by reference to
Eastern customs. Besides his *Outlines of a New Commentary on Solomon's
Song* (1768), from which the following extracts are taken, he published
*Observations on Divers Passages of Scripture . . . From . . . Books of Voyages
and Travels* (1764) and *Some Account of the Jewish Doctrine of the Resurrection* (1771). In the following extracts he comments on the use of perfumes
in Eastern weddings, seeks to date incidents referred to in the Song of
Songs by reference to the natural history alluded to therein and suggests a
parallel between Solomon's litter (Song of Songs 3, 7) and an Indian
prince riding in a howdah on board an elephant!

If my Readers should not be led, by what I have said, to adopt the sentiments
contained in these papers, I am willing however to hope, that this way of
explaining this obscure part of Scripture will not appear, to the candid and
ingenuous, an U N N A T U R A L Attempt: What can be more likely to
lead us into the *literal sense* of an Ancient Nuptial Poem, than the comparing it
with similar modern productions of the East, along with Antique Jewish
Compositions of the same kind? especially if we enlarge our Plan, by carefully taking in every *additional* account relating to the Marriages of Princes in
those countries, mentioned in the Holy Scriptures, as well as modern Travellers? This *general* management however, as well as the *more dubious particulars*
contained in these sheets, I chearfully leave to the Judgment of the Public . . .
(pp. xxiii f).

Observation IV

In *what manner* the Royal Bridegroom's Vestments were made fragrant, the
Psalmist doth not inform us, but besides *Unctions, Sprinkling* of odoriferous
Waters on the Clothes, and *Fumigations in confined places*, they sometimes *burn*
these sweet Odours in a more *unconfined* way in the Levant, and in particular
at their Weddings.

So Lady M. Wortley Montague, in the account which she gives of the
Reception of a beautiful young Turkish bride at the Bagnio . . . tells us
Perfumes were burnt there after this manner, *two Virgins met her at the Door,
two others filled Silver Gilt Pots with Perfumes, and began the Procession, the rest
following in pairs to the number of thirty — in this order they marched round the three
large rooms of the Bagnio.* This was done in an open Bagnio, and in a Procession
round the several large rooms; in common the head is *wrapped up in a sort of*

Veil, or the smoke by some means confined, in order that the Hair may the better imbibe the Fragrancy.

Agreeably to this, the Bride of Solomon is represented here, (in ch. iii. 6), as perfumed in a solemn Procession made upon occasion of the King's entering with her into Jerusalem. The *Virgins* went out to *meet them*, ch. iii. 11; they burnt Odours before them, ver. 6, with a profusion that became a Royal Wedding, so that the smoke ascended up like Pillars, it seems . . . Or these Pillars of Smoke may refer to the burning Perfumes in Jerusalem, as a Preparative for the Reception of the Royal Pair: so Maillet describing the Entrance of the Ambassadors of an Eastern Monarch, sent to propose Marriage to an Ægyptian Queen, into the Capital of that country, tells us, *the Streets through which they passed were strewed with Flowers, and* precious Odours *kept burning in the Windows from very early in the Morning, embalmed the Air there*, besides other expressions of regard that were made use of on that occasion. Let. v.

Observation V

A Litter, Palanquin, or something of that kind, was used, it should seem, in this Procession for the conveyance of the Bride; and was something so magnificent, and perhaps so unusual too, as to be thought worthy of being celebrated in these Songs.

The xlvth Psalm, I think, whether it refers to these Nuptials, or to some other Royal Wedding, takes notice of this manner of conveying the Bride, 'The King's Daughter is all glorious W I T H I N; her Clothing is of wrought Gold,' ver. 13. Where the word *within*, is not that which is used to signify within a *man's self*, but expresses the being *within some place*. Glorious within therefore, which is said of the King's Daughter, means her being covered with Vestments of wrought gold, *within some Vehicle* in which she rode.

Agreeably to this, when it is said, Cant. iii. 7, 'Behold *his Bed* which is Solomon's,' it is to be understood, I presume, of the Bed, the Litter, the Palanquin, or whatever other name better suits it, which Solomon *prepared* for his Bride, and in which *she rode* on this solemn occasion. The Description of it follows, ver. 9, 10, and puts those that have read Mandelslo in mind of that pompous Vehicle, which is depicted in his Book, and in which he saw an Eastern Governor carried. I will not take upon me to affirm that Solomon's Bed was precisely the same, but I think I may venture to say, that if it's top and bottom had been made of Cedar of Lebanon; if this top had afterwards been covered with Purple; if the Pillars had been of Silver; the Carpet underneath of Cloth of Gold; and the Furniture on which this East-Indian Viceroy sat had been Needle-work, wrought by the Daughters of Jerusalem, and presented as a Token of Duty and Love; no words could have given a more lively description of this Vehicle in short, than this passage of the prophetic Poet. All that is wanting is the transferring it from an *Elephant*, which it seems this East-Indian used, to a Camel, which would better suit, I presume, the state of things in Judaea in the days of Solomon . . . (pp. 123–7).

Observation XII

All the *Notes of the Season* that occur in this book, so far as they are understood, agree to the time of the *blossoming of the Vine* . . .

Ibrahim makes the Singing of the *Nightingale* and Roses, contemporary things with the *blossoming of the Vine*.

"The Nightingale now wanders in the Vines;
"Her Passion is to seek Roses.
"I went down to admire the Beauty of the Vines;
"The Sweetness of your Charms hath ravished my Soul."

As the Song of Solomon makes the time of *Singing*, and of the Vines with the *tender Grape giving a good Smell*, conincident.

The time when Roses blow and Vines blossom *with us* is about the end of June, and consequently about the end of April, I imagine, in Palestine; for though I do not remember to have observed in any Traveller an account when *they* blossom there, I have remarked, that other vegetable productions are, according to their reports, about two months forwarder than with us . . .

Agreeably to this Lady Montague, in a letter dated the first of April, (it is to be remembred she used the Old Style,) tells us the country was *then* full of *Nightingales*, whose Amours with the *Roses* is an Arabian fable, as well known there, as any part of Ovid among us, and consequently the Singing of the Nightingale and blossoming of the Rose must be supposed to be *contemporary* things: and indeed that ingenious Author directly remarks, that these lines of Ibrahim were a description of that *Season of the year* there.

Solomon's Song joins the time of the singing of birds, (of Nightingales it without doubt means,) and the voice of the Turtle together; and Lady Montague in the same Letter, or in one of the same date at least, April 1. O.S, speaks of Turtles as cooing on the Cypress-Trees of her Garden from morning till night . . . (pp. 146–9).

Query XLVI

Doth not the mention of the injuriousness of the *Dew* here, allowing a former Observation I made, that this Jewish Poet closely follows Nature in his descriptions, show that the Transactions mentioned in this Song are supposed to have followed one another pretty closely, and not to have taken up much time?

The invitation to this Lady to go into the Country, previous to the Marriage, in the 2d chapter, appears from the circumstances mentioned there, in so amusing a manner, to have been about the middle of April O.S, and this complaint, *concerning the Dew*, places this transaction before the end of May, for it should seem, by the latter end of that month, O.S, there is no apprehension from the Dews, in that country: for Dr. Pococke was entertained at Supper on the House-Top, at Tiberias in Galilee, and was afterwards lodged there, towards the close of that month, consequently there were no apprehensions then of any danger from the Dew.

Agreeably to this, Dr. Russell informs us, that the inhabitants of Aleppo, who make their Beds *in the Summer*, from the end of May to the middle of September, in their Court-Yards, or on the House-Tops, yet in Winter choose the lowest and smallest rooms they have for their bed-chambers, and often have charcoal burning in them; and he attributes the disorders the Natives of that place are wont to have in their Eyes, in great multitudes, to their laying exposed to the Dews, which begin to fall towards the close of Summer. It was not then Summer, it was not so late as the close of May that Solomon made this attempt; consequently he endeavoured Reconciliation presently after his *New* Nuptials, probably as soon after as he well could.

From [Thomas Harmer], *The Outlines of a New Commentary on Solomon's Song, Drawn by the help of Instructions from the East*, 'By the Author of Observations on divers Passages of Scripture', Corrected with Care (London, J. Buckland, 1768), pp. xxiii–iv, 123–7, 146–9, 311–12.

(iii) A visit to a Sikh community

Sir Charles Wilkins (1749?–1836) went to Bengal in 1770 as a merchant in the service of the East India Company. He was the first English person to gain a thorough grasp of Sanskrit and to study Sanskrit inscriptions. He helped Sir William Jones in the formation of the Asiatic Society of Bengal and also assisted in establishing a printing press for oriental languages. Because of ill-health he returned to England in 1786 and busied himself in making translations from Sanskrit manuscripts. In 1800 he became librarian to the East India Company – mainly in order to take care of the company's oriental manuscripts – and from 1805 was examiner and visitor to its college, Haileybury. In 1828 the Royal Society of Literature awarded him their medal as 'princeps litteraturae Sanscritae' and in 1833 he was knighted. Four of his five articles for *Asiatick Researches* are on Sanskrit inscriptions. He also published works on the Sanskrit language and translations from various works including the *Bhagavadgita*. The following passage is the complete text of a paper by him which, according to a letter to him by Sir William Jones, was read to the Asiatic Society 'who expressed themselves highly obliged to you for your attention, and much pleased with the paper'. It is a pioneering piece and is a good example of how a sympathetic inquirer might report on his first acquaintance with the adherents of another faith. It speaks well, incidentally, both of Wilkins' liberal attitude and of the Sikh community's openness and hospitality to him.

I found the college of the *Seeks*, situated in one of the narrow streets of *Patna*, at no very considerable distance from the Custom-house. I was permitted to enter the outward gate, but, as soon as I came to the steps which led up into the Chapel, or public hall, I was civilly accosted by two of the Society. I asked them if I might ascend into the hall: they said it was a place of worship open to me and to all men; but at the same time intimated that I must take off my shoes. As I consider this ceremony in the same light as uncovering my head upon entering any of our temples dedicated to the Deity, I did not hesitate to comply, and I was then politely conducted into the hall, and seated upon a carpet, in the midst of the assembly, which was so numerous as almost to fill the room. The whole building forms a square of about forty feet, raised from the ground about six or eight steps. The hall is in the center, divided from four other apartments by wooden arches, upon pillars of the same materials, all neatly carved. This room is rather longer than it is broad. The floor was covered with a neat carpet, and furnished with six or seven low desks, on which stood as many of the books of their law; and the walls, above the arches, were hung with *Europe* looking-glasses in gold frames, and pictures of *Mussulman* Princes, and *Hindoo* Deities. A little room, which, as you enter, is situated at the left-hand end of the hall, is the chancel, and is furnished with an altar covered with a cloth of gold, upon which was laid a round black shield over a long broad sword, and, on either side, a *chowry* of peacock's feathers, mounted in a silver handle. The altar was raised a little above the ground, in a declining position. Before it stood a low kind of throne plated with silver; but rather too small to be useful; about it were several silver flower-pots and rose-water bottles, and on the left-hand stood three small *Urns* which appeared to be copper, furnished with notches to receive the donations of the charitable. There stood also near the altar, on a low desk, a great book of a folio size, from which some portions are daily read in their divine service. It was covered over with a blue mantle, on which were printed, in silver letters, some select passages of their law.

After I had had a long conversation with two of the congregation, who had politely seated themselves, on each side of me, on the carpet, and whom I found very intelligent, notice was given, that it was noon, and the hour of divine service. The congregation arranged themselves upon the carpet, on each side of the hall, so as to leave a space before the altar from end to end. The great book, desk, and all, was brought, with some little ceremony from the altar, and placed at the opposite extremity of the hall. An old man, with a reverend silver beard, kneeled down before the desk with his face towards the altar; and on one side of him sat a man with a small drum, and two or three with cymbals. The book was now opened, and the old man began to chant to the time of the drum and the cymbals; and, at the conclusion of every verse, most of the congregation joined chorus in a response, with countenances exhibiting great marks of joy. Their tones were by no means harsh; the time was quick; and I learnt that the subject was a Hymn in praise of the Unity, the Omnipresence, and the Omnipotence, of the Deity. I was singularly delighted with the gestures of the old man: I never saw a countenance so expressive of infelt joy, whilst he turned about from one to another, as it were bespeaking their assents to those truths which his very soul seemed to be engaged in chanting forth. The Hymn being concluded, which consisted of about twenty verses, the whole congregation got up and presented their faces with joined hands towards the altar, in the attitude of prayer. A young man now stood forth; and, with a loud voice and distinct accent, solemnly pronounced a long prayer or kind of liturgy, at certain periods of which all the people joined in a general response, saying *Wä Gooroo!* They prayed against temptation; for grace to do good; for the general good of mankind; and a particular blessing to the *Seeks*; and for the safety of those who at that time were on their travels. This prayer was followed by a short blessing from the old man, and an invitation to the assembly to partake of a friendly feast. The book was then closed and restored to its place at the altar, and, the people being seated as before, two men entered bearing a large iron cauldron, called a *Curray*, just taken from the fire, and placed it in the center of the hall upon a low stool. These were followed by others with five or six dishes, some of which were of silver, and a large pile of leaves sewed together with fibres in the form of plates. One of these plates was given to each of the company without distinction, and the dishes being filled from the caldron, their contents were served out till every one had got his share: myself was not forgotten; and, as I was resolved not to give them the smallest occasion for offence, I ate up my portion. It was a kind of sweetmeat, of the consistence of soft brown sugar, composed of flour and sugar mixed up with clarified butter, which is called *Ghee*. Had not the *Ghee* been rancid, I should have relished it better. We were next served with a few sugar-plums; and here ended the feast and the ceremonies of the day. They told me the religious part of the ceremony was daily repeated five times. I now took my leave, inviting some of the principal men amongst them, who were about to return to their own country through *Banares*, to pay me a visit.

In the course of the conversation I was engaged in with the two *Seeks* before the service, I was able to gather the following circumstances. That the founder of their faith was called *Náneek Sah*, who flourished about four hundred years ago at *Punjab*, and who, before his apostasy, was a *Hindoo* of the *Kshétry*, or military tribe; and that his body disappeared as the *Hindoos* and *Mussulmans* were disputing for it; for upon their removing the cloth which covered it, it was gone. That he left behind him a book, composed by himself, in verse and the language of *Punjab*, but a character partly of his own invention; which teaches the doctrines of the faith he had established. That they call this character, in honour of their founder, *Gooroo-Mookhee: from the mouth of the preceptor*. That this book, of which that standing near the altar, and several others in the hall, were copies, teaches that there is but one God, omnipotent and omnipresent, filling all space, and pervading all matter, and that he is to be worshipped and invoked; that there will be a day of retribution, when virtue will be rewarded and vice punished (I forgot to ask in what manner); that it not only commands universal toleration, but forbids disputes with those of another persuasion; that it forbids murder, theft, and such other deeds as are, by the majority of mankind, esteemed crimes against society; and inculcates the practice of all the virtues, but particularly an universal philanthropy, and a general hospitality to strangers and travellers. This is all my short visit would permit me to learn of this book. It is a folio volume, containing about four or five hundred pages.

They told me further, that some years after this book of *Náneek Sah* had been promulgated, another made its appearance, now held in almost as much esteem as the former. The name of the author has escaped my memory; but they favoured me with an extract from the book itself in praise of the Deity. The passage had struck my ear on my first entering the hall, when the students were all engaged in reading. From the similarity of the language to the *Hindoovee*, and many *Shanscrit* words, I was able to understand a good deal of it, and I hope, at some future period, to have the honour of laying a translation of it before the Society. They told me I might have copies of both their books, if I would be at the expence of transcribing them.

I next inquired why they were called *Seeks*, and they told me it was a word borrowed from one of the commandments of their founder, which signifies "*Learn thou;*" and that it was adopted to distinguish the sect soon after he disappeared. The word, as is well known, has the same import in *Hindoovee*.

I asked them what were the ceremonies used in admitting a proselyte. A person having shewn a sincere inclination to renounce his former opinions, to any five or more *Seeks* assembled together, in any place, as well on the highway as in a house of worship, they send to the first shop where sweetmeats are sold, and procure a small quantity of a particular sort, which is very common, and as I recollect, they call *Batasa*, and having diluted it in pure water, they sprinkle some of it on the body, and into the eyes of the convert, whilst one of the best instructed repeats to him, in any language with which he is conversant, the chief canons of their faith, exacting from him a solemn promise to abide by them the rest of his life. This is the whole of the ceremony. The new convert may then choose a *Gooroo*, or preceptor, to teach him the language of their scriptures, who first gives him the alphabet to learn, and so leads him on, by slow degrees, until he wants no further instruction. They offered to admit me into their Society; but I declined the honour; contenting myself with the alphabet which they told me to guard as the apple of my eye, as it was a sacred character. I find it differs but little from the *Dewnager*: the number, order, and powers, of the letters are exactly the same. The language itself is a mixture of *Persian, Arabic*, and some *Shanscrit*, grafted upon the provincial dialect of *Punjab*, which is a kind of *Hindoovee*, or, as it is vulgarly called by us, *Moors*.

Charles Wilkins, 'Observations and Inquiries concerning the Seeks and Their College, at Patna,' being a Report to the Asiatick Society dated 1st March 1781 and printed in *Dissertations and Miscellaneous Pieces Relating to the History and Antiquities, the Arts, Sciences, and Literature of Asia*, by Sir W. Jones, W. Chambers, Esq., W. Hastings, Esq., . . . and Others (London, G. Nicol, J. Walter, and J. Sewell, 1792), II, pp. 68–75

VII

Controversy

In the following passages we have three examples of the use of 'other religions' for controversial purposes, showing how a knowledge of other religions was sometimes used in debates within Christianity – by Herbert of Cherbury to criticise priestcraft, by an anonymous French author to attack Socinian views, and by Middleton to expose the character of Roman Catholic ways. (For the use of other religions to attack 'deism' *cf*. also Clarke, II (iii), Skelton, II (iv) and Prideaux, IV (iii).)

(i) The corruption of religion by priestcraft

For Edward Herbert, first Baron Herbert of Cherbury (1583?–1648) see II (i) *supra*. While Herbert of Cherbury maintains that in principle all people will acknowledge as true the common notions of authentic religion once they are brought to their attention, he also recognises that in practice the actual religions to be found in the world are far from pure expressions of such religious understanding. They are corrupted not only by human misunderstanding but also – and to a large extent – by priestcraft. In *De Religione Laici* (1645 – *On religion for the people*) Herbert argues that the 'lay' person can decide, on the basis of faith, prayer and reason, which religion ought to be followed, by determining which of the actual religions between which he has to choose most closely coheres with the principles declared in the five common notions of religion. In *De Religione Gentilium* (1663 – *On the religion of the world*) he makes several attacks on the priesthood for perverting the pure religion of the common notions for their selfish interests. The following extracts indicate how he perceives the clerical manipulation of religion to provide prestige, authority and material benefits for the members of the priesthood. Although his references are particularly related to the ancient world, his comments on the threats posed to religion by 'Crafty Priests' are probably to be understood as applying in his view to all ages, at least 'where the cap fits'! The extracts thus provide an example of the way in which discussions of 'other religions' could be used, implicitly if not explicitly, to direct criticisms at the role in Christianity of those who are ordained.

Tho' the Heathens had but very lame and imperfect Notions of the Supream GOD, either from the Villainy or Madness of the Priests, seducing Men from the Knowledge or the true Principles, by which they might arrive at the Knowledge of GOD, grossly imposing on them and impudently boasting, that they only had the Knowledge of the Mysteries of Religion, and that there was no access to GOD but by them, and without their Assistance it was impossible to please him. This brought a dark Cloud over the Minds of the Vulgar, which intercepted those bright Rays of Divinity; and involved them in such profound Ignorance, that they durst not stir or move a foot, unless led by the hand or directed by the Mouth of the Priest . . . (p. 269).

Tho' I must lay this down for an Establisht Truth, That the Religion of the Antient Heathens was not so absurd and stupid as is generally imagin'd, being receiv'd for so many Ages by the most Learned Philosophers, the Greatest and Best Magistrates and most Valiant Heroes. Tho' I shall notwithstanding discover those gross and foul Errors with which it every where abounds. When the Heathens had receiv'd the Notion of the Attributes of the Supream GOD mention'd before, there sprung up a Race of Crafty Priests, who not thinking it sufficient there should be but one GOD in all this Universe, judg'd it would conduce much to their Interest, to join and associate some others to this Supream Deity; and that it would be no obstacle, but that the one Most Good and Great GOD should have the Pre-eminence over all others. Their Design of Introducing other Gods, drove farther: they thought they could embarass the Minds of the People more with the Notion of Plurality of Deities, than by the Worship of One only, tho' never so Great; especially after they had invented and dispersed a different way of Worship for each of them. They also expected to reap more Profit, and have larger Stipends from the various Rites, Ceremonies and Sacred Mysteries which they contriv'd and divulg'd, than if Men of all Ages should continue to perform the same Duties of Piety and Virtue. For tho' this were the true way of Worshipping the Supream GOD, their Country was preserv'd against Enemies, the Citizens lived in Peace and Amity together; yet there was nothing in all this that did redound so to their own Private and Particular Advantage: wherefore with wonderful Artifice they interwove Truths with Probabilities, Possibilities and Falsities . . . to insinuate into, and prevail upon the Populace . . . (pp. 270 f).

When the most part of Men had imbib'd these empty Notions and Opinions, they little regarded what was true, probable, possible or false, but had an implicite Faith for what their Guides the Priests told them, and by degrees, gave themselves entirely up to them. That Maxim of Eternal Truth, did not obtain amongst them, *That all Deities are Ador'd in the Supream God*; but enquir'd of their Priest who those *Deities* were, and how they ought to Worship them; for, they would not be so ungrateful to receive Favours from them, and not return them due acknowledgments, if the Priests would but inform them how it was to be done. In the whole, it was very evident to them, that all *Good* did proceed from *Heaven*, but from what *Deity, Star, Power* or *Influence*, or by the Co-operation of what Causes, they were entirely ignorant, unless they were inform'd: This gave the Priests a fine opportunity . . . (p. 274).

They brought Matters to that height, that tho' their Tenents were very questionable, and their Oracular Answers prov'd eventually false, yet it was esteem'd most notoriously Impious, so much as to seem to doubt of their Truth, or to make any other interpretation of them, than what they had given them: But the Priests did not stop here, for having discarded the most solid Parts of their own Religion, they debauch'd the Minds of Men with most tremendous Rites and Ceremonies, offering up Humane Sacrifices to their *Gods*; until that Custom was at last abolish'd by the *Romans* and other Nations.

Still notwithstanding the pure Worship of the *Supream God* was made to consist of no other *Sacrifices*, but such as they devour'd; *Prayers*, but such only as were put up by them; *Sacred Mysteries*, but to be performed by them alone; *Oracles* but of their own, Invention; *Auguries*, but they must expound them; *Rites* and *Ceremonies*, which were contrived by them also; *Feasts* and *Games*, of their own Institution; and *Dreams* in their Temples, which none did interpret but themselves. Thus the most Certain and Fundamental Articles of *Divine Religion*, as *Faith* in the *Supream God*, a firm and solid *Hope* in him, and *Love* which unites Man with G O D, were either totally neglected, or at least postponed . . . (pp. 290 f).

They did not preach up the serious Practice of *Virtue*, nor *Sorrow* or *Repentance* for *Sin* to the People; but perswaded them to an entire belief of the *Oracles, Dreams* and *Revelations*, which every Day and Night they dreamed and invented to impose upon their Credulity. These *Oracles, Dreams* and *Revelations*, they still made more unintelligible, obscure and intricate, by their absurd and incoherent Interpretations, that the People might rely altogether on their Fantastick *Commentaries*; and Common Experience tells us, That they gave those the Characters of the most profound *Theologists*, and intimately acquainted with the *Divine Mysteries*, whom they had most perverted from the Rules of right Reason: but whether this was to be attributed most to the stupid Credulity of the People, or the Villainy of the *Priests*, I shall not presently determine; tho' at the same time it will not appear strange, that there was so much *Superstition* and *Juggling* doings of the *Priests*, formerly introduc'd into *Religion*, when they produc'd the Authority of a *God* for them. So they that give a Peasant some base Metal, or perhaps Leather with the Image of an *Emperour* stampt on it, and tell him he must take it for what is bought of him, he will be afraid to refuse it, because of the *Emperour's* Edict. Thus when the *Priests* had invented some New *Rites*, or set up *Oracles*, they always pretended they were instituted by the Authority and Command of *Jupiter*, or some other *Deity*; and the poor wretched Populace had neither Courage nor Will to suspect them of being adulterate, and reject them as such.

But the Sober and Judicious part of Mankind esteem'd all things of this nature, meer Humane Inventions; and sometimes they desir'd that they might be admitted into these more Holy and Secret Recesses of their Temples, and be Ear-witnesses of those things which proceeded from the Mouths of their *Gods*; for the *Priest's* only being there, was but a single Evidence, which would be much corroborated by the Accession of another; and promis'd that they would be entirely devoted to the *Priests* and their *Doctrines*, if this Satisfaction were but permitted them.

But this was only design'd to ridicule them; for they did not in the least suppose that *God* spoke with an Articulate Voice, or deliver'd his Commands or Inspirations in a soft Whisper . . .

From Edward, Lord Herbert of Cherbury, *The Antient Religion of the Gentiles, and Causes of their Errors Consider'd*, translated by William Lewis (London, J. Nutt, 1705), pp. 269–71, 274, 290–91, 293–4.

(ii) Socinianism and Islam compared

The French author of the *Historical and Critical Reflections upon Mahometanism and Socinianism*, from which the following extracts are taken, has not yet been traced. What the preface reveals is that the author is not a Roman Catholic for he speaks of 'the Errors' of 'the Romish Church' and sees its decisions as manipulated by the French Court which is in turn under the control of the Jesuits. On the other hand he sees 'the abundance of Knowledge and Light' among the opponents of Rome as also of restricted effectiveness because 'in our Churches' there has been some 'Corruption of Doctrines'. Since the 'Heterodox' attempt to camouflage their opinions, the author of this piece has decided to publish his *Reflections* on them in order to expose their character. He seeks to show that whereas in the early period of Christianity such views were unable to

prevail, they were revived by Mahomet and that now 'his Sect is so like
. . . Socinianism, that it is impossible to distinguish them'. In this way,
as the following passages illustrate, he hopes to scare the Socinians 'back
to *true Religion*'. He also attacks Pelagian views – which he sees as the
initial step on the way to Unitarianism and a '*Religion* perfectly human,
more like a Moral Philosophy' than like Christianity – and a 'critical'
approach to the Bible which fails to appreciate its status as 'God's Word'.
This work is thus an example of the way in which 'other religions' were
occasionally used in doctrinal debates within Christianity.

We are a great deal better inform'd at this day, than those of former Ages, of
the Doctrines and Manners of the false Prophet *Mahomet*. . . . The first and
principal Article of their Faith, is *the Unity of God, and the Certainty of*
Mahomet's *Mission*, who gives himself the Title of *the Prophet and Messenger
of God*. 'Tis certain, that this Article once admitted, in the sense that the
Mussulmans give it, the other Doctrines necessarily follow from it. This
Unity of God is, in the Sense of *Mahomet* himself, the chief, or rather only
Cause of his prophetick Mission. The *Christians*, said he, having fall'n into
Error, corrupted this Dogma by the Doctrine of the Trinity; and God, who
would not leave the essential Truths without Testimony, sent his Prophet to
re-establish them. This is the reason why the *Mahometans* give themselves the
Title of *Unitarians*, in opposition to the *Orthodox Christians*, who are call'd
Associants in the *Alcoran*; because, according to the false Prophet *Mahomet*,
they associate with God other Objects of Adoration and religious Worship.
There is a Proof of it in a whole Chapter of the *Alcoran*, which contains their
chief Confession of Faith. The *Mahometans* have so much Veneration for this
Chapter, tho 'tis one of the shortest in the whole Book, that they look upon
it, and would have others do so too, as the third Part of their Law. 'God is
one, God is eternal, he neither begot nor is begotten; nothing is equal to him.'
One sees evidently that the false Prophet had the Mystery of the Trinity in his
Eye . . . (pp. 171 f).

This false Prophet had very fine natural Talents: He was agreeable, polite,
taking pleasure in obliging People, and fit to converse with all the World.
This Testimony is given of him by an *Eastern Christian* . . . As to what
concerns his Mind, 'tis easy to conclude, that he was a Man of an extraordinary Genius, and any one may easily perceive this even in the Translations of
the *Alcoran*; altho by the Confession of all those who understand the Tongue
in which it was writ, they very imperfectly represent the Beauty and Majesty
of the Original.

I don't believe that, in the Confessions of Faith which I have related, the
Socinians find any thing that, according to their own Principles, they can
condemn as erroneous or impious. Nay, I am persuaded, that if they acted

with Sincerity, they would own that the *Mahometans* are *Orthodox*: And indeed they must be so by the Principles of all those who have embrac'd the *Socinian* Religion. These two Sects are proud to be call'd *Unitarians*; a name that signifies the same thing with both Parties. Therefore I cannot see with what reason the *Socinians* should make such a bustle as they do, when they are accus'd of entertaining the same Opinions of the Deity with the *Mahometans*. The chief of the Sect has acted herein with more Sincerity; and whether he did not foresee the Consequences of this Confession, or whether he was little concern'd about them, he owns, that the *Alcoran* speaks of the Unity of God in the same sense, that he spoke of it himself, and that his Predecessors in *Poland* and *Transylvania* had spoke of it before him.

Moreover, *Mahomet*, the better to shelter himself from plain Texts of the *New Testament*, made his Followers believe, that that *Holy Book* was corrupted by the *Christians*. In which this Impostor acted a very cunning part; for truly his Religion cannot subsist, if the *New Testament* takes place: The Divinity of our *Saviour*, and that of the *Holy Ghost*, which are clearly establish'd there, manifestly overturning all the Blasphemys of that *fanatical Prophet* against the Mystery of the Trinity. The *Socinians* have acted in this with greater Caution, altho they don't stick to insinuate that the principal Texts are corrupted, which they do in some Places with as little Judgment as Honesty. Add to this, that the Hypothesis of *Mahomet* is more favourable to his Doctrines, and puts them in a way not to receive any *New Testament*, but what may serve to support their Opinions; an Advantage the *Socinians* have been aspiring at to this time, without being able to obtain it. The Method of the former has likewise this Conveniency in it, that it does not oblige them to wrest those Passages, in which all true *Christians* find the greatest Evidence and Clearness; whereas the *Socinians* are liable to this Inconvenience, not only upon the Article of the Trinity, but likewise upon many others, where they depart farther from the Truth than the *Mahometans*.

The *Socinians* have many Subterfuges, by the help of which they might perhaps strain to clear themselves from the Reproach of favouring *Mahometanism*. But I believe there is scarce any of these, from which it were not very easy to chase them. The ignominious Death of our Lord Jesus Christ, which the *Mahometans* deny, puts no great difference between them; since the *Socinians* don't own the Fruit and Necessity of that Death . . . To deny this Satisfaction, and to deny the Death that made it, is the same.

I shall say nothing here of the outward Ceremonys and Abstinences of the *Mahometans*; I don't believe the *Socinians* would be inclin'd to make an Objection of these, more than of abundance of false Imputations formerly laid on *Mahomet* and his Disciples . . .

'Tis then an Advantage reserv'd to the Orthodox Religion, to be able invincibly to refute the *Mahometans* by express Texts of the New Testament. They would have it believ'd that this Holy Book is corrupted; but we can shew them the same Passages, which we make use of to oppose them, in the Versions that preceded *Mahomet*, and in the Fathers of the six first Centurys. We must oblige them to prove their sensless Accusation, and ask them the Epocha of the Corruption. When they are shewn that it was impracticable from the time of the Apostles till that of their false Prophet, it may be hop'd, they will open their Eyes to the knowledg of the Truth, and condemn the Seduction by which both they and their Ancestors were abus'd.

In vain would the *Socinians* attempt to attack them by the same Method; they have put themselves out of a condition to do it with Advantage to Christianity. They agree with the *Mahometans* in the essential Article of their Separation: And I dare say, that they could not dispute with them but to their own disadvantage. If they deny the Mission of *Mahomet*, an able *Mussulman* will shew them the necessity of it, by Principles that are common to both Sects; and wheresoever they are pinch'd, they will have the worst, unless they have recourse to the Method of the Orthodox, which they could not do without abandoning *Socinianism* . . . (pp. 181–4).

These were the beginnings of that unhappy and cursed Sect. *Poland* and *Germany* shar'd with the *Turks* the Ruins of the Dispersion of *Venice*; but the *Turks* had the greatest Lot: And indeed they seem'd to have the best Right to it. *Michael Servetus*, who was the first that dogmatiz'd in the sixteenth Century against the Mystery of the Trinity, had dip'd into the *Alcoran*, upon the Briars of which (they are words of *Lubinietski*) like a Bee, he gather'd the Honey of his Doctrine. He had travel'd from *Spain* to *Africa*, doubtless with a Design to communicate his Sentiments to the *Mahometan* Doctors, and profit by their Instructions. Altho his Doctrines were not agreeable in all things to those of *Mahomet*, yet they did not differ so far from them, as to deserve to be entirely rejected by the *Mussulmen*, among whom there are certain Doctors who go yet farther than *Servetus*, when they speak of our Saviour.

We ought not therefore to be supriz'd, if the *Unitarians* of *Transylvania*, in the Infancy of their Sect, cited the *Alcoran* as one of the Classick Books of their Religion. When I come to speak of *Socinus*, I shall describe the vain Efforts he made to remove the Scandal which such dishonourable Quotations occasion'd to Persons who were not willing to pass for Renouncers of the Christian Religion . . . (pp. 212 f).

After all that has been said, I think I may conclude, that a Conformity with *Mahometanism* is not the heaviest Accusation that might be brought against the Sect of *Socinus* . . . I know that they intrench themselves within their Morality; and by this perhaps, they would endeavour to make the Parallel odious, which I have drawn between their Sect and that of *Mahomet*. But nothing will be more easy than driving them from that Intrenchment: The *Alcoran* permits Polygamy; and it was no fault of the Patriarchs of the *Unitarians* that it was not establish'd among them. *Lewis Hetzer*, a *Bavarian*, the first *German* that wrote in the sixteenth Century against the Divinity of

our Lord Jesus Christ, marry'd twelve Wives, as is attested by many contemporary Authors. *Sandius* places him in the number of Martyrs for *Socinianism*, tho he was beheaded at *Zurich*, rather for his Crimes than for his
Errors. *Bernard Ockin*, another Hero of the *Unitarians*, wrote concerning
Polygamy; and believes it not only permitted, but to be likewise profitable
and edifying . . .

From: *Historical and Critical Reflections upon Mahometanism and Socinianism*
(London, 1712), pp. 171–2, 181–4, 212–13, and 242–3. This work is part of
*Four Treatises Concerning the Doctrine, Discipline and Worship of the Mahom-
etans* (London, printed by J. Darby for B. Lintott and E. Sanger, 1712),
pp. 151–244.

(iii) Paganism lives on in Rome

Conyers Middleton (1683–1750) entered Trinity College, Cambridge,
in 1700 and became a fellow in 1706. He was known for his musical tastes
more than for his studies. Through his wife he became for a short time
from 1726 rector of Coveney and was also presented to the living of
Hascombe in 1747. He was involved in a pamphlet war with Richard
Bentley over payments of a fee on his being made a D D in 1717. In 1721
the post of Protobibliothecarius (head librarian) was created for him at
£50 p.a. In 1724–5 he visited Rome for the sake of his health and made a
collection of antiquities which he later sold to Horace Walpole. The
Letter from Rome appeared in 1729. As the following extracts from it
show, Middleton suggests in it various ways in which the contemporary
Roman Catholic church incorporates ancient pagan beliefs and practices
in its rituals and religious objects. Middleton himself says that the
argument is not new, only his way of putting it. The work was well
received by Protestant divines in England. When, however, he criticised
Waterland for wanting to claim against Tindal that every statement in
the Bible is historically accurate, his orthodox contemporaries began to
suspect him of sceptical tendencies. His works on miraculous powers in
the Church were ostensibly to deny the credibility of reports of post-
apostolic miracles but he was widely understood to be implicitly casting
doubt on earlier reports and this created a lively controversy. In 1750 his
examination of Sherlock's views on prophecy confirmed many people's
views on his lack of orthodox beliefs. The following extracts show his
lively style as well as providing a classic example of the use of the 'other

religion' of ancient paganism to attack Roman Catholic beliefs and practices as being not authentically Christian. (For another use of 'other religions' to attack Roman Catholicism, *cf.* Leslie I I I (iii).)

As therefore my general studies had furnished me with a competent knowledge of *Roman History*, as well as an inclination, to search more particularly into some branches of it's antiquities, so I had resolved to employ my self chiefly in inquiries of this sort; and to lose as little time as possible, in taking notice of the fopperies and ridiculous ceremonies of the *present Religion* of the place. But I soon found myself mistaken; for the whole form and outward dress of their worship seemed so grossly *idolatrous and extravagant*, beyond what I had imagined, and made so strong an impression on me, that I could not help considering it with a particular regard; especially when the very reason, which I thought would have hindered me from taking any notice of it at all, was the chief cause, that engaged me to pay so much attention to it: for nothing, I found, concurred so much with my original intention of conversing with the ancients; or so much helped my imagination, to fancy myself wandering about in *old Heathen Rome*, as to observe and attend to their *religious worship*; all whose ceremonies appeared plainly to have been copied from the *rituals of primitive Paganism*; as if handed down by an uninterrupted succession from the *priests of old*, to the *priests of new Rome*; whilst each of them readily explaned and called to my mind some passage of a *classic author*, where the *same ceremony* was described, as transacted in the *same form and manner*, and in the *same place*, where I now saw it executed before my eyes: so that as oft as I was present at any religious exercise in *their Churches*, it was more natural, to fancy myself looking on at some *solemn act of idolatry in old Rome*, than assisting at a worship, instituted on the principles, and formed upon the plan of Christianity . . . (pp. 130–32).

   The very first thing that a stranger must necessarily take notice of, as soon as he enters their *Churches*, is the use of *incense* or *perfumes* in their *religious offices*: the first step, which he takes within the door, will be sure to make him sensible of it, by the offence, that he will immediately receive from the smell, as well as smoak of this *incense*; with which the whole Church continues filled for some time after every solemn service. A custom, received directly from *Paganism*; and which presently called to my mind the old descriptions of the *Heathen temples* and *altars*, which are seldom or never mentioned by the *ancients* without the epithet of *perfumed* or *incensed* . . . (pp. 133 f).

   In the *old bas-reliefs*, or *pieces of sculpture*, where any *Heathen sacrifice* is represented, we never fail to observe *a boy in sacred habit*, which was always white, attending on the *priest*, with a little *chest* or *box* in his hands, in which this *incense* was kept for the *use of the altar*. And in the same manner still in the *Church of Rome*, there is always a *boy in surplice*, waiting on the *priest* at the *altar* with the sacred utensils, and among the rest, the *Thuribulum* or *vessel of incense*, which the *priest*, with many ridiculous motions and crossings, waves several times, as it is smoaking, around, and over the altar in different parts of the service.

The next thing, that will of course strike one's imagination, is their use of *holy water*: for nobody ever goes in or out of a *church*, but is either *sprinkled by the priest*, who attends for that purpose on solemn days, or else serves himself with it from a *vessel*, usually of marble, placed just at the door, not unlike to one of our *baptismal fonts*. Now *this ceremony* is so notoriously and directly transmitted to them from *Paganism*, that their *own writers* make not the least scruple to own it . . . The very composition of this *holy-water* was the same also among the *Heathens*, as it is now among the *Papists*, being nothing more than a *mixture of salt with common water*: and the form of the *sprinkling-brush*, called by the ancients *aspersorium* or *aspergillum* (which is much the same with what the *priests* now make use of) may be seen in *bas-reliefs*, or *ancient coins*, wherever the *insignia*, or *emblems of the* Pagan *priesthood* are described, of which it is generally one . . . (pp. 136–8).

No sooner is a man advanced a little forward into their *Churches*, and begins to look about him, but he will find his eyes and attention attracted by a number of *lamps* and *wax candles*, which are constantly burning berfore the *Shrines* and *Images of their Saints*. In all *the great Churches of Italy*, says *Mabillon, they hang up lamps at every altar*: a sight, which will not only surprize a stranger by the novelty of it, but will furnish him with another proof and example of the *conformity of the Romish with the Pagan worship*; by recalling to his memory many passages of the *Heathen Writers*, where their *perpetual lamps* and *candles* are described as continually burning before the *altars* and *statues of their Deities* . . . In the collections of *old inscriptions*, we find many instances of presents and donations from private persons, of *lamps and candlesticks* to the *temples and altars* of *their gods*: a piece of zeal, which continues still the same in modern *Rome*; where each Church abounds with *lamps of massy silver*, and sometimes even of *gold*: the *gifts of Princes*, and other persons of distinction: and it is surprizing to see, how great a number of this kind are perpetually burning before the *altars* of their *principal Saints*, or *miraculous Images* . . . But a stranger will not be more surprized at the number of *lamps*, or *wax lights*, burning before their *altars*, than at the number of *offerings*, or *votive gifts*, which are hanging all around them, in consequence of *vows*, made in time of danger; and in gratitude for deliverances and cures, wrought in sickness or distress: a practice so common among the *Heathens*, that no one *custom of antiquity* is so frequently mentioned by all their writers; and many of their *original donaria*, or *votive offerings* are preserved to this day in the *cabinets of the curious* . . . (pp. 143–6).

As oft as I have had the curiosity to look over these *Donaria*, or *votive Offerings*, hanging around the *Shrines of their Images*, and consider the several stories of each, as they are either expressed in painting, or related in writing, I have always found them to be *mere copies*, or *verbal translations* of the *originals of Heathenism*: for the *vow* is often said to have been *divinely inspired*, or *expressly commanded*; and the cure and deliverance to have been wrought, either by the *visible apparition, and immediate hand of the tutelar Saint*, or by the notice of a *dream*, or some other *miraculous admonition* from heaven . . . And what is all this, but a revival of the *old impostures*, and a repetition of the same *old stories*, of which the *ancient inscriptions* are full, with no other difference, than what the *Pagans* ascribed to the imaginary help of *their Deities*, the *Papists* as foolishly impute to the favor of *their Saints?* . . . (pp. 152 f).

When a man is once engaged in reflections of this kind, imagining himself in some *Heathen Temple*, and expecting as it were some *sacrifice*, or other *piece of Paganism* to ensue, he will not be long in suspence, before he sees the finishing act and last scene of *genuin Idolatry*, in crouds of bigot votaries, prostrating themselves before some *Image* of *wood or stone*, and paying divine honors to *an Idol* of their own erecting. Should they squabble with us here about the meaning of the word, *Idol*, St. *Jerom* has determined it to the very case in question, telling us, that by *Idols are to be understood the Images of the Dead*: and the *worshippers of such Images* are used always in the *stile of the Fathers*, as terms synonymous and equivalent to *Heathens* or *Pagans* . . . (p. 156 f).

But their *temples* are not the only places where we see the proofs and overt-acts of their *superstition*: the whole face of the country has the visible *characters* of *Paganism* upon it; and where-ever we look about us, we cannot but find, as St. *Paul* did in *Athens* clear evidence of it's being possessed by a *superstitious and idolatrous* people.

The *old Romans*, we know, had *their Gods*, who presided peculiarly over the *roads, streets* and *highways*, called *Viales, Semitales, Compitales*: whose little *temples* or *altars* decked with flowers, or whose *statues* at least coarsely carved of wood or stone, were placed at convenient distances in the public ways, for the benefit of travellers, who used to step aside to pay their devotions to these *rural Shrines*, and beg a prosperous journey and safety in their travels. Now this custom prevails still so generally in all *popish countries*, but especially in *Italy*, that one can see no other difference between the *old* and *present superstition*, than that of changing the name of the *Deity*, and *christening* as it were the *old Hecate in triviis*, by the new name of *Maria in trivio*; by which title, I have observed one of their Churches dedicated in this city: and as the Heathens used to paint over the ordinary *Statues of their Gods*, with *red* or some such gay color, so I have oft observed the coarse *Images of these Saints* so daubed over with a gaudy red, as to resemble exactly the description of the *God Pan* in Virgil . . .

But besides these *Images* and *Altars*, there are frequently erected on the road huge *wooden crosses*, dressed out with flowers, and hung round with the trifling offerings of the country people; which always put me in mind of the *superstitious veneration*, which the *Heathens* used to pay to some old *trunks of trees* or posts, set up in the highways, which they held *sacred*, or of that *venerable Oak* in *Ovid*, covered with *garlands* and *votive offerings* . . .

> Reverend with Age a stately Oak there stood,
> It's Branches widely stretch'd, itself a Wood,
> With Ribbands, Garlands, Pictures cover'd o'er,
> The Fruits of pious Vows from Rich and Poor.

This description of the *Pagan Oak* puts me in mind of a story, that I have met with here, of a *Popish Oak* very like it, *viz.* how a certain person devoted to the worship of the *Virgin*, hung up a *picture of her* in an *Oak*, that he had in his vineyard, which grew so famous for *it's miracles*, that the *Oak* soon became covered with *votive offerings, and rich presents* from distant countries, so as to furnish a fund at last for the building of a *great Church* to the *miraculous picture*; which now stands dedicated in this city, under the title of *St. Mary of the Oak*.

But what gave me still the greater notion of the superstition of these countries, was to see those *little Oratories*, or *rural Shrines*, sometimes placed under the cover of a *tree* or *grove*; agreeably to the descriptions of the *old idolatry*, in the *sacred* as well as *profane* writers; or more generally raised on some *eminence*, or, in the *phrase of Scripture*, on *high places*; the constant scene of *idolatrous worship* in all ages; it being an universal opinion among the *Heathens*, that the Gods in a peculiar manner loved to reside on *eminences* or *tops of mountains*: which *Pagan notion* prevails still so generally with the *Papists*, that there is hardly a *rock* or *precipice*, how dreadful or difficult soever of access, that has not an *Oratory*, or *Altar*, or *Crucifix* at least planted on the *top* of it . . . (pp. 180–5).

If I had leisure to examine the *pretended miracles*, and *pious frauds* of the *Romish Church*, I should be able to trace them all from the same source of *Paganism*, and find, that the *Priests of new Rome* are not degenerated from *their predecessors*, in the art of forging these *holy impostures*; which, as *Livy* observes of *old Rome, were always multiplied in proportion to the credulity and disposition of the poor people to swallow them*.

From Conyers Middleton, *A Letter from Rome, Shewing an exact Conformity between Popery and Paganism: Or, The Religion of the Present Romans, derived from that of their Heathen Ancestors* (London, Richard Manby, fifth edition, 1742), pp. 130–32, 133–4, 136–8, 143–6, 152–3, 156–7, 180–85, 193.

VIII

Missionary activity

The following three passages briefly illustrate the ways in which missionary activity overseas was understood, advocated and practised at the end of the eighteenth century. When compared with each other, the passages illustrate on the one hand the confidence of many Christians in the benefits which they had to bestow on the adherents of other religions and, on the other, the enormous difficulties and dangers which faced some of those who attempted to undertake missionary work. (For another comment on missionary work, *cf.* Jones V (vii).)

(i) The civilising benefits of Christianity

East Apthorp (1733–1816), after studying at Cambridge University, was accepted in 1759 by the Society for the Propagation of the Gospel as a 'missionary' to Cambridge, Massachussetts. Described by Archbishop Secker as a young man of 'temper and prudence and abilities', he was sent to prevent the 'poysoning the Foundation of Education' there by Socinian and Deistic notions. Although some opposition was expected from the Congregationalists in Cambridge, Mass., in practice Apthorp had a better than anticipated reception. While there he founded Christ Church and defended the S P G from accusations that it was misappropriating funds in that a large part of its missionaries in New England was not engaged in the conversion of the Indians to Christianity. Apthorp's reply was that the society's charter gave it the right to establish missions in colonies in general and that the phrase 'orthodox clergy' is to be interpreted as Anglican clergy. This interpretation, though, was challenged by Congregationalists who argued that the S P G had no right to send ministers where there was already provision of Protestant ministers. While Apthorp saw America as becoming an asylum for the persecuted where personal enrichment, liberty and reason could prevail, he also was careful to distinguish civil liberty from licentiousness and urged grateful and conscientious subjection to the lawful government of Britain. He returned to England in 1765 and became rector of St Mary le Bow in London and vicar of Croydon. In 1778 he wrote a reply to Gibbon, *Letters on the Prevalence of Christianity*, and in 1785 delivered the Warburton Lectures, *Discourses on Prophecy*, from the final one of which the following extract is taken. In it Apthorp indicates the many secular benefits which he considers will follow the spread of Christianity throughout the world. His remarks are an example of the self-confidence, optimism and, in effect, condescension with which missionary activity was often viewed.

> The conversion of the heathens, Jews, and mohammedans is predicted as an essential in the amplitude and felicity of the Church.
>
> The system of African Slavery is a powerful obstacle to the humane business of conversion. A distinguished prelate hath excited the public compassion to *mitigate* its horrors: but a politic and peaceful sect have set the example in their own district of *abolishing* it. They have freed their slaves, and allow them wages for their labour.
>
> How pleasing would it be to indulge our hopes, that the present General Peace might be improved to extend the glories of the Gospel to the remotest regions of either hemisphere! and to multiply as well as edify the Churches! How happy, should God dispose and enable the kingdoms of Europe at this time, to extend the knowledge and influence of the pure Gospel, among the Gentile inhabitants of the East and West; that the untutored Indian might derive from Europe the riches of Christ, in return for that ill-omened opulence which they have showered on us. In particular, the mild and gentle temper of the Gentoos, and of many casts and tribes in the vast empires of Persia, Hindostan, Tibet, and China, their frugal simplicity, and their commercial intercourse with Europe, are predisposing circumstances very favourable to their illumination by the Christian Faith. But alas! *how shall they believe in* H I M, *of whom they have not heard? and how shall they hear without a preacher?* . . .
>
> Would it not be practicable, for the East India Companies, aided by their respective Governments here and abroad, to place Protestant Missionaries, acquainted with the popular languages of the East, in all their factories; and to favour their communication with the Mohammedans? For this purpose, the H O L Y   S C R I P T U R E S, especially the New Testament may be dispersed over the East in Arabic, Turkish, and Persian Translations. Such is my idea of that inspired book, that it finds it way directly to the heart, and conquers unbelief by a more than human energy.

There are circumstances in the Mohammedan countries favourable to Christianity. In the past year 'the Grand Signor hath permitted to all Christians, whether Catholicks, Protestants, or Greeks, the free exercise of their religion throughout his states. The Catholic merchants highly extol the toleration of the present Sultan, and the protection which he grants to all Religions.'

It were easy to demonstrate from the interior constitution of the Christian Religion, that it includes all the principles of personal and public good. With respect to the felicity of nations, a Religion prescribing moderation, temperance, industry, and frugality, will tend to the populousness and competent support of any country in any climate: prescribing godlike charity, it will mitigate the sufferings of human nature, and even the inclemency of climate and situation. It will also promote that firmness of mind and body, which averse to aggression, furnishes the means of defence. The wisdom and sublimity of its principles have a direct tendency to improve human reason; to excite enquiry, meditation, comparison; to enable intellect in man to be superior to sense; and thus to re-establish the rights of conscience. The equity and kind affection, that predominate in this Religion, will have the best effects on Legislation, which, when tempered by Christianity, becomes not so much a strict executive justice as a kind of protection, asylum, and chancery, that tempers even punishments with lenity, and reforms or prevents vice, as well as protects virtue.

When I consider the Christian Religion as an institute of happiness, I do not mean Christianity as it is now practised in the world: I do not mean the Popish Christianity, which is either a profligate hypocrisy, or a gloomy superstition, which would exterminate the passions by a slow and dreadful suicide; of which we have memorable examples in some of the best men that Communion. I exclude from my ideas of the Gospel, that antinomian fanaticism, which makes Religion consist in inexplicable Theories: much less, has the libertinism of the vulgar Protestants, and the customs of the present age, any pretensions to the name and honours of true Christianity. By this august name I mean that Religion which is described and exemplified in the New Testament, a Religion of personal, domestic, and public virtue: in which the passions are not extirpated, but governed: in which, God is adored through Jesus Christ, with love, admiration, fear, and gratitude: by which Society is continually improved and meliorated; while the individual is daily renewed and prepared both by the blessings and adversities of the present life for the endless felicity of the future.

From East Apthorp, *Discourses on Prophecy* (London, J. F. and C. Rivington, 1786), II, pp. 339–44.

(ii) The need for Christian missionaries

George Burder (1752–1832) originally studied to be a line engraver and
began in that business in 1773. Influenced by the preaching of William
Romaine and George Whitefield, he became a member at the Tabernacle
in 1775 and, with the encouragement of John Fletcher of Madeley, began
to preach the following year. In 1778 he was ordained as minister of an
Independent church at Lancaster, moving to West Orchard Chapel,
Coventry, in 1783, where he initiated Sunday Schools. While there he
helped to found the Warwickshire Association of Ministers which did
much to encourage overseas missions, and the Religious Tract Society.
Having become a director of the Missionary Society (later the London
Missionary Society), at its formation in 1795, he moved in 1803 to
Islington to be its (unpaid) secretary, a post which he held until 1827, and
to be minister of the Independent church in Fetter Lane, an appointment
which he held until his death although he resigned his salary for it in
1830. He edited the *Evangelical Magazine* for many years and was one of
the founders of the British and Foreign Bible Society. He published
several volumes of sermons, a defence of evangelical truth and a collection of papers on the rumour that among the Indians of North America
were some who spoke Welsh, being the descendants of the followers of a
Welsh prince who went there in the eleventh century. The following
passage is taken from his sermon at the inaugural meetings of the
Missionary Society. It was delivered in Crown Court Meeting House,
Covent Garden, before a packed but, it is said, attentive congregation.
Burder's emphases in the sermon on the evils of pagan practices and the
relief which the Christian gospel had to offer as well as on the duty of
Christians to practise their faith both by observing its commands and by
spreading its message illustrate the kind of appeal which was made to
gain support for Christian missions overseas.

> The discoveries of C O O K, and other celebrated navigators, have lately
> opened to our view, a new world, equal perhaps in population to America
> itself – Clusters of inhabited islands, scattered throughout the vast Pacific
> Ocean, and all these inhabited by poor benighted Pagans.
>   Those who are acquainted with the state of the world, need not be
> informed, that the heathen tribes, are in general, shockingly uncivilized. I
> have a view more particularly to the inhabitants of the South Sea Islands.
> Some of their customs are far too indelicate to be rehearsed in a Christian
> audience. On the coast of Terra del Fuego, they are elevated but a small

degree above the very brutes. Ought we not to pity fellow-men so degraded in the scale of society; and knowing the vast advantages of a civilized state, endeavour to civilize, may I not say, to *humanize* them?

Where ignorance so awfully prevails, is it any wonder that men are extremely wicked? Drunkenness is dreadfully prevalent among some. Lasciviousness is the reigning vice of others. Theft is almost universal among the inhabitants of the South Sea Islands. Cruel revenge and bloody murders are too frequent. Who can read without horror, the account of the death of Captain Furneaux's people, or the slaughter of the famous, but unhappy Captain Cook? It is a fact, but too well established, that the inhabitants of New Zealand, who are frequently at war, neither give quarter, nor take prisoners, but are absolutely canibals, and feast on the flesh of their slaughtered enemies.

Their superstitions are also very affecting to a pious mind. How strange, how absurd, are their ideas of a Divine Being! Who can enumerate the multiplied gods of the Heathen? What has reason, with all its boasted powers, effected for man with regard to divine worship? Natural religion has not much to be proud of . . . Some of the Heathen rites are acts of abominable lust, and others of savage cruelty. The Deities themselves were examples and patrons of vice, and the most filthy and abominable deeds were committed under the notion of consecrated acts, acceptable to their gods, and beneficial to their souls. Human sacrifices, as before observed, are still common in the South Sea Islands: when a king is going to war with another Island, he invokes his Eatooa to succeed his bloody designs: he sends some of his servants privately to murder one or more of his subjects. The unhappy victim is called Taata taboo, or the consecrated man; he is presented at the Morai, to their god, who is supposed to feed with much delight upon the sacrifice. Ten such wretched victims were presented on a single occasion; and no less than forty-nine skulls were found at a Morai, which, not being much altered by the weather, were supposed to have been collected in a short time.

In other parts of the world, incredible tortures are endured on a religious account; whether as a penance enjoined to expiate crime, or as the means of attaining higher degrees of perfection, by a greater abstraction of mind, and mortification of the animal nature. "Some are hung up forty feet high in the air, by flesh hooks fastened in their backs, and thus swung and whirled round for a considerable time. Others have threads, thirty yards long, passed through both their sides, in six different places, the ends being fastened, while they dance backward and forward as in a rope walk. Others pass a spit four feet long through their tongue, drawing it backwards and forwards. Others have fixed themselves in a certain position, for several years, exposed to the extremes of heat and cold."

O Sirs! can you hear these things, without longing to go, or send to them, and to tell them of Jesus Christ, that he is able and willing to save them, "without money, without price," without torture? That *his yoke*, altogether contrary to the Devil's, *is easy*, that *his burden is light*, and that *none of his commandments are grievous?* It is a pleasing anecdote which was related to Mr. Thomas, at Calcutta, respecting one of the Malabarian Missionaries:

"A certain man on the Malabar Coast, had enquired of various devotees and priests, how he might make atonement for his sin; he was directed to drive iron spikes, somewhat blunted, through his sandals, and on these he was to place his naked feet, and walk (if I mistake not) 250 coss, or 480 miles; if through loss of blood, or weakness of body, he was forced to halt, he might wait for healing and strength: he undertook the journey, and while he halted under a large shady tree, where the gospel was sometimes preached, one of the Missionaries came, and preached from these words – *The blood of Jesus Christ cleanseth from all sin.* While he was preaching, the poor man rose up, threw off his torturing sandals, and cried aloud – This is what I want; and he became a lively witness, that the blood of Jesus Christ, does indeed cleanse from all sin."

Who can tell, till a trial be made, how many wretched men may be found, labouring under fearful apprehensions of divine wrath, and trying in vain, by the superstitions of their country to obtain peace, who would gladly listen to gospel ministers, – *Preaching peace by Jesus Christ. He is Lord of all!* . . . (pp. 35–8).

My brethren, the honour of the christian name requires some exertions at our hands – I blush for my country, when I reflect, that the peculiar impiety and unbridled lusts of Englishmen, have left a stain on the christian religion, wherever they have resided. O cruel Britain, not content with the honour of discovery and the gain of commerce, thou hast, with a christian name, communicated vice and disease to the poor helpless Pagan Islanders! Christians! if you deserve that honourable appellation, for Christ's sake, endeavour to retrieve the forfeited glory of our religion, and let these abused people know that our Saviour came *not to destroy men's lives but to save them*, – to save them *from their sins*, not to promote their dreadful reign.

What a cutting reproach was lately conveyed to our country by a letter from the East Indies, written by some persons lately converted to christianity. "O great Sir, though we thought that many nations had many kinds of *Shasters*, (or holy laws) yet in the country of the English we thought there was no Shaster at all: for, concerning sin and holiness, those that are here have no judgment at all. We have even thought that they were not men, but a kind of other creatures like devourers."

It has been objected to the truth of christianity, that it is so partially established in the world. "If, say the infidels, it were of God, how is it that the larger part of the globe is, after 1700 years, confessedly destitute of the Gospel?" I deeply feel the severe reproach, for reproach it is . . . But the partial distribution of the Gospel is to be ascribed to the cold, the cruel, the criminal neglect of christians; their want of love to God and man. Let us rouze ourselves from this wicked indifference, and by our utmost exertions try to remove this fatal stumbling block out of the way.

We may reasonably hope, that besides the success which we trust will crown our efforts abroad, no small advantage will accrue to us at home . . . A pious friend of another denomination thus expresses himself to me on this subject.

"Had I no hope of success attending future efforts among the Heathen, yet I could not but rejoice in the effects which I am persuaded will attend the present exertions at home. In proportion as christians enter into the real spirit of missions, so will their personal piety be promoted . . . Nor can I class it among the least advantages which will result from the present emulation among christians of different names, to distinguish themselves by their efforts to evangelize the Pagan world, that a more free and affectionate intercourse will be opened among ministers and others in England, who being separated in situation and denomination were hardly known to each other before. Now one common cause unites us all: we see, we feel, that whatever hard thoughts we previously indulged, the honour of Christ, and the happiness of souls prevails over every other feeling in our brother's bosom, as well as in our own. To mark this temper must be to love its owner. Love will promote intercourse, and intercourse in its turn strengthen love. Party spirit, abashed, will hide its head, and so the unity of the spirit be preserved in peace. Jealousies, invective, insinuations, sneers and bigotry will be banished from the churches; and thus the way will be prepared for the watchmen's seeing eye to eye, and the Lord's name becoming *one* over all the earth."

From George Burder, 'Jonah's mission to Nineveh', a sermon preached 22 September 1795 and printed in *Sermons Preached in London at the Formation of the Missionary Society, September 22, 23, 24, 1795* (Published by Order of the Directors for the Benefit of the Society, London, T. Chapman, 1795), pp. 35–8, 41–4.

(iii) Landing missionaries

James Wilson, the son of a sea–captain, spent his early years at sea. He was present at the Battle of Bunker's Hill and later went to India where he was involved in the relief of Sir Eyre Coote's force and suffered greatly as a prisoner of Hyder Ali. Finally he settled in Horndean, Hampshire, and was converted under the ministry of the Reverend John

Griffin of Orange Street Chapel, Portsea. Having accompanied him to the inaugural meetings of the Missionary Society (*cf.* V I I I (ii) *supra*), he offered his services to the society as a sea-captain, on condition that he received no remuneration. His offer was accepted, and in the autumn of 1796 he sailed in the ship Duff with 'a select crew of pious mariners' to take thirty persons to serve as missionaries in the South Seas. Having landed the majority on Tahiti ('Otaheite') in March 1797, he sailed for Tongatabu in the Friendly Isles. The following extract is from a letter which he wrote to the Missionary Society on his return journey, reporting how the remaining missionaries were put ashore. The report illustrates the precarious situation that faced missionaries as they ventured into what were then remote parts. Of the thirty missionaries who sailed, only four were ordained ministers. The rest were artisans, the aim of the Missionary Society being to establish a self-sustaining community which would attract converts among the natives by the example of its members. The group of ten who were landed at Tongatabu consisted of a shopkeeper, a tailor, a shoemaker, a cotton manufacturer, a weaver (who was ordained at Tahiti), a hatter, a cabinet maker, a bricklayer, a carpenter and a person described as a 'probationer' who had accepted a place in the crew of the Duff in order to accompany the missionaries and who was chosen by them to join them when they were approaching Tahiti. Of these ten, Isaac Nobbs had to return to England immediately because of ill-health, one (George Veeson) was soon excommunicated by the others, and three were killed by natives in May 1799 during civil wars, when the islanders failed to appreciate the missionaries' notion of neutrality in such affairs. The rest, except for Veeson, eventually left for Port Jackson (Sydney Harbour, Australia) in 1800; Veeson himself returned to London in 1802. As Captain Wilson's letter also reports, William Pascoe Crook (1775–1846), who is described as having been a 'gentleman's servant', stayed alone on Santa Christina (Tahuata) in the Marquesas. He found food scarce and in June 1798, being on a visit to an American ship, was carried away when a storm blew up. He was landed some sixty miles away on Sir Henry Martyn's Island (Nukuhiva). After staying there seven months, he sailed in two whalers for London since he could not expect to be found by the Missionary Society's ship when he was no longer on the island where it had landed him. As a piece of missionary activity, then, the venture was not a success.

Having no time to spare, we made all sail to the Friendly Islands; this was the twenty sixth of March; the first of April made Palmerston Islands; and on the ninth, Tongataboo; the next day we anchored about the place Captain Cook lay, according to his bearings. The anchor was no sooner gone than the ship was surrounded with canoes, and a number of Chiefs came on board, who informed us that two Europeans were on the Island, and to our great joy, they soon afterwards made their appearance; but of all the men we ever saw, these were certainly the most wicked looking fellows; and they soon gave us proof they were as bad as they appeared to be: one of them was an Irishman, named John Kennelly: the other Benjamin Ambler, of London: they told us a strange story respecting their coming to these islands; but this was a matter of little consequence to us, firmly believing that the Lord had sent them as our interpreters; for though we had provided, as we thought, sufficient instruments for the purpose, by bringing Peter and two Otaheitans with us, we should have been much at a loss, the language differing so much, that they could not understand one word in ten: but these two men, Ambler and Kennelly, who had only been thirteen months on the island, could talk the language well. After some time our business was partly told them; they readily agreed to give all the assistance in their power. After giving them and the Chiefs present, they all went on shore, highly gratified apparently. Very early the next morning, we were surrounded with a prodigious number of single canoes, besides ten or twelve large double ones. From the peaceable manner they left us the night before, we had not the least suspicion, until the two Europeans came and told us, they intended to take the ship. This you may easily conceive, alarmed us much. We got the people to their quarters as privately as possible. After getting thus ready, we scaled two of our guns; on this the large canoes began to sheer off, and a number of the single ones followed; whether their intention was really to attack us we know not – but it was very alarming to see so many canoes and people round the vessel presenting their clubs and spears for sale, which might in a moment be turned against us.

Our fears in a great measure being done away, Ambler pointed out four Chiefs, which he said were the only ones we need to care for. Tibo Mamoe, the present king, was then at the point of death and his son Tugahowè, the least of the four, would certainly succeed his father (which was actually the case); he therefore would recommend the Missionaries being placed under his care: after talking with them on the subject, they readily agreed to go. I told them that they could not expect to keep their chests, and if they were the least afraid, I would take them back to Otaheite; their answer was, the property was only a secondary object with them, that they would go with an humble dependance on that God, who had brought them safe over the mighty ocean, and had enabled them to leave their country and friends. After a most solemn season in prayer, six of them went with the Chief and Ambler, but not before they promised they should want for nothing; the other Chiefs wanting each to have one, but we thought it best for the present they should be all together, promising them that when the ship returned, if they then chose to separate, each should have some of them; this satisfied them all. After receiving presents, they all went on shore before dark, and all the canoes left us. The next morning we weighed, and run further out, that we might have plenty of room, in case of an attack. About noon two of the Missionaries returned, with the pleasing intelligence that the natives did not attempt to steal, but treated them with the greatest respect; we then loaded the canoes with the remainder of their things, and with such stores as they thought they should want.

We now got under weigh to endeavour to find a channel to the Westward of the spot where Captain Cook got aground: after some time a very good one was found, which we sailed through; this we conceived to be a very valuable acquisition, as we should now, in case of being attacked, be able to sail out of the harbour, either to the East or West. Being now without the reefs, we intended to spend two or three days to see how the natives would behave to our people; but the Lord saw fit to send us a smart gale from the North West, so that at day light we found ourselves in a critical situation, not being able to weather the reefs on either tack; but to our comfort we just fetched the channel which we had only discovered the day before: thus we narrowly escaped shipwreck; and before we cleared the harbour, we were nearly cast away the second time. What cause have we to praise our God, for thus preserving us in such imminent danger. Having now cleared the harbour, April the 16th, we made the best of our way towards the Marquesas . . . and on the 4th of June made the Island Christiana, and the next day anchored in Resolution Bay, after a long disagreeable passage of fifty days. Our rigging being now in a bad state, it was necessary to get it on deck. I shall only remark, that on getting the fore shrouds down, we found two of them gone, so that, had we been on the starboard tack, instead of the larboard, during the gales we had in this passage, we must have been dismasted. O what cause of gratitude for all His kindness to us! We no sooner arrived, than we were visited by many of the natives, amongst them the Chief, whom, after a few visits, we gave to understand that the two Missionaries were to stay with him. On hearing this he could not contain himself, but jumped about the cabin for joy. He said they should have a house, and that they should never want while he had to give, which we have reason to believe will be the case. The young lad Crook went immediately with the Chief, but Harris staid on board to get the things ready, as he said; however, I am sorry to say in this place, that though he was the first that proposed coming to these islands, and was the cause of two others not coming, he seemed now to have lost his Missionary spirit, which was visible to every one, though he denied it. After a little time he went on shore, but with such a gloomy countenance, that the natives soon took a dislike to him; the young lad, on the contrary, was chearful and obliging, so that the whole village was remarkably fond of him. This being the case, I was under the necessity of carrying Harris back to Otaheite. I would have brought Crook away likewise, but he begged to be left, which was agreed to; and I have no doubt but he will prove a blessing to those poor, good natured Heathens.

Having now refitted our rigging, supplied Crook with everything needful, we took an affectionate leave of each other, and sailed for Otaheite the 27th of June . . . and on the 18th of August anchored off Tongataboo, nearly in our old birth, where we were soon visited by our dear people, who informed us they were all well (except one), and how the Lord had preserved them from the machinations of their countrymen, who had done all in their power to make the poor heathens destroy them, and that some of them had separated with a view to counteract their villainous plots. During my stay, Messrs. Buchanan and Galton went to live with another Chief, which I trust will not only be the means of gaining their affections, but will likewise facilitate the knowledge of the language, which is of the greatest importance. After doing every thing in our power for them with the Chiefs, and dividing the articles, we parted with many tears on both sides. I brought away Mr. Nobbs, by their advice, as he had not his health from the time he landed. Our intention was now to touch at the Fegee islands, and, if possible, to have some intercourse with the natives. On the 7th of September we left Tongataboo, and on the 9th, in the evening, made the Fegees; but after six days toil, trying to find anchorage, we were under the necessity of quitting them without finding any, or having any intercourse with the natives . . .

From a letter from Captain J. Wilson, dated Canton, 16 December 1797 and printed in *Four Sermons Preached in London at the Fourth General Meeting of the Missionary Society, May 9, 10, 11, 1798* (published by Order of the Directors for the Benefit of the Society, London, T. Chapman, 1798), pp. 29–33.

Notes

Notes to Chapter I: Introduction

1 For the story of comparative religion in the period following this present study, cf. Eric J. Sharpe, *Comparative Religion, A History* (Duckworth, 1975).

2 R. G. Collingwood, *An Autobiography* (Oxford University Press, 1939), p. 31.

3 Hugo Grotius, *The Truth of the Christian Religion*, translated by John Clarke (London, 1729), p. 178.

4 Charles Leslie, *The Truth of Christianity Demonstrated* (first published in 1711) in *The Theological Works of the Reverend Mr. Charles Leslie* (London, 1721), I, p. 164; cf. p. 169 where Judaism is held to be 'but Christianity in type, tho' in time greatly corrupted', heathenism as even more corrupted and Islam as 'but a heresy of Christianity'. The other religions are but 'delusions', which 'the Devil has set up in imitation of Christianity'.

5 Joshua Toulmin, *Dissertations on the Internal Evidences and Excellence of Christianity: and on the Character of Christ, Compared with that of Some Other Celebrated Founders of Religion or Philosophy* (London, 1785), p. xiii.

6 Adrian Re[e]land, *Of the Mahometan Religion, Two Books*, printed in *Four Treatises Concerning the Doctrine, Discipline and Worship of the Mahometans* (London, 1712), pp. 9, 83; cf. pp. 8 f, 17 f, 101 f.

7 G. E. Lessing, *Nathan the Wise, A Dramatic Poem*, first published in 1779, translated by W. Taylor (London, 1805), p. 153 f.

8 Henry Smith, *Gods Arrow Against Atheists*, first published in 1593 (London, 1628), pp. 1, 96, 18, 42.

9 Beilby Porteus, *A Summary of the Principal Evidences for the Truth and Divine Origin of the Christian Revelation*, first published in 1800 (London, 1812), p. 65; cf. Robert Hodgson, *The Life of the Right Reverend Beilby Porteus, Late Bishop of London* (London, 1812), p. 280 n for a report about the translation of this work and its use in attempting to convert the 'Cingalese' to Christianity.

Notes to Chapter II: Background

1 Richard Baxter, *The Reasons of the Christian Religion* (London, 1667), p. 198; cf. Readings I (i).

2 Henry More, *An Explanation of the Grand Mystery of Godliness* in *Theological Works* (London, 1708), p. 364. The liberty, though, was for those who believed in God and immortality.

3 John Locke, *An Essay Concerning Human Understanding* (London, 1690), Book 4, chapter 17, para. 24; for Locke's assertion of the canon of reason in general and for religious belief in particular, cf. *ibid.*, Book 4, chapters 16–20.

4 Matthew Tindal, *Christianity as Old as the Creation: or, The Gospel, A Republication of the Religion of Nature*, I (no other volume was published) (London, 1730), p. 220. Tindal's work is often described as a classical expression of 'deism' but the designation is debatable since there are many – and sometimes fundamental – differences between those who are so classified.

5 Charles Leslie, *A Short and Easy Method with the Jews*, first published in 1699, in *Works*, I, p. 91.

6 A classical statement of this position is given in the Boyle Lectures for 1704–5: Samuel Clarke, *A Discourse of the Being and Attributes of God, the Obligations of Natural Religion, and the Truth and Certainty of the Christian Revelation* (London, 1705–6), first published with this joint title in 1716. The edition cited hereafter is the eighth edition (London, 1732).

7 John Rogers, *The Necessity of Divine Revelation, and the Truth of the Christian Revelation Asserted*, (London, second edition 1729), pp. 60 f.

8 *Ibid.*, pp. 157 f.

9 Charles Blount, *Anima Mundi: or, An Historical Narration of the Opinions of the Ancients Concerning Man's Soul after This Life* in *Miscellaneous Works* (London, 1695), pp. 11 f.

10 Benjamin Whichcote, *Several Discourses* (London, 1707), IV, p. 24.

11 David Hume, *The Natural History of Religion*, edited by A. W. Colver (Clarendon Press, Oxford, 1976), p. 70.

12 Alexander Ross, *Pansebeia: or, A View of All Religions in the World* (London, sixth edition, 1696), preface, pp. A3–A5.

13 Joseph Pitts, *A Faithful Account of the Religion and Manners of the Mahometans*, (London, fourth edition, 1738), pp. xi f.

14 John Toland, *Letters to Serena* (London, 1704), p. 124.

15 Hume, *op. cit.*, *passim*.

16 Sir William Temple, 'An Essay upon the Ancient and Modern Learning' in *Miscellanea, The Second Part* and printed in *The Works* (London, 1740), I, p. 159.

17 Cf. Edward [Herbert], Lord Herbert of Cherbury, *The Antient Religion of the Gentiles and Causes of their Errors Consider'd*, translated by William Lewis

(London, 1705), *passim*; Thomas Halyburton, *Natural Religion Insufficient; and Revealed Necessary to Man's Happiness*, first published in 1714 (Montrose, 1798), *passim* but especially pp. 189–291.

18 East Apthorp, *Letters on the Prevalence of Christianity before its Civil Establishment: with Observations on a Late History of the Decline of the Roman Empire* (London, 1778), pp. 251 f.

19 *Ibid.*, pp. 355–8, 388–91.

20 *Ibid.*, pp. 251–391 (The numbering of pp. 353–62 is duplicated).

21 John Z. Holwell, 'The Religious Tenets of the Gentoos' from *Interesting Historical Events relative to the Provinces of Bengal and the Empire of Indostan*, II, 1767, printed in P. J. Marshall, *The British Discovery of Hinduism in the Eighteenth Century* (Cambridge University Press, 1970), p. 50.

22 Cf. Warren Hastings, 'Letter to Nathaniel Smith' from *The Bhagvat-Geeta, or Dialogues of Kreeshna and Arjoon*, 1785, printed in Marshall, *op. cit.*, pp. 185 f. A similar protest had been made earlier in the century in relation to the understanding of Islam, cf. Henri, Comte de Boulainvilliers, *La Vie de Mahomet* (1730) – an example of his view on the matter is included in the extract in the Readings, IV (vi).

23 Alexander Dow, 'A Dissertation concerning the Customs, Manners, Language, Religion and Philosophy of the Hindoos' from *The History of Hindostan*, I, 1768, printed in Marshall, *op. cit.*, p. 107.

24 Cf. Readings, V (iv).

25 Toulmin, *op. cit.*, pp. 145 n, 141 n.

26 Humphrey Prideaux, *The True Nature of Imposture Fully Display'd in the Life of Mahomet*, (London, sixth edition, 1716), pp. 259–74.

27 Cf. *ibid.*, pp. iv f. Although, then, his life of Mahomet is not satisfactory and repeats many of the errors found in earlier material, Prideaux seems to have been aware of the need to find trustworthy authorities for his work and is perhaps not to be as strongly criticised as N. A. Daniel suggests in *Islam and the West* (Edinburgh University Press, 1960) – cf. pp. 283, 286, 295 etc.

28 Reland, *op. cit.*, p. 12.

29 Translated into English as *A Treatise Concerning the Turkish Liturgy, the Pilgrimage to Mecca, Circumcision, Visiting the Sick, &c.* by Albertus Bobovius and printed in *Four Treatises Concerning the Doctrine, Discipline and Worship of the Mahometans* (London, 1712).

30 Simon Ockley, *The History of the Saracens* (Cambridge, third edition, 1757), p. xv.

31 'Memoir of Simon Ockley' in Simon Ockley, *The History of the Saracens* (Bohn's Standard Library, London, 1847), p. x.

32 Ockley, *op. cit.*, 1757 edition, pp. xv f.

33 Ockley, *op. cit.*, Bohn edition, 1847, p. xi.

34 Garland Cannon (ed.), *The Letters of Sir William Jones* (Clarendon Press, Oxford, 1970), I, p. 36.

35 Apthorp, *Prevalence of Christianity*, p. 389; Toulmin, *Excellence of Christianity*, p. 141 n.

36 Pitts, *op. cit.*, cf. account of his conversion in Readings, IV (iv).

37 George Burder, 'Jonah's Mission to Nineveh' in *Sermons Preached in London at the Formation of the Missionary Society* (London, 1795), pp. 35 ff – cf. Readings VIII (ii).

38 Edward Herbert, Lord Herbert of Cherbury, *Religio Laici*, printed in 'An unpublished manuscript by Lord Herbert of Cherbury entitled 'Religio Laici', edited by Herbert G. Wright, *Modern Language Review*, 28, July 1933, p. 296.

39 Cf. Herbert, *Religion of the Gentiles*, pp. 2 f.

40 Cf. *ibid.*, pp. 100 f, 138 – and cf. Readings VII (i).

41 Cf. *ibid.*, pp. 49, 110, 384 f; cf. also the view that the parables of the ancients contained important insights in Francis Bacon, *De Augmentis Scientiarum*, in *Philosophical Works of Francis Bacon*, Ellis and Spedding, edited by J. M. Robertson (Routledge, London, 1905), pp. 441 ff, and *De Sapientia Veterum*, *ibid.*, pp. 822 ff.

42 Porteus, *Evidences of the Christian Revelation*, p. 18.

43 Samuel Horsley, *Nine Sermons on the Nature of the Evidence by which the Fact of our Lord's Resurrection is established to which is prefixed A Dissertation on the Prophecies of the Messiah dispersed among the Heathen* (London, 1815), p. 116.

44 *Ibid.*, pp. 114, 108.

45 Dow in Marshall, *op. cit.*, pp. 138 f.

46 Holwell in Marshall, *op. cit.*, p. 55; cf. p. 101.

47 Nathaniel Brassey Halhed, 'The Translator's Preface' to *A Code of Gentoo Laws, or Ordinations of the Pundits*, 1776, printed in Marshall, *op. cit.*, pp. 144 f.

48 Hastings in Marshall, *op. cit.*, p. 187.

49 *Ibid.*, pp. 185 f; Halhed in Marshall, pp. 164 ff.

50 Cf. Boulainvilliers, *op. cit.*, – see Readings IV (vi).

Notes to Chapter III:
The question of natural religion

1 Edward [Herbert], Lord Herbert of Cherbury, *De Veritate*, translated and introduced by M. H. Carré (University of Bristol, 1937), p. 304. The five common notions of religion are stated and expounded on pp. 289–303, cf. also Readings II (i) for his outline of them in *De Religione Gentilium*.

2 *Ibid.*, p. 299.

3 *Ibid.*, pp. 302 f.

4 *Ibid.*, p. 304.

5 Cf. p. 20 *supra* on how he deals with the evidence to make it amenable to his position.

6 Cf. Locke, *Essay concerning Human Understanding*, Book I, chapters 2–4.

7 [Edward Herbert], Lord Herbert of Cherbury, *De Religione Laici*, edited and translated by H. R. Hutcheson (Yale University Press, 1944), p. 89.

8 The brilliant Renaissance scholar, Pico della Mirandola (1463–94) learnt Hebrew and Arabic as well as Latin and Greek in order to facilitate his search for the truth common to all philosophies and religions.

9 Daniel Defoe, *Robinson Crusoe*, first published in 1719 (Everyman, 1945), pp. 157–9; cf. *The Farther Adventures of Robinson Crusoe* in *ibid.*, pp. 320 ff for the story of how Will. Atkins' native wife converts her husband to a real Christian faith by her religious questions and insights.

10 Cf. passage by Robert South in Readings II (ii).

11 Cf. Richard Hooker, *Of the Lawes of Ecclesiastical Politie* (London, 1661), Book I, chapter 8, p. 13: 'The general and perpetual voyce of men is as the sentence of God himself'; Herbert of Cherbury, *De Veritate*, p. 77.

12 Nathanael Culverwel, *An Elegant, and Learned Discourse of the Light of Nature* (London, 1661), p. 2.

13 Ross, *Pansebeia*, preface (p. A4).

14 Ralph Cudworth, *The True Intellectual System of the Universe . . . Wherein, All the Reason and Philosophy of Atheism is Confuted; and Its Impossibility Demonstrated* (London, 1678), p. 634; cf. pp. 208 ff, 233 ff, 453 ff.

15 Cf. Locke, *Essay concerning Human Understanding*, Book I, chapter 3, para. 9 and Book I, chapter 4, paras 8 and 9.

16 *Ibid.*, Book III, chapter 9, para. 23; cf. Book I, chapter 3, para. 13.

17 *Ibid.*, Book I, chapter 4, para. 11.

18 Charles Blount, Mr. Gildon and others, *The Oracles of Reason* (London, 1693), pp. 82, 85 (published also in *The Miscellaneous Works*); the original is to be found as 'Appendix. De Brachmanis hodiernis apud Indos, eorumque dogmatibus' in Thomas Burnet, *Archaeologiae Philosophicae: sive Doctrina Antiqua de Rerum Originibus* (London, second edition, 1728), pp. 477–86.

19 Joseph Glanvill, *The Vanity of Dogmatizing: or Confidence in Opinions* (London, 1661), p. 5 f.

20 Robert South, *Twelve Sermons Preached upon Several Occasions* (London, third edition, 1715), pp. 44–75 (an extract is quoted in Readings II (ii); cf. also Toland, *Letters to Serena*, pp. 69 ff on the original simple religion being lost through the depravity of human reason.

21 Apthorp, *Prevalence of Christianity*, pp. 253 f, 256.

22 [Andrew Michael Ramsay] Chevalier Ramsay, *The Philosophical Principles of Natural and Revealed Religion* (Glasgow, 1748–9), II, pp. 12, 14 f.

23 *Ibid.*, II, pp. 26 f; cf. p. iv where he claims to have surveyed the views of 'the antient Hebrews, Chinese, Indians, Persians, Egyptians, Greeks and

Romans'.

24 *Ibid.*, p. 7. He holds that these principles are reducible to six threefold heads: the existence of God with three essential attributes, three persons in the Trinity, three manifestations of the Messiah, three states of human nature, three states of angelical nature and three means of reuniting the soul to God.

25 Prideaux, *Life of Mahomet*, pp. 253, 256.

26 John Leland, *The Advantage and Necessity of the Christian Revelation* (London, 1764), I, pp. 88 f; cf. pp. 90 ff.

27 Cf. Locke, *Essay concerning Human Understanding*, Book I, chapter 3, paras. 19 f.

28 Bernard Mandeville, 'A Search into the Nature of Society' added to the 1723 edition of *The Fable of the Bees*, edited by P. Harth (Penguin, Harmondsworth, 1970), pp. 334 f.

29 Halyburton, *Natural Religion Insufficient*, pp. 222, 225; cf. pp. 220–34.

30 Thomas Stackhouse, *A Compleat Body of Speculative and Practical Divinity*, (London, third edition, 1743), p. 531; cf. pp. 533 f.

31 Cf. *ibid.*, pp. 517 ff.

32 Cf. Readings II (iv) for such an argument given by Philip Skelton.

33 Ross, *Pansebeia*, pp. 364 f.

34 Thomas Hobbes, *Leviathan* (London, 1651), pp. 54 f.

35. Hume, *Natural History of Religion*, pp. 37, 38 f, 82.

36 Voltaire, *Philosophical Dictionary*, translated and edited by P. Gay (Harcourt, Brace & World, New York, 1962), p. 244 – article entitled 'Dogmes'.

37 Defoe, *Robinson Crusoe*, p. 339; cf. pp. 125, 168 f where Crusoe allows that cannibalism may not be a crime for the natives as it is not against their conscience.

38 Charles Leslie, 'A Letter from the Author to a Deist upon his Conversion by Reading his Book' printed in *A Short and Easy Method with the Deists* (S P C K, London, 1828), pp. 43 f. (This letter is not published in *The Theological Works of the Reverend Mr. Charles Leslie*.) After reading this quotation I am tempted to reply 'tu quoque'!

39 Charles Leslie, *Truth of Christianity Demonstrated* in *Works*, I, p. 169.

40 John Wesley, *The Works*, 16 vols (London, 1810–13); Sermon L X V I I I, 'The General Spread of the Gospel', I X, pp. 233 f.

41 Wesley, *Works*, X, p. 341: Sermon C X, 'On Faith'.

42 Wesley, *Works*, I, p. 224, Journal for 9 July 1737. Wesley's inconsistency comes out when this passage from his Journal and the one from the sermon on 'The General Spread of the Gospel' is compared with the idyllic picture which he presents in his *Thoughts on Slavery* (*Works*, X V I, pp. 442–66). Here, in order to make his point about the evil of slavery, he describes the heathens of West Africa as examples of good social and moral behaviour and asks: 'Where shall we find, at this day, among the fair-faced natives of Europe, a nation generally practising the justice, mercy, and truth, which

are found among these poor Africans?' (p. 448). Wesley picks his evidence according to his case!

43 Thomas Secker, *Fourteen Sermons Preached on Several Occasions* (London, 1766), pp. 116 f.

44 George Anson, *A Voyage Round the World*, edited by Richard Walker (London, 1748) – new edition by G. S. Laird Clowes (London, 1928), p. 389; cf. pp. 329 f, 375.

45 [Edmund Gibson], The Bishop of London, *Three Pastoral Letters to the People of his Diocese* (London, 1732), p. 88; cf. pp. 89 ff.

46 *Ibid.*, pp. 132–6; the material in square brackets gives *in situ* what Gibson provides in footnotes to his text.

47 Isaac Barrow, 'The Doctrine of Universal Redemption asserted and explained' in *The Works* (London, fourth edition, 1716), III, pp. 329 f.

48 Baxter, *Reasons of the Christian Religion*, pp. 300 f.

49 Theophilus Gale, *The Court of the Gentiles: or A Discourse touching the Original of Human Literature, Both Philologie and Philosophie from the Scriptures & Jewish Church* (Oxford, 1672), Part I, 'Advertissements', pp. A2 f.

50 John Edward, *A Discourse concerning the Authority, Stile, and Pefection of the Books of the Old and New Testament* (London, 1693), p. 269.

51 *Ibid.*, p. 274; cf. also Daniel Waterland, *The Works*, edited by W. Van Mildert (Oxford, 1843), V, pp. 1–30 for another expression of the argument that 'The Wisdom of the Ancients' was 'borrowed from Divine Revelation' in 'A Charge delivered to the Clergy of Middlesex' in 1731.

52 Edward Stillingfleet, *Origines Sacrae: or A Rational Account of the Grounds of the Christian Faith, as to the Truth and Divine Authority of the Scriptures* (Cambridge, 1701), p. 396 (Book III, chapter 5).

53 Prideaux, *Life of Mahomet*, pp. 256 f. This theme is developed at length in John Ellis, *The Knowledge of Divine Things from Revelation, Not from Reason or Nature*, (London, second edition, 1747).

54 Humphrey Prideaux, *The Old and New Testament Connected in the History of the Jews and Neighbouring Countries*, Part I (sixth edition, 1719), pp. 402, 475 f; cf. Halyburton, *Natural Religion Insufficient* who holds that while some religious understanding may be attained by 'the mere light of nature', many of the most notable things were initially revealed and, in the case of the Greeks, came to them from the Jews by way of the Egyptians (pp. 235 ff).

55 Leland, *Necessity of the Christian Revelation*, I, p. 13. Later he repeats the suggestion that such nations as the Chinese and Persians may have some knowledge of God, even though it was soon corrupted, since their law-givers were among the early descendants of Noah – I, p. 74 n, cf. p. 104 f. (If what has survived is corrupted, how does Leland know what its original pure state was?)

56 [Patrick Delaney,] *Revelation Examined with Candour* (London, 1763), III,

pp. 58 f, 46 f, cf. p. 50 ff for writing. On the other hand Delaney does not accept that the gift of prophecy was confined to the Jews and so finds nothing incongruous in supposing that Socrates was 'appointed by God as a kind of prophet to the Grecians' (p. 76).

57 But cf. Grotius, *Truth of the Christian Religion*, pp. 25 f where he suggests that the Greeks' letters and most ancient laws are derived from Moses.

58 *Ibid.*, pp. 27 ff, 41, 43, 49.

59 Hobbes, *Leviathan*, pp. 62, 53 ff.

60 Hume, *Natural History of Religion*, pp. 25, 93 professes in this work to accept the argument from design but he powerfully attacks it in his *Dialogues concerning Natural Religion*.

61 *Ibid.*, p. 94.

62 *Ibid.*, p. 26; cf. the views of Prideaux and Leland that monotheism was the most primitive form of religion. The conclusions reached by Hume on the one hand and by Prideaux and Leland on the other were probably determined by their theological convictions and apologetic needs since the evidence they considered was much the same in each case.

63 Cf. *ibid.*, pp. 27 f. This argument apparently provides Hume with a defence of his interpretation of the evidence of other religions but his case is somewhat undermined by his later claim (on pp. 51 ff) that in practice humanity oscillates between monotheism and polytheism – although here the monotheistic position is as little a matter of reason as the polytheistic one.

64 Cf. *ibid.*, pp. 33 ff.

65 William Robertson, *A Historical Disquisition Concerning the Knowledge which the Ancients had of India* (London, 1791), pp. 315 f: cf. Readings I (ii).

66 Cf. Hume, *Natural History of Religion*, pp. 58 ff, 81 ff.

67 These reservations are presumably to deflect the criticism that he was basically anti-Christian – see also note 60 *supra*.

68 Hume, *Natural History of Religion*, p. 63.

69 *Ibid.*, p. 95.

70 Robertson, *Historical Disquisition of India*, p. 313.

71 *Ibid.*, pp. 318 ff; cf. Readings I (ii).

72 Cf. *ibid.*, pp. 322 ff. Robertson admits, though, that it is difficult to communicate rationally sound insights into religion to the people – cf. p. 331 ff.

73 Henry St John, Viscount Bolingbroke, *The Works* (London, 1754), V, pp. 228 f.

74 Cf. Voltaire, *Philosophical Dictionary*, pp. 464 ff and 479 f where he contrasts the worship of God with the claims of the actual religions.

75 *Ibid.*, pp. 480 f – article entitled 'Théologien'.

76 John Tillotson, *The Works . . . Being All that were Printed after his Grace's*

Decease, edited by R. Barker (London, 1712), I, p. 148.

77 *Ibid.*, p. 402.

78 Prideaux, *Life of Mahomet*, p. 251.

79 Tindal, *Christianity as Old as the Creation*, pp. 11, 13; cf. pp. 219 f, 232 ff for his view that reason is the only way out of religious error.

80 Henry Chadwick (ed.), *Lessing's Theological Writings* (A. & C. Black, London, 1956), pp. 105 f (from the fragment 'On the Origin of Revealed Religion'); cf. also pp. 82 ff – 'The Education of the Human Race'. Lessing's view of positive religions is also expressed in the parable of the three rings in *Nathan the Wise* referred to earlier. The touchstone of the preferred religion given by Lessing in the passage quoted is close to Herbert of Cherbury's advice in *De Religione Laici*.

81 Gibson, *Three Pastoral Letters*, p. 136. Similar arguments are found, though for different ends, in Voltaire's *Philosophical Dictionary* – cf. pp. 463 ff, 467, 482 ff – and in Mandeville's *Fable of the Bees*, p. 87: reasonableness in other fields does not guarantee reasonableness in religious affairs.

82 Culverwel, *The Light of Nature*, p. 59.

83 Archibald Campbell, *The Necessity of Revelation: or An Enquiry into the Extent of Human Powers with Respect to Matters of Religion* (London, 1739), pp. 385 f; cf. pp. 223 f. On p. 45 he states his view of the content of 'the religion of nature'.

84 Ellis, *Knowledge of Divine Things*, passim.

85 Leland, *Necessity of the Christian Revelation*, pp. ix, xi.

86 Bacon, *De Augmentis Scientiarum* in *Philosophical Works*, p. 631; cf. also pp. 91 ff, 168 ff.

87 Cf. Apthorp, *Prevalence of Christianity*, pp. 251 f; cf. Leslie, 'Letter to a Deist upon his Conversion', p. 43 for the claim that all religions 'pretend to revelation for their original'.

88 Clarke, *Being and Attributes of God and the Christian Revelation*, pp. 283 f; cf. Tillotson, *Works*, I, pp. 402, 422 f (referred to earlier) for a similar view that natural religion cannot in practice adequately meet the moral and religious needs of humanity.

89 Baxter, *Reasons of the Christian Religion*, p. 198; cf. pp. 191 ff, 300 ff, and his *More Reasons for the Christian Religion* where he criticises Herbert of Cherbury.

90 Gibson, *Three Pastoral Letters*, pp. 136, 95. Gibson particularly cites the ancient philosophers' ignorance of many important things in religion that have since been revealed, the obscurity and uncertainty of several of their important religious ideas, their endless and apparently irreconcilable disputes about basic religious matters, their teaching of doctrines which encourage wickedness, and their ineffectiveness in reforming humanity.

91 Halyburton, *Natural Religion Insufficient*, p. 5.

92 Toulmin, *Excellence of Christianity*, pp. 49, 108, 133.

Notes to Chapter IV: Pride and prejudice in the study of actual religions

1 Cf. such cases as those of Bobovius (Bobowski or Ali Beigh), a Pole who had been captured by Tartars, sold to the Turks and eventually became 'Prime Interpreter' to Mahomet IV (see Bobovius, *The Turkish Liturgy*, pp. 105 f), Joseph Pitts (see Readings IV (iv)), and Adam Neuser, a Socinian who was arrested for writing a letter to Selim II in which he invited him to 'reduce the idolatrous Christians to the Knowledg of one only God' as well as to 'aggrandize' his empire but who escaped to Constantinople (see *Historical and Critical Reflections upon Mahometanism and Socinianism* (London, 1712), printed in *Four Treatises Concerning the Doctrine, Discipline and Worship of the Mahometans*, 1712).

2 Thomas Hyde in preface to Bobovius, *The Turkish Liturgy*, pp. 106 f.

3 Grotius, *Truth of the Christian Religion*, p. 178; cf. Baxter, *Reasons of the Christian Religion*, p. 198 (see Readings I (i)).

4 Wesley, Sermon C X, 'On Faith', in *Works*, X, pp. 340–43.

5 William Carey, *An Enquiry into the Obligations of Christians to Use Means for the Conversion of the Heathens* (Leicester, 1792) – cf. his survey of the world and its religions on pp. 38–62. Although he admits that no reliable population figures are available for 'many countries, as Turkey, Arabia, Great Tartary, Africa', and most of America and the 'Asiatic Islands', he estimates that of the approximately 731 million inhabitants of the world, 420 millions are 'still in pagan darkness', 130 millions are Muslims, 100 millions 'catholics', 44 millions 'protestants', 30 millions 'greek and armenian' and 'perhaps' 7 millions Jews.

6 One exception is Boulainvilliers who, in his study of Mahomet and Islam, advocates the recognition of something akin to modern notions of the cultural relativity of understanding – cf. *The Life of Mahomet*, translated from the French original by the Count of Boulainvilliers (London, 1731), pp. 172 ff (see Readings IV (vi)). On the other hand Boulainvilliers' somewhat deistic interpretation of Mahomet's views indicates the hermeneutical difficulty of applying such notions in practice when dealing with other religions and other cultures.

7 Reland, *Of the Mahometan Religion*, pp. 12 f.

8 Hyde in preface to Bobovius, *The Turkish Liturgy*, p. 108 – Hyde is speaking of Muslims whose faith he has earlier described as laughable.

9 Holwell, 'Religious Tenets of the Gentoos', in Marshall, *British Discovery of Hinduism*, pp. 48 f and Marshall's comment on p. 18; cf. also Alexander Dow, *ibid.*, p. 107 f.

10 Richard Baxter, *More Reasons for the Christian Religion and No Reason Against*

It, first published in 1672, in *The Practical Works*, edited by W. Orme (London, 1830), X X I, p. 562.

11 Charles Wilkins, 'The Translator's Preface' from *The Bhagvat-Geeta* printed in Marshall, *op. cit.*, p. 194.

12 'On the Literature of the Hindus, from the Sanscrit, communicated by Goverdhan Caul: with a Short Commentary' in Sir William Jones, W. Chambers, W. Hastings *et al.*, *Dissertations and Miscellaneous Pieces Relating to the History and Antiquities, the Arts, Sciences, and Literature, of Asia* (London, 1792), I I, p. 115; cf. also Sir William Jones, 'On the Gods of Greece, Italy, and India' in *ibid.*, I., pp. 5–[80]. In another paper Jones linked together 'the *Mosaick* and *Indian* chronologies' – cf. *ibid.*, I, pp. 341 f.

13 William Whiston, *A Supplement to the Literal Accomplishment of Scriptural Prophecies* (London, 1725), p. 127; cf. pp. 106–34.

14 Cf. *ibid.*, pp. 110 ff, 130 ff.

15 William Whiston, *Memoirs of the Life and Writings* (London, 1749), p. 575; cf. pp. 576 ff.

16 Marshall, *op. cit.*, p. 43. Such images, of course, can have negative as well as positive forms.

17 Cf. Sir William Temple, 'Of Heroick Virtue' in *Works*, Part I, p. 196, where he suggests that parts of the world as yet 'known only by common and poor Relations of Traders, Seamen, or Travellers' may be found, when better reported, to provide matters to consider even in relation to their 'Laws and Customs'.

18 Hooker, *Ecclesiastical Politie*, Book V, chapter 1, pp. 136 f.

19 Stackhouse, *Compleat Body of Divinity*, p. 533 f.

20 Wesley, Sermon C X, 'On Faith', in *Works*, X, pp. 341 f; cf. also Barrow, *Works*, I I I, p. 329, on the working of divine grace among the heathen.

21 Hyde, preface in Bobovius, *The Turkish Liturgy*, pp. 107 f.

22 Halhed, 'Translator's Preface' in Marshall, *op. cit.*, p. 145; cf. also Hastings, 'Letter to Nathaniel Smith' in *ibid.*, pp. 185 ff.

23 Cf. Barrow, 'Of the Impiety and Imposture of Paganism and Mahometanism' in *Works*, I I, pp. 152 ff; Leslie, 'Letter to a Deist upon his Conversion', pp. 43 f; Andrew Fuller, *An Apology for the Late Christian Missions to India* in *Complete Works* (London, 1856), pp. 811 ff.

24 Grotius, *Truth of the Christian Religion*, pp. 180 ff, 198 ff; Barrow, *Works*, I I, p. 154; Gibson, *Three Pastoral Letters*, p. 133; Hume, *Natural History of Religion*, pp. 81 ff; Tillotson, *The Works*, I I, p. 597.

25 Holwell, 'Religious Tenets of the Gentoos' in Marshall, *op. cit.*, p. 72.

26 Herbert of Cherbury, *Religion of the Gentiles*, p. 44: cf. *passim* for numerous other examples of such symbolic understanding.

27 Dow, 'Dissertation concerning the Hindoos' in Marshall, *op. cit.*, pp. 126 f.

28 Cf. Isaac Watts, 'A Caveat Against Infidelity' in *The Works*, compiled by George Burder (London, 1810), I V, pp. 80 f; Fuller, *op. cit.*, pp. 812 f.

29 William Paley, *The Evidences of Christianity* in *The Works*, edited by D. S.

Wayland (London, 1837), III, p. 328.

30 Joseph White, *Sermons Preached before the University of Oxford in the Year 1784 at the lecture founded by the Rev. John Bampton*, (London, third edition, 1789), pp. 503 ff – the citation is from a separate university sermon about missionary work in India which was added to these Bampton Lectures. They are usually referred to as 'A View of Christianity and Mahometanism in their History, their Evidence, and their Effects' – the title given on a preliminary leaf.

31 The accusation that priestly ambition has corrupted religion is found throughout the period – cf. Herbert of Cherbury, *Religion of the Gentiles*, pp. 12 ff and *passim* (see Readings VII (i)); Fuller, *op. cit.*, pp. 811 f.

32 Bernard Picart, *The Ceremonies and Religious Customs of the Various Nations of the Known World*, with Additions and Remarks Omitted by the *French* Authors, Faithfully Abridg'd from the French Original (London, 1741), p. 294.

33 John Jortin, *Discourses Concerning the Truth of the Christian Religion* (London, second edition, 1747), p. 37.

34 Grotius, *Truth of the Christian Religion*, p. 197; cf. pp. 189 ff and 193 ff for the lack of support from miracle and prophecy.

35 Tillotson, *Works*, II, pp. 500 f.

36 Cf. *Ibid.*, I, p. 609; John Tillotson, *Works: . . . Being All that were Published by his Grace Himself* (London, third edition, 1701), pp. 532 f. (In future these will be described as 'Works, III'.)

37 *Ibid.*, I, p. 148.

38 Francis Atterbury, *Sermons and Discourses on Several Subjects and Occasions*, edited by T. Moore (London, third edition, 1745), III, p. 12.

39 Paley, *Evidences of Christianity* in *Works*, III, pp. 328 f.

40 Baxter, *Reasons of the Christian Religion*, p. 353.

41 Conyers Middleton, *A Letter from Rome, Shewing an extract Conformity between Popery and Paganism* (London, fifth edition, 1742), p. 193 (see Readings VII (iii)).

42 So far as Conyers Middleton's work was concerned, such doubts were aggravated by his critical examination of reports of post-apostolic miracles published in 1749 as *A Free Enquiry into the Miraculous Powers . . . in the Christian Church*.

43 Paley, *Evidences of Christianity* in *Works*, III, p. 331.

44 Jortin, *op. cit.*, pp. 37 f.

45 Toulmin, *Excellence of Christianity*, p. 140.

46 *Ibid.*, p. 170; cf. also Delaney, *Revelation Examined with Candour*, pp. 72 ff and Tillotson, *Works*, II, p. 361 for the suggestion that Socrates had divine inspiration.

47 Toulmin, *op. cit.*, pp. 183, 190, 180, 214.

48 *Ibid.*, p. 230; Temple, *Works*, I, p. 200 describes Confucius' teaching as 'a Body or Digestion of Ethicks' based on what people find through using their 'own Natural Reason'. Since Confucius was human, Hugh Farmer accuses the Chinese of idolatry in worshipping him, in *The General Prevalence of the Worship of Human Spirits in the Antient Heathen Nations Asserted and Proved* (London, 1783), p. 41. Stackhouse, *Compleat Body of Divinity*, p. 533, though, is complimentary about Confucius' teaching but Leland attacks it for denying immortality – Leland, *Necessity of the Christian Revelation*, pp. 329 ff.

49 Toulmin, *op. cit.*, p. 243; (see Readings V (vi)).

50 Stackhouse, *Compleat Body of Divinity*, pp. 527, 533 n (see Readings V (iv) and, for Leslie's story of 'Sommonocodom', V (ii)).

51 Farmer, *Worship of Human Spirits*, p. 126.

52 Jones, 'On the Hindu's' in *Dissertations on Asia*, I, p. 108.

53 Jones, 'On the Arabs' in *ibid.*, I, p. 129.

54 Jones, 'On the Chronology of the Hindus' in *ibid.*, I, p. 293.

55 *Ibid.*, I, pp. 291, 297 f.

56 *Ibid.*, I, p. 300.

57 Contemporary Parsees are mentioned by Prideaux, *Connection of Old and New Testament*, I, p. 231 and Picart, *Ceremonies and Religious Customs*, pp. 417 ff.

58 Cudworth, *True Intellectual System*, pp. 285, 290 f.

59 Cf. *ibid.*, pp. 288, 294.

60 Cf. Prideaux, *Connection of Old and New Testament*, I, pp. 211 ff and Thomas Stackhouse, *A New History of the Bible from the Beginning of the World to the Establishment of Christianity* (London, 1760), II, pp. 1176 ff (see Readings V (v)).

61 Leland, *Necessity of the Christian Revelation*, I, p. 75 n; cf. p. 172 n.

62 Holwell, 'Religious Tenets of the Gentoos' in Marshall, *op. cit.*, pp. 62, 63 f.

63 Cf. Prideaux, *Connection of Old and New Testament*, I, p. 213; Stackhouse, *History of the Bible*, I, p. 1177.

64 Farmer, *Worship of Human Spirits*, pp. 52 f, 54. His footnotes identify the 'gentlemen' as John Richardson and William Jones.

65 Holwell, *op. cit.*, p. 64.

66 Prideaux, *Connection of Old and New Testament*, I, pp. 212, 216.

67 *Ibid.*, I, p. 230.

68 *Ibid.*, I, p. 231; cf. Picart, *Ceremonies and Religious Customs*, p. 434, on the situation in Persia.

69 Toulmin, *Excellence of Christianity*, pp. 6 f.

70 *Ibid.*, pp. 9 f.

71 *Ibid.*, p. 17.

72 *Ibid.*, p. 51.

73 *Ibid.*, pp. 1, 230.

74 Jones, 'On the Chronology of the Hindus' in *Dissertations on Asia*, I, p. 280; cf. 'On the Gods of Greece, Italy, and India' in *ibid.*, pp. 7 f.

75 Cf. Jones, 'On the Gods', p. 7: 'Either the first eleven chapters of *Genesis*, all due allowances being made for a figurative Eastern style, are true, or the whole fabrick of our national religion is false.'

76 Voltaire, *The Questions of Zapata* (written in 1766), printed in *Selected Works of Voltaire*, edited by J. McCabe (London, 1935), pp. 48 f.

77 Halhed, 'Translator's Preface' in Marshall, *op. cit.*, pp. 158, 162.

78 Voltaire, *Philosophical Dictionary*, p. 336; cf. pp. 61, 204 on Jewish borrowings.

79 Halhed, 'Translator's Preface', p. 162.

80 Jones, 'A Supplement to the Essay on Indian *Chronology*' in *Dissertations on Asia*, I, p. 339 f.

81 Jones, 'On the Chronology of the Hindus' in *ibid.*, p. 319.

82 [Andrew Michael Ramsay], Chevalier Ramsay, *The Travels of Cyrus*, new edition, (London, n.d.), I, p. xvi; cf. also the views discussed earlier which identify true natural religion with the original religion of humanity. For the contrary notion which allows antiquity to heathenism but denies its truth, cf. Tillotson, *Works*, I I, p. 597 and I I I, p. 322.

83 Col. Pearse, 'On Two Hindu Festivals, and the Indian Sphinx' in *Dissertations on Asia*, I I, p. 193; Reuben Burrow, 'Memorandums concerning an Old Building in the Hadjipore District' in *ibid.*, I I, pp. 266, 269 f.

84 Holwell, 'Religious Tenets of the Gentoos' in Marshall, *op. cit.*, p. 61; cf. p. 46.

85 Sir William Jones, 'On the Persians' in *Dissertations on Asia*, I, p. 199.

86 Cf. *ibid.*, pp. 206 ff, 233.

87 Jones, 'On the Gods of Greece, Italy, and India' in *ibid.*, I, p. 2; cf. pp. 2 ff for his identification of the gods of one country with those of the others.

88 *Ibid.*, p. 75.

89 Delaney, *Revelation Examined with Candour*, I I I, p. 58.

90 David Collyer, *The Sacred Interpreter* (Oxford, new edition, 1815), I, p. 215 (first edition appeared in 1723).

91 Grotius, *Truth of the Christian Religion*, pp. 201, 204.

92 Voltaire, *Philosophical Dictionary*, p. 60.

93 *Ibid.*, p. 215; cf. also Hume, *Natural History of Religion*, pp. 55 f for a similar comparison of Magians, Muslims and Roman Catholics as having high doctrines of God combined with absurd practices to aid salvation.

94 For example, cf. Leland, *Necessity of the Christian Revelation*, I, p. 261 n; Robertson, *Historical Disquisitions of India*, pp. 324 ff (see Readings I (ii)); Paley, *Evidences of Christianity* in *Works*, I I I, pp. 328 f.

95 Edward Lord Herbert of Chirbury [Cherbury], *A Dialogue between A Tutor and his Pupil* (London, 1768), p. 4.

96 George Fox, *Gospel-Truth Demonstrated in a Collection of Doctrinal Books*

(London, 1706), pp. 207 ff; cf. also for other expressions of Fox's summons to the world, pp. 35 ff, 171 ff, 327 f.

97 While later studies of religions have recognised what may be called the cross-national characteristics of different religions, especially in the more artificial national divisions of the modern world, they may be criticised for having lost this sense of the integratedness of a living religious faith with the total life of its followers, both individually and corporately.

98 Herbert of Cherbury, *De Religione Laici*, p. 121; cf. the fourth of his common notions of religion which would provide a way of salvation available to all.

99 Blount, *Oracles of Reason*, p. 198.

100 Richard Kidder, *A Demonstration of the Messias. In which the truth of the Christian Religion is proved especially against The Jews* (London, 1684), p. 9; cf. Fox, *Gospel-Truth Demonstrated*, p. 209.

101 Halyburton, *Natural Religion Insufficient*, pp. 167, 147.

102 Thomas Rymer, *A General Representation of Reveal'd Religion* (London, 1723), p. 88; Tindal, *Christianity as Old as the Creation*, p. 414 ff quotes others of this opinion.

103 Barrow, *Works*, III, p. 332.

104 Rymer, *op. cit.*, pp. 118, 122.

105 Wesley, Sermon C X, 'Of Faith' in *Works*, X, p. 341.

106 Ross, *Pansebeia*, pp. 361 f.

107 Cf. Baxter, *More Reasons for the Christian Religion* in *Works*, X X I, pp. 569 ff.

108 *Ibid.*, pp. 557 f.

109 Cf. *ibid.*, pp. 558 ff.

110 Tillotson, *Works*, II, p. 361.

111 Watts, *Caveat against Infidelity* in *Works*, IV, p. 65.

112 Thomas Wilson, *The Knowledge and Practice of Christianity Made Easy to the Meanest Capacities: or, An Essay toward an Instruction for the Indians*, first published in 1741 (London, twentieth edition, 1815), p. xxi.

113 Stackhouse, *Compleat Body of Divinity*, pp. 260 f.

114 *Ibid.*, p. 535.

115 Defoe, *Farther Adventures of Robinson Crusoe*, p. 401.

116 Tillotson, *Works*, II, p. 598.

117 Cf. *ibid.*, III, p. 20.

118 Leslie, *Truth of Christianity* in *Works*, I, p. 165.

119 Watts, *Caveat against Infidelity* in *Works*, IV, p. 91; cf. also pp. 74, 98 f.

Notes to Chapter V:
The treatment of Judaism

1 Ross, *Pansebeia*, pp. 2–21 and 21–41. Ross also distinguishes in the first part between the religious practices of the Jews before Moses (though not saying very much – cf. p. 4) and those after Moses.

2 *Ibid.*, p. 26 f.

3 See Readings III (iv), for extracts from Picart.

4 See J. Howell, *Epistolae Ho-Elianae: Familiar Letters Domestic and Foreign* (London, for R. Ware, J. and P. Knapton, T. and T. Longman *et al.*, 1754), pp. 251–4 (Book I, Section 6, Letter XIV) and pp. 308–10 (Book II, Letter VIII), for the kind of information in general circulation.

5 Barrow, *Works*, II, p. 157 (see Readings III (i)).

6 Thomas Chubb, *The Posthumous Works* (London, 1748), II, pp. 29, 19.

7 E.g. Voltaire, *Questions of Zapata*, numbers 1–49; *Philosophical Dictionary*, *passim*, but for lively fun see the articles on Abraham, David and Solomon.

8 More, *Theological Works*, p. 52.

9 Voltaire, *Philosophical Dictionary*, p. 463.

10 Voltaire, *Questions of Zapata* in *Selected Works*, p. 48.

11 Baxter, *Reasons of the Christian Religion*, p. 202.

12 William Romaine, 'A Modest Apology for the Citizens and Merchants of London' in *Works* (London, 1796), VIII, p. 252. ('A Modest Apology' was first published in 1753.)

13 Cf. Leslie, *Short Method with the Jews* in *Works*, I, p. 62, where this is raised as an objection by the Jews to Christianity.

14 Barrow, *Works*, II, p. 157 (see Readings III (i)).

15 *Ibid.*, pp. 161 ff. Barrow's argument is not wholly convincing when it tries to claim that the goodness of God, together with the need of men, shows that revelation may be reasonably expected, while at the same time holding that God may properly delay giving all or part of what is needed. It was on the basis of the principle expressed in the first claim (i.e., by taking God's goodness as having discernible implications) that Tindal and others argue that the gospel revelation must be as old as the creation if religion is to be based on revelation.

16 Thomas Burnett, *The Demonstration of True Religion, In a Chain of Consequences from certain and undeniable Principles*, Boyle Lectures for 1724 and 1725, printed in *A Defence of Natural and Revealed Religion: Being a Collection of the Sermons Preached at the Lecture founded by the Honourable Robert Boyle, Esq., (From the Year 1691 to the Year 1732)* (London, 1739), III, p. 541. (This collection will be referred to as *Boyle Lectures 1691–1732*).

17 *Ibid.*, p. 542.

18 Ross, *Pansebeia*, p. 11; cf. Laurence Echard, *A General Ecclesiastical History*,

(London, sixth edition, 1722), I, p. 5.

19 Barrow, *Works*, II, p. 160; cf. p. 159; Grotius, *Truth of the Christian Religion*, pp. 213 ff.

20 Cf. Tillotson, *Works*, II, p. 597; Stackhouse, *Compleat Body of Divinity*, pp. 727 ff; Toulmin, *Excellence of Christianity*, pp. 110 f.

21 There was, as will be noted later, controversy over whether the Jews believed in immortality. The question overlapped that of whether the Old Testament affirmed personal immortality and, if not, what was the significance of this fact.

22 Barrow, *Works*, II, p. 163, 159.

23 Tillotson, *Works*, II, p. 597.

24 Watts, *The Harmony of All the Religions which God ever Prescribed* in *Works*, IV, p. 33.

25 John Leland, *A View of the Principal Deistical Writers*, (London, fifth edition, 1766), I, p. 203.

26 Cf. Farmer, *Worship of Human Spirits*, pp. v ff on the Jewish revelation as superior to pagan beliefs.

27 Cf. Barrow, *Works*, II, p. 166 where he states that the Christian revelation is 'not . . . consistent with that particular and partial law'.

28 Cf. Farmer, *op. cit.*, pp. xviii ff.

29 Grotius, *Truth of the Christian Revelation*, p. 207; cf. also P. Allix, *Reflexions Upon the Books of the Holy Scriptures to Establish the Truth of the Christian Religion* (London, 1688), II, pp. 256 ff.

30 Barrow, *Works*, II, pp. 165, 167; cf. Grotius, *op. cit.*, pp. 207, 225 f; Leslie, *Short Method with the Jews* in *Works*, I, pp. 39, 62 ff; Watts, *op. cit.*, IV, pp. 20 ff; Allix, *op. cit.*, II, pp. 314 ff.

31 Ross, *Pansebeia*, p. 18.

32 William Berriman, *The Gradual Revelation of the Gospel; From the Time of Man's Apostacy*, Boyle Lectures for 1730, 1731 and 1732, in *Boyle Lectures 1691–1732*, III, pp. 652 f.

33 Cf. Kidder, *Demonstration of the Messias*, pp. 394 ff.

34 Leland, *Necessity of the Christian Revelation*, II, p. 444.

35 Farmer, *Worship of Human Spirits*, pp. xix f, xxvii ff.

36 More, *Theological Works*, pp. 51 f.

37 Burnett, *op. cit.*, in *Boyle Lectures 1691–1732*, III, p. 578.

38 Cf. William Warburton, *The Divine Legation of Moses Demonstrated* (London, tenth edition, 1846), III, p. 340 (first published in 1737–41).

39 Burnett, *Demonstration of True Religion* in *Boyle Lectures 1691–1732*, III, p. 578

40 Leland, *Necessity of the Christian Revelation*, II, p. 447.

41 Burnett, *op. cit.*, III, p. 578.

42 Cf. Grotius, *Truth of the Christian Revelation*, p. 244; Tillotson, *Works*, II, p. 597. Edward Gibbon comments on the perplexing stubbornness of the

Jews who keep their religion increasingly pure as heaven's protection is removed from them – *The History of the Decline and Fall of the Roman Empire*, edited by J. B. Bury (London, 1897), II, p. 4.

43 Burnett, *op. cit.*, III, p. 577.

44 Picart, *Ceremonies and Religious Customs*, p. 53.

45 Cf. Berriman, *op. cit.*, III, pp. 672 f; Echard, *Ecclesiastical History*, I, p. 384.

46 Picart, *op. cit.*, pp. 47, 48–62.

47 Kidder, *Demonstration of the Messias*, p. 140.

48 *Ibid.*, pp. 161, 163; cf. pp. 162–71.

49 Leland, *Deistical Writers*, I, p. 204.

50 George Stanhope, *The Truth and Excellence of the Christian Religion Asserted: Against Jews, Infidels and Hereticks* (Boyle Lectures for 1701 and 1702), printed in *Boyle Lectures 1691–1732*, I, pp. 645 ff; cf. also More, *Theological Works*, pp. 95 ff.

51 Cf. Grotius, *Truth of the Christian Religion*, pp. 208 ff, 235; Leslie, *Short Method with the Jews* in *Works*, I, p. 37 ff; F. Atterbury, *Sermons and Discourses*, I, p. 134; III, pp. 13 f.

52 Leslie, *op. cit.*, I, p. 37.

53 Cf. Jacob Bryant, *A Treatise upon the Authenticity of the Scriptures, and the Truth of the Christian Religion*, first published in 1791, (London, third edition, 1810), p. 41: 'How then was it possible for a few illiterate men of Galilee, and their adherents, to win over to the gospel such a variety of people, whom they could neither understand nor be understood by them? . . . nothing but the Divine assistance could have brought it to perfection.'

54 F. Atterbury, *op. cit.*, I, p. 131.

55 Grotius, *op. cit.*, p. 132.

56 Atterbury, *op. cit.*, I, p. 136.

57 Bryant, *op. cit.*, p. 38.

58 Fox, *Gospel-Truth Demonstrated*, pp. 243 ff, 397 ff.

59 Leslie, *Short Method with the Jews* in *Works*, I, pp. 39, 74; cf. More, *Theological Works*, p. 195 for another example of the claim that the Jews seek to evade the 'plain sense' of Old Testament prophecies; also p. 237.

60 Bryant, *op. cit.*, p. 29 – see Leslie, *op. cit.*, in *Works*, I, pp. 46 ff for a list of Messianic claimants since the time of Jesus.

61 Kidder, *Demonstration of the Messias*, pp. 376 f.

62 *Ibid.*, p. 393.

63 Cf. Richard Kidder, *Demonstration of the Messias, preached at the Honourable Robert Boyle's Lecture*, printed in *Boyle Lectures 1691–1732*, I, pp. 92 ff; cf. also Stanhope in *Ibid.*, I, pp. 645 ff.

64 Cf. *ibid.*, I, pp. 94 ff; cf. also Stanhope in *ibid.*, I, pp. 650 ff.

65 Cf. *ibid.*, I, pp. 100 f; cf. also Stanhope in *ibid.*, I, pp. 652 ff, 657 ff.

66 *Ibid.*, I, p. 101; cf. also Stanhope in *ibid.*, I, pp. 652 ff, 657 ff.

67 Cf. Grotius, *Truth of the Christian Religion*, pp. 236 ff; Tillotson, *Works*, II, p. 597; Collyer, *Sacred Interpreter*, I, p. 59; Stackhouse, *Compleat Body of Divinity*, pp. 727 f; Porteus, *Evidences of the Christian Revelation*, pp. 86 ff.

68 Kidder, *Demonstration of the Messias*, Preface.

69 Cf. Kidder in *Boyle Lectures 1691–1732*, I, pp. 117–52; cf. also Jortin, *Discourses concerning the Truth of the Christian Religion*, pp. 7–37.

70 Picart, *Ceremonies and Religious Customs*, p. 67.

71 Echard, *Ecclesiastical History*, I, pp. 373, 383; cf. Grotius, *op. cit.*, p. 244. Echard, in II, p. 401, applies a similar interpretation of divine vengeance to the great fire of Rome.

72 Cf. Romaine, 'Modest Apology' in *Works*, VIII, p. 255.

73 *Ibid.*, VIII, p. 248; cf. William Romaine, *An Answer to A Pamphlet, entitled, Considerations on the Bill to Permit Persons Professing the Jewish Religion to be Naturalized* (London, 1753), printed in *Works*, VIII, p. 299.

74 Cf. *ibid.*, VIII, p. 249.

75 *Ibid.*, VIII, pp. 251 f.

76 *Ibid.*, VIII, pp. 256, 258; cf. Romaine, *Answer to a Pamphlet*, in *ibid.*, VIII, pp. 290 ff.

77 *Ibid.*, VIII, p. 260.

78 *Ibid.*, VIII, p. 254.

79 Romaine, *Answer to a Pamphlet* in *ibid.*, VIII, p. 322 f.

80 Tobias Smollett, *Continuation of the Compleat History of England* (London, 1760), I, p. 143.

81 Cf. Kidder, in *Boyle Lectures 1691–1732*, I, pp. 117–52.

82 Cf. Grotius, *Truth of the Christian Religion*, pp. 258 ff, 261 ff.

83 Tillotson, *Works*, II, p. 584; cf. pp. 599 ff for an exposition of these charges; cf. also Kidder, in *Boyle Lectures 1691–1732*, pp. 104 ff.

84 Jortin, *Discourses Concerning the Truth of the Christian Religion*, p. 3.

85 Cf. *ibid.*, pp. 21, 29, 32 f; cf. also Kidder in *Boyle Lectures 1691–1732*, pp. 104 ff, 108 f.

86 Cf. Porteus, *Evidences of the Christian Revelation*, pp. 92 f; cf. Ross, *Pansebeia*, p. 29.

87 Stackhouse, *Compleat Body of Divinity*, pp. 726 f; cf. pp. 728 f for what is required of Christians to secure the conversion of the Jews.

88 Barrow, *Works*, II, p. 165 (see Readings III (i)).

89 Ross, *Pansebeia*, p. 27.

90 *Ibid.*, p. 28.

91 Romaine, *Modest Apology*, in *Works*, VIII, pp. 258 f; cf. *Answer to a Pamphlet*, in *Works*, VIII, p. 272.

92 Romaine, *Answer to a Pamphlet*, in *Works*, VIII, p. 274.

93 Baxter, *Reasons of the Christian Religion*, p. 363.

94 Cf. Leslie, *Short Method with the Jews* in *Works*, I, pp. 62 f, 91 f.

95 See Readings III (iv).

96 Picart, *Ceremonies and Religious Customs*, pp. iii, i.

97 *Ibid.*, p. iii; cf. pp. 42 ff, 45 ff, 71 ff.

98 *Ibid.*, p. 45; cf. pp. 68 ff, 72 ff.

99 Cf. Ross, *Pansebeia*, pp. 4–21 for the Biblical period and pp. 21–41 for current Judaism.

100 Leslie, *Short Method with the Jews*, p. 108.

101 See Readings I I I (iii) for Leslie on this problem.

102 Cf. Kidder in *Boyle Lectures 1691–1732*, I, pp. 104 f, 112–16.

103 *Ibid.*, I, p. 114; cf. pp. 114 f.

104 Prideaux, *Connection of the Old and New Testaments*, I, pp. 212 ff; cf. Stackhouse, *History of the Bible*, I I, p. 1177: (see Readings V (v)); Stillingfleet, *Origines Sacrae*, Book I I I, chapter V, pp. 395 ff.

105 Gale, *Court of the Gentiles*, Advertissements, pp. A2 f; cf. Burnett in *Boyle Lectures 1691–1732*, I I I, pp. 543 f, 566 ff; Allix, *Reflexions upon the Holy Scripture*, I, p. 118 has the Chinese borrowing from the Jews.

106 Burnett, *Demonstration of True Religion* in *Boyle Lectures 1691–1721*, I I I, p. 565.

107 Anthony, Earl of Shaftesbury, *Characteristics of Men, Manners, Opinions, Times*, first published in 1711, edited by John M. Robertson (Bobbs-Merrill, New York, 1964), I I, p. 192; cf. pp. 188 ff.

108 Ramsay, 'A Discourse Upon the Theology and Mythology of the Pagans' in *Travels of Cyrus*, I I, p. 222; the phrase about 'the sublime knowledge of the first men' is used by Daniel on p. 124 of the *Travels*.

Notes to Chapter VI: The treatment of Islam

1 Reland, *Of the Mahometan Religion*, p. 13.

2 Bryant, *Authenticity of the Scriptures*, p. 172; Paley, *Evidences of Christianity* in *Works*, I I I, p. 331.

3 Smith, *Gods Arrow against Atheists*, pp. 42–52 (see Readings I V (i)) – among others attacked are unbelievers, infidels, Roman Catholics, Brownists and Barrowists.

4 Hodgson, *Life of Beilby Porteus*, p. 55.

5 Cf. Porteus, *Evidences of the Christian Revelation*, p. iv.

6 Cf. Robert Jenkin, *The Reasonableness and Certainty of the Christian Religion*, (London, sixth edition, 1734), I, p. 399.

7 Chubb, *Posthumous Works*, I I, p. 31.

8 Cf. Jenkin, *op. cit.*, I, p. 400. The unreliability of the materials, though, is not all on one side: cf. Ockley, *History of the Saracens*, 1757 edition, I, 'Life of Mahomet' p. 10 (this is by Roger Long and separately paginated) for a criticism of Boulainvillier's inventions in his approving *Life of Mahomet*.

9 Cf. Ross, *Pansebeia*, pp. 118 f.

10 Cf. Blount, *Oracles of Reason*, pp. 84 f. This charge is challenged by Ockley, *op. cit.*, I, pp. vii ff and Boulainvilliers, *op. cit.*, pp. 3 f: even the burning of the Library at Alexandria is seen as an expression of devotion to the Koran (cf. Ockley, I, p. 315; Boulainvilliers, pp. 46 f) rather than, as most commentators treat it, as evidence of Muslim hostility to reason and true learning.

11 Reland, *Of the Mahometan Religion*, p. 47; cf. pp. iii f.

12 Cf. Ockley, *op. cit.*, I, pp. xv ff; II, pp. xxxii, for his account of his problems in using them.

13 Ockley, *op. cit.*, II, pp. iv f.

14 *Four Treatises Concerning the Doctrine, Discipline and Worship of the Mahometans*: the summary and the refutation constitute Reland, *Of the Mahometan Religion*; the treatise by a convert is Bobovius, *The Turkish Liturgy*; as well as *The Life and Actions of Mahomet*, the volume also contains *Reflections on Mahometanism and Socinianism* (see Readings I V (v) and V II (ii)).

15 Cf. George Sale, *The Koran: Commonly called The Alcoran of Mahommed; Translated into English immediately from the Original Arabic; with Explanatory Notes . . . To which is Prefixed A Preliminary Discourse* (London, 1850), p. vii for comments on this and other translations.

16 Cf. *ibid.*, pp. viii f; E. D. Ross, in an introduction to a modern (undated) edition of *The Preliminary Discourse* (F. Warne, London and New York), holds that research indicates that Sale had done little first-hand work on the Arabic commentators to whom he refers – cf. pp. vii f.

17 Reland, *op. cit.*, p. 8.

18 Cf. *ibid.*, pp. 47 f (see Readings I V (v)); cf. also Pitts, *Religion and Manners of the Mahometans*, pp. x f which indicates what Pitts had discovered of Christian misrepresentations of Islam.

19 Reland, *op. cit.*, pp. 17 f.

20 Cf. Sale, *op. cit.*, pp. 3 n3, 33, 37, 39 nl, 73 ff, 83, 94 ff for examples of his corrections.

21 *Ibid.*, p. vi.

22 Even less acceptable, of course, as well as exceptional, was Boulainvilliers' attempt to portray Mahomet's teaching as a form of rational theism whose moral precepts produced accord between nature and the Law (cf. *Life of Mahomet*, p. 131) and whose doctrines were commendably simple (cf. pp. 223 f, 293 f). In spite of Boulainvilliers' assertion that he is a sincere Christian (cf. p. 243), his remarks on the plausibility of Mahomet's doctrines as 'agreeable' to reason and morality and on their power to convince (cf. p. 244), made his work seem like a piece of Muslim apologetics when compared to other studies of Islam at that time (see Readings I V (vi)).

23 Cf. Jenkin, *Reasonableness and Certainty*, I, p. 398.

24 Gibbon, *Decline and Fall*, V, p. 333n.

25 Cf. Davenport's outline of the life of Sale in Sale, *op. cit.*, p. xii.

26 *Ibid.*, p. iii.

27 Cf. Chubb, *Posthumous Works*, I I, pp. 30 ff – but Chubb's methodological scepticism is somewhat eccentric.

28 Cf. *ibid.* where he argues that it is not important to him to discover the facts about Islam since they would be no help to him as he accepts only the truth of natural religion. For Chubb the choice between Christianity and Islam is as inconsequential as that between a red and a blue coat. In effect, the advocates of the sufficiency of natural religion react to theological arguments over Christian and Muslim revelations by pronouncing 'a plague on both your houses'.

29 As well as Boulainvilliers' favourable *Life of Mahomet*, Henry Stubbe wrote a defence of Islam in the 1670s which was circulated in manuscript although not printed until 1911 – cf. Edmund Bosworth, 'The Prophet Vindicated: A Restoration Treatise on Islam and Muhammad', *Religion*, V I, spring 1976, pp. 1–12.

30 Sale, 'Preliminary Discourse' in *The Koran*, p. 12; cf. pp. 27 f; cf. Baxter, *Reasons of the Christian Religion*, p. 203.

31 Sale, *op. cit.*, p. 45; cf. p. 77; cf. Picart, *Ceremonies and Religious Customs*, pp. 525 f also gives a favourable account but it is by a Muslim (cf. p. 526).

32 Richard Simon, *The Critical History of the Religions and Customs of the Eastern Nations*, translated by A. Lovell (London, 1685), pp. 156 f.

33 Pierre Bayle, *A General Dictionary, Historical and Critical*, translated and augmented by J. P. Bernard, T. Birch, T. Lockman and others (London, 1738), V I I, p. 345.

34 Gibbon, *Decline and Fall*, V, pp. 338 f; cf. pp. 394 f.

35 *Ibid.*, V, p. 346; cf. also p. 395 for a claim about the lack of ambition in the clergy of Islam; for Gibbon on the status of the Koran, cf. pp. 342 f, 376 f.

36 *Ibid.*, V, p. 396

37 *Ibid.*, V, pp. 376, 311.

38 More, *Theological Works*, p. 114; Bryant, *Authenticity of the Scriptures*, p. 172; cf. Baxter, *Reasons of the Christian Religion*, pp. 202, 302; Sale, 'Preliminary Discourse', p. 78; Simon, *Critical History of the Religions*, pp. 148 f.

39 Simon, *op. cit.*, p. 150.

40 Cf. Thomas Woolston, *Third Discourse on the Miracles of our Saviour* (London, 1728), p. 66.

41 Barrow, *Works*, I I, p. 154 (see Readings I V (ii)).

42 Cf. Porteus, *Evidences of the Christian Revelation*, p. 66.

43 Cf. Barrow, *op. cit.*, I I, p. 154: Islam's age, extensiveness and claims to be God's final revelation mean that it must be given special treatment; cf. Paley, *Evidences of Christianity* in *Works*, I I I, pp. 331 f.

44 The use of references to Islam in anti-Socinian apologetics is discussed in Chapter V I I I *infra* – see Readings V I I (ii).

45 John Locke, 'A Discourse of Miracles' in *Works* (London, 1768), I V, pp. 226 f.
46 Cf. Porteus, *op. cit.*, pp. 70 f. Boulainvilliers, though, rejects the demand for such credentials: he argues that Mahomet asserted his message on the basis of reason and eloquence, not by the aid of 'juggling pretence' (*Life of Mahomet*, p. 137). 'Practical and moral truths' are their own justification and do not need miraculous support, while Mahomet's doctrinal truths are such as are 'demonstrable by mere human reason' (*ibid.*, p. 249). The stories of Mahomet's miracles are rejected as later inventions (cf. pp. 195 f). In this way Boulainvilliers presents Mahomet as a rationally acceptable teacher and, by implication, those Christian apologists who demand miracles as persisting in unwarranted credulities.
47 Locke, *op. cit.*, p. 226.
48 Clarke, *Being and Attributes of God . . . and the Christian Revelation*, p. 320; cf. Joseph Butler, *The Analogy of Religion Natural and Revealed, to the Constitution and Course of Nature* (London, fifth edition, 1765), pp. 352 f.
49 Cf. Charles Leslie, *A Short and Easy Method with the Deists*, in *Works*, I, p. 18. On the other hand, those who allow Mahomet did perform wonders may claim, like Henry Smith, that Mahomet was 'thoroughly instructed in Satans schoole, and well seene in Magicke' (*Gods Arrow Against Atheists*, p. 44).
50 White, *Mahometanism and Christianity*, p. 276.
51 Paley, *Evidences of Christianity* in *Works*, I I I, pp. 332, 335; Bryant, *Authenticity of the Scriptures*, p. 174.
52 Porteus, *Evidences of the Christian Revelation*, p. 71; Gibbon, *Decline and Fall*, V, p. 344.
53 Long, 'Life of Mahomet' in Ockley, *History of the Saracens*, I, p. 37.
54 Simon, *Religions and Customs of the Eastern Nations*, p. 150.
55 More, *Theological Works*, p. 111.
56 The first and second rules for authentic revelation, according to Leslie, are that its supporting facts should be empirically observable and public – *Short Method with Deists* in *Works*, I, p. 11. These criteria were not met by Mahomet's alleged miracles – *Truth of Christianity Demonstrated* in *Works*, I, p. 137; cf. also Tillotson, *Works*, I I, p. 501; Prideaux, *Life of Mahomet*, pp. 46 ff, 55 ff, 80, 107.
57 Leslie, *Short Method with Deists* in *Works*, I, p. 18.
58 Prideaux, *Life of Mahomet*, p. 46; cf. pp. 27 ff, 42 f. Sale sees it as an 'artful' fiction by which Mahomet successfully enhanced his reputation ('Preliminary Discourse', p. 33). *The Life and Actions of Mahomet* (in *Four Treatises Concerning the Mahometans*) recognises that the story may have been invented by Mahomet to please or to test his followers but prefers to hold that Mahomet may have been deceived by a dream rather than that he deliberately invented a story to secure credence for his teaching.

59 Long, 'Life of Mahomet' in Ockley, *History of the Saracens*, I, p. 7.

60 Cf. Leslie, *Short Method with Deists* in *Works*, I, p. 11 where the third and fourth criteria of supporting facts for authentic revelation require them to be commemorated by 'monuments' and activities which date from the time of the events. On this basis, too, Leslie rejects the stories of Mahomet's miracles as 'legendary fables' which even 'the wise and learned' among the Muslims reject (p. 18).

61 Paley, *Evidences of Christianity* in *Works*, I I I, pp. 333 f; cf. similar views in Grotius, *Truth of the Christian Religion*, pp. 274 f; Prideaux, *Life of Mahomet*, pp. 102 f, 226 ff; Toulmin, *Excellence of Christianity*, pp. 158 f.

62 Cf. *Life and Actions of Mahomet* in *Four Treatises Concerning Mahometanism*, p. 55, reminds readers that 'every *Orthodox Mussulman*' believes in Mahomet's night journey as firmly as 'the best Christian' believes anything in the gospel.

63 *Ibid.*, p. 6 f.

64 Cf. *ibid.*, p. 7; Leslie, *Short Method with Deists* in *Works*, I, p. 18.

65 Jenkins, *Reasonableness and Certainty*, I, pp. 396 f. Jenkin was doubtless ignorant of the edited state of the Bible!

66 White, *Mahometanism and Christianity*, pp. 203, 257, 277.

67 Cf. Chubb, *Posthumous Works*, I I, p. 35.

68 Cf. White, *op. cit.*, pp. 276 f; Smith, *Gods Arrow Against Atheists*, p. 48.

69 Cf. *ibid.*, p. 271 for the significance of this ability.

70 Smith, *op. cit.*, p. 48; cf. pp. 45 f (see Readings I V (i)).

71 Cf. *The Life and Actions of Mahomet*, p. 9, where it is held that he did make such claims. They are not specified but his followers are said to hold that they were fulfilled to the letter.

72 Prideaux, *Life of Mahomet*, p. 226; cf. Toulmin, *Excellence of Christianity*, pp. 158 f; Porteus, *Evidences of the Christian Revelation*, p. 70. Boulainvilliers seeks to defend Mahomet by claiming that his title of 'Prophet' does not imply predictive power but only that he had such power of reason and eloquence that the people 'thought God was the author' of his teaching (*Life of Mahomet*, p. 250). The title among Arabs primarily refers to natural powers of insight (p. 246).

73 Leslie, *Short Method with the Jews* in *Works*, I, p. 63.

74 Porteus, *op. cit.*, p. 69.

75 Prideaux, *op. cit.*, p. 137.

76 White, *op. cit.*, p. 272; cf. pp. 272 ff; cf. *Life and Actions of Mahomet*, p. 9.

77 Grotius, *Truth of the Christian Religion*, p. 285.

78 Thomas Newton, *Dissertations on the Prophecies, which have Remarkably been Fulfilled and at this Time are Fulfilling in the World* (London, 1848), pp. 481 f; cf. also pp. 308 ff, 401 ff. (The work first appeared in three volumes, 1754–8.)

79 Cf. White, *op. cit.*, pp. 161 ff.

80 Boulainvilliers, though, does point out that attacks on Mahomet as an impostor are in the end self-defeating, for they mean that his success can only be explained as a result of supernatural support or of Mahomet's having immense personal qualities (cf. *Life of Mahomet*, pp. 168, 179, 251). Boulainvilliers thus attributes much of Mahomet's success to his qualities, speaking of him as compassionate (p. 225), courageous, resolute, generous, faithful, discreet, prudent (pp. 239 f) and perceptive (p. 224) – see Readings I V (vi).

81 Smith, *Gods Arrow Against Atheists*, p. 49; Jenkin, *Reasonableness and Certainty*, p. 400; Bryant, *Authenticity of the Scriptures*, p. 180.

82 Sale, 'Preliminary Discourse', p. 29; cf. Gibbon, *Decline and Fall*, V, pp. 335 f, 366.

83 White, *op. cit.*, p. 167; cf. Boulainvilliers' argument on this point mentioned in n. 80 *supra*.

84 Toulin, *Excellency of Christianity*, p. 150.

85 Prideaux, *op. cit.*, pp. 17 f; cf. p. 18 n★ for the 'authorities' for this claim; cf. Smith, *op. cit.*, p. 44.

86 Ockley, *History of the Saracens*, I, p. 262; Sale, *Koran*, p. 469 n. 'r'; cf. Gibbon, *op. cit.*, V, p. 373 n. 161.

87 More, *Theological Works*, p. 109.

88 *Life and Actions of Mahomet*, p. 29; cf. Prideaux, *op. cit.*, pp. 199 f.

89 Sale, 'Preliminary Discourse', p. 28. Sale says, though, that he cannot decide whether Mahomet acted from enthusiasm or ambition; cf. also Gibbon, *op. cit.*, V, p. 376.

90 Toulmin, *op. cit.*, pp. 150 f; cf. Prideaux, *op. cit.*, pp. 199 ff.

91 Sale, 'Preliminary Discourse', p. 28; cf. p. 29 but also p. 50 where he speaks of Mahomet as having 'pretended' to be a prophet.

92 Cf. Prideaux, *op. cit.*, pp. 141, 246, 250 f; cf. Leslie, *Short Method with Deists* in *Works*, I, p. 10.

93 Cf. *ibid.*, p. 144; cf. pp. iv f, 145–246 for arguments that these marks of imposture are found in the case of Islam (see Readings I V (iii)).

94 Halyburton, *Natural Religion Insufficient*, p. 5.

95 *Life and Actions of Mahomet*, pp. 46, 5; White, *op. cit.*, pp. 56, 196.

96 Cf. Prideaux, *op. cit.*, pp. 21, 43; Prideaux sees Mahomet's claim to revelatory insight as falsified by the fact that he was not divinely warned of the poison which was administered to him – cf. pp. 104, 112.

97 Sale, *op. cit.*, pp. 27 f; cf. Hyde in Bobovius, *The Turkish Liturgy*, pp. 107 f.

98 Long, 'Life of Mahomet' in Ockley, *History of the Saracens*, I, p. 74: 'the governing principles of his soul were ambition and lust'.

99 *Life and Actions of Mahomet*, p. 26.

100 Prideaux, *op. cit.*, p. 146.

101 Toulmin, *op. cit.*, p. 161. Boulainvilliers, though, argues that Mahomet's teaching is the result of rational reflection (*Life of Mahomet*, pp. 223 f,

240 f), not the consequence of a conspiracy with an ignorant monk (see Readings I V (vi)).

102 Barrow, *Works*, I I, p. 155.

103 Porteus, *Evidences of the Christian Revelation*, p. 83.

104 Cf. Prideaux, *op. cit.*, pp. 12 f, 116 f.

105 Toulmin, *op. cit.*, p. 262.

106 Cf. Barrow, *op. cit.*, pp. 154 f (see Readings I V (ii)); cf. Toulmin, *op. cit.*, pp. 142 ff; Prideaux, *op. cit.*, p. 169 seems to allow that the wickedness of a teacher does not necessarily condemn his teaching (it is an 'inference' which people are inclined to make 'too precipitately'), nevertheless, the tenor of his study is that Mahomet's faults disprove his claims.

107 More, *Theological Works*, p. 110.

108 Cf. Prideaux, *op. cit.*, pp. 45 f; Reland, *Of the Mahometan Religion*, pp. 95 ff; Sale, 'Preliminary Discourse', p. 29, for defences of Mahomet's conduct.

109 Cf. Gibbon, *Decline and Fall*, V, p. 378.

110 Prideaux, *op. cit.*, p. 127; cf. pp. 117 ff for his conduct with women.

111 White, *Mahometanism and Christianity*, pp. 197 f; cf. Long, 'Life of Mahomet' in Ockley, *History of the Saracens*, I, pp. 51, 59 f, 74; Porteus, *op. cit.*, p. 68; Smith, *Gods Arrow Against Atheists*, p. 49; Jenkin, *Reasonableness and Certainty*, p. 401.

112 Porteus, *op. cit.*, p. 69; cf. Smith, *op. cit.*, p. 44 on the story of a dove taught to peck at Mahomet's ear.

113 Grotius, *Truth of the Christian Religion*, p. 274.

114 Leslie, *Truth of Christianity Demonstrated* in *Works*, I, p. 167; Edwards, *Authority, Stile and Perfection of the Old and New Testament*, pp. 405 f; cf. also Grotius, *op. cit.*, pp. 279 f.

115 White, *op. cit.*, p. 334.

116 Cf. *ibid.*

117 Baxter, *Reasons of the Christian Religion*, p. 203 (see Readings I (i)); cf. p. 302; cf. also Bryant, *Authenticity of the Scriptures*, pp. 175 f; Porteus, *op. cit.*, pp. 81 f; Ross, *Pansebeia*, p. 116.

118 Cf. Reland, *Of the Mahometan Religion*, pp. iii f, 11 ff for his aim. On p. 47 he begins an extensive defence of Islam from 'several Things falsly charg'd' against it (see Readings I V (v)) although he describes its doctrine as an 'Infection and Contagion' which has 'poison'd almost the whole Earth'.

119 Cf. Sale, 'Preliminary Discourse', p. 77.

120 Smith, *op. cit.*, p. 44.

121 Cf. White, *op. cit.*, pp. 351 f.

122 Cf. *ibid.*, p. 267.

123 cf. Prideaux, *Life of Mahomet*, pp. 18 ff (see Readings I V (iii)), 31 ff but cf. also p. 43; Ockley, *op. cit.*, I, pp. 101 ff. Muslim claims that the style of the Koran shows its divine origin are rejected – cf. Sale, *op. cit.*, pp. 43 f; Toulmin, *op. cit.*, pp. 161 f; Porteus, *op. cit.*, pp. 79 ff.

124 White, *op. cit.*, p. 343; cf. pp. 338 ff, 347 ff.

125 *Mahometanism and Socinianism*, p. 161.

126 Cf. Sale, 'Preliminary Discourse', pp. 47 f.

127 White, *op. cit.*, p.360; cf. pp. 245 f.

128 Cf. *ibid.*, p. 415.

129 More, *Theological Works*, p. 110.

130 Cf. Sale, *op. cit.*, p. 28; White, *op. cit.*, pp. 341 f; *Mahometanism and Socinianism*, pp. 174 f.

131 Cf. Grotius, *Truth of the Christian Religion*, pp. 161 ff, 271 ff; White, *op. cit.*, pp. 273 ff. Some critics make the counter-charge that Mahomet or his followers altered the text – cf. John Pearson, *An Exposition of the Creed* (London, 1880, first edition was published in 1659), p. 200.

132 Cf. *Life and Actions of Mahomet*, pp. 54 f; Prideaux, *Life of Mahomet*, pp. 204 f.

133 Prideaux, *op. cit.*, p. 83; cf. pp. 80 ff, 97 ff, 160 f, 221 f; *Life and Actions of Mahomet*, p. 70.

134 Paley, *Evidences of Christianity* in *Works*, I I I, p. 339; cf. Sale, 'Preliminary Discourse', pp. 68 ff; Toulmin, *Excellence of Christianity*, pp. 149, 152 f; but note that Reland, *Of the Mahometan Religion*, pp. 74 ff and Bobovius, *The Turkish Liturgy*, p. 142 n 'd' protest that these descriptions should perhaps be understood as allegories and not as literal descriptions of heaven.

135 Cf. Prideaux, *op. cit.*, pp. 89 f, 221 f; *Life and Actions of Mahomet*, p. 63 f; Paley, *op. cit.*, I I I, p. 339 f.

136 Cf. Prideaux, *op. cit.*, pp. 118 f, 124 f, 127 ff; Sale, 'Preliminary Discourse', p. 37, 45 f.

137 Cf. Paley, *op. cit.*, p. 335; Porteus, *Evidences of the Christian Revelation*, p. 71.

138 Grotius, *op. cit.*, p. 270.

139 Baxter, *Reasons of the Christian Religion*, pp. 203 f; cf. p. 428; cf. also Ross, *Pansebeia*, p. 125; Reland, *op. cit.*, pp. 13 f holds that if Muslims cannot argue about the individual contents of the Koran, they must argue about the justification of their assent to its contents.

140 Prideaux, *op. cit.*, p. 77; cf. pp. 222 f.

141 Cf. Grotius, *op. cit.*, pp. 270 f; Richard Watson, *Two Apologies, One for Christianity . . . The Other for the Bible* (London, 1820), p. 5 f where Watson links Muslims with Roman Catholics in contrast to Protestants as to their openness to the guidance of the human intellect.

142 Cf. Smith, *Gods Arrow Against Atheists*, pp. 49 f; Grotius, *op. cit.*, p. 278; Toulmin, *Excellence of Christianity*, pp. 154, 156 ff; Porteus, *op. cit.*, pp. 75 f.

143 Ross, *Pansebeia*, pp. 120 f.

144 Cf. White, *Christianity and Mahometanism*, Sermon I X, pp. 385 ff. White suggests that there may be geographical and racial reasons for the success of

Islam in certain areas (pp. 385 f, 455 f).

145 *Ibid.*, pp. 449 (this presumably refers to the ban on alcohol and the fast of Ramadan), 443, 456; cf. pp. 352 f – where Mahomet takes up Christian moral teaching, he corrupts its original beauty and majesty.

146 Wesley, Sermon L X V I I I, 'The General Spread of the Gospel' in *Works*, I X, p. 234.

147 Cf. *ibid.*, I X, pp. 234 f; X, pp. 341 f; *Mahometanism and Socinianism*, p. 253; Sale, 'Preliminary Discourse', pp. 21 ff.

148 Toulmin, *op. cit.*, pp. 150, 147; cf. pp. 146 ff for his comparison of the two; White, *op. cit.*, pp. 353 ff; Bryant, *Authenticity of the Scriptures*, pp. 175 f.

149 Barrow, *Works*, I I, p. 156; cf. White, *op. cit.*, pp. 343 f; but cf. Reland, *Of the Mahometan Religion*, pp. 64 f, *Mahometanism and Socinianism*, pp. 179 f and Sale, 'Preliminary Discourse', p. 75 for the value of the Muslim ceremonies. Bobovius, *The Turkish Liturgy*, pp. 109 ff gives a description of them.

150 Cf. Grotius, *op. cit.*, p. 280; cf. Hume, *Natural History of Religion*, p. 54; White, *op. cit.*, p. 414; but cf. Reland, *op. cit.*, pp. 21 ff, 52 ff for claims that these descriptions are not to be taken literally.

151 Cf. Grotius, *op. cit.*, pp. 281 f; cf. also Prideaux, *op. cit.*, pp. 8 f, 25 ff, 203 ff; *Life and Actions of Mahomet*, pp. 12 ff, 19 ff, 23 f, 47, 71 f, but cf. pp. 8, 37 f.

152 Baxter, *Reasons of the Christian Religion*, p. 204; cf. Prideaux, *op. cit.*, p. 205; Collier, *Sacred Interpreter*, I, p. 123 f.

153 White, *op. cit.*, p. 336.

154 Cf. Grotius, *op. cit.*, p. 272; White, *op. cit.*, pp. 356 ff.

155 Cf. Grotius, *op. cit.*, pp. 278 f; Ross, *Pansebeia*, p. 126; Jenkin, *Reasonableness and Certainty*, I I, pp. 396 f; Bryant, *Authenticity of the Scriptures*, pp. 180 ff; but cp. *Mahometanism and Socinianism*, pp. 177 ff and Jones in *Dissertations on Asia*, I, p. 240 for suggestions that in some respects Muslim moral teaching is superior to Christian.

156 Thomas Hyde, preface to Bobovius, *The Turkish Liturgy*, pp. 107 f; cf. Sale, 'Preliminary Discourse', p. 27: but Sale is unsure of Mahomet's real intentions.

157 Cf. letter from Leibniz printed at end of *Mahometanism and Socinianism*, p. 245.

158 Cf. Chubb, *Posthumous Works*, I I, pp. 37 ff where the treatment of Islam seems to reflect contemporary Christian debates. Woolston and Lessing both link Muslim doctrine with 'deistic' forms of natural theology and it is interesting to note that the views of the 'Muzerim' on revelation as presented in *The Life and Actions of Mahomet*, pp. 40–46 are similar to the views on revelation and the Bible to be found in Tindal and other critics of traditional Christian understanding.

159 Paley, *Evidences of Christianity* in *Works*, I I I, p. 344.

160 Cf. Paley, *ibid.*; White, *op. cit.*, p. 57.
161 Stackhouse, *Compleat Body of Divinity*, p. 720.
162 Robertson, *Historical Disquisitions of India*, p. 92.
163 Jenkin, *op. cit.*, I, p. 394.
164 White, *op. cit.*, p. 50; cf. pp. 57 ff, 101 ff.
165 Stackhouse, *op. cit.*, p. 720; cf. Paley, *op. cit.*, III, pp. 344 f.
166 Cf. Porteus, *Evidences of the Christian Revelation*, p. 72; White, *op. cit.*, p. 345. Boulainvilliers, *Life of Mahomet*, pp. 169 f rejects this view.
167 Cf. Reland, *Of the Mahometan Religion*, p. 45, n. 'h' on obedience for no other reason than that it is demanded by God; cf. Gibbon, *Decline and Fall*, V, p. 348 on almsgiving.
168 Cf. Prideaux, *op. cit.*, pp. 91 ff; cf. also *Life and Actions of Mahomet*, pp. 66 f.
169 Prideaux, *op. cit.*, p. 220; cf. Paley, *op. cit.*, III, pp. 340 f.
170 Ross, *Pansebeia*, p. 125; cf. p. 126.
171 Cf. Smith, *Gods Arrow Against Atheists*, pp. 48 f; Grotius, *op. cit.*, pp. 102, 282; Tillotson, *Works*, III, p. 253; Prideaux, *op. cit.*, pp. 23 f; Paley, *op. cit.*, III, p. 339; Porteus, *op. cit.*, p. 74; Bryant, *op. cit.*, pp. 177 f. There are some who challenge the literal interpretation of the Koranic descriptions of heaven – cf. Simon, *Religions and Customs of the Eastern Nations*, p. 154; Reland, *op. cit.*, pp. 74 ff; Bobovius, *The Turkish Liturgy*, p. 142 n. 'd', – but this view is doubted by Sale, 'Preliminary Discourse', p. 73.
172 Gibbon, *op. cit.*, V, p. 351.
173 Cf. Paley, *op. cit.*, III, pp. 338 f.
174 F. Atterbury, *Sermons and Discourses*, I, p. 130.
175 Cf. Barrow, *Works*, II, pp. 154 f (see Readings IV (ii)); cf. also White, *op. cit.*, 73 ff.
176 Cf. Grotius, *op. cit.*, p. 134; Prideaux, *op. cit.*, pp. 223 ff; Toulmin, p. 164.
177 Cf. Paley, *op. cit.*, III, pp. 341 ff; White, *op. cit.*, p. 92.
178 White, *op. cit.*, pp. 84 f; cf. pp. 261 f.
179 Ross, *Pansebeia*, p. 125; cf. Grotius, *op. cit.*, pp. 265 ff; F. Atterbury, *op. cit.*, p. 129; Stackhouse, *Compleat Body of Divinity*, p. 720. More, *Theological Works*, p. 115, holds that Muslims remain unconverted because of the continuing evils in Christianity.
180 White, *op. cit.*, pp. 66, 68, 70; cf. Sale, 'Preliminary Discourse', pp. 23 ff.
181 *Mahometanism and Socinianism*, pp. 168 f.
182 Cf. Boulainvilliers, *Life of Mahomet*, who claims that God 'has thought to make use of' Mahomet 'to destroy and confound those bad Christians of the East', to overthrow the Romans and Greeks and Persians, and 'to spread the knowledge of the unity of GOD from India to Spain, and to suppress every other worship besides his own' (pp. 165 f; cf. pp. 30 f).
183 Gibbon, *op. cit.*, V, p. 333.
184 White, *op. cit.*, pp. 170 f.
185 Toulmin, *Excellence of Christianity*, pp. 162 f.

186 Paley, *op. cit.*, III, p. 336; cf. Porteus, *op. cit.*, p. 67.
187 Grotius, *op. cit.*, p. 23; cf. p. 133 and White, *op. cit.*, pp. 101 f; cf. also
    Gibbon, *op. cit.*, V, p. 394 who finds not the rise but the persistence of
    Islam to be surprising.
188 Tillotson, *Works*, I, p. 148.
189 Sale, 'Preliminary Discourse', p. 35; cf. Grotius, *op. cit.*, pp. 133 f, 276 f;
    Prideaux, *op. cit.*, pp. 76 f, 241 ff; Gibbon, *op. cit.*, V, p. 359; White, *op. cit.*,
    pp. 86 ff; Toulmin, *op. cit.*, pp. 154 ff, 159 f; Paley, *op. cit.*, III, pp. 343 ff;
    Porteus, pp. 75 ff.
190 Cf. Sale, *op. cit.*, p. 25.
191 Cf. Grotius, pp. 276 f.
192 Chubb, *Posthumous Works*, II, p. 48 n.: he also points out that Christianity
    too has used the sword to establish itself when it was available; *Mahometan-
    ism and Socinianism*, p. 170.
193 Ross, *Pansebeia*, p. 126.
194 Barrow, *Works*, II, p. 154 (see Readings IV (ii)).
195 Leland, *Deistical Writers*, I, pp. 204 f.
196 White, *op. cit.*, p. 97; cf. contrast to Christianity, pp. 109 f; Gibbon notori-
    ously not only offered such a natural explanation of the rise of Islam but also
    one for the rise of Christianity.
197 Cf. Smith, *Gods Arrow Against Atheists*, p. 48.
198 Prideaux, *op. cit.*, p. 116; cf. p. vi; cf. also Grotius, p. 269; Sale, 'Pre-
    liminary Discourse', p. 26; Ross, p. 127. Chubb, out of step as ever, even
    suggests (*op. cit.*, II, pp. 37 ff) that Mahomet may have been a divinely
    ordered reformer of a corrupt Christianity.
199 Ross, *Pansebeia*, p. 130; cf. p. 127.
200 Cf. Grotius, *op. cit.*, pp. 279, 282 ff; Prideaux, *op. cit.*, pp. 215 f; Halybur-
    ton, *Natural Religion Insufficient*, pp. 5 f; Toulmin, *op. cit.*, pp. 166 ff.
201 Cf. Marshall, *British Discovery of Hinduism*, pp. 20, 43 f for a similar conclu-
    sion about the treatment of Hinduism.

Notes to Chapter VII: The uses of 'other religions' for instruction

1 Cf. Montesquieu (Charles-Louis de Secondat), *Persian Letters*, translated by
   C. J. Betts (Penguin Books, Harmondsworth, 1973), p. 238.
2 *Ibid.*, p. 182.
3 Cf. *ibid.*, p. 125. This comment is presumably taking up Christian views of
   Islam as a heresy.
4 *Ibid.*, p. 88.
5 *Ibid.*, p. 89.

6 *Ibid.*, p. 101; cf. pp. 101 f, 126.
7 Cf. Oliver Goldsmith, *The Citizen of the World or Letters from a Chinese Philosopher residing in London to his friends in the East* (Folio Society, London, 1969), pp. 57, 111 f.
8 Cf. *ibid.*, pp. 50 f, 281 f.
9 Cf. *ibid.*, pp. 133 ff.
10 *Ibid.*, p. 47.
11 *Ibid.*, p. 317.
12 *Ibid.*, p. 80.
13 *Ibid.*, pp. 122 ff.
14 Cf. *ibid.*, pp. 40, 120 f, 151 f.
15 *Ibid.*, p. 114. When lists of so-called 'deists' are attempted, the placing of this Archbishop of Canterbury is a nice point.
16 Halyburton, *Natural Religion Insufficient*, p. 57.
17 Cf. William Lithgow, *Rare Adventures and Painful Peregrinations*, edited by G. Phelps (Folio Society, London, 1974), pp. 173 ff, 90 ff, 210.
18 *Ibid.*, pp. 141, 251.
19 *Ibid.*, p. 94.
20 Cf. Defoe, *Robinson Crusoe*, pp. 320 ff; cf. also pp. 157 ff.
21 Voltaire, *Zadig*, chapter 12 in *Zadig/L'Ingenu*, translated with an introduction by J. Butt (Penguin Books, Harmondsworth, 1964), p. 66.
22 *Ibid.*, chapter 18, pp. 97 f.
23 Voltaire, *L'Ingenu*, chapter 10 in *ibid.*, p. 145.
24 'Salignac De La Motte Fenelon (Francis de)' in Bayle, *A General Dictionary, Historical and Critical*, I X, pp. 37 f. (This article is not by Bayle but was added by one of the British contributors to this edition.)
25 'Eloge Historique de Monsr. de Fenelon, Archevêque-Duc de Cambray', p. xl f in François de Salignac de la Mothe-Fenelon, *Les Avantures de Télémaque, Fils d'Ulysse* (Hambourg, 1731). The article in Bayle's *Dictionary* (see the preceding note), p. 33, suggests the piece is by Durand.
26 Cf. Ramsay, *Travels of Cyrus*, I, p. xiii f for the differences between Fenelon's Télémaque and Ramsay's Cyrus.
27 *Ibid.*, I, p. xiii.
28 *Ibid.*, I, p. viii.
29 *Ibid.*, I, p. xiv.
30 I, p. xvi.
31 *Ibid.*, I, p. xix; cf. p. xvi.
32 Cf. remarks on the 'Gymnosophists' in *ibid.*, I, p. 67.
33 Cf. *ibid.*, I, p. xix; cf. also p. xvi.
34 *Ibid.*, I, pp. xvi f.
35 *Ibid.*, I, p. xvii.
36 *Ibid.*, I, pp. xix f.
37 *Ibid.*, I I, p. 132.

38 *Ibid.*, I, pp. 150 f.

39 *Ibid.*, II, pp. 65–78.

40 *Ibid.*, II, p. 78; cf. p. 110.

41 *Ibid.*, II, p. 135.

42 *Ibid.*, I, p. xviii.

43 For Descartes and Malebranche, cf. *ibid.*, II, pp. 29 ff; Hobbes, I, pp. xvi f; Newton, I, pp. 87 f; Berkeley, II, pp. 27 ff; Tindal, II, p. 130; Butler, II, p. 35; Leibniz, II, pp. 111 ff; Bayle, II, pp. 122 f.

44 Cf. Ramsay's defence of the identification of ancient and modern thinkers in his 'Discourse upon the Theology and Mythology of the Pagans' in *ibid.*, II, pp. 186 ff: on p. 188 he states the principle of his position in these terms: 'The history of former times is like that of our own: Human understanding takes almost the same forms in different ages, and loses its way in the same labyrinths; there are periodical diseases of the mind as well as of the body.'

45 Cf. *ibid.*, I, pp. ix ff for Ramsay's acknowledgement of his indebtedness to Cudworth and others.

46 Voltaire, *Philosophical Dictionary*, 'China', p. 169.

47 *Ibid.*, 'Religion', p. 448.

48 *Ibid.*, 'Sect', p. 465.

49 Cf. *ibid.*, 'Theologian', p. 480; 'Necessary', pp. 407 f.

50 Cf. *ibid.*, 'Common Sense', p. 468.

51 *Ibid.*, 'Chinese Catechism', pp. 145 f.

52 Cf. Marshall, *British Discovery of Hinduism*, p. 8.

53 [Philip Dormer Stanhope, Fourth Earl of Chesterfield], *The Oeconomy of Human Life*, (London, seventh edition, 1751), p. vi – see Readings VI (i).

54 *Ibid.*, p. xiv.

55 Cf. *ibid.*, p. xvii.

56 Cf. *ibid.*, p. xvi.

57 [Philip Dormer Stanhope, Fourth Earl of Chesterfield], *The Oeconomy of Human Life . . . Found soon after that which contained the Original of the First Part*, (London, eighth edition, 1787), p. v. (This will be referred to as *Oeconomy, Part 2*.)

58 T. W. Rhys Davids, 'The Wisdom of the East, and How it came to the West', in *Inaugural Lectures Delivered by Members of the Faculty of Theology*, edited A. S. Peake (Manchester University Press, 1905), pp. 292 f.

59 Cf. *Oeconomy of Human Life*, pp. xxii ff.

60 *Ibid.*, p. 30.

61 *Ibid.*, p. 52: 'demands' is apparently a misprint for 'depends'.

62 *Ibid.*, pp. 82 f.

63 *Oeconomy, Part 2*, p. 57.

64 *Ibid.*, pp. 92, 94.

65 *Oeconomy of Human Life*, p. 69.

66 *Ibid.*, p. 68.

67 Cf. *Oeconomy, Part 2*, p. 58.
68 Cf. *ibid.*, p. 97.
69 *Ibid.*, p. 100; see Readings VI (i) for its views on religion.
70 According to Rhys Davids, *op. cit.*, p. 292, the work had fifty editions by 1812.
71 Wilson, *Knowledge and Practice of Christianity*, pp. v, vii; cf. pp. xxiii f.
72 *Ibid.*, p. viii.
73 *Ibid.*, p. 220.
74 *Ibid.*, p. 217.
75 *Ibid.*, 'Advertisement'.
76 Stillingfleet, *Origines Sacrae*, pp. 405 f; cf. pp. 395–410.
77 Cf. Gildon in Blount, *Oracles of Reason*, pp. 184 f.
78 Allix, *Reflexions upon the Books of the Holy Scripture*, p. 110.
79 Jones, 'On the Gods of Greece, Italy and India', in *Dissertations on Asia*, p. 76.
80 Cf. Jones, 'On the Chronology of the Hindus' in *ibid.*, pp. 290, 324.
81 Jones, 'On the Hindu's', in *ibid.*, pp. 116 f.
82 Bryant, *Authenticity of the Scriptures*, pp. 245, 250; cf. pp. 245–53.
83 Whiston, *Supplement to the Literal Accomplishment of Scriptural Prophecies*, pp. 109, 125 f.
84 Whiston, *Memoirs*, p. 580.
85 Picart, *Ceremonies and Religious Customs*, p. ii.
86 Collyer, *Sacred Interpreter*, II, p. 305.
87 *Ibid.*, II, pp. 305–16.
88 Tindal, *Christianity as Old as the Creation*, p. 342.
89 Thomas Harmer, *The Outlines of a New Commentary on Solomon's Song, Drawn by help of Instructions from the East* (London, 1768), pp. viii–xvi, see Readings VI (ii) for extracts from this Commentary.
90 Cf. *ibid.*, pp. xvii f, 126 f.
91 *Ibid.*, pp. 80 ff.

Notes to Chapter VIII: The uses of 'other religions' in controversy

1 Cf. Fox, *Gospel-Truth Demonstrated*, pp. 1075 ff for attacks on the customs of Shrove Tuesday, May Day and other 'Relicks of Heathenism' (p. 1077) still found to be practised.
2 Ross, *Pansebeia*, p. 381.
3 *Ibid.*, p. 379
4 Cf. David A. Pailin, 'Herbert of Cherbury and the Deists' in *The Expository Times*, XCIV, No. 7, April 1983, pp. 197 ff.
5 Herbert of Cherbury, *De Veritate*, pp. 289 f.

6 *Ibid.*, pp. 294 f; cf. p. 303.

7 Herbert of Cherbury, *De Religione Laici*, p. 107; cf. pp. 111, 123.

8 See Readings V I I (i).

9 Herbert of Cherbury, *Religion of the Gentiles*, p. 11.

10 *Ibid.*, p. 41; cf. pp. 46, 55, 113, 208.

11 Cf. *ibid.*, pp. 73 f, 138 f.

12 *Ibid.*, pp. 380 f.

13 *Ibid.*, p. 3.

14 *Ibid.*, p. 358.

15 Cf. article cited in n. 4 *supra* for doubts about this description of Herbert of Cherbury.

16 Cf. Charles Blount, *Anima Mundi: or, An Historical Narration of the Opinions of the Ancients concerning Man's Soul After this Life according to Unenlightened Nature* (London, 1679), p. 64; Charles Blount, *Great is Diana of the Ephesians: or, The Original of Idolatry, Together with the Politick Institution of the Gentiles Sacrifices* (London, 1695), 'Preface'.

17 Blount, *Great is Diana*, 'Preface' and p. 3.

18 Cf. *ibid.*, pp. 25 f.

19 *Ibid.*, p. 4; cf. pp. 13 ff, 29 ff, 36 ff.

20 Cf. *ibid.*, pp. 8 ff, 11 f.

21 Cf. *ibid.*, pp. 13 ff.

22 Cf. *ibid.*, pp. 10 ff.

23 Cf. Anthony Collins, *A Discourse of Free-Thinking, Occasion'd by the Rise and Growth of a Sect call'd Free-Thinkers* (London, 1713), pp. 37 ff.

24 *Ibid.*, p. 42; cf. pp. 43 ff.

25 Cf. *ibid.*, pp. 25 f.

26 Toland, *Letters to Serena*, p. 104; cf. pp. 105 ff for his list of what the priests invented, including 'Augurys and Auspicys, Extispicys, Necromancy and Necyomancy, Pyromancy, Psychomancy, Nephelomancy, Hydromancy, Capnomancy, Sortileges, with other numberless and superstitious Vanitys' (p. 106).

27 Cf. *ibid.*, pp. 114 ff.

28 *Ibid.*, p. 104; cf. similar charges in Hobbes, Leviathan, pp. 80 f; Bolingbroke, *Works*, V, p. 124 f where priests are held to threaten civil liberty by flattering rulers.

29 *Ibid.*, p. 123.

30 Middleton, *Letter from Rome*, p. 221; cf. p. 205 for the charge that priests invent stories of prodigies for their own gain.

31 *Ibid.*, p. iii; see Readings V I I (iii) for examples.

32 *Ibid.*, p. vi.

33 *Ibid.*, p. 159.

34 Cf. *ibid.*, pp. 160, 133–55, 190–93.

35 *Ibid.*, p. 211; cf. pp. 195–211.

36 *Ibid.*, p. 188.

37 *Ibid.*, p. 224; cf. pp. 246 f.

38 Hobbes, *Leviathan*, pp. 516 ff.

39 Herbert of Cherbury, *Religion of the Gentiles*, p. 365.

40 Joseph Mede, *The Apostasy of the Latter Times, or The Gentiles Theology of Daemons Revived in the Latter Times* (London, fourth edition, 1663), printed in *The Works of the Pious and Profoundly-Learned Joseph Mede* (London, 1664), p. 767 (title-page).

41 *Ibid.*, pp. 794, 796, 767 (title-page).

42 Cf. Toland, *Letters to Serena*, pp. 123, 127; cf. also Voltaire, *Philosophical Dictionary*, pp. 310 ff, 324.

43 Gale, *Court of the Gentiles*, Part III: *The Vanitie of Pagan Philosophie Demonstrated* (London, 1677), Book 2, chapter 2, pp. 148–238.

44 *Ibid.*, pp. 237 f.

45 Leslie, *Short Method with the Jews* in *Works*, I, p. 80 – the reference is to Philippus A. Limborch, *De Veritate Religionis Christianae Amica Collatio cum Erudito Judaeo* (Gouda, 1687), p. 102. Leslie was a non-juring divine who uses Jewish difficulties also as a way of criticising non-episcopal structures in some churches – cf. pp. 81 f, see Readings III (iii).

46 Kidder in *Boyle Lectures 1691–1732*, I, pp. 113 f; cf. Tillotson, *Works*, II, pp. 599 f attacks Roman Catholics for perpetuating the Jewish error in rejecting Christ.

47 Prideaux, *Life of Mahomet*, p. 14.

48 Whichcote, *Several Discourses*, IV, pp. 24 f.

49 *Life and Actions of Mahomet* in *Four Treatises concerning Mahometanism*, p. 80.

50 *Ibid.*, p. 82; cf. pp. 82 f.

51 Rogers, *Necessity of Divine Revelation*, pp. 157 f; in his 'Reasons against Conversion to the Church of *Rome*' in *Seventeen Sermons on Various Occasions* (London, 1736), pp. 413 f, Rogers again takes up a comparison of the authority of the Koran and that of the Bible. Here he argues that if a Muslim claimed to believe the miracles of Mahomet because they were ascribed to him in an infallible Koran, it would be a sufficient rebuttal to show that the Koran contains some 'plain Contradiction to any manifest Truth'. Rogers goes on to point out that if the doctrine of transubstantiation were declared in the gospel, this would also prove it not to be infallible.

52 Tillotson, *Works*, II, pp. 284, 512; cf. Marshall, *British Discovery of Hinduism*, p. 24.

53 Hume, *Natural History of Religion*, p. 68.

54 Reland, *Of the Mahometan Religion*, p. 8; cf. pp. 8 ff.

55 Hooker, *Of the Lawes of Ecclesiastical Politie*, Book 7, chapter 20, p. [57]; cf. also Book 4, chapter 7, p. 103.

56 More, *Theological Works*, pp. 106 f; cf. pp. 113 ff, 171 ff, 188.

57 Ross, *Pansebeia*, 'Preface' (pp. A4 rev.–A5).

58 Prideaux, *Life of Mahomet*, pp. 141 f; cf. pp. 248 ff.

59 Apthorp, *Prevalence of Christianity*, p. *353

60 Gibbon, *Decline and Fall*, chapters 15 and 16.

61 Prideaux, *op. cit.*, p. 257.

62 Letter from 'A.W.' in Blount, *Oracles of Reason*, p. 201; cf. Blount, *Anima Mundi*, pp. 14 ff on the way people pretend to revelations to gain authority for their views.

63 Another group attacked by Leslie are the Latitudinarians. He argues by comparison with the Jews that the adoption of Latitudinarian principles would cause a loss of identity – cf. *Short Method with the Jews* in *Works*, I, p. 82.

64 Gibbon, *op. cit.*, V, p. 339; cf. p. 353.

65 John Edwards, *The Socinian Creed: Or, A Brief Account of the Professed Tenents and Doctrines of the Foreign and English Socinians* (London, 1697), p. 221.

66 *Ibid.*, p. 227; cf. pp. 228 f; Leslie, *The Socinian Controversy Discuss'd in Six Dialogues* in *Works*, I, pp. 217 f.

67 Sale, 'To the Reader', in *The Koran*, p. vi.

68 Cf. Leslie, *Socinian Controversy* in *Works*, I, p. 205. The letter is printed on pp. 207–11.

69 *Ibid.*, pp. 209 ff; cf. p. 211.

70 Leslie, *Truth of Christianity Demonstrated* in *Works*, I, p. 167.

71 Cf. *ibid.*, *Socinian Controversy*, I, pp. 216 ff, 337 ff; Prideaux, *Life of Mahomet*, pp. 17 n. 't', 60.

72 Leslie, *Socinian Controversy* in *Works*, I, p. 218.

73 *Ibid.*, I, p. 339.

74 *Mahometanism and Socinianism*, p. 156, see Readings V I I (ii) for this work.

75 Cf. *ibid.*, pp. 177 f.

76 *Ibid.*, p. 182; cf. pp. 193 f.

77 *Ibid.*, cf. p. 184.

78 Cf. *ibid.*, pp. 183, 194.

79 Cf. *ibid.*, pp. 184 ff.

80 Cf. *ibid.*, pp. 188, 191.

81 Cf. *ibid.*, p. 242.

82 *Ibid.*, p. 212; cf. pp. 190, 235 f.

83 *Ibid.*, p. 221; cf. p. 229 where Neuser and Sylvan are accused of seeking a 'Syncretism' of Socinianism and Mahometanism.

84 *Ibid.*, pp. 188 f; cf. p. 183.

85 *Ibid.*, p. 230; cf. pp. 182 f, 207, 288 ff, 242.

86 'A Letter from Mr. Leibnitz to the Author of the Reflections upon the Origin of Mahometanism' appended to *Mahometanism and Socinianism*, pp. 252 f.

87 *Ibid.*, pp. 248 f.

88 *Ibid.*, p. 245.
89 William Berriman, *An Historical Account of the Controversies that have been in the Church concerning the Doctrine of the Holy and Everblessed Trinity* (London, 1725), p. 412.
90 White, *Mahometanism and Christianity*, 'Notes', p. lxi.
91 *Ibid.*, 'Notes', pp. lxi ff.
92 *Ibid.*, 'Notes', p. lxiii.
93 Bolingbroke, 'Fragments or Minutes of Essays' in *Works*, I V, p. 501 n.
94 Toulmin, *Excellence of Christianity*, p. 249; cf. pp. 249 ff, 264 ff.
95 *Ibid.*, pp. 260 f; cf. pp. 262 f.
96 Cf. *ibid.*, pp. 263 ff.
97 For an exception cf. Gibbon, *Decline and Fall*, V, p. 339 who gives a favourable outline of Muslim views.
98 Ross, *Pansebeia*, 'Preface' (p. A3 f).
99 Echard, *Ecclesiastical History*, I I, p. 429; cf. pp. 538, 698.
100 Cf. Gibbon, *Decline and Fall*, chapters 15 and 16.
101 Apthorp, *Prevalence of Christianity*, p. ★356; cf. pp. 265 ff.
102 Cf. *ibid.*
103 More, *Theological Works*, p. 71; cf. pp. 71–107.
104 *Ibid.*, pp. 85, 87, 103.
105 *Ibid.*, p. 88; cf. p. 103.
106 Stanhope in *Boyle Lectures 1691–1732*, I, p. 635.
107 Horsley, 'Dissertation on the Prophecies of the Messiah' in *Sermons on the Evidence of the Resurrection*, pp. 6, 24, 28, 68; cf. pp. 114 ff.
108 Jones, 'On the Gods of Greece, Italy, and India' in *Dissertations on Asia*, I, p. 2; cf. pp. 7, 109 ff ('On the Hindu's').
109 Edwards, *Authority, Stile and Perfection of the Books of the Old and New Testament*, pp. 405 f.
110 Cudworth, *Intellectual System of the Universe*, pp. 288, 547; cf. pp. 546 ff; cf. Horsley, *op. cit.*, p. 114.
111 Cf. Ramsay, *Natural and Revealed Religion*, I I, pp. 119 ff.
112 Cf. Cudworth, *op. cit.*, p. 548.
113 Ramsay, *op. cit.*, I I, p. 119.
114 *Ibid.*, I I, p. 111.
115 Fox, *Gospel-Truth Demonstrated*, p. 336.
116 Cf. Middleton, *Letter from Rome*, p. 194; cf. pp. 82, 88 f for his comments on Leslie's tests for miracles.
117 Bolingbroke, 'Essay the Second Containing Some Reflections On the Folly . . . of Philosophers . . . On the Propagation of . . . Superstition And on . . . Attempts . . . to Reform . . . Human Reason' in *Works*, I V, p. 170; cf. 'Essay the Fourth Concerning the Authority of Religion' in *ibid.*, I V, p. 250.
118 Cf. Bolingbroke, 'Essay the Fourth' in *ibid.*, I V, pp. 260 ff; cf. Collins,

Discourse of Free-Thinking, pp. 30 ff.

119 Bolingbroke, 'Fragments or Minutes of Essays' in *Works*, V, p. 228.

120 Boulainvilliers, *Life of Mahomet*, pp. 223 f.

121 *Ibid.*, p. viii; cf. p. vii.

122 Howell, 'The Religious Tenets of the Gentoos' in Marshall, *British Discovery of Hinduism*, pp. 76 f; cf. pp. 65, 70; Dow, 'A Dissertation concerning the Hindoos' in Marshall, *op. cit.*, p. 138.

123 Cf. Marshall, *op. cit.*, p. 28.

124 Prideaux, *Life of Mahomet*, p. 258.

125 Cf. Ross, *Pansebeia*, 'Preface', pp. (A4 f), 125, 361.

126 *Ibid.*, p. 385; cf. pp. 357 ff for his views on permissible toleration.

127 *Ibid.*, p. 127; cf. pp. 129 f. Ross also suggests that this challenge makes Christians exercise their armies abroad and not at home!

128 Leslie, *Short Method with the Jews* in *Works*, I, p. 81, see Readings, III (iii); cf. also Kidder in *Boyle Lectures 1691–1732*, I, p. 114 for another claim that divisions within Christianity are an obstacle to the conversion of the Jews.

129 Burder, 'Jonah's Mission to Nineveh', in *Sermons at the Formation of the Missionary Society*, p. 44, see Readings VIII (ii).

130 Fuller, *Apology for Christian Missions* in *Works*, p. 816; but cf. p. 805.

131 *Ibid.*, p. 824; but cf. p. 805 for anti-Roman Catholic remarks.

Notes to Chapter IX: Missionary activity and 'other religions'

1 Cf. Dr Coke and Mr Moore, *The Life of the Rev. John Wesley, A.M., including an Account of the Great Revival of Religion in Europe and America* (London, 1792), pp. 472 ff.

2 *Sermons at the Formation of the Missionary Society*, p. xi.

3 David Bogue, 'Objections Against a Mission to the Heathen Stated and Considered', in *ibid.*, pp. 130 f.

4 Cf. the enlightenment attitude to actual religions expressed in the parable of the three rings in Lessing's *Nathan the Wise*.

5 Collins, *Discourse of Free-Thinking*, pp. 32 f.

6 Secker, *Fourteen Sermons*, p. 111; cf. pp. 123 ff. The need to send missionaries to the colonists because of their moral decline is also to be found in Fuller, *Apology for Christian Missions* in *Works*, p. 800.

7 Wesley, Sermon LXVIII, 'The General Spread of the Gospel' in *Works*, IX, pp. 233, 245, 240; cf. pp. 239–46.

8 Cf. Carey, *Obligations of Christians*, pp. 38–61.

9 *Ibid.*, pp. 62 f; cf. p. 84 where he holds that there is enough room in the world for the different denominations to act without interfering with each

other.

10 *Ibid.*, p. 65.

11 Cf. *ibid.*, pp. 81 f.

12 *Ibid.*, p. 13.

13 Secker, *op. cit.*, p. 117; cf. pp. 129 ff; cf. also White, *Mahometanism and Christianity*, pp. 473 ff.

14 Burder in *Sermons at the Formation of the Missionary Society*, p. 27, see Readings VIII (ii).

15 Greatheed in *ibid.*, pp. 52, 56 f.

16 East Apthorp, *Discourses on Prophecy* (London, 1786), II, pp. 339 f, see Readings VIII (i).

17 Cf. White, *Mahometanism and Christianity*, pp. 502 ff.

18 Fuller, *Apology for Christian Missions* in *Works*, p. 811.

19 *Ibid.*, p. 797; cf. pp. 797 ff, 811 ff. Fuller quotes with approval the judgement of Sir William Jones that while the Hindu Institutes of Menu contain many beautiful pieces, they are 'a system of despotism and priestcraft . . . filled with strange conceits in metaphysics and natural philosophy, with idle superstitions, and with a scheme of theology most obscurely figurative, and consequently liable to dangerous misconceptions . . . with ceremonies generally absurd, and often ridiculous . . . ' p. 811.

20 Cf. *ibid.*, p. 807.

21 White, *op. cit.*, p. 475; cf. pp. 475 ff.

22 *Ibid.*, pp. 480, 482.

23 Cf. *ibid.*, pp. 485 f.

24 *Ibid.*, p. 488; cf. Bogue in *Sermons at the Formation of the Missionary Society*, pp. 148 ff.

25 White, *op. cit.*, pp. 495 f.

26 Bogue in *Sermons at the Formation of the Missionary Society*, p. 126; cf. pp. 126 ff.

27 White, *op. cit.*, p. 500; cf. Bogue, *op. cit.*, pp. 148 ff.

28 Cf. George Berkeley, *A Proposal for the Better Supplying of Churches in Our Foreign Plantations, and for Converting the Savage Americans to Christianity* in *Works*, edited by G. N. Wright (London, 1843), II, pp. 281, 301 ff.

29 Secker, *Fourteen Sermons*, p. 121; cf. pp. 112 f, 121 ff; cf. also Fuller, *Works*, pp. 797 ff.

30 Secker, *op. cit.*, p. 123.

31 *Ibid.*, pp. 126 f.

32 *Ibid.*, pp. 128 f.

33 Coke and Moore, *Life of John Wesley*, pp. 472 f.

34 Cf. Fuller, *Apology for Christian Missions* in *Works*, pp. 806, 811.

35 Cf. *ibid.*, pp. 796 ff, 799 f, 801–9, 815 f.

36 Cf. *ibid.*, pp. 797 ff.

37 *Ibid.*, p. 799.

38 Cf. *ibid.*, pp. 815 ff, 824.

39 Cf. *ibid.*, pp. 800, 827.

40 Cf. White, *Mahometanism and Christianity*, pp. 516 ff.

41 Secker, *Fourteen Sermons*, p. 123. Was it, then, the lack of missionaries and not taxation that really led to the bother at Boston?

42 *Ibid.*, p. 124.

43 Cf. Bogue in *Sermons at the Formation of the Missionary Society*, pp. 148 ff.

44 More, *Theological Works*, pp. 364 f.

45 Collins, *Discourse of Free-Thinking*, p. 33.

46 Cf. sermon by Thomas Pentycross in *Four Sermons Preached in London at the Second General Meeting of the Missionary Society* (London, 1796), pp. 67 f, where he suggests that all that may be lost 'is the *blood*' of those who are sent but 'this will be no loss. Not to the church: for it will be propagated, established and adorned by it; Not to the Missionaries: for to them *to die* will be *gain* . . .'

47 Carey, *Obligations of Christians*, pp. 67–75; see Readings V I I I (iii) for an example of the risks faced by missionaries.

48 Cf. Bogue, *op. cit.*, pp. 124–41.

49 Cf. *ibid.*, p. 153.

50 *Ibid.*, p. 157.

51 Ross, *Pansebeia*, p. 29; cf. Apthorp, *Prevalence of Christianity*, p. ★353 on the ineffectiveness of the use of force to gain converts.

52 Cf. Fuller, *Apology for Christian Missions* in *Works*, pp. 822 f.

53 Berkeley, sermon to the S P G on 18 February 1731, in *Works*, I I, p. 300.

54 Apthorp, *Discourses on Prophecy*, I I, p. 341, see Readings V I I I (i).

55 Carey, *op. cit.*, p. 63.

56 Cf. Defoe, *Robinson Crusoe*, pp. 320 ff.

57 Wesley, Sermon L X V I I I, 'The General Spread of the Gospel' in *Works*, I X, pp. 242 f.

58 Robertson, *Historical Disquisitions of India*, p. 229; cf. White, *Mahometanism and Christianity*, pp. 472 f.

59 Paley, *Evidences of Christianity* in *Works*, I I I, pp. 327, 330; cf. pp. 326 ff; cf. Fuller, *op. cit.*, *Works*, p. 822.

60 Apthorp, *Prevalence of Christianity*, pp. ★353 ff.

61 Tillotson, *Works*, I I, p. 256; cf. pp. 283 f; a similar claim was made by Grotius in a comment on Matthew 16, 17; Middleton criticises the claim – cf. *Free Enquiry into Miraculous Powers*, pp. xviii f.

62 Tillotson, I I, p. 512.

63 *Ibid.*, I I, pp. 283.

64 Cf. Middleton, *Letter from Rome*, pp. xcvii ff; cf. *Free Enquiry into Miraculous Powers*, p. xviii f.

65 Middleton, *Free Enquiry into Miraculous Powers*, pp. xvii ff, xx f.

66 Cf. Carey, *Obligations of Christians*, pp. 64, 83; Defoe, *Robinson Crusoe*,

pp. 322 f. Kidder in *Boyle Lectures 1691–1732*, I, p. 116 refers to cases of the bad behaviour of supposed converts from Judaism.

67 Tindal, *Christianity as Old as the Creation*, p. 405; cf. pp. 404 f for other references on this theme.

68 Baxter, *Reasons of the Christian Religion*, p. 440; cf. pp. 438 ff.

69 Wesley, *op. cit.*, I X, p. 242. As for the conversion of those outside normal contact with Christians, Wesley suggests that the providence of God will be able to send missionaries to such nations (by more Robinson Crusoe incidents?) – pp. 243 f. Grotius, *Truth of the Christian Religion*, p. 3, describes his book as an aid to sailors travelling to heathen lands.

70 Berkeley, sermon to the S P G in *Works*, I I, pp. 299 f; cf. White, *Mahometanism and Christianity*, pp. 498 f; Fuller in *Works*, pp. 820 ff holds that the absence of miraculous powers is not a proof that the missionaries have no authority.

71 Secker, *Fourteen Sermons*, p. 120.

72 Apthorp, *Discourses on Prophecy*, II, pp. 341 f.

73 Cf. John Hey in *Sermons at the Formation of the Missionary Society*, pp. 83 f.

74 Stackhouse, *Compleat Body of Divinity*, p. 728 n. 'o'.

75 Sale, *The Koran*, pp. v f.

76 White, *op. cit.*, p. 496.

77 Apthorp, *op. cit.*, II, p. 340.

78 Berkeley, *Proposal for the Better Supplying of Churches* in *Works*, I I, p. 282; cf. Wilson, *Knowledge and Practice of Christianity*, pp. xvi f.

79 Secker, *op. cit.*, p. 127.

80 *Ibid.*, p. 114; cf. pp. 114 f; cf. Berkeley, sermon to the S P G in *Works*, I I, p. 302.

81 Wilson, *Knowledge and Practice of Christianity*, p. xvi.

82 Beilby Porteus, *Sermons on Several Subjects* (London, twelfth edition, 1810), I, p. 417 n., on converted slaves being better workers.

83 *Ibid.*, I, p. 416; cf. pp. 395–428.

84 Cf. *ibid.*, pp. 419 f; cf. Hodgson, *Life of Beilby Porteus*, pp. 85 ff on Porteus' attempt to persuade the S P G to implement his ideas.

85 Hodgson, *Life of Beilby Porteus*, p. 217.

86 Cf. *ibid.*, p. 223.

87 Watts, *Works*, I V, p. 394.

Index